# A Practical Guide to Government Management

# A Practical Guide to Government Management

## Vince Meconi

Lanham • Boulder • New York • London

Published by Bernan Press
An imprint of The Rowman & Littlefield Publishing Group, Inc.
4501 Forbes Boulevard, Suite 200, Lanham, Maryland 20706
www.rowman.com
800-865-3457; info@bernan.com

16 Carlisle Street, London W1D 3BT, United Kingdom

**Library of Congress Cataloging-in-Publication Data**

Library of Congress Cataloging-in-Publication Data Available
ISBN 978-1-59888-752-5 (cloth : alk. paper) -- ISBN 978-1-59888-753-2 (electronic)


∞ ™ The paper used in this publication meets the minimum requirements of American
National Standard for Information Sciences Permanence of Paper for Printed Library
Materials, ANSI/NISO Z39.48-1992.

Printed in the United States of America

To Senator Tom Carper, Governor Ruth Ann Minner, and County Executive Paul Clark, who honored me beyond measure by letting me practice my trade.

And to Sharon, Lindsay, Steve, Jack, Jamie, and Mike (not to mention Dad, Honey, Michel, Yannick, Kevin, Shelley, and the other Mike)—the ones whose love I need.

# Contents

# Introduction

Our nation's elected leaders are seldom voted into office because of their managerial ability. Government administrators on all levels are too often selected and then promoted for their program and policy expertise rather than their operational acumen. Once in office, they receive limited or no management training, and at higher levels, focus more on policy than management, with negative consequences for the agencies they manage, not to mention the American public. The best public policy in the world cannot succeed without execution, and execution requires management.

In America we do not let anyone practice medicine without a medical degree. Every lawyer has graduated from law school. You cannot become a social worker, a landscape architect, an engineer, a nurse, or a police officer without the right education and training. In most places, you can't even cut hair or manicure nails without a government license. But many people without any management training try to manage government agencies. "You would never deduce from the job descriptions of government executives and managers that they are, collectively, responsible for managing billions of dollars, property and equipment worth billions of dollars, and the performance of millions of employees. The sad fact of the matter is that the word 'management' is itself virtually taboo in the public sector."[1]

The following sentences were written to describe high level British government leaders, but they might as well have been written about America's as well. "Senior civil servants were not trained for management and did not care about management." And, "Like cabinet secretaries in any large nation, few ministers even saw management as their job."[2] Closer to home, a retired city manager has this to say: "It would be incorrect to say that political appointees are anti-management—they are not. But they do not *practice* management. They may or may not be interested in management. They are about the political values of the elected officials they work for."³ I have seen administrator after administrator—on all levels—underperform because they were policy experts who could not manage. Management is its own special kind of expertise, very distinct from program knowledge, something that many elected officials do not understand.

There is a dearth of training, education, and written material for the public sector managerial cadre to make use of. Most of the scholarly work on public administration appears to be written for a scholarly audience, not the practitioner one. There are far more works on public policy than on public management. And the relatively small percentage of government books that are devoted to management are, for the most part, more descriptive than prescriptive—necessary but not sufficient. Even schools of public administration (from one of which I am proud to have graduated) in many cases either emphasize policy rather than management, or aim their entire syllabi at the federal government, or both. This book is predicated on the notion that government can and should be managed better than it has been.

Regardless of legislation passed by Congress, the states, or localities to improve government operations, and regardless of executive branch studies on ways to improve government by blue ribbon bodies dating back to the Hoover Commission in 1947, *government performance will not improve across the board unless more emphasis is placed on management and fewer non-managers are placed in management positions.*

Much of today's critique of government is ideological, not rational, dating at least to Homer Ferguson's 1928 "A Plea For Inefficiency In Government."⁴ But some of the critique—that government is often poorly run—has validity. Partly this inefficiency stems from the nature of democracy itself, especially in this country, with its checks and balances and separation of powers. The framers of the Constitution did not design our government to run smoothly. They chose limited government over effective government. But part of this inefficiency is the result of a lot of bad management in government. I am proud to say that my government career has included service in all three parts of each of government's two dimensions. I have served in all three branches of government: legislative, executive, and judicial, and on all three levels of government: federal, state, and local. Everywhere I've worked, I have seen dedicated, hardworking employees—but I have not always seen employees who were well managed or properly led.

I have also worked on over a hundred political campaigns at one level or another, doing everything from passing out brochures door-to-door to serving as the campaign manager. This book is not about politics, but I hope that it benefits from an understanding of what makes elected officials, both executive and legislative, tick.

The purpose of this book is to provide a comprehensive yet one-volume work on high-level government management, structured as a training manual for an incoming cabinet-level official working for a governor, county executive, mayor, or other elected executive. However, I believe it will also be useful to other upper level government managers, public administration students, and anyone interested in public sector management.

To successfully lead a government organization, an individual needs to

1. effectively self-manage,
2. run his own agency well, and
3. smoothly navigate the often treacherous waters of his agency's environment.

Doing one or two of the three well is insufficient; the public manager must do all three. Accordingly, the book is organized into three parts.

The first part is titled "You" because you have to have your own house in order before you start telling anybody else what to do. It includes chapters on self-management, leadership, and ethics, all areas in which what you do is as important as what you say. The second part is "Your Organization," that is, aspects of responsibility that are within your direct purview: people, prioritization, money, decision making and problem solving, and gaining control of your organization. Finally, "Your Environment" covers all the things outside of your control but with which you have to deal anyway—an environment that grows more turbulent with each passing year. Its topics are working for elected officials, the legislative branch of government, the media, and more (interest groups; agencies that should help you—and sometimes do; contractors, vendors and privatization; lawsuits; and a few last random thoughts).

When I was first appointed cabinet secretary, I was given no special training and found no instructions on my desk. Obviously, agency head positions do not come with owner's manuals. This absence is unfortunate, because it results in a lot of on-the-job training and reinventing, not of government, but of wheels. In fact, often the higher up you go in government, the less guidance you are likely to get, if your immediate supervisor is an elected official who is very busy with other priorities. At the very top of the administrative apex, cabinet positions customarily change with administrations, and transitions may be less than amicable, particularly if the new leader told the voters for the last six months of the campaign how bad things were under the old regime. Each new administration seemingly starts from scratch, and a huge amount of productivity is lost with every new leader's learning curve.

In addition to what this book is, there are a few things that it is not. First, although I personally have strongly held views on a wide variety of public policy issues, this volume is not about the best government policies or specific programs. As previously stated, there are many works on the policy aspects of government, but fewer on the management of government. It does, however, take as a given that government, whatever its policies and programs, is necessary for a properly functioning, just society. "The most important [institution] is our own democratic form of government. Every other social, religious, economic, scientific, and political institution is enhanced and shared in by the people because of our democracy."[5] No elected executive, regardless of his or her political ideology, wants poor management of government agencies under his or her control. Even those who want to downsize government still want the government that remains to run well. Whatever your political party or philosophy of governance, "As a manager, your mission must be, first and foremost, to make government work."[6]

Other books describe how government ought to operate. Perhaps you are lucky enough to work in a jurisdiction that has decentralized administrative controls, organizational deregulation, reinvention laboratories, extensive waiver policies, beta sites, and rules sunsets,[7] among others. If you work in such a bureaucracy-free government, you may not need many of these coping strategies. But that is not the environment in which I have spent my government career, nor is it the environment of most of my counterparts from around the country. *This* book is intended to assist people in the world most of us live in, not the world as it should be. It is intended to help you understand yourself, the agencies and programs you run, and the environment that surrounds you.

Finally, it is not a book of theory. As the book's title indicates, it describes what has worked—and equally important, what has not worked—for me, my bosses, my colleagues, and my staff, over the years, in my state and around the country. It should work for you, too.

The seed for this book was planted when the Delaware Governor's Chief of Staff requested that a colleague and I conduct a mini "cabinet secretary school" for the newest member of the cabinet. Being asked to do so forced me to finally write down a lot of thoughts that had been running around in my head for years. It got me thinking about why so many cabinet-rank and other high officials, both in administrations I had been a part of and administrations I had observed from the outside, had either performed poorly or been outright failures. I saw other top government managers leave absolutely no imprint on their organizations during their tenure. It also made me realize that to really do the job right would require a book, not an afternoon.

Preparing to teach cabinet secretary school also made me think about why government administrators enter and stay in the field. After all, public management has never been a glamour profession. And, it is today more difficult than ever to get the job done. The problems and issues have never been more complex, far more so than when I entered the field almost 40 years ago. You can never rest on your laurels. If you had a good year this year, that's terrific, but there is likely nothing to look forward to next year except more of the same challenges, or even bigger issues and problems to manage. The level of scrutiny public officials undergo has never been higher, and we are in a media environment where every problem is a headline, while successes are routinely ignored. "You can have 99 successes and nobody notices, and one mistake and you're dead."[8] The resources available to handle responsibilities and fix problems have never been more limited. Austerity is not sporadic or cyclical problem, but is endemic. A positive budgetary year may be the one when you do not have to give back some of your money midway through that **fiscal year** (terms in bold appear in the glossary at the end of the book). Seemingly, the public's understanding of how government actually works has never been lower, on both ends of the political spectrum. Our field changes constantly. Whenever I get the notion that I have seen it all, that is a good harbinger that shortly, I will encounter something I have never encountered before. And "Every day there is more and more to manage...."[9]

In addition, the image of public service, historically not very high, has never really recovered from a President of the United States himself declaring in his inaugural address (among other occasions) that "Government is the problem." He was not the first to say it, but he gave it the most currency. Surely this statement is one of the greatest examples ever of a bird fouling its own nest. At times, it seems that government employees rank in public esteem somewhere below used car salesmen, if slightly above serial killers. "Public management is not a profession for the faint of heart, for those who want always to be loved and admired, or for those who think there is nothing to running the public's business but a little common sense and acumen."[10]

So why do we do it? I believe that there are multiple reasons. First, public service earns those of us in government an amount of **psychic income** that few other professions can match. Psychic income in government comes in the form of helping people, individually and/or collectively, and in making our society function a little bit better. In the public sector you are almost always doing one or the other, so your psychic paycheck arrives daily, not just once or twice a month. Second, as a manager, you double your rewards via the opportunity to make solid managerial decisions and get things done. At the end of the worst day I ever had as a cabinet secretary, I could still point to half a dozen things that I had accomplished that day. You can "make a difference," as one of the governors in whose cabinet I served told us repeatedly. What we do matters—a great deal. It matters to the clients our agencies serve, who are often less fortunate than we are, and it matters to the citizenry in general. Ultimately, we managers are the ones who determine performance—whether public services really serve the public well. There is no more noble profession than public service!

And, you are in the arena, which is where the action is. Your work may be challenging, even frustrating, but it is never dull or boring. The average citizen might find much of what we do tedious, but those of us in the business know that we are truly in the middle of "the show that never ends." During my first cabinet assignment, I told everyone that I never had a slow day. In my second cabinet posting, which featured 10 times the budget and 20 times the number of employees, I revised the description of my working environment: I never had a slow hour. If that were insufficient motivation to go to work every day, the best part of my job has always been working with the people—dedicated, hardworking, altruistic, and not especially motivated by money. For all its difficulties, if you don't love your job, it's time to take a long look in the mirror and think about another career. If you do love your job, you'll want to keep getting better at it via every means possible.

Observers of public management debate whether it is an art or a science. My graduate school advisor, a wonderful man, disliked it when anyone tried to portray government management as an art. The implication of that statement in his mind was that it is a talent, not something you can learn. Other analysts feel that government administration is strictly an art. "Public management is an art, not a science—and a people art at that." In my view it is both a science and an art. There are numerous scientific aspects to management that never vary, but it is an art, too, if for no other reason than that sometimes you have to go with your instinct and intuition because what you encounter is neither in your previous experience nor any textbook. Whether it is an art, a science, or both, though, no matter how talented you are, you can and should get better at it. I did, and I hope to help others get better via this volume.

To experienced managers reading this book, many of the suggestions may seem very basic, even obvious. I have included basic material precisely because some of the basics are not at all obvious to, and not always used by, individuals in leadership positions who are not managers.

Finally, if the tone of this book appears overly pedantic or even omniscient, please bear in mind that for every imperative that is based on my own insight, two derive from the wisdom of someone more knowledgeable and experienced than I, and three stem from mistakes I made. I may not have made all the missteps described in this book, but I made a lot of them. As I once said to my teenagers in a different context, "You don't have to make *every* mistake I made."

## NOTES

1.  Wilson, *Rethinking Public Administration*, 47.
2.  Osborne and Plastrik, *Banishing Bureaucracy*, 24.
3.  Wilson, *Rethinking Public Administration*, 10.
4.  Frank, *The Wrecking Crew*, 130-131.
5.  Ashworth, *Caught Between the Dog and Fireplug*, 182.
6.  Chase and Reveal, *How to Manage in the Public Sector*, 178.
7.  Osborne and Plastrik, *Banishing Bureaucracy*, 221.
8.  Osborne and Gaebler, *Reinventing Government*, 21.
9.  Gawande, *The Checklist Manifesto*, 12.
10. Chase and Reveal, *How to Manage in the Public Sector*, 179.

*Part I*

# You: Managing Yourself

Management, leadership, and ethics have one thing in common: the most important thing is what you yourself do. Giving orders to others will do you little good if you cannot set a good example. Before you make a single policy decision, before you hire or fire anyone, before you spend the first taxpayer dollar, you must have your own personal house in order. If you are personally disorganized, there is no way you are going to run an organized agency. It is as simple as that. To handle the wide variety and high volume of responsibilities and tasks that come with the top job, you must properly manage your own resources, starting with your time and your direct interactions with your staff. You must also practice good leadership, something not separate and distinct from good management, but the other side of the same coin. And you must conduct yourself ethically at all times, as well as promote, encourage, and demand ethical behavior throughout your organization. The rules for proper self-management, leadership, and ethics are universal within government; they do not vary, regardless of the responsibilities, location, or size of the agency you run.

Chapter 1, "Self-Management," includes the following topics: "Your Time," "Keeping Lists," "Meetings," "Using Your Immediate Staff," and a few others in "Miscellaneous." Chapter 2 covers "Leadership," with these subchapters: "Setting the Tone," "Your Leadership Style," "Coaching Your Team," and "Dealing with Adversity." Chapter 3 is "Ethics."

*Chapter One*

# Self-Management

"Manager, Manage Thyself"

## INTRODUCTION

The Gospel According to Luke, 15:32, contains the proverb, "Physician, heal thyself," probably because Luke was himself a doctor. Had Luke instead been, say, head of the Antioch Housing Authority, he might have coined the phrase, "Manager, manage thyself." If you cannot manage yourself properly, regardless of your policy expertise, you have no business running a government agency.

Effective self-management includes but is not limited to:

1. efficient use of your time,
2. making and using lists to manage your work, keep track of details, and aid your memory,
3. properly using meetings, and
4. appropriately utilizing your immediate staff.

## YOUR TIME

Some individuals wear their workaholism like a badge of honor. But if you are working 24/7 and have no time for family and friends, no time to exercise and be healthy, and no time to take a vacation, you are probably not a good manager and/or your organization is not in good shape. I love to go to work every day, but I love to come home to my family at night too. You may be either micromanaging or spending too much time on unimportant matters—

3

or both. The flood of input that all managers receive, from e-mails, smart phones, text messages, and the like, has made time management more important than ever. This surfeit of distractions acts as a centrifugal force pulling you away from the center of things to the periphery. You must manage your time so that you can focus on big picture and priority items and avoid wasting time and energy on matters that can be satisfactorily handled by subordinates and/or have no bearing on the ultimate success of you and your agency.

To properly allocate your time, first recognize that you cannot and should not do everything. You need to spend as much time as possible on what is most important to your organization and minimize the time you spend on time-sensitive and routine matters. Self-help guru Steven Covey has the best discussion of this imperative with his Time Management Matrix. He explains that people spend too much time doing the things that are both urgent and important (handling crises, dealing with pressing problems, and working on deadline-driven projects) and not enough time on matters that are important but not urgent (prevention, recognizing new opportunities, planning, and prioritizing).[1] It is very easy to get caught up in daily activities, in meeting after meeting, in micromanagement. Do not get into a situation where "Inevitably, the crisis of the day must be addressed before the crisis of the year, much less the decade."[2] If you make this mistake, over time you will be better at getting some detail work done, but you will not be able to give the time to the major issues and problems facing your organization. Some of those problems will be very obvious to you and to others, but other problems will not be obvious. Some leaders schedule unstructured time on a daily basis to deal with what is important. As one manager put it, "I need an hour and a half once a day to think."[3] Personally, I do not regularize such time, but have found over the years that I do a lot of strategic thinking and prioritizing during my morning shower, on my daily commutes, and while driving to and from meetings—all times when there are no distractions.

One important way to accomplish the goal of effective time management is to get control of your schedule. Do not overschedule yourself. The higher up you are in an organization and the more demands on your time, the more you need a scheduling meeting. At the scheduling meeting, you decide how much time to allocate to your varied responsibilities and determine which invitations you should accept. Attendees at the scheduling meeting should include your secretary or scheduler, your deputy and/or executive assistant if you have one, and your media person (again, if you have one). Scheduling meetings should be held weekly, at a regular time if at all possible, and rescheduled (not canceled) if you are off or have an unavoidable conflict. These days it is very easy to keep your own schedule on a smartphone. Resist that temptation; add nothing to your schedule yourself on an ad hoc basis, unless it is a request you get directly from your boss or another elected official. Even in the case of the latter—and in every other case—tell them your secretary/scheduler will call them, and you can add that you no longer schedule yourself because you would just screw it up. That statement is self-deprecating and also very likely true.

Similarly, your scheduler/secretary should not add anything to your schedule absent your and your team's input (with such automatic exceptions as you may wish to delineate in advance—say, your boss, your cabinet colleagues, and other elected officials). All decisions as to whether to attend a particular event or agree to a meeting can thus be made not in a vacuum, but in the context of all competing demands on your time, and with the input of your key aides, so that you can schedule strategically. As mentioned, do not overschedule yourself, particularly when it comes to invitations. What value are you adding to the event? As the head of your agency, you have some responsibility to act as the public face of your entity, but that is not your only or even your most important responsibility.

When making up your schedule, be sure to allow sufficient time between meetings to collect your thoughts, review any notes you may have from previous meetings on the same subject (see "Meetings", below), and focus on what you want to accomplish at the next meeting. You may need only five minutes for this purpose or you may need a longer period of time. But you will need it. The larger and more diverse your department, the higher the number of different matters you will need to deal with. As an agency head, one of the things that will mark your performance as superior instead of mediocre will be your ability to deal with multiple issues, problems, and initiatives contemporaneously.

In addition to controlling your schedule, you need to get rid of the routine stuff to the maximum extent possible. That is what deputies, assistants, and secretaries are for. Handle the routine matters you *do* have to handle as efficiently as possible. To start with, identify someone to manage your correspondence, both written and electronic. Otherwise, that correspondence is going to manage you. I still want to see the majority of what comes addressed to me via postal mail or e-mail, but not all of it. At a minimum, have your secretary or administrative assistant 1) remove any correspondence that is marketing, and 2) direct constituent service-related inquiries to the appropriate part of your organization for response (making sure that there is some tracking mechanism). When you get your hands on written correspondence that passes this screening, you will still end up delegating a great deal of it. To that end, you may want to use formal transmittal slips that offer a checklist of options, everything from "**FYI**" to "Prepare a letter for my signature" (or the signature of the elected official for whom you work). Or you may simply use post-it notes for that purpose. But in either case, have your secretary or assistant track what you send out, if a response is required, so that you can be sure that your subordinate has handled your request. Much more often than not, such tracking will prove to be unnecessary as your employee will comply with the request in a timely fashion. But even the very best employee loses a request in the crush of day-to-day business, and you need a simple fail-safe mechanism. Similarly, when you forward an e-mail to a subordinate for handling, copy your secretary or assistant so they can log and track the response.

It will also be helpful to examine your signature policy. You should not be signing documents unless you are legally required to do so (you as the **CEO** may be the only official who can officially terminate an employee, for example) or if you are **adding value**. By adding value, I generally mean, are you actually reviewing the document for content before signing it, or are you signing it because it has been placed in front of you for signature? If you are not adding value by signing, you should delegate signature authority to the employee at the appropriate level below you. If someone else could sign the document just as well as you could, if they were in your shoes, that person should be the one doing the signing. It is all part of matching responsibility with authority; if you have given an employee below you the responsibility to handle a matter, you should give him or her the authority to sign documents relating to that matter. Also, I prefer not to use autopens for ordinary matters. If the document is so routine that you need not examine it individually before signing, it is very likely that it should be signed by a subordinate instead. In my first cabinet assignment, I realized that I was spending a huge amount of time every day simply signing documents. So I had my secretary log everything I signed for a couple of months, and then used the log summary to decide which items were more appropriately handled at a lower level.

As with many rules, there is an exception. I have never delegated the signing of recognition letters or certificates, nor have I signed them by autopen, even if I am presented with a hundred of them at a time. The autopen signature—easily discernible to your employees—cheapens the recognition, in my view. The least I can do is sign the certificate or letter personally, and if it is a letter, I like to add a note at the bottom, sometimes only a phrase or a sentence, particularly if I have met the employee. A little thing like that can mean a lot to the employee. As discussed in Chapter 4, employee recognition is extremely important.

Once you have narrowed the number of documents you need to sign, you are still going to spend a lot of time signing things. To speed things along, you should insist that any document requiring your signature be **idiot-proofed** (you know who the idiot is) by affixing a "sign here" stickie. Especially with a thick contract or grant application, which may require your signature in multiple places, you do not want to spend any time searching for signature blocks. If you have a high volume of documents to sign, you should also have your staff prepare color-coded sheets indicating the time sensitivity of the document. Pink could represent "sign this document before you leave work today," green could indicate "sign this by the next business day" and blue "sign when you get a chance." Finally, I advise my staff with regard to documents that I am required to sign but am not going to read (e.g., contracts) that my rules are the following. I will sign whatever they put in front of me, but I expect that the document will have been reviewed thoroughly before it gets to my level. Don't ever burn me by not reviewing it or try to slip something by me; that will subject the person who did so to a future level of scrutiny that he will find very uncomfortable.

In addition to saving time by not signing documents, there are many other ways to save time on routine matters. Note pads and to-do lists (see next section) may be first generation time management, but they are essential. I carry them everywhere I go. I also carry loads of post-its and transmittal slips. In down time while traveling or between meetings, it is easy to manage your correspondence in this fashion.

What you are trying to do via effective time management is negate the **Pareto principle** as it applies to your schedule. In economics, the Pareto principle holds that 80 percent of one's results come from 20 percent of one's activities. If you are wasting your time on non-essential tasks, it is very likely that the Pareto principle applies to you. Your goal should be to free up as much of that 80 percent of your time as possible to become even more productive. If you have scheduled your time properly, and if you have off-loaded non-essential duties from your pallet, you will have adequate time to focus on your major issues and priorities. If you have to throw time at a really serious problem, and you will, you will have that time available to throw. One chief executive explained how he knew he was spending time on important matters: "My desk was always a mess, even when I was CEO, because I actually concentrated on a few things that were important."[4]

## KEEPING LISTS

Write it down. Nothing will improve your personal productivity more than making and maintaining lists. I recommend that you have two lists in front of you at all times: a list of phone calls to make or return, and a to-do list. Mine are on paper, but yours can be on your smartphone or tablet or desktop computer. You should also have a checklist for activities or projects, to make sure that you do not leave anything out or forget a step. I further recommend keeping a pen and note card in your pocket to jot down notes of things you need to take care of. You might be on the job—in a meeting on another subject, or driving to an appointment—or off the job. When you are running a large organization, you are often thinking about things related to work even when you are not physically at your workplace. In the words of one of my cabinet colleagues, "To really do the job right, you are probably thinking about it all the time." You remember something then that you may not remember at another time—when you actually need it. Some people prefer pocket recorders, but they have one defect: you cannot use them if you are in a meeting. Smartphones can also serve the same purpose, but have the same defect. If you write something down while in a meeting, you look like you are paying attention. If you enter something into your smartphone, you look like you are distracted.

There are two basic reasons to keep lists. The first is that it will greatly aid your memory. A checklist is simply a reminder to remember. My father once said, "The mind has a major fault. It thinks of things at the wrong time." You can remember it, but not necessarily recall it (retrieve it) when you need to. With a list in front of you, you do not need to worry about whether you remembered it. My family makes great fun of the fact that I have a master packing list (not to mention a master grocery list) but it never fails that we are on vacation and we have to find a store to purchase something they have forgotten. But I don't forget anything, because I do not have to remember anything.

The master packing list is an example of the checklist that helps with activities or projects where you do not want to leave anything out. Sometimes leaving something out can be harmful or fatal to the effort. It is analogous to an internet address or travel directions. If you mistype just one character in the **URL**, you will not get to the website you are seeking. If there are twelve turns between your home and your destination, directions that include only eleven of those turns will get you lost.

The second reason is that lists greatly aid in organizing and prioritizing your time. If you have your to-do list in front of you, you can look at your responsibilities holistically and determine, often at a glance, what your top priorities are. Yes, there will absolutely be days when your lists will look exactly the same at quitting time as they did at the start of the workday, because you will have been **overtaken by events** and unable to get to anything on the list. But making lists and sticking to them keeps those days to a minimum. Unquestionably, making and sticking to lists requires discipline. You have to be self-disciplined, and you have to get your subordinates to be disciplined, too.

The great thing about a list is that, once you have created it, you do not have to create it again, merely update it. And if said list is on a computer, it is even easier.

## MEETINGS

I think I can state without fear of contradiction that more time has been wasted in meetings than in any other governmental activity. As one CEO stated, "I believe that the majority of meetings could easily be cut to a third of what they are and accomplish much more. People just lose track after some point, and it doesn't matter what's being said."[5] It need not be thus. A few basic rules, if followed religiously, will greatly shorten your meetings and make them more productive. Having a successful meeting is equal parts preparing, conducting, and following up.

Preparation consists of understanding what kind of meeting you are having, and composing a suitable agenda. Are you problem-solving, monitoring a given program or project, or seeking or providing information? In the case of the latter, you may be looking for information on a given topic, or you may be providing information to staff about policies or new developments. Any meeting that you convene should have an agenda, prepared by you or an aide, in advance. Agendas have two purposes: focus and tracking. The agenda need not be lengthy, but should include the items that need to be discussed and the decisions that need to be made; that's the focus part. The second purpose of the agenda, especially at regular meetings, is tracking. My staff always knows that a given item does not get removed from the agenda unless it is 100 percent resolved or fixed. It might move up or down on the agenda as it fluctuates in relative priority, but it never leaves the list until it is completely finished. This tactic almost always has the effect of making sure that important matters get done.

When you conduct the meeting, if even one person is unknown to other participants, begin with introductions. This can take the form of each person introducing himself or, if there are multiple "teams," each team leader can introduce her team. The goals of introductions are 1) to make the discussions more informal and familiar—the more contentious the meeting is likely to be, the more important this is—and 2) to make sure that the attendance of each person is acknowledged as appropriate, and signal that everyone can contribute if they have something to say. Although there are exceptions, I prefer not to sit at the head of the table, even (or especially) if I am running the meeting. It is marginally more informal and democratic.

Following the introductions, unless it is a regularly recurring meeting, always begin the discussion with a brief statement regarding the purpose of the meeting and what you expect to accomplish. Then, follow the agenda, keeping extraneous discussion and digressions to a minimum. Let everybody talk, but keep on topic. Announcing the purpose of the meeting and keeping it on point maintain the focus of the group on what needs to done.

All discussion must be courteous. Vigorous debate and dissent are permissible, even encouraged; personal attacks and any effort to label someone else's opinion as invalid are *verboten*. It is your job as the person leading the meeting to politely but firmly call an immediate halt to anyone violating these ground rules. Another thing you should not do at a meeting is have a lengthy discussion about a problem and/or its solution when key information germane to that problem is still missing, and cannot be obtained by the meeting's end. You are wasting everyone's time. Have the discussion about that particular topic once the information is at hand.

You can specify who should attend a given meeting, but I generally defer to my section chiefs as to whom they want to attend. For example, if I need a meeting to discuss a personnel issue, the human resources office head will attend and can bring whomever she wants to the meeting. I encourage my directors to bring anyone who has information that will bear on the matter at hand. I disagree strongly with the old saw that the fewer people in a meeting, the better the decisions will be. In today's increasingly complicated world, the more complex the issue, the more unlikely it is that any one person (or even a few people) will have all the information necessary to make an informed decision. I have been in construction progress meetings on large projects with 30 people in the room and that was not too many. Your division leaders are free to attend alone—but they had better know the answers to all the questions. A division leader seldom has all the answers himself, and that's fine. I hired him to get things done, not to know every detail personally. If I have a meeting to make a decision on something, I want to make the decision at that meeting, with the people at the meeting who have the information. I do not want to wait to have another meeting where someone else can attend. If that happens, I have wasted everybody's time at the first meeting.

A second reason to have more rather than fewer people at a meeting is that it can be a great learning experience for staffers, regarding not just content but also how decisions are made and meetings conducted. On the other hand, do not hesitate to excuse some attendees midway through a meeting when the matters that concern them have been covered. They may prefer to use the time differently. Of course, do not eject them; give them the option.

To the greatest extent possible, start your meetings on time. Also, except in very limited circumstances, you should insist on technology-free meetings: no cell phones, smart phones, pagers, laptops, or tablet computers. They are distracting to everyone, not just the user, and employing them is rude. Obviously, someone reading e-mail is not focusing on the issue before the group. The technology ban applies to you, too. Route calls to your secretary or other aide during the meeting. Unless the call is coming from someone on your phone interrupt list (see below) or someone you have specifically instructed your secretary to interrupt you for, do not take any calls during the meeting. Just as you should have the attendees' undivided attention, they should have yours. As one leader put it, "When we're in a meeting it starts on time, it ends on time, no technology. It's just, let's stay focused, and we have a much more healthy conversation."[6] If I am in a large meeting in my office and *do* have to take a phone call, by the way, it is only polite in my view that

I step outside the office to take that call, rather than ask everyone else to leave while I take it at my desk. In addition, my departure enables them to continue the discussion in my absence.

Speaking of technology, video conferencing and teleconferencing are obviously tools that you can use, and sometimes must use, depending on how geographically large your jurisdiction is. But if I have the choice, I always prefer face-to-face meetings. I like to read facial expressions and see body language. I also prefer to convey information, especially regarding anything new (programs, policies, developments, etc.) in a meeting as opposed to via e-mail. If you are making a simple announcement about, say, a new staff member, e-mail is great for that purpose. But if you are preparing to issue a new dictum, you need to get feedback in an interactive forum, not via e-mail.

If the meeting has been called for the purpose of reaching a decision, or you have to make a decision in the course of regular business, and the final say is yours, do not make your decision until you have given everyone a chance to express herself. Specifically, as you approach decision time, ask anyone who has not yet spoken, one at a time, what her thoughts are. If you want to poll the members for their final "vote," make sure you ask for their opinions in ascending order of rank. That sequence may ameliorate the tendency of employees to defer to their bosses.

You need to make clear who has the responsibility for any follow-up actions, such as who needs to acquire a key bit of information, who has a task to complete, and who heads up the team charged with solving a problem. If you keep discussing the same problem at repeated meetings, it is because no one has been given the job of fixing it.

Follow-up is made much easier if at each meeting, you or a subordinate take a few notes—*not* minutes, which are generally a waste of time. The notes should cover three things:

1. what decisions were made,
2. what courses of action need to be taken and/or what agreements were reached regarding how given situations will be handled, and
3. most important, who has the responsibility for said actions.

If I am doing the notes myself, and I usually do them myself, I just jot them on the agenda. It is important that you retain those notes and refer to them, whether there is a follow-up meeting or not. If a follow-up meeting takes place without those notes (or without an agenda), it is very likely that old ground will be plowed over again. Eventually, usually, everyone will get back to where they left off at the previous meeting, but only after wasting a considerable amount of time. And if there is no additional meeting, you need the notes to make sure that the action steps are taken by the staffers to whom the assignments were given.

Although you should try to avoid scheduling back-to-back meetings, sometimes they are unavoidable. If you do have consecutive meetings scheduled, and again as sometimes happens, the first meeting runs more than a few minutes long, be polite to the individuals waiting for the second meeting. Either bring the first meeting to a close or reschedule the following meeting. In any event, as mentioned above, even if the meetings run up against each other, always take five minutes between them to clear your head, forget the previous meeting, and review your notes or agenda for the coming meeting. You will be able to make the second meeting much more productive if you do so.

All of the foregoing rules also apply when you are attending someone else's meeting. If it is sufficiently important that you cannot delegate it to someone on your staff, give the convener the courtesy of your distraction-free attention. Also, unless it is your boss and he or she has specifically directed otherwise, or the subject is confidential, bring whomever you need to the meetings. A status-conscious aide of mine once cautioned me not to bring staffers to a certain meeting because that would make me look like less of a "player." Even though I was not certain what it took to be a "player" in the first place, or why that was important, I complied with her counsel that one time, but never again. If a subordinate of yours has information that would bear on the meeting subject that you yourself do not have, and you leave her behind, you are doing your boss and/or your counterparts a disservice.

For major problems or issues, especially those involving parties external to your agency (vendors, legislators, your boss), and those which involve a public presentation, you will likely need a meeting before the meeting. While this sounds like something out of the *Dilbert* comic strip, it is a very necessary and important activity. The meeting before the meeting allows you to understand the nuances of the issue, determine what your goals are for the subsequent meeting, and devise a strategy for achieving those goals. It allows you to engage in the kind of frank discussion about the matter at hand that should never occur in front of external parties. Nothing reflects more poorly on you and your organization than for folks in your department to disagree on factual matters or offer competing approaches, let alone argue, in front of outsiders.

Hearings before legislative bodies are a special case, which will be discussed in Chapter 10.

## USING YOUR IMMEDIATE STAFF

Effectively using your immediate staff, to the extent you have them in your agency, can greatly enhance your personal productivity. These individuals include but are not limited to your deputy, administrative assistant, personal secretary, and director of your administrative division. First, empower them with both responsibility and authority (and make sure the two match). It is very important that everyone in your department understand that when this select group of people calls, staff should react the same as they would react if you yourself were to call. If you do not specifically articulate this to your staff, it is a certainty that the level of cooperation you expect will not always be forthcoming. The other side of this coin is that your staff should operate smoothly when interacting with the rest of your agency, some of whom they will outrank and some of whom they will not outrank. They should never throw their weight around or put on airs. Anyone who has to invoke his position or rank in making a request for information or action lacks the appropriate finesse for the job. If you have communicated how the rest of your department should interact with your immediate staff and the appropriate cooperation is not occurring, the request for correction should be made by you, not your staffer, to the offender's superior.

Never use your immediate staff for a personal errand, no matter how busy you are and no matter how minor the chore. Doing so would demean them and their professionalism. No staffer of any rank should get your lunch, go to the dry cleaner for you, run an errand, or, to use an extreme example, help with your child care.

Your confidential secretary or assistant should have two primary qualities. First, they should have people skills sufficiently developed that their interactions with your colleagues, your boss, other elected officials, and the public always reflect favorably on you and your bureau. Said people skills should include recognizing by name elected officials who will be calling. Elected officials may not notice if your secretary knows them by name, but they will most certainly notice—and probably say something to you—if your secretary does not. Obviously, you can provide your assistant with the list of key names, but it is up to him or her to memorize it. Over the years, I have been blessed with a number of secretaries whom my colleagues have made a point to praise. That is what you should aim for. Second, your confidential secretary or assistant should possess enough organizational ability to handle your scheduling. You do not want to spend time doing it yourself, as mentioned above, and you especially do not want to spend time fixing scheduling problems. Your assistant should never send you to the wrong location or at the wrong time. You should have a limited tolerance for such mistakes; if they happen more than rarely, you should probably replace your secretary.

As a bonus, it can be helpful if your secretary is attuned to the personalities and conflicts of your immediate office personnel. It is an axiom of human nature that in any group of 10 people, two are going to dislike each other. It is not necessarily your job to deal with that dynamic personally, but you should be aware of it, and your secretary can keep you informed.

If you have an administrative assistant in addition to a personal secretary, the assistant can manage your correspondence, postal and e-mail. Otherwise, your secretary should do it.

Those are the most important things I look for in a secretary. Anything else is gravy and not really essential to the job. In these days of universal computing power and e-mail correspondence, your assistant's ability to take dictation or even compose correspondence for you is really superfluous. I have found that the qualities I am seeking are most often found in an individual of some maturity, as opposed to a more youthful person, no matter how energetic and intelligent he or she may be.

You should never raise your voice or publicly demean any of your agency's personnel, but especially not your support staff. (More on this in Chapter 4.) If you need to be stern be stern—not abusive.

Hire a complementary individual to be your deputy, if you have one, rather than a similar one. For example, if you are strong in money matters, your Deputy should be strong in different areas; conversely, if budget management is not your specialty, it would be good if your number two were strong in that area. Use your number two (it could be your Deputy or your Executive Assistant if you have no Deputy) to manage your office. He or she should have ultimate responsibility for office scheduling, disciplinary matters, vacation approvals, correspondence, and the like. The reason that you should not handle any of these matters is that you need to have time to deal with big picture items. All employees in your immediate office, whether professional or support, including your confidential secretary, should report to her, not you. Beyond managing your office, you can deploy her to do anything else that needs doing.

As will be discussed in greater detail in Chapter 4, you should expect your immediate staff to be very free when speaking with you. They should tell you at all times what they think—what you need to hear—which includes bringing you bad news and telling you anything you should or should not have done.

## MISCELLANEOUS

I strongly recommend that you belong to your national association, if there is one. You need a peer group, and it is likely that your counterparts from around the country are the only people who are truly your peers. Your cabinet colleagues in your state or county may have some of the management problems that you do, but none of the policy problems that you do. Nor, obviously, do your boss, the Governor or Mayor, or your key subordinates share the same difficulties. Across the three national associations to which I have belonged, it was sometimes astonishing how often and how closely my problems tracked those of other jurisdictions around the country, down to the smallest detail. When I ran my state's health and social services department and had difficulty with the seemingly arcane issue of how to provide services to the handful of individuals who had both development disabilities and sexual behavior issues, I was surprised to find that most of my colleagues in other states faced the identical situation. Information exchange with your compatriots is of great value.

Equally valuable is benchmarking your organization against other jurisdictions at national conferences—where are you ahead or behind everybody else? Even if all you find out is that nobody is currently doing anything different from or better than what you are doing, that can be extremely valuable information.

Even if your organization is not one that offers services on a 24/7 basis, you always need to make a chain of command designation when you are absent from your state, city, or county for a vacation, conference, or any other purpose. There should be an unbroken chain of command at all times. You never know when a problem might arise. The name of your designee and the duration of the designation should be communicated both to your boss's executive office and to your **leadership team** in advance. Even if you are going to be reachable via cell phone and e-mail, there should be someone with a physical presence in your jurisdiction should circumstances require it.

You need to establish ground rules for how and when your key subordinates should reach you after hours. Decide what you want and then communicate it to everybody. My own instruction to my key staffers was, call 24/7 if there is an emergency, just make sure it *is* an emergency. My aides never abused the privilege.

By the way, many individuals convey time-sensitive information via e-mail or text message, in the expectation that I and other recipients are constantly monitoring our electronic communications. While I regularly check e-mails after hours, that should not be the expectation—and sometimes, of course, it is not even an option. In a true emergency, always use the phone and instruct your subordinates to do the same. That goes for anything requiring a dialogue, as well. E-mail is the greatest method ever invented for conveying straight information, but inadequate when interaction is required. Again, use the phone instead.

You should have a **"phone interrupt list"** so that your staff knows when to interrupt a meeting or phone call. Staff should not have to guess whether a call is worth interrupting you or not—and there always seems to be a new employee or a temporary one who answers the phone. A sample of one such memo I wrote is below. Who you want on that list is obviously up to you. For everyone else, staff takes a message. I find it very discourteous to interrupt a meeting in my office unless it is a priority call.

The same goes for cell phone calls. The corollary of the phone interrupt list is that I give out my cell phone number selectively—key aides and phone interrupt list names only. During office hours, I seldom take a cell phone call if I am on the phone with someone else or in a meeting. Everybody knows my office number and can call that number if there is something urgent or time-sensitive. In any event, I never answer a cell phone call if I do not recognize the number. If it is important, they will leave a message or call back. I prefer not to be blind-sided, ever.

Finally, you should personally approach every day as a learning experience. From your first day on the job to your last, you should never stop learning about your agency and your employees, even after you are very far up on the learning curve. From a results point of view, you will have successes and failures—but you should learn from them all. It is the only way to operate.

February 10, 2001

Memorandum

TO: Karryl Hubbard
Office of the Secretary Personnel Who May Answer My Phone
Division of Public Health Personnel Who May Answer My Phone
FROM: Vince Meconi
RE: Phone Interrupt List

Normally, when I am on the phone or in a meeting, I would prefer to have whoever answers my phone take a message if a new call comes in, unless the caller specifies that it is urgent.

However, if certain persons call, I would always like to be interrupted, so that I can decide whether to take the call or not.

This list of persons includes:

—Governor Ruth Ann Minner

—Lt. Governor John Carney

—Lee Ann Walling, Senior Advisor to the Governor

—Matt Denn, Counsel to the Governor

—Greg Patterson, Communications Director for the Governor

—Any State Senator or State Representative

—My wife Sharon and daughters Lindsay and Jamie

Thanks for your assistance. I would appreciate your sharing this memo with anyone who might be answering my phone, even if briefly.

—vpm

## NOTES

1. Covey, *The 7 Habits of Highly Effective People*, 151.
2. Wilson, *Rethinking Public Administration*, 13.
3. Conde interview, *New York Times* 1-17-10, Business 2.
4. Leahy interview, *New York Times* 2-3-13, Business 2.
5. Babbitt interview, *New York Times* 7-8-12, Business 2.
6. Rosensweig interview, *New York Times* 7-11-10, Business 2.

*Chapter Two*

# Leadership

## "They Are Two Halves of the Same Coin"

### INTRODUCTION

Before you understand what leadership is, you should understand what it is not, because there is a wealth of wrongheaded information in circulation about this key subject.

First and most important, some people think that control and power by themselves make you a leader; they emphatically do not. No matter how "powerful" you are, as the old saying goes, if you look behind you and there is no one following you, by definition you are not leading.

Second, there is a school of thought that says that management and leadership are two distinct qualities. You can be a good manager but a poor leader, or a poor manager but a good leader, goes this line of thinking. I strongly disagree. Management and leadership are two halves of the same coin. You cannot be a good manager without being a successful leader, and vice versa. It is true that "No management success can compensate for failure in leadership."[1] But is also true that a so-called "inspirational leader" who cannot manage will accomplish very little.

In the private sector, a frequent approach is to have a leader as Chief Executive Officer and a manager as Chief Operating Officer, and the federal government appears to contemplate the same arrangement. The **GPRA** (Government Performance and Results Act) Modernization Act of 2010 (actually enacted in early 2011) formalizes the role of the number two position in every federal department as that agency's COO.[2] This statute follows on the heels of administrative directives by the three consecutive presidential administrations to the same effect. While the latter arrangement is certainly

19

an improvement over having a manager in neither of the two top agency positions, it is not a substitute for having the agency head manage his organization. And that is assuming that the deputy does, in fact, concentrate on management. But interviews with individuals who have recently held such positions leave much doubt. Two years into his tenure, one stated, "The job of the Deputy Secretary is still a little unclear to me."[3] Occupants of those jobs described six roles they fill in addition to that of COO, some managerial in nature and others not so: "alter ego for the cabinet secretary... convenor, policy advisor, leader of departmental initiatives, crisis manager, [and] liaison to stakeholders."[4]

The CEO/COO split does not work well in government, in my view. Marshaling resources and overcoming bureaucratic and political obstacles are too difficult and too essential to any success your organization may have to hand off to a subordinate while you concentrate only on policy and being the public face of the organization.

The President of the United States is both head of the government (the person who is responsible for submitting budgets, proposing legislation, and running the executive branch) and head of state (the nation's ceremonial leader who addresses the nation, for example, following a great tragedy). As the head of a government organization, as manager you are its head of government, and as leader you are its head of state.

Third, do not put much stock in standard leadership texts that purport to see differences between transactional, innovative, transforming, charismatic, etc., leaders—they do not apply in government agencies.

There are many, many definitions and descriptions of leadership. Over the years I have developed my own. To me, a good leader has a vision for her organization, sets the tone and leads by example, has the right style (has a positive attitude, is energetic, is mentally tough, is reliable, and is informal), coaches her team, and can handle adversity. Vision is covered in Chapter 5, "Prioritization;" more on each of the other characteristics below.

## SETTING THE TONE

When I had my Senate confirmation hearing to take the position of the state health department secretary, a senator asked why I was qualified to run the department, inasmuch as I was not a doctor. My response spoke in equal parts to the management aspects of the job (setting priorities, fiscal responsibility) and the leadership aspects of the job (setting the tone, leading by example). My point was that a physician might well possess those qualities, but there is nothing in medical training that guarantees that a doctor will be a good manager or leader.

In the same way that you must manage yourself properly, as described in Chapter 1, you must lead yourself properly. "You can't lead anybody if you can't lead yourself."[5]

To that end, leading by example and setting the tone for your organization are key elements of being a good leader. Leadership is more about behavior than skills. Never underestimate the degree to which you set the tone of an organization. "It's a real cliché to say that the boss is the one that sets the tone, but it's absolutely true."[6] On matters large and small, your staff takes their cues from you, whatever the behavioral or managerial dimension (civility rather than arrogance, ethical behavior, proper money management, etc.). They are always watching you, so you had better lead by example.

Never ask your team to do something that you would not do yourself. If it is budget cutback time, for example, your office budget needs to take a cut along with everybody else's. Never exempt yourself from anything that is mandatory for all other employees. If every staffer is required to attend a certain kind of training, be sure that you are in the front row, where everybody can see you, at one of the sessions. "Do as I say, not as I do" is not a good way to parent your children, and it is not a good way to lead your organization. One chief executive had this to say about leading by example: "We've done mission and vision and value statements. But I think what you write on a piece of paper is not as important as how you behave every day. People will see and take clues from your day-to-day behaviors far more than from a plaque on a wall. Your words in action speak far greater than your words in print."[7]

Leading by example includes the necessity of being on an even keel at all times. It is important because both key staffers and line employees will be affected by your demeanor—if you are in a bad mood and broadcast it, it is a downer for everyone. States one CEO, "Consistency is important to me. I think my partners and employees appreciate the fact that you get the same…every day, regardless of the circumstances. You don't have to think about whether to approach me. If one of my employees told me that they had to think about what my mood was on a particular day—'How is he?' 'Can we talk?'—I'd quit. I never want to be that person."[8] And as we used to say in my departments, no matter what is going on that inclines you to show anger, you have to "put the gun down."

## YOUR LEADERSHIP STYLE

Good leaders have a positive attitude and a lot of energy—to solve problems, to take on challenges, to deal with setbacks, sometimes even just to come to work each day. Displaying that positive attitude and energy will mean that when you lead, people will follow. A big part of leadership is confidence;

you must look, feel, and act like you can handle the problems and issues that come your way.

Except for the most extreme circumstances, there is no reason for you to have anything but an informal, open, relaxed style of doing business. You should not be a mystery to your personnel; they should know what kind of a person you are and that you are approachable. You motivate people by letting them do their jobs, encouraging them, and acknowledging their good work. You do not motivate them by fear, threats, or micromanagement. Attempting to lead through fear and intimidation may work temporarily, but cannot work in the long run. (There will be more on this subject in the "How to Manage Your Employees" section of Chapter 4.) Humility should be the order of the day. Try to be on a first-name basis with as many people as you can. Do not spend a minute worrying about any amenities that might come with the job (other than a reserved parking space that will save you time during a busy day, which will be almost every day). Forget about the size of your office, the office furniture, or anything of a similar nature. Your focus should be wholly on the job at hand. In fact, any focus on amenities will quickly become known to your employees and be a significant negative in their eyes. Any fame or prestige that happens to come with the job (and there may be very little of it) should be irrelevant to you. And subscribe to the old cliché, "...take your work seriously, but don't take yourself too seriously. What we do is important, but let's make sure we can laugh at ourselves now and again."[9] By all means, keep a sense of humor about yourself and about what is going on—if you do not have a few good laughs at every staff meeting, something is probably wrong.

A very important aspect of your leadership style is keeping your word. Whether the recipient of your commitment is a legislator, an employee, a colleague, your boss, or any other outside party, if you say you will do something, you must do it without fail. If you say you will not do something, you cannot do it. You should follow this rule even when (as sometimes seems to be the case) everyone else appears to have abandoned it. The result will be that you will gain enhanced credibility as a leader. Conversely, if you fail to honor your commitments, you will wreck your reputation, especially if any of the recipients of your promises have made decisions and taken action based on your assurances. One chief executive summed it up in the following way: "I don't think there's anything worse... than somebody who gives you their word and then goes back on it. If you give somebody your word internally or as a rep..., it has to be done—no ifs, ands, or buts. Whether it's a good idea or bad, if you committed to do it, you have to do it." If you later decide it was a mistake, you have to do "it anyway because that's more important."[10] A corollary of keeping your word is never to promise things that you cannot do. As another leader recalled, "One of my early bosses...gave me a few tips. He said, 'No. 1, don't make any promises you can't keep. No. 2, keep the promises that you make.... If you do all those things, you'll be successful.' They were very simple lessons, and I've never forgotten them."[11]

## COACHING YOUR TEAM

When you take the reins of an organization, you become the coach of a team, in both senses of the word. You are leading them, but you are always trying to help them become better. It does not matter that you inherited 95 percent of the employees in your chain of command, or that (if you come from outside the organization) you know very few of the staff. They are now all part of your flock. Treat them accordingly, and treat them well even if they do not always return the favor.

Leaders care about their people; they protect their people and look after their welfare. Always regard them as the most important part of your organization. (More on this topic as well in Chapter 4.) If you as head of the agency have the attitude that employees are interchangeable—that employees are overhead, not resources—all the other leaders in your department will eventually behave the same way. You can then expect both morale and productivity to decline. "Leaders take the blame and spread the credit.... Even when a subordinate is to blame for some mistake within the organization, the executive should take the hit in public; she can settle accounts with the employee in private."[12]

One of the worst trends in government these days is the tendency for leaders to abandon their employees when the going gets tough. It is bad enough that some politicians and bosses stand by and watch as their employees are eviscerated; some are worse by actively throwing people under the bus. It happens so often that one of my former cabinet colleagues observed, "It's getting pretty crowded under the bus."

Never throw a subordinate under the bus by scapegoating them. Do not deflect responsibility. You are the captain of the ship. If an employee's conduct is sufficiently egregious that termination is merited, do so. But anything short of that is a private personnel matter, even if discipline is called for, and not fodder for the legislature or the press. Everybody makes mistakes, including you.

A version of this reprehensible maneuver is dissociating oneself from anyone who is under fire. It is called "letting someone twist in the wind." Your approach should be just the opposite. When a senator did not like the policies of one of my division directors, he publicly called for her resignation. In response to media inquiries, I issued the clearest and most unequivocal statement I could think of, declaring that she "is a dedicated public servant doing an outstanding job and there will be no change." It helped a great deal that both of those attributes were true. The senator never forgave me (later on he was calling for *my* resignation), but that was one time the political cost was well worth it. My attitude, and I hope yours, is summed up nicely by this CEO: "I say this explicitly. I am always there; I will always put myself in the line of fire for people. There's never been an exception. I take the bullet. That's my job."[13] Another leader put it this way: "...there is a selflessness to really good leaders and...they [are] willing to sacrifice for the sake of the team."[14]

A different chief executive summed up how to handle his team as follows: "Another technique I use [is] captured in a quote I once read about leadership from Russell Ewing, a British journalist, who said, "A boss creates fear; a leader, confidence. A boss fixes blame; a leader corrects mistakes. A boss knows all; a leader asks questions. A boss makes work drudgery; a leader makes it interesting. A boss is interested in himself or herself; a leader is interested in the group."[15]

Leadership is cheerleading and empowering, but it is also empathy and coaching. "Leadership is getting people to exceed their own expectations."[16] Always be coaching your troops about the rules of the game. One former member of one of my leadership teams made the comment that I ran the leadership team meetings somewhat like seminars; "You were always trying to teach us stuff." I like to think it was a compliment.

## DEALING WITH ADVERSITY

As the leader of an organization, you will be challenged by adversity every day of the week. You will be challenged by your organization, by your environment, by circumstances, and by difficult people—sometimes all at once. Running a government agency is a constant battle against constraints—political, resource, organizational, and especially bureaucratic. Your job is to manipulate those constraints to your advantage and surmount the obstacles that circumstances place in your path, one at a time. Whatever the hurdles, your organization should always see you as undaunted (even if you are feeling somewhat less than dauntless at a given moment).

Mental toughness is a prerequisite for dealing with ever-present critics, be they in the legislature (Chapter 10), the media (Chapter 11), or elsewhere inside or outside government (Chapter 12). Remember that you are making your decisions in real time, while critics are almost always using 20-20 hindsight when they are composing their reviews of your performance. Leaders do not quit easily. Hang in there, because "The devil's happy when the critics run you off."[17]

·You will not succeed at everything. You will not win them all, because nobody does. The President and Vice President of the United States both lost elections on their way to the two highest offices in the land, so it is unlikely that you are going to be undefeated over the course of your career. You may even be unfortunate enough to have to play in a game or two that no one, including you, can win (see "Crisis Management" in Chapter 7). You cannot be afraid to fail. If you try something and it does not succeed, so be it. I am not saying that I don't mind failing—I hate it. It is said that championship athletes are the ones who don't just like to win; they hate to lose. But I would rather try 10 things and succeed at half of them than try two and get 100 percent of them done. When—not if—you get knocked down, get back up. Learn from every loss so you will win the next time around.

As for those difficult people, I love the desk plaque given to me by a cabinet colleague when I was in the middle of a crisis situation: *Illegitimi non carborundum* (mock Latin for "don't let the bastards grind you down".) Words to live by.

## NOTES

1. Covey, *The 7 Habits of Highly Effective People*, 102.

2. US Government Printing Office, http://www.gpo.gov/fdsys/pkg/BILLS-111hr2142enr/pdf/BILLS-111hr2142enr.pdf.

3. Lawrence and Abramson, *What Government Does*, 36.

4. Ibid., 37.

5. Hart interview, New York Times 1-6-13, Business 2.

6. Bryant, *The Corner Office*, 212.

7. Murray interview, *New York Times* 12-23-12, Business 2.

8. Duffy interview, *New York Times* 11-4-12, Business 2.

9. Hicks interview, *New York Times* 6-24-12, Business 2.

10. Babbitt interview, *New York Times* 7-8-12, Business 2.

11. Gumz interview, *New York Times* 2-13-11, Business 2.

12. Ashworth, *Caught Between the Dog and the Fireplug*, 173.

13. Fields interview, *New York Times* 10-2-11, Business 2.

14. Sheehan interview, *New York Times* 6-3-12, Business 2.

15. Flemming interview, *New York Times* 8-12-12, Business 2.

16. Hart interview, *New York Times* 1-6-13, Business 2.

17. Jami, *Venus In Arms*, 28.

*Chapter Three*

# Ethics

## "Not Only Is It Wrong, You'll Get Caught."

As the leader of your organization and a public servant, you have a duty always to act in the public interest. You represent the citizens and taxpayers.

As a career public servant, I am always a little disheartened to see public corruption or misbehavior, especially the hypocrisy of some of our leaders who preached morality right up until the day before they were arrested. I never have a good feeling when reading a headline about bad behavior, even when someone whose politics I loathe is exposed as a wrongdoer, and even if the misbehavior occurs three states away. As much as I would like it not to, his corruption reflects on me and on everyone else in our profession. What is it about public officials and public corruption? I believe that 98-99 percent of all public servants are honest, but it seems that there is a very consistent one to two percent who are not. That percentage does not seem to vary much over time.

I always tell my staff that there are two reasons not to get involved in illegality: not only is it wrong, you'll get caught. I firmly believe that in this day and age, it is almost impossible to get away with wrongdoing in the government arena. There is too much transparency and too much scrutiny, there are too many controls, and there are too many people who can see exactly what you are doing. Depending on what is being done wrong, there may even be significant financial rewards for turning the miscreant in. Sooner or later, just about everybody who is misbehaving is found out.

More specifically, in addition to the moral imperative to do the right thing, unethical conduct can subject an organization to unwanted scrutiny by the media and investigations by outside agencies (legislators, auditors, special panels, etc.), not to mention lawsuits and, if the conduct is outright illegal, indictments and arrests, all of which lead to ruined reputations, career-ending scandals, and public humiliation.

Ethics is one area where you absolutely must lead by example—where your actions, indeed, do speak louder than your words. As the Speaker of my state's House of Representatives wisely remarked to me, "You never take the [leadership] hat off." Your employees, your staffers are always watching you. Regardless of what you say or write to the contrary, they will naturally assume that whatever you do, it is okay for them to do.

In my observation, academic literature on government ethics is of limited value to managers when attempting to deal with common ethics dilemmas. Take this bit of tautology: "Simply put, 'integrity' means having a genuine, wholehearted disposition to do the right and just thing in all circumstances, and to shape one's actions accordingly."[1] Another leading tome advises that, when dealing with ethical dilemmas, you should develop as many alternatives as possible to a given course of action.[2] While there is nothing wrong with a structured approach to any difficult situation, unfortunately, many ethical matters in the end come down to binary decisions; you are going to do something or you are not going to do it (some examples are listed below). I prefer a much simpler but still quintessential guiding principle once articulated to me by a Congressman's Chief of Staff: whatever you are doing, how would it look if it were described on the front page of your local paper? More specifically, there are some standard dos and don'ts regarding situations that normally arise.

Never ask for or accept special treatment because of your position. In large matters and small, you have to be treated the same as John Q. Citizen. Once when I was hosting a meeting of my national association, we arranged to have an evening visit to a state park. Shortly after entering the park, driving a car with three of my out of state counterparts as passengers, I was stopped for speeding by a park policeman. I received an unpleasant lecture, but no ticket. After we went on our way, my colleagues asked me why I had not identified myself. I laughed and told them that I might have identified *them* to the officer, but never myself. To do so, even for this relatively minor matter, would have violated **the John Q. Citizen rule**.

I also prefer not to appear on my jurisdiction's gift registries. I have given back more than one gift, including one that was painful to do. An architect who was doing business with my department, and who shared my alma mater, returned from a campus visit with a memento, a brick from the old football stadium when it was remodeled. I had seen similar items advertised in alumni publications, so I knew what it cost. They play a little football at our alma mater, so I would have preferred to take it home with me. But it was just cleaner to decline it. A few years later, I was disappointed to learn that the group Christmas gift my leadership team gave me exceeded the threshold value for gift reporting, so I had to report it, even though its value was about equivalent to the collective value of the gifts I gave them.

You and all your staff must avoid any potential or actual **conflict of interest**. A conflict of interest results from any situation in which a government employee has an outside interest that might interfere with his judgment in a government matter over which he has authority. Conflicts of interest are probably the most common ethics situations you and your organization will encounter. It does not matter whether the outside interest actually does interfere with a manager's judgment. The conflict must be avoided, period. A prime example that may arise is if, in the course of your daily business, you encounter a family member, possibly in terms of a service your agency provides or a contract your department issues. They may be seeking a service to which they are fully entitled, or may be eminently qualified to perform the work they are seeking. Nevertheless, to avoid any conflict of interest, you must recuse yourself immediately and completely from any involvement with the service or contract. Let someone else in the agency handle the matter. Offer that someone else no advice or instructions, even generic, other than to handle the matter as if the name of the individual were Bob or Mary Smith. Do not ask for or receive briefing(s) on how things turned out. If said family member eventually receives the service or obtains a contract, your recusal continues.

The conflict of interest that results from a superior and a subordinate engaging in a romantic relationship is covered in "Problem Employees" in Chapter 4.

Financial conflicts of interest are also very problematic. To that end, you need to consider your own outside activities and monitor those of your employees—things like boards of directors, participation in non-profit organizations, and especially, private businesses. You need to know what they are and that they present no conflict of interest. An employee should have no role (even if non-financial) in an outside organization that has a current or prospective contractual relationship with your department. This is an area where, in my judgment, recusal is insufficient.

If your jurisdiction requires financial disclosure, make sure that your disclosure form and the forms of all of your subordinates who must file them are filed on time, and personally review those of your employees to make sure there is nothing that presents a financial conflict of interest or other problem.

The selection process for contracts, vendors, consultants, etc., should always be fair and impartial. To that end, neither you nor your subordinates should ever accept a meal, favor, or anything of value from someone trying to sell your agency something. I am an absolutist on this rule. I have lost track of the number of times I have turned down lunch invitations from prospective or current vendors over the years. I do not mind meeting with people, even when I know a sales pitch is likely to be on the agenda, but I always refer them to my secretary for scheduling purposes (see the section on "Time" in Chapter 1). My secretary is instructed to tell the prospective vendor that, whatever the day the lunch is requested, I have a prior engagement, and to schedule the meeting at a non-mealtime. This slight subterfuge avoids hard feelings on the part of the vendor. Before I adopted this system, and simply told vendors that I would not share a meal with them, some were taken aback, feeling that I was accusing them of bribery, when all they were engaging in was, to them, a standard business practice. (Of course, I could also avoid any problems by paying for any meal myself. But I'm almost always a brown bagger, anyway.)

Unfortunately, selection of outside vendors is not generally a simple matter. Procurement can and should be as objective as possible, and your jurisdiction likely already has codified certain procedures. But in reality, almost all procurement processes have some degree of subjectivity. When you are buying certain commodities, where every vendor will be supplying the same item, a truly subjective low-bid-wins system is possible. But for many other commodities, and for all services, a low bid system is counterproductive. Due to this subjectivity, as a political appointee you may receive political pressure to "tilt" the selection in favor of a particular vendor. On a couple of different occasions, I have been the recipient of either strong pressure or subtle pressure. Each time I demurred.

This is a good juncture to point out that government ethics and business ethics are not one in the same, the foregoing discussion of lunch being a prime example. This is not to say that business ethics are inferior and government ethics superior, merely that they are different. This difference often comes into play when someone joins your department directly from the private sector. You need to be sure that the newcomer understands that there is a difference. In my experience, the adjustment is not always automatic.

You should hold members of your leadership team, especially those who are de facto members of the administration because they serve at the pleasure of the elected official, to a higher standard than rank and file employees. I have had to dismiss key aides for criminal justice system involvement and sleeping with subordinates, offenses that would not necessarily have merited firing were the employees in the merit system. (For a further discussion of this issue, see Chapter 4.)

As for your employees, do not assume that they are conversant with the laws, rules, and procedures that govern their behavior. At a minimum, they should be provided with written material on this subject and have it explained to them. Better yet, hold a training session or sessions on the subject. At the training session, be sure to devote time to the grey areas.

Grey areas are important. Some unethical behavior is easy to spot: fabricating data, forging documents, theft, withholding requested information, lying, and disregarding laws. But there are areas that are not black and white, creating dilemmas. There are plenty of outmoded laws on the books, and you cannot follow them all to the absolute letter of the law, 100 percent of the time. When does it make perfect sense to ignore the law and when should it absolutely not be ignored? Is an absolute, strict interpretation or application of a rule foolish, wasteful, counterproductive, or even harmful? Do you have to ignore, bend, or break rules to achieve important goals in a timely or effective manner? Unfortunately these are easier questions to ask than to answer. Case-by-case decisions are often required.

If your county or city has an independent ethics or public integrity board or commission, you should take advantage of them in any grey area. If there is any doubt in your mind as to whether an activity by you or any of your employees is permissible, seek an opinion from that body. If you get their seal of approval, you should have no further worries.

My strong advice to rely on their instructions is not to say that every decision issued by ethics boards is wise or even fair. Sometimes public integrity boards want to insert their value or policy judgments into areas that really have nothing to do with ethics. Unfortunately, I have also seen such bodies make arbitrary, inconsistent, and hypertechnical decisions. Worse, I have seen them play favorites—for the same or similar activities, someone whom they do not like or has quarreled with them gets disapproval, while someone else receives approval. But if you or your staffers are on the wrong end of such a decision, you have one option and one option only: accept it. Never get into a private or especially a public battle with an ethics commission. You cannot win—you cannot get the commission to change its mind and you will be found guilty in the court of public opinion—so do not bother trying. Ethics is an area where appearance truly is reality. You also run the risk of being on the wrong end of one or more future decisions should the board be one of those that plays favorites.

I have never been offered a cash payment or any other thing of value, either obviously or subtly, in exchange for engaging in illegal conduct. If I were, I would not just refuse it, I would report it to law enforcement, and do so immediately. In such an instance, I would almost be less concerned with bringing the offender to justice than in making a semi-public statement that I would never even consider such an offer. But again, it has never happened to me, and hopefully it will never happen to you. Years ago a veteran state senator told me that the reason why he and I had never been offered such a payment is because the wrongdoers know whom to approach and whom not to approach. I take that as an encouraging sign.

Of course, ethics matters are not just confined to outright illegalities. A legislator once asked me for the unlisted phone number of one of my employees in whom he apparently had a romantic interest. I politely declined. Another legislator wanted me to declare some property owned by my agency in his district to be surplus, and then sell it to him (undoubtedly at a discount below fair market value), so he could remodel it and sell it at a profit. Under the lax surplus property laws in effect at the time, it would have been perfectly legal. Eventually, the property was declared surplus, but disposed of through public advertisement. I would like to think I saved that legislator a huge public embarrassment (not to mention saving myself one), but I don't think he saw it that way. Some of your trickiest dealings are with legislators, tricky not because they are more dishonest than others, or ask what others do not, but because the consequences of telling them "no" can be more severe. (The ethics of hiring or not hiring individuals recommended by legislators, and the handling of legislative requests for services for their constituents are covered in "What Legislators Want From You" in Chapter 11.)

I would also add that, in my opinion, ethics is not only about wrongdoing like stealing money or accepting a sexual favor—although, obviously, those are important no-nos. It is also about values; about treating people fairly. It is about treating people, as one of my governors said repeatedly, as you would yourself wish to be treated. There is also an ethic in never taking credit unfairly and in never shifting blame when you make a mistake. (For more on this topic, see Chapter 4.)

Finally, unethical behavior observed or uncovered should be dealt with immediately. If you are unfortunate enough to come upon outright wrongdoing yourself, or have it brought to your attention, report it to law enforcement immediately. If it is improper but does not involve illegality, deal with it promptly yourself. Never look the other way on an infraction. It is not just wrong to hide it; it is stupid. And never discipline, let alone fire, the employee who has uncovered improper behavior. Do not try transferring such an employee to some remote corner of your operation, either. The whistleblower may not be an ideal employee, and the disclosure of that improper behavior may be deeply embarrassing to you and your organization, but shooting the messenger compounds the problem. Sometimes an individual who is no whistleblower successfully manipulates the outside world, at least temporarily, into perceiving that he is one. If so, tread carefully with any proposed discipline or termination. Beginning (as opposed to concluding) disciplinary action against an employee *after* that employee's whistleblowing activity will undoubtedly be regarded by the media, the public, and possibly the legislature as prima facie evidence of your organization's efforts to cover up wrongdoing—and it ought to be similarly regarded by you if it comes to your attention. (There is more on the subject of spurious whistleblowers in the "Problem Employees" section of Chapter 4.)

But just as you should always deal with unethical behavior, you should also deal with ethical behavior. Ethical behavior is difficult to reward because much of it comes in the form of not doing something. But if you do see it or it comes to your attention, find a way to acknowledge it favorably.

Finally, ethics is the one area where your responsibilities will outlast your tenure in office. Because we appointed officials do not occupy our positions permanently, we hold them in trust for the public, so to speak. I therefore believe that it is a gross breach of ethics for anyone in a management or regulatory position to go to work for an entity that did business with or was regulated by your department during his or her tenure, if the employee had any authority or responsibility (no matter how small) for those business dealings or regulation. Many jurisdictions have **revolving door laws** that prohibit such employment, but others do not or cover only certain positions. And of those that do, often there is a time limit of only a year or two. The restricted time period ought to be 10 years or more, in my opinion.

## NOTES

1. Fleischman, *Self-Interest and Integrity*, 53.
2. Cooper, *The Responsible Administrator*, 17-25.

*Part II*

# Your Organization: Managing Internally

Every organization has resources that it can draw on to perform its mission. How well your organization does its job is partly a function of how many of those resources you have, but mostly it is a function of how well you use the resources you do have. You may or may not be able to increase the level of those resources—primarily people and money—because those resources are allocated via a political process that is outside of your organization and which may or may not reflect your genuine needs. But you as the organization's leader can always make the use of those resources more efficient and effective, provided that you have control of the organization's personnel and agenda, a condition that does not occur automatically. By managing your people and your money carefully, by treating the most important things as the most important, by making good decisions, and by solving the problems that you encounter, you can get the most out of what you have available to you.

The five chapters of "Part II: Your Organization" describe how you can manage the resources and situations that are internal to that organization. Chapter 4 deals with your most important resource, and is titled "People," it includes sections on "Whom To Hire," "How to Manage Your Employees," "Your Leadership Team," "Problem Employees," "Making Your Organization's Culture Managerial," and "Managing Change in a Bureaucracy." Chapter 5 covers "Prioritization." Chapter 6, "Money," discusses "The Budget Game" and "Cutback Management." Chapter 7 explores the process of "Making Decisions and Solving Problems." Its subheadings are "Making Decisions" and "Solving Problems," plus "Negotiations" and "Crisis Management." The topic of Chapter 8, "Gaining Control of Your Organization," does not come up for discussion in management texts very often. The chapter features sections on "Control—What It Is and Who Needs to Know," "Assessing Your Organization," "Gaining Control of Your Personnel," and "Gaining Control of Your Agenda."

*Chapter Four*

# People

"People Issues Are Always the Toughest"

## INTRODUCTION

People are the most important resource in your department. Surprisingly, though, many organizations do not recognize that the most vital part of their operation is their personnel. People are also the most difficult part of management. For you and your organization to succeed, you need to hire the best people—especially the members of your leadership team. Then, you have to manage your good employees properly, while doing everything you can to excise your problem employees. To get the maximum out of your people, do as much as you can to make your organization's culture managerial. And finally, in a world where everything changes, and changes faster all the time, there are some specific techniques to manage change in the bureaucracy that you lead.

## WHOM TO HIRE

In any organization, the ability of the leader to surround himself with top flight individuals will be the single biggest determinant of whether he will be successful. Hiring decisions are among the most critical decisions a manager will make. If there is one thing that leaders of organizations agree on more than any other, it is the importance of having a good team around you. Says one, "A big part of leading becomes your ability to pick and guide the right people...you're only as good as the leaders you have underneath you."[1] Urges a second, "Surround yourself with amazing people. In this more net-

worked, interconnected world, it's all about the people you work with....
Surround yourself with only the best you can find."² Each of the governors
and county executive for whom I worked felt the same way. Having the right
people is far more important than the structure of your organization. Un-
wieldy structures with really good people can and do work well, but a completely rational organizational setup without good people will not produce
good results. Your people will make you a hero or a bum, so hire the best. It
is the only sane way to manage. Hiring top people will result in less work for
you and less stress.

In fact, your goal as the top manager should be to have such a good staff
that you yourself have almost nothing to do, because those below you are
handling everything perfectly. In the words of one top executive, "The trick
is to get truly world class people working directly for you so you don't have
to spend a lot of time managing them."³ Another suggests that you "...make
yourself dispensable—what greater accomplishment is there than the organization running well without you? It means you picked great people, prepared
them, and inspired them. And if executives did this, the world would be a
better place."⁴ Of course, it is an unattainable goal; at best, you can attain an
**asymptotic relationship** with it. Also, even with the very best staff around
you, as the organization's leader you always have to spend time setting
priorities. But it should be your goal nevertheless.

Is the notion that one should hire the best obvious to you—a truism? If it
is, you may wish to skip to the next section. I assure that it is not at all
obvious to many, many people who do hiring. There are many reasons why
managers do not hire the best. First of all, it may be a lot of work to sort
through a huge number of applicants for a position or go out looking for
someone to fill a position that is not advertised. It is much easier to hire
friends or acquaintances or those who are referred to you. The educational
system is notorious for hiring starting teachers this way. It is much simpler
than plowing through 200 resumes. Second, there are those managers who do
not want the best people around them because, in their insecurity, they do not
want anyone nearby smarter than they are or who might conceivably be a
threat to their position. It is ultimately a self-defeating attitude, but one I have
seen more than once. Sometimes hiring the best will indeed mean hiring
someone smarter than you.

Third, some people like to hire people similar to themselves: the ex-
athlete who likes people with sports backgrounds or the woman who prefers
to surround herself with other women. Overt or covert discrimination in
hiring is bad on two levels: it is wrong, but equally important, *it restricts the
available talent pool.* If I am a man who only hires men, I have just eliminated half of the people who might be able to do the job. There is always,
everywhere, a shortage of good people, so you should never do anything to
exacerbate that shortage. And finally, there are those who hire based on

loyalty considerations rather than competence, hiring their cronies at every opportunity.

Your hiring process should be a relentless search for the very best. But what (or who) constitutes the very best?

Generally speaking, as agency head you will be hiring three types of personnel:

1. top managers and supervisors,
2. knowledge workers whose duties do not include supervising others, and
3. support personnel.

Your agency will also hire rank and file employees; you will not participate directly in those hirings, but you should establish some hiring principles for your organization.

*The most fundamental rule for hiring management positions is to hire good managers, not the most knowledgeable experts.* Very strong managers can succeed in almost any management position. Unfortunately, most people (elected executives, legislators, the media, and the public) fundamentally misunderstand this important principle. And when government managers succeed, government departments succeed. "The performance of an institution and the performance of its management are the same thing."[5] On the other hand, if poorly managed, it is perfectly possible for an agency to have almost all good employees but accomplish little.

By good managers, I mean people who have the following attributes:

1. people, leadership, and supervisory skills and experience,
2. the ability to prioritize,
3. political (small p) sensitivity,
4. problem solving skills,
5. the ability to manage budgets,
6. the ability to handle problem employees, and
7. the willingness to be a team player.

For almost every top management post, technical expertise is of secondary importance. Expertise is not irrelevant, but it is a lot easier for a good manager to learn policy than for a policy expert to learn management. No matter how much program expertise someone has, if she is not a good manager she will always be a problem. Specialists and experts are essential for your organization, but not in management positions. A good policy person who is not a good manager usually cannot prioritize, but even if he does know where he wants his unit to go, he will not possess the skills to get it there.

Supervision is not for everyone. Some very talented people do not want to supervise. Others should not supervise because they lack the temperament for it. One of the almost universal attributes of poor managers is their inability to deal with problem employees. Unfortunately, in many civil service systems, a key determinant of pay (if not the only determinant) is the number of employees one supervises. The only way to earn higher pay is to supervise (or supervise a higher number of employees). Some classroom teachers who love teaching become administrators because that is the way to increase their compensation. A rational personnel system should have a dual track scheme for many job classifications: a technical or expertise track, and a supervisory track. That way, talented individuals not cut out for management can still advance in pay. Dual track systems are hardly new. In the federal government, they date from their 1971 establishment in the Internal Revenue Service.[6] Unfortunately, they do not seem to have spread very far.

A recent study of government managers identified a series of characteristics of individuals unsuited for heavy-duty management jobs (if not for other government jobs), including "A tendency to like working on and looking at only big issues," and "Low to moderate interest in the nitty-gritty details of the operations of the organization."[7]

Making the right calls in selecting managers is one of the most important ingredients for your organization's success. Your agency will never achieve its full potential unless you follow this rule religiously. If you hire a policy or program expert who cannot manage well, you risk hearing what I heard an experienced legislative leader say about one of my former cabinet colleagues: "She's a great consultant." You can expect that plans will not turn into action, and for things to go wrong, sooner or later. Bad managers also negatively impact employee morale. Worse, you can expect that someone in a leadership position who does not understand management will either hire or influence the hiring of other people who cannot manage. Bad managers, in other words, propagate. It can really be a downward spiral for an organization.

The lack of good managers in top and middle management positions has been common to everywhere in government I have worked, and I have never had a cabinet colleague in my state or counterpart in any other state tell me his or her department was different. More than one of my division directors over the years have told me that below their deputy directors, the upper reaches of management were filled exclusively with program experts but not good managers.

There are multiple reasons for this dearth of managers in government. Some professional training is either lacking in or antithetical to good management. Also, governments (and often, the private sector) tend to promote based on knowledge and productivity. While these are admirable qualities, they do not necessarily correlate with management ability. How many times have you observed this scenario, or one just like it? An office has five engineers and an engineering supervisor. (Or, five accountants and an accounting supervisor.) The supervisor leaves, and who gets the job? The best line engineer. After all, he has earned it, hasn't he? But the best engineer may not be the best supervisor. "Sometimes the brightest find it the hardest to make that transition [to management] because they've always been better than the people around them. They find it hard to trust the people around them to do the work. They think, 'Well, I know best.'"[8] A second top executive described the pattern: "Most people start out as doers, and they have a function. They get really good at doing that, as they gain more experience. The reason they usually get promoted is not because someone innately thought that the person would make a great manager. They get promoted because they were a great doer. Is the same person going to be a great manager? Sometimes yes, sometimes no."[9]

Some of the traits that make the best line employees (e.g., intense attention to detail) are not the best traits for a good supervisor. Hear the words of various executives. A newly minted state Attorney General told me that his Department of Justice had always promoted based on legal ability, not management ability. As a result, none of his supervisors had the ability to supervise—not even the basics like telling a subordinate how to perform better. A corporate CEO admitted, "I tend to be a perfectionist, and that doesn't always make for the best supervisor. Sometimes the best employees can't make the transition to managers."[10] Another CEO stated, "Just because you're the biggest producer, you often get put in the management role. But just because you're a great producer doesn't mean you're a great manager."[11]

Areas where professional training is lacking in management skills include law, science, medicine, and law enforcement. They teach expertise, not management. There is nothing problematic about this emphasis; I would certainly rather have my personal physician be a great doctor than a great manager. But it does have potential implications for hiring in your agency. Medical school is completely lacking in management training. Doctors, accustomed to a lot of both autonomy and deference, seldom make good managers. As a famous work on scientific culture explained, "Scientific training is not well designed to produce the man who will easily discover a fresh approach."[12] Law enforcement personnel have spent their lives sitting across the table from criminals. Sometimes they do not understand that, once they have left law enforcement, the individuals sitting across the table from them with different opinions are not bad guys, just people with contrasting views.

It is well known in the field of court management that legal training, with its emphasis on *stare decisis* (precedent), is inimical to good management.[13] When confronted with a problem, turning first to what has been done in the past is almost always the wrong approach, since what you have done in the past is what got you to the problem state of the present. The notion propagated by law schools that "law school is great preparation for anything" is, to put it baldly, specious. It is not good preparation for anything but the practice of law, and it is bad preparation for management. If you have ever watched a top lawyer prepare for a case, you have watched him learn each and every possible fact, nuance, argument, and counterargument he can, down to the smallest detail. By knowing every last detail, that lawyer puts himself in the best possible position to win the case. Lawyers (and a few lawyers who become elected officials) sometimes try to manage the same way: by knowing every detail. Managers cannot operate that way. No one, not even the most brilliant, hardworking individual, can know every detail, because there are not enough hours in the day. Nor should they, if they are to effectively use staff. One top lawyer turned top executive described her adjustment: "As general counsel, you're taught research, research, find out every case, find out every opinion, think about it. It's almost like you're a judge. So when I went from being general counsel to CEO, that's the way I first approached it. Well, that doesn't work. I had to learn to make decisions quicker, and follow my gut. You're not going to be able to run the numbers and come up with perfect answers."[14] When a manager gets too far into the minutiae of some problem without resolving it, we refer to him as "managing like a lawyer."

I have had many conversations with young people working for me who were considering a return to school on a part-time or full-time basis for an advanced degree. I have always suggested that they consider a master's degree in public administration instead of a law degree, if they intend to remain in government rather than practice law.

Certainly there are excellent physician-executives and lawyers who are terrific managers. I have had both in the departments I ran. But the training they have received and experiences they have had practicing law or medicine have not helped, and may have hindered them in managing. (For more on the clash between scientific or legal cultures versus managerial cultures, see "Making Your Organization's Culture Managerial", below.)

During the transition period before I took my first cabinet assignment, one well-regarded outgoing cabinet secretary advised me to "Just hire the smartest people you can find. They'll figure it all out." I did not follow his advice, because, in the words of one of my mentors, "Smart people are a dime a dozen." A study of ostensibly successful federal government managers pointed out that "We continue to find many examples of the presumption that all jobs are the same and that any smart person can fill any of them. This is not the case."[15] All the **IQ** points in the world will not make a good employee, let alone a leader, out of someone who lacks people skills, who cannot prioritize, and who cannot figure out what is important versus what is not so important.

Avoid people with toxic personalities, no matter how competent or intelligent they are, people with big egos, people who lack integrity or loyalty, and non-producers (people who can talk as opposed to people who can do). Avoid hiring the suck-up, kick-down personality—although it not so easy to spot them. Commented one executive, "Some people were really good at what they did, but they were really difficult to work with. I can teach people [particular] skills. I can't teach them how to play in the sandbox."[16]

It is also advisable to hesitate before appointing individuals who are very intelligent but under, say, 30 years of age to middle or upper management positions. They generally lack the maturity necessary for good people skills. A chief executive points out that "When you're in your 20s and have that leadership gene, the bad thing is that you don't know when to shut up. You think you know all the answers, but you don't. What you learn later is to just listen to everybody else."[17] Some things cannot fully be taught, only learned through experience, and leadership is one of them. In my experience, too often, these individuals are considerably smarter than those whom they would supervise, but unable to avoid broadcasting that superior intelligence in their dealings with their subordinates, and/or unable to effectively delegate to staffers. "[It] can be the hardest for young leaders: to trust the people you lead. It's about letting go, and allowing people to grow.... At the end of the day, it's okay if they make a mistake or they fall down. Because as leaders, it's your job to pick them back up."[18] Another CEO says, simply, "There are certain things you can't learn without years of experience."[19] (Of course, as with any rule, there are exceptions, in this case for young people of exceptional maturity.)

So how do you go about finding good managers? Start by making a realistic assessment of how large your real talent pool is, especially in light of where you are in the **life cycle of the administration**. Your greatest flexibility will occur if you have taken a position in an administration when your county executive or mayor has just been elected for the first time, and has the opportunity to be reelected. Depending on term limits, prospective hirees who are considering whether to join your organization will have at least four years and possibly eight or even more, providing they do well. You may have the opportunity to draw from individuals all over the country, if you wish to consider them. The closer you get to the next election, the smaller your talent pool will be, because a higher percentage of people will be unwilling to uproot themselves when future employment cannot be guaranteed for any length of time. In an election year, unless public opinion polls are showing your elected boss to be unbeatable, your available talent pool is likely to consist primarily or exclusively of candidates already in your state, county, or city government. When a term-limited candidate approaches the end of her tenure, the pool will be the smallest of all, probably confined to your department.

What this means is that you are going to do a fair amount of internal hiring, either internal to your jurisdiction or internal to your department.

Whatever jurisdiction you are working for, you should make it your business to know who the top people are (the top managers, that is, not the top experts) in your department, and who the top people elsewhere in the state or county are. Always observe, always ask, always file away in your mind, because you never know when you will need to hire someone. Ideally, when a vacancy occurs, you will already have a mental list of people to consider. When making hiring decisions, personal observation is the very best predictor of future success, far superior to interviews or especially resumes. I like to hire people whose performance I have seen first hand because I can be sure in advance that I am getting a quality product. But I am hiring them because I know they can handle the job, not simply because I know them. It is a huge mistake to hire someone if you are the least bit unsure of his ability to do the job, let alone if you are certain he cannot.

You should go out of your way to identify outside sources of evaluation if you do not know a candidate yourself. A CEO says to anyone under consideration, "I'll find out whether you and I have a common acquaintance. It may take me a while, but I'm going to know a couple of people you know. So before you're hired, I'm going to hear them talk to me about you."[20] If I have personal experience with my prospective hire or get recommendations from people whose judgment I trust, my hiring success rate is over 90 percent. Absent such recommendations, and relying only on an interview and a resume, it's more like 50 percent.

References are always more important than the interview. In the words of one CEO, "I am notorious...for warning people not to place too much emphasis on interviews. References, and what somebody has done, are more important than what somebody tells you in an interview. Well done is better than well said, and there's no substitute for good referencing."[21] In this context, references are not resume references, because they have been supplied by the applicant and are in almost every case individuals who will speak only positively of the applicant. What you want is the personal observations or recommendations from people whose judgment you value, or references from previous employers. You want to know whether applicants have the necessary management, leadership, and people skills to succeed, and whether they have a track record of accomplishment. People who get negative ratings from previous bosses or colleagues should not get to the interview stage. Contact references by phone (or even face to face, if that's possible), never by letter, so that you can assure them of confidentiality. Ask the people you call for additional names of individuals who are familiar with the applicant.

Just as references are more important than interviews, interviews are more important than resumes. One CEO stated frankly that "I don't look at a resume. I go by referrals. I go by people I trust. I've always said, there's something about a resume. You can make it say what you want it to say."[22]

Sooner or later, though, you will face a pool of applicants, none of whom you know and none of whom come recommended by anyone you are familiar with. So you are still going to interview people, but you should be aware of the interview's limitations. It is easy to determine via that interview whether a candidate for a job is articulate or poised, but you cannot determine through an interview what kind of a worker he or she is. As one top executive puts it, "It is too easy to let the person with great presentation skills buffalo you into thinking they are better or more knowledgeable than someone who might not necessarily have that particular set of skills."[23] Another went further: "What I find is that interviews are just a miserable way to screen people. It's hours of unnatural conversation, and some people are just really good at giving job interviews, and some people are awful at giving job interviews. I've learned that those things don't necessarily coincide with performance."[24]

Start by conducting interviews in person, never by phone. Never hire someone sight unseen. I have plenty of experiences to back up these statements. Understand that being interviewed is a skill; some people have it and some do not. One of the best managers who ever worked for me bombed his initial interview with me, omitting his greatest accomplishment in his interview (and his resume). Fortunately I was familiar with it from local newspaper accounts. On another occasion, I insisted that a division director hire a certain individual whom I knew was an outstanding performer from his having worked for me previously. I seldom interfered with hiring by my directors, but this time I did. As I anticipated, I received a report that he gave a poor interview, so poor that my director begged me, not once but twice, to hire another individual who was already in our department. I did not relent. Six months later the director admitted that I had been right. My pick was doing a terrific job, while her preferred candidate, she now knew, "blew a lot of smoke in his interview."

If I am conducting interviews for a management position I almost always ask the applicants questions in the following areas.

1. What do you know about the position?
   These days, it is easy to do a little research about the job and organization. Have they bothered to do it?
2. What is your management philosophy?
   There is no one best answer to this question, of course, but any competent manager has given some thought to it.
3. How do you deal with problem employees? Have you ever fired anybody?
   Handling problem employees is often the toughest nut in public sector management, testing both a manager's resolve and his skills. One top manager asked the question this way. "I would... ask them, 'What do you think is the most important thing in deciding to fire

someone?' They might go through some business-school buzzwords, and then I say, 'Well then, how do you actually do it?' If they send a note, or they delegate it, or they arrange three people in the room with them, then I know that they're not prepared to take full, personal responsibility. When I had to fire someone, I did it one-on-one."[25] (For more on dismissal, see *Your Leadership Team* later in this chapter.)

4. Describe a significant management problem you faced and how you solved it.

   The advantage of asking about real world experience is that not only do you get insight into how someone approached a problem, you also get an idea of what she thinks is important.

5. Why do you want the job?

   Do they really want to work in your department, or do they just want the position?

6. Of the many people we're talking to, why are you the very best person for the job?

7. What are you going to do on their very first day—your first week?

   This question gives you a sense of how organized they are, and if they have a plan for going about this job, or any job.

8. What questions do you have of us?

   In the words of a top business executive, "I also ask if they have questions for me. That's important.... It tells me several things. Sometimes people don't have a single question. And if you have any curiosity here is your window."[26]

If a prospective hire is coming from the private sector, additional questions are in order, starting with, what do you know about the difference between the private sector and government? Public sector management and private sector management certainly have some similarities: management of personnel, handling of problem employees, the need to deliver a product (in government, a service) in a cost-effective manner, and the necessity to provide good customer service. And while the private sector appears to emphasize management more so than the public sector, their performance is not uniformly better. For every government management failure like the botched response to Hurricane Katrina or the more recent Veterans Affairs Hospitals patient care scandal, there is an Enron or a Toyota in the business world.

There are also stark differences between business and government. Some of the major ones are as follows. First, in many private companies, every employee is an at-will employee, lacking the merit system (and sometimes union) protections of government employees (in the case of the educational system, tenure). Second, to balance its budget, government usually does not (and sometimes, cannot) lay off masses of employees, nor can government get out of unprofitable lines of business. If the Acme Widget Corporation is not selling enough curved black widgets, it can stop making them. But if the county government I worked for found that the costs of operating the sewer system started outrunning the sewer fees, it did not have the option of getting out of the wastewater treatment business.

Government's time horizons, tied to election cycles, are different from the ability of business to engage in long-term planning. The for-profit sector has a single bottom line, money, whereas government has multiple measures of success or failure. The fishbowl environment of government service contrasts sharply with the trade secrets world of business.[27] The number of actors involved in making any decision is almost always much larger than in the private sector. "Making change in public organizations requires far more political effort... because public organizations live in a political sea, while businesses live in a market economy."[28] For this reason, in government it is difficult to reorganize (see *Managing Change in a Bureaucracy,* below). Finally, ethical considerations are different.

Be very sure that your jobseeker knows the difference between working in the public sector and the private sector. You need to probe this one and not just rely on their assurances.

You should also ask why they are leaving the private sector. If they have been laid off and are searching for more employment stability, there is nothing wrong with that, but my suspicion would be that they do not know what they are getting into and think that it will be easier working for the government. Having seen it so often, I am no longer surprised, but I do find it interesting how many individuals with only private sector experience think that government employees do not work very hard. I usually sit down with anyone I have hired from the private sector after they have been on the job for six months and ask them whether government is easier or harder than they expected. They almost always sheepishly admit that they had not appreciated how hard we work in the pubic sector and how difficult the challenges are: the complicated issues, the resource constraints, the number of people involved in making any changes. In my experience, frankly, the success rate of individuals moving from the private sector to high-level management positions in government is probably only 50 percent.

As stated, interviews do not rate as highly in my book as recommendations. But they can reveal things that are more likely to make you reject an applicant. One interviewee whom I had considered a likely contender for a post answered a question about management philosophy by talking about how it was usually her preference just to do things herself. Here was someone who did not understand management; she fell out of contention instantly.

I generally do not ask questions about an applicant's technical knowledge of the position, although there are exceptions. There are a few areas (facilities management comes to mind) where I would not hire a management generalist. But they are the exceptions, not the rule.

In filling top management positions, there should be no hard sell. More than once, I was turned down by a person to whom I had offered a leadership post. I always accepted that answer without argument. Never try to talk someone into a leadership position who is not sure she wants it. Anyone you hire absolutely has to want to take on the additional responsibilities and headaches in order to do the job properly. Self-confidence is a key ingredient to success in a top management slot, and someone who does not think she is ready for such a job does not yet possess sufficient self-confidence.

When it comes to hiring knowledge workers who will not be supervising, this is the time to hire the smartest people you can find, *as long as they have the requisite people skills.* Examples of these positions are executive assistants, policy advisors, and legislative liaisons. Experience is less important for these jobs than brain power.

The executive assistant slot is ideal for someone young, bright, and energetic, who displays the attitude that nothing is too much for him or her. Do not let an executive assistant make a career out of that particular job, however. There is a tendency for **EAs** serving high-level officials to get very comfortable in their positions. They are at the top of the information pyramid, and there is always something interesting and challenging going on. But after two or three years, they have learned all they are going to learn in your office and it is time for them to move to something different.

Generally the only support person you should hire yourself is your own— let everybody else pick theirs. I have never replaced a personal secretary/ scheduler when assuming a new position. They always have a great deal of institutional knowledge, and will be very loyal to you if you give them the opportunity by retaining them. And if I do have to hire one when a vacancy occurs, I always let my team pick my secretary, for two reasons. First, it is another way of empowering my staff by delegating. I want the new person to be a team player whom other staffers are comfortable with. Second, I want the new person to understand that she is part of a team, that she needs to work cooperatively with that team, and that my number two is her direct supervisor, not me (see Chapter 1, "Self-Management"). I have never been disappointed with this approach.

When it comes to hiring by your organization, you should try to institutionalize these same practices to the maximum extent possible, either through rules or through training, preferably both. The first and most important of these is that they, like you, should hire the best managers, not the best program experts, for management positions. The second rule is that in their selection process, as in yours, the highest priority consideration is what an applicant's current and past employers say about her, followed by the interview, followed by the resume. Hiring based on credentials is pervasive in government but the wrong way to go for management positions. What too often happens in hiring is that people look for a resume with many years of progressively responsible experience in a given field, disregarding (or never considering) previous bosses' analyses. The importance of thorough referencing cannot be overstated, particularly in government where sister agencies are not above playing a **game of Old Maid** on you. Unable or unwilling to terminate an employee, they are frequently quite willing to give him a glowing recommendation so they can foist him off on you. I make it an ironclad rule not to allow my troops to play that game on others. If we have a problem employee, it is our job to deal with him or her, not someone else's (see "Problem Employees", below).

I also want my agency to do open/competitive hirings to the maximum extent possible, even for promotional positions. Promotions are too often based on seniority, because employees expect it. Union and non-union employees alike want all positions filled internally and through seniority—but that is not the approach that will necessarily get the best managers and/or introduce creativity, extra energy, and new blood into your organization. If an internal candidate is truly superior, given that observation and recommendations are the most important criteria, he should have no trouble getting the job. As will be discussed below, bringing in new employees can be a very effective tool, possibly *the* most effective tool, in promoting change within your organization.

You should encourage your organization to make full use of internships, paid and unpaid. Have one in your own office if possible. Internships are very valuable because you can actually see the quality of work by the intern, which will make a decision as to whether to hire her permanently very easy.

Merit systems are not the ideal for any aspect of personnel, which will be covered under "How to Manage Your Employees", below—and this includes the selection process. Improve it as much as you can, if you have the ability to do so (often you will not if it is controlled by a central personnel agency).

Finally, if allowed by statute, drug test and perform criminal background checks on *every* prospective employee. Before you recoil at this idea because you find drug testing distasteful on civil libertarian grounds, consider that many if not most organizations around you already do such testing. You do not want to be the organization of choice for those individuals with drug and alcohol problems, but if you do not test, you risk becoming exactly that. Be aware that the drug and alcohol abusing communities trade information about which organizations test and which do not. A criminal history may or may not disqualify an individual from consideration, but it is certainly information you should be aware of. Criminal background checks should also be done periodically on current employees, if your statute permits it. Sometimes they commit crimes while off the job. You may find that, unbeknownst to you, an employee has just become a registered sex offender, or a worker who drives as part of his job just received a ticket for reckless driving, or been charged with driving under the influence of alcohol.

In addition to hiring people, sometimes you have to fire people. As the head of your organization, it is likely that the terminations you handle will be those of your leadership team. They will be covered in that section, below.

## HOW TO MANAGE YOUR EMPLOYEES

You have hired and/or inherited your staff. Now you have to manage them. The how of employee management starts with setting the tone via some overarching principles. Here are mine.

1. Treat your employees properly.
2. Communicate with your employees by listening as well as speaking.
3. Support your employees at every opportunity.

Treating your employees properly starts with relating to them as human beings. By this I mean, you should interact with your staffers the same way you would interact with any other people you encounter (friends, family, or neighbors). I will quote an old friend of mine, who once summed up her philosophy of dealing with humanity by saying, simply, "Why not be nice to people? Doesn't cost you anything." Why not indeed? Treat your staff well, which covers of multitude of behaviors. "You treat people well, and they will return the favor. And if you treat them poorly, they will return the favor."[29] You should treat all your staff with respect. To that end, never raise your voice or be verbally abusive to any of your employees. If you have to criticize someone, it should always be done privately. (More below on giving praise and criticism.)

Always consider your employees to be not just a resource, but the most valuable resource. They are your flock, your team, your community—even your second family. So, act accordingly. Unfortunately, the trend in government these days seems to be to emulate some companies in the private sector and regard employees as interchangeable parts or commodities—even overhead.

Say hello to everyone; in a large organization, you may not know who they all are, but they all know who you are. If your operation has fewer than 300 employees, you should try to get to know them all personally. (If you have a superior memory, you might extend that number to 400 or 500.) In the smaller department I ran, I met with each of my new employees individually right after they were hired, or if more than one employee was hired in a given week, those two or three new ones. It was nothing heavy duty, just a "hi how are you" session. I would ask them a little about their background, tell them a little bit about mine, and give them the department's lapel pin. (I have always loved my agencies' lapel pins, and wear one every day.) If nothing else, when I saw the new employees in the future while out and about, I could greet them by name.

However many employees you do know personally, you cannot befriend them, because you still have to be the boss. (Friendship must await your departure from the agency.) But you do have to know what is going on in their lives. If an individual is going through a divorce, recently suffered the death of a parent, has just received a diagnosis of cancer, or has a very sick child, you need to be aware of those things, so that you can relate to each staffer as an individual. Such situations are almost certainly going to affect employee performance. It's a matter of "Striking the right balance of being friendly, though not friends, with the people [you] manage, and learning how to be a boss without being bossy."[30]

You are also not there to be loved. Employees do not necessarily have to like you personally for you to be an effective manager, but they do have to respect you. "As a leader, I never expected people to like me, but it matters if they trust you or respect you."[31] Conversely, employees are perfectly capable of liking you as a person while evaluating you—correctly—as a poor manager. In high school, my daughter complained about one of her coaches, but when the season was over, she came back from a sleepover at the coach's house saying how much she had enjoyed it. When I asked what had changed, because she had been complaining all season long, she said, "Oh, we all like her as a person. She just wasn't a very good coach."

You must present a consistent, positive demeanor on the job. If you radiate negativity, then everybody else will be negative, too. You will have to work hard at it. Every job has days when nothing goes right, and the top job has more such days than most, but you cannot let it show. A top executive summed it up perfectly thus: "I can't have a bad day. If I walk into a meeting and I'm grumpy—not good.... I think anybody in a leadership position where people depend upon you has to simply realize that you can't have that one off day because you're going to affect a lot of people."[32]

When something goes right, it is vitally important that you share credit with your subordinate(s), give credit to your subordinate(s), sometimes even avoid crediting yourself if your staffers had any part in the success. It is not just a best management practice; it's an ethical imperative. For one thing, it is very unlikely that you accomplished the job all by yourself, because most successes today are the result of teamwork. It is all the more important to highlight others' contributions if you yourself had little or no role in the success. Usually, as department head, you directly control your organization's media apparatus, so it is very easy for you to capture accolades yourself, but that is exactly the opposite of what you should do. When something goes wrong is the time to put it all on your shoulders, not when things go right. Sharing the credit motivates your employees and builds their loyalty. And if one of my team, especially one of my top aides, does something good, the way I see it is that I am the guy who was smart enough to hire (or retain) him.

The final part of treating your employees properly is dealing with everyone fairly and equally. Never play favorites. The only thing that should count when you evaluate the performance of people who work for you is results. You should be unconcerned about such irrelevancies in employees as what clothes they wear, their hair length, and their personal lives (as long as the latter is not affecting their workplace performance). And last but not least, remember that *every* staff member is a resource, be they male or female, gay or straight, black, white, or Hispanic, etc. All of them can help get the job done.

My second operating principle is to communicate with your employees by listening as well as speaking. Part of good listening is hearing what they say, but an equally important part of it is making sure they know in advance that you will hear them if they talk to you. Therefore, to encourage input from your troops, I recommend informality. I myself certainly prefer an informal work environment. When serving as a cabinet officer, I always asked my employees to address me as Vince rather than "Mr. Secretary." If I am meeting with anyone in my office, except for the briefest conversations with immediate staff, I prefer to get out from behind my desk. As a fellow top executive says, "Too much formality or reverence can get in the way of a good exchange of ideas."[33]

Almost the only times my door was closed when I was in my office were when I was eating lunch (never more than 30 minutes, but I wanted those 30 minutes to read, uninterrupted if possible), and when I was having a confidential meeting or phone call. Other than that, people could wander in without an appointment if they wanted to.

In any meeting with an individual or group, keep things relaxed, even if there is every reason for there to be tension due to the subject matter. Give the individual or group your undivided attention—no cell phones or other multitasking. Another chief spells it out: "When you are with somebody, you've got to make that person feel like nobody else in the world matters. So I don't have a mobile phone turned on because I'm talking to you. I don't carry a Blackberry. I don't want to be sitting there thinking I've got an e-mail message and I'd better look at that while talking to you."[34]

Another part of making sure that your employees know that you will hear them is accomplished by properly asking questions when in a meeting. Do not cross-examine your staff; you are not starring in a courtroom drama. Feigning ignorance, even if it is not very good feigning, is a good way to go. When I was a state representative, the Speaker of the House was the master of this method. Although he was very likely the smartest person in the House chamber, and almost always knew the answer to any question before he asked it, he invariably phrased them thus: "Help me with...." And whether you are asking questions of your employees or simply listening to their comments, always read their body language and facial expressions. If you are looking for secret techniques on how to decipher body language, you will not find them here; I do not know any. But you do not need special skills, or even have received any training, in my opinion. I discovered, pretty much by accident, that most people are not very good at hiding their feelings, even if they are not saying anything. Simply by paying attention, you can figure out most of them. Are they confused, unhappy, uneasy, or feeling defensive? You need to know why. Be sensitive to such appearances. For your part, keep poker faced.

Poker faced, that is, until it is time for some humor, and it's almost always time for some humor. Nothing cuts tension like a display of humor. Maintain your sense of humor at all costs, and encourage your staff to do the same. Public sector jobs can be extremely stressful, especially at the upper management level. Humor is the great stress reliever. Ideally, a sense of humor should be present in all your hires, although it is difficult if not impossible to ascertain that in the course of an interview. There is no science behind the following observation, but I almost never had a bad line employee or a bad leader who possessed a good sense of humor.

The most important reason to listen to your employees is that whatever the task at hand, there are almost always multiple points of view about how your agency should proceed. It is vitally important that you get the benefit of everyone's best thinking. You are not doing this to be polite; you need the information because you do not know everything. You have to know what you do not know. It is also the case that in government, although you want to make as many choices based on data as you can (see "Making Decisions and Solving Problems" in Chapter 7), other decisions will end up being judgment calls—and you need everyone's perspective. Never adopt this attitude, described by one top executive: "For whatever reason, people believe that when they get to that spot [CEO], they have to know everything. They've got to be in total control, and you can never show weakness."[35] You are only going to get the best thinking from those around you if you tolerate and even encourage alternate viewpoints, disagreement, criticism, and dissent. Let your staff say exactly what is on their minds, and tell you you're crazy if they want to. Another executive put it like this. "The lesson I learned is the value of an environment where truth telling is valued.... It takes a lot of spine to tell the truth, especially in a large organization."[36] You have to give a variation of the following speech over and over. "Tell me what you think, not what you think I want to hear. Keeping your concerns to yourself does none of us, especially me, any good. If you don't like something, say so." Having run for office and endured professionally prepared calumny, printed and distributed thousands of copies at a time, I tell my staff that it is almost impossible to hurt my feelings, and certainly not merely by telling me that I'm wrong. You also never want to find out that someone did not think you wanted to know some key fact or piece of information. The sins of omission in this context far outweigh the sins of commission.

The ability to withstand criticism was embodied by George C. Marshall, Chief of Staff of the United States Army during World War II, architect as Secretary of State of the Marshall Plan that enabled postwar European recovery, and one of the greatest leaders this country has ever produced. Here is Marshall's biographer on relations between Marshall and his subordinate at the time, General Dwight Eisenhower: "Eisenhower...had tried to please the chief of staff, who disliked that in subordinates. 'When you disagree with my point of view,' Marshall instructed, 'say so, without an apologetic approach; when you want something that you aren't getting, tell me and I will try to get it for you.'"[37] As Secretary of State, in a conversation with another deputy, Dean Acheson (who later became Secretary of State himself), Marshall "...declared that he would expect from Acheson nothing less than 'the most complete frankness, particularly about myself.' He had no feelings, he explained, 'except those I reserve for Mrs. Marshall.'"[38] If one of the most accomplished men in American history could handle criticism, the rest of us ought to make room for it, too.

Marshall had apparently learned that lesson from *his* World War I and interwar commander, General Jack Pershing. Marshall's biographer quotes him on Pershing. "I have never seen a man who could listen to as much criticism.... You could say what you pleased as long as it was straight, constructive criticism."[39] There is a lot to learn about management from how certain generals managed, some of whom had what at first glance might seem to be quite unmilitary management styles.

This attitude goes double when you have explained your preliminary thoughts on a subject. It is only human for subordinates, no matter how self-confident, to decline to state their opinions if they contradict yours. After all, they may be thinking, he already has his mind made up. "You suppress, even though you don't intend to, the conversation by jumping in a little bit too early with your view or your perspective. No matter how you couch it, everybody sort of goes, 'Okay, this is the way the boss wants to go,' and you risk losing the engagement and that participation that you're looking for."[40]

For this reason, in any discussion or meeting, you should try to be the last one to verbalize your thoughts, even if you have a pretty clear idea of where you want to go. If you speak first, it is just too easy for others to fall in line. This lesson was a hard one for me to learn. I am very analytical, and I tend to "get there" ahead of others. I had to discipline myself. "If you want to get the best out of people, you have to really hear them."[41] Adds a top government executive, "I expect to have a back and forth with [staff], where I respect what they say and they respect what I say. I think that creating that kind of respect and openness makes employees feel better and then work better."[42]

It is very difficult to foster an atmosphere of receptivity to criticism. It is easy to say it but it is one of the toughest things to do in government, which can be very hierarchical. You are probably a strong personality or you would not be in the lead spot in your organization, and everyone around you knows it. You have to emphasize and reemphasize that openness to other viewpoints is your standard operating procedure. As one chief executive put it, "When you become a CEO, you effectively step inside a bubble. Not by choice—it's a fact of the job. Nobody comes to you anymore without an agenda. It doesn't matter how open-minded you are. People will tailor their views, their positioning and everything else to suit you."[43]

Wanting to hear differing views does not mean that you accept them at face value. If someone disagrees with me, I am certainly going to probe him and analyze his views to see what is behind his thinking and how thoroughly he has thought things through. I do not mind when staffers challenge my assumptions, so I have no hesitation in challenging theirs on occasion. Once I have done that, I may or may not change my mind. But regardless, I will treat their views with respect. Never, ever belittle someone for disagreeing (even if, as sometimes happens, his ideas are less than fully baked). Almost everyone has had the experience somewhere down the line of having been told that his opinion was not just wrong, it was stupid. It has happened to me. Nobody likes that, and it certainly does not encourage one to speak up the next time around.

After you have made a final decision, assuming you have given all parties a fair opportunity to voice their opinions, it is time for everybody to fall in line. I am not interested in having issues "relitigated," to use President Barack Obama's term. When we have finished with a decision, there is always a long list of other matters to work on. We do not have the luxury of revisiting issues once we have decided what we are going to do. As one leader puts it, "I am very clear with people that I will respect their opinion, and I will listen to the range of issues on the table, but once a decision is made, even if you don't agree with it, it's your job to make me right."[44] Respecting the final decision is particularly essential if your boss, the elected official, has made that decision. At that point, it is time for your whole department to get behind it. The only exception I would make to my "no revisitation" policy is if I have failed to consult a **stakeholder** and she wants to weigh in after the fact. Since I did not give her the chance beforehand, I need to give her the chance to do so now.

Of course, when communicating any decision to subordinates, always detail your reasons. Your employees will be more receptive to any decision or change if they understand your thinking on the subject.

Another important reason to listen is that you need to know what is going on so you can monitor and evaluate individual and organizational performance. You can never know everything that is going on around you; in fact, inevitably some things are going to be willfully withheld from you. But you have to do your best. The larger your organization, the more important this information gathering is. Your managers themselves are the best source of information about what is going on. Regular reporting mechanisms are described in "Your Leadership Team", below. But you need other sources of information as well. As Admiral Hyman G. Rickover once said, use your chain of command to give directions, but get information from all levels, including the rank and file. When I have a meeting on a given subject, I want my aides to bring anybody who has information that will bear on the issue at hand. Explains one top executive, "Listen to the people below you because they are on the front lines... at any given moment any one of those people, from the highest to the lowest, can be the most important person that day in your operation."[45]

In the course of listening to your staffers, you will naturally hear all manner of complaints. Pay attention to all of them, but recognize that some people are chronic complainers. Nothing is ever going to suit them. On the other hand, there are other individuals who almost never complain. It helps to know which employees fall into which category, because when you get a complaint from someone who almost never speaks out, it is time to consider carefully what that person is saying.

Making site visits, talking with groups of employees, and taking any questions they choose to ask can be both very informative and good for employee morale. I try to do as much of it as I can. "I would have employee meetings and they could give me questions anonymously, and I promised them I would read them and answer any question. And there were some pretty ugly questions. I answered every one."[46]

My third basic principle is to support your employees in every way you can. To start with, although your options may be very limited in this regard, always try to get as much money for your people as you can, for two reasons. First, getting the best for your team is part of your job as their leader; second, the higher the pay for a position, the easier the recruitment process will be if the position becomes vacant. Also, never stand in the way if one of your employees has a chance to advance, even if it means that they will be leaving your organization (more on this in "Your Leadership Team", below).

Encourage employee-friendly human resources policies: casual Friday for those staffers not meeting with the public, flex time, 4-day workweeks, and the like. There are a few situations (24/7 worksites, for example), where such policies are inappropriate. But aside from those exceptions, and provided that middle management is properly trained in supervising alternate work arrangements, such policies can almost always be adopted with no loss in productivity, but big gains in employee satisfaction.

Always do your best to give your people the resources they need to do their jobs adequately—facilities, tools, equipment, supplies, etc. Do not underestimate the importance of your physical plant (comfortable chairs, fresh paint, building renovations, and others) in maintaining or improving employee morale. Above all, you have a duty to provide safe working conditions for your employees. All of the foregoing contribute to a supportive environment for your staff.

Employee recognition is a terrific way to support your troops. For minimal cost and effort on the part of management, you can have an enormously positive effect on employee morale. Depending on how large your organization is, you can have employee recognition events or ceremonies annually, semi-annually, or quarterly. Designate an employee and a team of the month, quarter, and/or year for exceptional performance. If you have more than one person doing an outstanding job per period, somebody can get the "Exceptional" award and somebody else the "Distinguished" award. Recognize longevity milestones with certificates, plaques, and, for the longer milestones, reading aloud of the employees' career histories. When you or another official are reading names and bios, by the way, be very sure you pronounce all the names correctly. Get a pronunciation guide in advance of the ceremony, if necessary. Nothing is worse than mispronouncing the name of an employee at a recognition event. I have seen it happen too often. Regardless of whatever else you say or do that day, if you mispronounce a name, you have just made it plain to your employees that you do not know the individual and that he is unimportant. It is the equivalent of receiving a letter from a company you deal with regularly that is addressed, "Dear Valued Customer." They have just told you loud and clear that you are an account, not a person.

Also, almost everywhere I have been in a leadership position, we have given out something for going the whole year without taking a single sick day off. My favorite is giving the zero-sick-day employee a day off with pay. Getting that extra day with pay was coveted sufficiently by some people that they would use a vacation day (or days) instead of a sick day or days when sick, to preserve their eligibility—precisely the desired outcome.

But the biggest success we had in both departments I ran was special awards that we instituted for good customer service. Conventional wisdom is that you always hear more complaints than praise about your employees, because human nature is to speak up when unhappy, but not bother when satisfied. In fact, though, I noticed that I tended to see far more complimentary e-mails and letters concerning my department's employees than complaints. So we decided to give out nice polo shirts (*not* t-shirts) with the department's logo on them to any employee who received such a letter or e-mail. The added benefit of those awards was that it emphasized good customer service, one of the touchstones of modern government performance. There were only a few guidelines. The praise had to be in writing (e-mail or letter); no "I heard him say." The compliment had to arise from outside the department; co-workers could not nominate each other. And no matter how many letters you received, we would note each one, but you could only get one shirt a year.

The shirts were a smash success in both departments I ran. Employees all but killed for them. A few cynics on our leadership team suggested that employees would generate them by requesting them from the citizenry. To which I replied, "Wonderful! If an employee makes a citizen sufficiently happy with his service that said citizen is willing to write a letter saying so, that is exactly what we are trying to accomplish." At each recognition ceremony, I called the beneficiary up to the podium to, as I announced to the audience, "bask in the admiration of your co-workers" while I read aloud the complimentary missive(s). A photographer was on hand to snap a photo of me presenting the award to the individual. One division was so large, and they received so many letters, that I could not read them all individually. But in every other case, for 16 years, I did. One reason I particularly liked the polo shirts (and, I suspect, why the employees liked them as well) is that they recognized employees just for doing a good job on a daily basis. To win the highly competitive "state employee of the year" award, an individual practically had to save someone's life or identify a million dollars in cost reductions. Worthy achievements, to be sure, but most employees have no opportunity to accomplish the equivalent. Almost every employee, however, can deliver good customer service.

Generally speaking, I prefer awards or recognition that many people can earn (rather than those with one "winner"), like the customer service shirts. If I wanted to incentivize my divisions to spend less money, say, on overtime, I would design the award with a threshold that multiple divisions (or even, theoretically, every division) could cross, rather than make a single award to the one division that spent the least. That keeps everybody interested and in the game. Obviously, any threshold must be set sufficiently high that there is some effort involved in attaining it. Then, as soon as everybody clears the hurdle, you can raise the bar for the next year.

I tried never to miss a recognition ceremony. I recall contemplating skipping one at some point, wondering if my presence would really add anything, but then decided to attend. Sure enough, an employee came up after the ceremony to thank me and tell how great it was to receive his award, "And I got a chance to meet the secretary!" I had no such further contemplations.

On occasion, we would hold a special event. In my second cabinet assignment, I discovered that there were almost 100 department employees (out of the department's nearly 5,000) who had worked continuously in our department from the date that it had been created 33 years before. So we held a

"Present at the Creation" luncheon in honor of those hundred (stealing the title from Secretary of State Dean Acheson's autobiography). No matter how tight your budget is, never curtail employee recognition to save a few dollars. Such a morale wrecker would be close to the ultimate in penny-wise, pound-foolish behavior.

It is important to emphasize that employee morale is not just something that feels good. The prime reason for its importance is that how you and your organization treat people will have an affect on your ability to hire the best talent. Explained a CEO, "You can be the smartest person...and if you can't attract talent, you're never going to succeed. Something that I have learned over time—and that I think not enough people recognize—is that when you are trying to recruit somebody, the first thing they are going to do is call someone you've worked with before, usually multiple people. And if they say it was a great experience, then half the job is done. If they say it wasn't a great experience, you've lost them. So making sure that you do take care of people who work with you along the way is such a great investment."[47] In recent years, I have had the identical situation recur. Somebody whom I have not yet decided to hire has already conducted her own interviews of people who have worked for me. David Halberstam, in his book *The Reckoning*, pointed out that the businesses that are the most successful over time are those that treat their employees as resources, not overhead.[48] Much research has shown the same. It is true of government agencies as well.

The more you treat your employees appropriately, listen to them, and support them, the higher their morale. Employees with high morale are far more productive and engage in less negative behavior than those without it. Employees with high morale are also less likely to exit your agency in search of greener pastures. Those with high morale will report problems to management, not contact auditors, legislators, or the media. It is the low morale employees who are far more prone to neglect their duties or be chronically late or absent.

Now it is time to do active management. What constitutes top quality management?

One year when I was a cabinet secretary, our department conducted a **360-degree evaluation** of each of the department's 350 top managers. In its broadest sense, 360-degree evaluation refers to an employee being evaluated not just by her superiors, but by her peers and subordinates as well. In our case, evaluations of those employees by their superiors were already extant, so we confined our 360-degree evaluations to confidential ratings of each manager by all of his or her direct reports. To the surprise of no student of management in the Office of the Secretary, the evaluation produced extremely consistent results across the board. Those managers rated highest by the employees had four things in common ("the four principles that separate

great managers from good ones" in the verbiage of the consultants we hired
to perform the evaluations). The common elements were:

1. giving praise and helpful feedback; encouraging development,
2. setting clear expectations and high performance standards,
3. engaging in participative planning and problem solving, and
4. delegating and empowering employees.

As a leader and manager, you will be both praising and criticizing your
employees. There are good and bad ways to do both. In general, you should
be handing out far more compliments than brickbats. A positive approach
will result in far better performance by your employees than a negative one.
"I've learned that you only get the best out of other people when you do
things in a positive way. There are negative styles of leadership... but it
doesn't get the best out of people and doesn't breed loyalty"[49] is how one
leader put it. The reason the positive approach works is that positive feedback is usually a very powerful motivator—more powerful than money.
"Psychic compensation is often more motivating than financial compensation."[50]

Never miss an opportunity to tell your team that you are pleased with
their performance, especially since "Bureaucracy will tend to lower self-
esteem... [but] if you consciously build people up so that they say, 'I matter
here and people respect me and they think I can contribute and they trust me
to contribute,' that really gets the best out of people."[51] Also, nothing is more
fun than praising people, especially those people (there are quite a few of
them) who do not dwell on what they have done well, and may not even
appreciate how well they *have* done. When it comes to congratulations, "It's
a universal language."[52] My rule of thumb is that at any meeting, *anything*
successful (a smooth public hearing, timely completion of a job, a satisfactory external evaluation, etc.), earns us five minutes of self-congratulation. I
believe that it is important to take that time, because in government, no
matter what went right today, there are new problems, issues, and challenges
tomorrow. It is very easy to gloss over the good job that just got done in
favor of the next assignment. Coaches preach that their players need to concentrate on the next game and forget yesterday's victory. But their seasons
are months long, with days or a week between contests. In government, there
is hardly ever an off day and never an off-season. To again quote the favorite
rock group of my youth, Emerson, Lake & Palmer, *we* are "the show that
never ends." Even if there is no particular positive outcome that just occurred, you should constantly thank your folks for the hard work and dedica-
tion that they put into their jobs, day after day. Tell them to be very proud of
their public service. "There's another way to get the best out of people,

which is to really motivate them and make them feel good about themselves."[53]

Praise your team in public, but do your criticizing, when you have to do it, behind the scenes. Whenever possible, give feedback instead of criticism. As the saying goes, be a coach, not a critic. As an experienced CEO put it, "You never, ever do anything to deprive a human being of dignity in work, in life. Always praise in public, criticize in private."[54] Another leader cited his own negative experience. "I remember a boss...who upbraided me in front of a group of colleagues. And I think substantively she was wrong, but that wasn't the point...you should have enough respect to come and talk to me...to say, 'Look, I want to pull you aside. This is what I think you should have done.'"[55] When a staffer makes a mistake, have a corrective conversation immediately and personally. Be clear, concise (focus on a few things, not ten), and direct when giving a critique. Another executive: "The most important time is not the review time. If you see something that you talked about, you have to pull them aside right then and there."[56] There is seldom a need to be heavy-handed. A third leader: "When they're awesome, I tell them they're awesome. When they mess up, they hear about it. But do it the right way. Do it consistently. Do it with respect. No yelling and screaming, but here's our expectation, and here's what you missed. What do you think you need to do to get better so this doesn't happen again? That's what creates the positive culture. That's what attracts amazingly talented people."[57] In the words of Lou Holtz, former football coach at the University of Notre Dame, criticize the performance, not the performer.

Never engage in **faculty-room admonitions**. Some principals have a tendency to address the faculty in the faculty room about a problem that only one or two teachers have. (Other managers do this too, or will send a mass e-mail requesting modified behavior when there is only one offender.) This approach is the wrong one, because invariably the offender(s) will ignore the directive, while everyone else will closely scrutinize their own behavior in an effort to determine what they might have done wrong. Sit the guilty party down one-on-one and tell him or her what behavior needs to be modified. Understand each staffer as an individual so that you can give constructive feedback tailored to his performance, not someone else's.

Some top managers and some elected officials, executive and legislative alike, view themselves as critics-in-chief. They seem to think that public shaming of government employees, individually and collectively, is a good idea. They will never get the most out of their employees—although unfortunately, the press and some members of the public will probably like them. "If you're the kind of leader who cuts people down and humiliates them, you leave scars on people that can eventually come back to haunt you."[58] One elected executive with an extensive business management background exhibited a more sensible attitude. He told me, "One thing I learned is that you can't ever trash your employees in public and then expect them to go out and work hard for you. It will never happen."

As previously stated, the annual review is not as important as real-time feedback, especially regarding matters that need improvement. But you should still have an annual review, even if things are going well. Consider having your direct reports prepare their own evaluations before you sit down with them. Almost invariably, individuals will underrate themselves, which will give you an opportunity to tell them that they are better than they thought.

Sometimes what warrants criticism is bad enough to warrant discipline, too. But it needs to be something serious. The occasional error seldom requires disciplinary action. If it is sufficiently serious, keep in mind the concept of **progressive discipline**; it is generally the best path. Sanctions are lighter for initial offenses and increase if they are repeated. (More on this subject below.) I also am not a believer in treating everyone with absolute equality when it comes to discipline. Human resources types tend to want to mete out exactly the same punishment for the same offense, but I disagree. In my mind there is a big difference between an otherwise good employee who made a mistake, versus one who is a constant problem and the current episode is only the latest in a series.

You should always be trying to improve your managers and your employees and give them an opportunity to develop their talents, abilities, and skills. Unfortunately, it is very likely that your efforts to develop your staff will not be helped, and may even be hindered, by your jurisdiction's personnel system. Government personnel systems generally have two problems: the systems themselves and the people in them. Human resources offices and state personnel agencies are too often populated by rules types, not creative types. They can quote you every rule, but not figure out how to use those rules to solve a problem or get what you need done. The customer service revolution seems to have bypassed them.

Merit systems are outmoded obstacles. They are the very latest advance in personnel management from 1930. In that bygone era, when Democrats came to power, they fired all the Republicans, and vice versa. Today, few elected executives, up to and including the President of the United States, can hire and fire even one per cent of executive branch employees. In my opinion, very little bad would happen if most merit systems were simply abolished. In the current era, the demand on government agencies for service is so great, and budgets so tight, that no one can afford to hire employees who are politically connected but incompetent. There is nowhere to hide them. Only an extremely foolish elected official would try a mass termination of competent employees for reasons of political patronage. Chaos would ensue, and that elected official's career would soon be over.

Most personnel systems are poor at selection, retention, discipline, and termination. If you do not find this statement self-evident, see, for example, former Duke University professor and public management expert Robert Behn's hilarious takedown of job classifications. Behn imagines Duke University basketball coach Mike Krzyzewski having to follow a personnel system's rules while coaching the team. Krzyzewski could not put his five best players on the court, regardless of position. No, Coach K would be forced to play one center, two forwards, and two guards. He would be required to prepare a job description for each position, which would have to be approved by a personnel department employee who has never played basketball, let alone coached it. After the months- or years-long process of creating the job descriptions, Coach K still might get into trouble if a forward filed a grievance because he had to perform some of the center's duties. **Scientific management**, Behn concludes, may be dead everywhere else, but it lives on in government personnel systems.[59]

If your jurisdiction's civil service rules resemble the foregoing, you may be on your own when trying to improve your managerial cadre. Personnel offices usually have training components, but even setting aside customary capacity issues, they tend to be better at serving line employees than managers. You may have to create your own management improvement program. If you cannot increase your training budget or do any reallocating, at least do not reduce it, even if you are in cutback management mode. Start or increase management roundtables where managers can discuss thorny personnel matters with peers. "I would get the young managers together in a room every two weeks, and we would share examples of times they had to deal with a difficult employee situation. I felt it would resonate more with them if they saw each other learn how to manage people."[60]

Another technique that can be very successful is to convene an annual leadership seminar or conference for your top managers—the top 5 percent, or the top 15 percent, or all the managers and supervisors you have, if you can afford it. Make it a full day and make it casual dress (no ties for the men, for example). As the leader of your organization, take questions from the audience at some point. Focus on management development (training, techniques, and information to help them better do their jobs), although you can usually kill two birds with one stone by adding an **alignment** component to the program. You can have segments on **emotional intelligence**, 360-degree evaluations, different generations in the workplace, hiring and firing techniques, Covey's *The 7 Habits*, e-mail etiquette, and others. There is certainly no shortage of possible topics. Make it as interactive as possible. Also, do not let the attendees sit with their friends. Instead, assign seating at random to increase cross-fertilization of ideas and discussion. Require participants to turn off all their electronic devices. In the event of a true emergency, staffs back at the home office know how to get in touch with the attendees. Allow breaks and lunchtime for your troops to make and receive the phone calls. One manager I know always got a big laugh by telling the audience that if he saw someone leaving the room to take a phone call, it had better be because the individual's organ transplant was ready.

As with any training session, you should pass out evaluation sheets. But I predict that you will find, as we did, that every time your department conducts a leadership seminar, your managers will rate it very highly.

The third high quality management rule is to communicate expectations (and everything else) clearly and repeatedly. Throughout my management career, 95 percent of the time when I did not get the product, information, or result I wanted, it was because I did not clearly communicate those expectations. Only 5 percent of the time did the poor outcome occur because my troops failed to do the job properly. Communicate with your employees just like a political or advertising campaign does: repeat everything. Never assume that any rank-and-file employee knows any particular piece of information. Listen to various top leaders on communication, repetition, and change. Said one, "You have to articulate. You have to tell people what you want."[61] Another: "When you're working with people, even if you think you've said something, maybe you need to say it two or three more times."[62] A university president: "One lesson about change in any organization—communicate, communicate, communicate."[63]

As for the expectations themselves, expect and demand the highest standards in everything you, your leadership team, and your rank and file do. That being said, everybody makes mistakes. You will make your share; I have certainly made mine. Unless you are in the midst of a crisis (see Chapter 7), some patience and understanding is called for. "One thing I've learned over time is a lot more patience and tolerance."[64] Every mistake is an opportunity for a teachable moment and improvement, not an occasion to browbeat the staffer who made the error. From time to time I quote an old friend who once said, "Just as soon as I stop making mistakes, I will criticize others for theirs. I suspect it may be some time." You, like everyone else, will commit errors. When (not if) you call one wrong, be open about it, both internally and externally. As the expression goes, "**put the donkey ears on**" and wear them around for a while.

Once you have clearly set expectations and goals, let your staff do their jobs the way they prefer to do them. You have hired the best (see "Whom To Hire", above); now it is time to "Give them the opportunity to do what they need to do."[65] It does not matter *how* they go about getting results, as long as they get them. To quote World War II General George S. Patton, "Never tell people how to do things, tell them what to do and they will surprise you with their ingenuity."[66] Too often, unfortunately, government works in exactly the opposite fashion. There may be no clear goals, but how one operates is heavily circumscribed by red tape.

I did not start off letting people do their jobs. When I became a cabinet secretary for the first time, I came from a job where I had supervised mostly recent college graduates who, while intelligent, had little or no experience. That being the case, and having done most of their jobs previously myself, my role as their boss was to give them detailed instructions about not just what to do, but how to do it. My first month in the cabinet was very troubling because I did not have the detailed knowledge about every one of my direct reports' jobs that I was accustomed to. Then I was fortunate enough to attend a meeting of my national association, where a speaker described his own evolution as a manager, from knowing everything about what his employees were doing to the realization that he no longer could (or should) do so as he moved up the management ladder. Instantly the light bulb went on over my head; I realized I needed to supervise my employees, not control them. In point of fact, you as the head of your agency will never know as much about *any* of your key aides' jobs as they will, let alone all of them. And if you try to stand over everybody to tell them how to do their jobs, there are not enough hours in the day. Said one CEO, "As you manage bigger groups…you become less of a specialist, less knowledgeable about specific issues."[67]

Micromanagement is the mortal sin of the management field. As a top executive states, "I think my worst bosses were hyper-controlling. I've learned that leaders do the opposite."[68] Working for the worst manager I ever had taught me the most I ever learned about management, because it taught me how not to treat people. Prior to that job, I may have engaged in some of the behavior he displayed; never again. This particular boss had many faults (he was a pedant, he relentlessly criticized his employees by tailoring his attacks to their particular emotional vulnerabilities, and he was unwilling to listen to opinions other than his own, among many others), but by far his worst was that he was the ultimate micromanager. In the days of typewriters, if this gentleman wandered by the mail tray and spotted a letter on which the typed address was not sufficiently parallel to the top and bottom edges of the envelope, he would yank it out of the tray and demand that it be redone. He issued precise instructions for clipping an article out of the newspaper and for making photocopies. And on and on. Right before my departure, he openly audited the petty cash drawer, which was my responsibility, to make sure that I had not stolen anything. It was the worst year of my professional life, bar none. It was only one year, because I only lasted one year, as did virtually everyone else who worked for him. As a top leader explains, "If you micromanage, the best ones leave."[69]

I am not the only one to have that experience. Having not been a varsity athlete in high school, I naively assumed that all youth sports coaches were pretty much the same. Then my daughter, who *is* a good athlete, had a terrible coach one season—a woman who beat her players down instead of building them up, and worst of all, played favorites. Naturally, her team performed well below their talent level. It was a rough season for my daughter, but a huge learning experience for her as well. Says a chief executive, "You learn a lot from the worst managers you've had. You learn more probably than from the great managers."[70] Another recounted that "I remember being publicly humiliated. I'd sent out an Excel spreadsheet that didn't have the first and last names broken out in separate fields, and he sent a 'reply all' to the entire company telling me how stupid I am and how bad I am at Excel. There were so many situations where I remember being just made to feel inferior and stupid, no matter how hard I worked. I was a kid out of college and I was not qualified to do some of the work I was being asked to do, but I did my best. And when my best wasn't good enough, I was told I was very stupid, essentially. And I just remember saying: 'I never want to make anybody feel this way.'"[71] In clear contrast, both governors in whose cabinets I served managed me the way I hope I manage my staff: they did not micromanage. They set goals for me that were few in number but of high importance, then expected me to accomplish them. Otherwise, I was free to run the department as I saw fit, while they held me accountable for its performance.

The final high quality management principle is to delegate and empower your employees. Effective delegation is one of the keys to management. As your organization's head, it is not your job to do things. It is your job to make sure that things get done. But what you need to practice is stewardship delegation, not gofer delegation. Amazingly, many leaders do not effectively use staff because they cannot delegate (or do not use staff at all). "Many people refuse to delegate to other people because they feel it takes too much time and effort and they would do the job better themselves."[72] As stated earlier in this chapter, anybody who says they would rather do the work themselves than delegate automatically flunks my interview. Some legislators with whom I dealt looked at me with disdain if I brought aides to a meeting. They did not want to see what they referred to as an "entourage." The legislature is traditionally at a disadvantage compared with the executive branch because so many legislators ineffectively use staff, or do not use them at all. When you are delegating, take care that there is always a match between authority and responsibility. If you give someone the responsibility to carry out a given task, make sure that they have the authority to get it done.

## YOUR LEADERSHIP TEAM

You need to identify a top management team in your department, which you will call your senior staff or leadership team. This team should include the department's deputy (if there is one), all the directors of your subordinate divisions, their deputies, and the professional members of your immediate office staff. Include your personal secretary or assistant too, as well as any other key support personnel. This is the group you will rely on to run your department. Best hiring practices for managers, knowledge workers, and support staff were discussed in "Whom To Hire", earlier in this chapter. Best practices for supervising employees were discussed in "How To Manage Your Employees", above. Once again, you want to hire the very best and then support them to the hilt. "You should always try to make the people around you as good and strong and talented as you can, because they make you shine."[73] When hiring and managing your leadership team, some additional rules apply. Managing managers is slightly different from managing line employees. In fact, in the large organization that you are running, you will only be managing managers. You should not be directly managing line employees, even in your immediate office. It is a task that can and should be delegated.

As stated in "Whom to Hire," above, the pool of talent from which you can draw will be greatest at the beginning of your elected official's administration, then decline steadily over the next four years. Then, if your boss is reelected, you will have another uptick in the talent pool, but the pool will decline still further over the remainder of the second term. Potential candidates become less likely to leave jobs for **exempt positions** when they face the possibility of being replaced just a short while later. Because your talent pool may shrink over time, always keep an eye out for talent in the merit ranks of your agency. The members of your leadership team are the most important individuals in your organization, and your success depends upon the quality of these individuals more so than any other factor; therefore, you should try to have a replacement plan in the back of your mind for every member of your senior staff. Turnover is inevitable, and you do not want to flounder around while searching for a new director. The more good people you hire, the more you have people around you who can advance. As one veteran government leader puts it, "The good people you hire will tend to move on and be hired away from you."[74]

In all but a few jurisdictions throughout the country, diversity in hiring is a key consideration. It goes double for your leadership team if the team consists primarily of exempt employees. Primarily, this is because leadership team members have the highest profile and will be seen as representing your personal commitment to diversity. Second, you will not be able to hide behind cumbersome merit system procedures as an obstacle to diverse hiring, because there aren't any. Diversity in hiring will be discussed further in Chapter 8.

Because of the shortcomings of civil service systems discussed in the previous section, the position of personnel director for your department is a critical one. Whether you have one person whose sole responsibility is human resources, or a director whose responsibilities include **HR** among others, it is essential that you get someone for the job who is results-oriented. Someone who can tweak the system to get out of it what you want is far more valuable than someone who merely knows all the rules forward and backward.

Think of your team *as* a team. If you have followed the rules described earlier in this chapter, and have hired good managers for your management positions, you can now deploy them with a great deal of flexibility. The best college football coaches recruit great athletes by position, but they do not worry about changing those positions once the young men enroll, if it is the best for the team. Your strongest managers are candidates for any management job that comes open, regardless of what their experience is in a particular area. If you join your department at the very beginning of an administration, you may have the opportunity to pick the members of your team first, then figure out which slots to put them in (see Chapter 8). Later, you will be mostly limited to changing your lineup when a vacancy occurs. When the position of director of my largest program came open, I replaced him with a very strong manager who was directing a different but much smaller division, even though his technical knowledge of his new position was limited. He was very successful at his new post. I never hesitated to move my troops around for the good of the organization.

Time is of the essence when filling a leadership team vacancy. Ideally, I want to announce the replacement the same day I announce the vacancy, and ideally, if Sarah leaves on Tuesday, I would like Carol to assume the reins on Wednesday. There are two reasons for this telescoped time frame. First, if a top management position is involved, I want to minimize if not eliminate the time when there is no permanent director. During an interregnum, routine or everyday business gets done, but nothing moves forward while there is an acting division head. Acting directors lack both the authority and the inclination to make substantive changes. Second, if a vacancy opens up and there is no announcement of a successor, outside parties like legislators and advocates will draw the correct conclusion that you do not have a replacement lined up, and they will feel free to offer their recommendations. "Do not keep high-level jobs open too long. It will... give interest groups, special constituencies, and other external players time to find and promote their own candidates."[75]

Unfortunately, I have found that my idea of who can do a top management job is quite at variance with the ideas of many legislators. Sometimes they are simply interested in patronage. Even if they are not, most legislators do not have management backgrounds and—very much like their constituents—have little concept of what it takes to successfully manage a government agency. Oddly, if you announce the replacement when you announce the vacancy, legislators rarely complain that they did not have an opportunity to suggest a name. But they may be unhappy if you do not hire somebody they do send your way. No matter how obvious it is to you that a recommended candidate cannot do the job, you will have to give him or her a **courtesy interview** that looks like a real one.

Advocates sometimes suggest names for leadership jobs. Also, you may occasionally be asked by a group that (or an individual who) has a stakeholder relationship with one of your department's divisions to go one step further—can they participate in the hiring of the vacant director position? Allowing outsiders a role in selecting your most important employees is fraught with peril. If you and the stakeholders ultimately agree on the same individual, you will have earned some good will. But the downside risks are large. If your preferred candidate is not the same as the third party's, you will have two equally unpalatable alternatives. You either have to defer to their preference, which you should never do, or go against their wishes and create far larger bad feelings than you would have by simply declining their request. Ultimately, your interests and the interests of the stakeholders may not align. Stakeholders who are advocates (and almost all of them are, in some form or other) tend to want experts, not managers, and want advocates, not team players, in key leadership roles. In addition, if the new appointee does not perform well, if anything goes south, or even if the new appointee merely comes under criticism, the outsiders will not be there to support the appointee, or you. You are responsible for the success or failure of anyone you hire into a leadership position, so you had better retain the authority to make the choice.

If no likely candidates are immediately available, you will have to consider whether to publicly post a vacancy, or alternatively, whether to employ a recruitment firm. (If any positions in your leadership team are non-exempt, you will of course have to post them anyway.) Occasionally I use both tactics, but generally I try to avoid using either, as they each have significant drawbacks. Posting an exempt position may or may not attract some good talent, but it definitely will attract recommendations from outside parties like legislators and advocates. When you do not immediately announce a replacement for a vacancy, they may *assume* that you have no candidate; if you post the job, they *know* it. Again, you will have to interview everyone who is recommended to you. Such job postings also attract an astonishing number of applicants who could not possibly handle the responsibilities. Executive search firms can identify good candidates, but the process is quite expensive. And sometimes the candidate looks great on paper and interviews well, but just does not fit right—a fact that no search firm, no matter how good, can tell you.

Having put your team in place, clearly and repeatedly communicate your expectations and ground rules to them. Areas to cover should include but not be limited to working hours/arrangements, who hires whom, reporting requirements, the need to provide accurate information, the necessity of dealing promptly and effectively with non-functional employees (as discussed in "Problem Employees", below) and disagreement, alignment, and team play. My own customary rules are as follows.

I expect my key staffers to work as long as necessary to get the job done. However, how and when they do their work is up to them. I do not care how many or few hours they put in at the office itself, or when they come and go. In other words, they are free to ignore the clock. If they want to work from home on occasion, that is fine, too. I am not hypervigilant about punctuality, as long as somebody is not keeping a group of people waiting. One of my predecessors in a cabinet position, an ex-Marine, was legendary for his rule that the door would be locked at the precise minute the meeting was scheduled to begin. If you arrived a minute late, you cooled your heels in the hallway until the meeting ended. I declined to institute a similar rule, lest I be the individual on the outside looking in.

Establish clear rules regarding who hires whom. Which positions will you as the head of the agency hire yourself, which positions can be hired by your directors but subject to your approval, and which positions can be hired by your directors without any review on your part? As cabinet secretary, I hired all the exempt (at will) professionals, and left the hiring of exempt support staff and merit system employees to my division heads. Create your own rules, but make sure everyone understands and follows them. If your jurisdiction allows the hiring of the lowest level of merit employees without engaging in merit rules of procedure, establish some ground rules for such hiring that you are comfortable with.

You should either meet biweekly with your division directors, or require them to submit a biweekly written report. The larger your organization, the more important this reporting is. You need the regular reports not so that you can micromanage your department, but for two reasons. First, you need to be conversant with what is going on in all corners of your bailiwick. Second, you need to know where the problems are in your agency. The reports are essentially **exception reports**, because you need to spend your time not where things are going well, but where things are not. I prefer that the biweekly reports be written either by the director or the deputy director, not a subordinate. Except for the statistics that might be included, the reports should be in narrative form. Writing in a narrative form, I have found, helps the director focus on what the most important matters are. Assuming that the reports are not subject to freedom of information act disclosure, I prefer personal, candid views. I prefer a prospective view as well as retrospective— I want to know what they think is going to happen next, not just what has already happened. If X occurs, will Y follow or will it be Z? The ability to accurately forecast what will happen next, by the way, is an excellent metric by which to judge your top people. The very best people have a preternatural ability to see what is coming around the corner. It is not an ability that you can ascertain during the hiring process, unfortunately. You have to see people in action.

The content of these reports should include, first and foremost, the major issues and problems facing your subordinate, be they press, legislative, policy, regulatory, and/or budgetary issues. If I have given the director an assignment, she can report on her progress through this medium. Major accomplishments and milestones should be announced. Any legislative contacts should be detailed. You always need to know if and when legislators have made an inquiry about anything. There should be a summary of all pending litigation (see "Lawsuits" in Chapter 12). Extraneous matters like quotations, travel plans, the director's schedule, and events attended by the division staff should be excluded. The distribution of these reports should be limited to you and a very few key aides.

When statistics on workload and performance measures are in the report, they should include a time comparison, i.e., what is the current number versus what was the number last month and/or last year. With any statistical measurement, the trend is as important as, if not more important than, the current situation. It is not necessarily where you are that indicates how you are doing, it is where you are going. If you have good metrics across the board, it can be very easy to assess your organization at a glance. Regular statistical reports can be somewhat drab when everything is going well, but spikes in numbers can be revealing when they occur.

You will be receiving other briefings from your leadership team regularly. Just as you should be concise when giving briefings to your boss, the elected official (see Chapter 9), your team should be concise when briefing you. Bottom line information, primarily concerning the cost and the due date, is what you need from your aides. Instruct them accordingly.

Chapter 10 will discuss the necessity of providing accurate information to others. Similarly, your top leaders must always provide accurate information to you. Everyone makes mistakes, but providing inaccurate information is the worst kind of mistake, because you make decisions based on the information that you have. Bad information inevitably yields bad decisions, which ultimately yield loss of control.

As was discussed in "How To Manage Your Employees", above, you should insist that your leadership team always speak their minds. However, once a final decision has been reached (whether by you, the elected official for whom you work, or the budget director if it is a money matter), it is time for all members of your team to align themselves in support of that decision, even if (or especially if) the decision is contrary to the personal views of a team member.

All the general rules about clearly communicating expectations and not micromanaging go double when dealing with your leadership team. One method I used to transmit expectations to my top managers was to give newly hired ones the "Vince Meconi Management Style Quiz." Corny it is in the extreme, but it got the message across.

Sample questions:

1.  In hiring employees, the most important thing to consider is

    a. what their previous employers say about them
    b. how extensive their previous experience is

2.  The best way to get one of your professional or supervisory employees to perform a task is to

    a. tell them what you want done and let them figure out how to go about it.
    b. give them clear, specific instructions on how to do the job.

3.  When confronted with non-functional employees, generally managers should

    a. take aggressive action as soon as possible.
    b. ignore or "cubbyhole" them.

4.  The new cabinet secretary should always be addressed as:

    a. Vince
    b. Mr. Secretary
    c. Excellency
    d. Your grace

5.  You have asked the cabinet secretary, two times, politely, to do something (sign a document, approve a proposal, etc.) that is time sensitive. He has failed to take action. You next move should be:

    a. Say, "Hey stupid. I need this now!"
    b. Politely remind him a 3rd time.
    c. Be patient. He's a busy man.

6.  You have just heard a joke from the secretary. At least, you think it's a joke, because he's smiling. You should:

    a. Laugh whether you get the joke or not. It just saves time.
    b. Ask that the joke be repeated. Maybe it will be clearer the 2nd time.
    c. Ask that the joke be explained.

7.  The secretary has just announced that he will be taking a certain action. In your view, it is a bad idea. You should:

    a. Say what is on your mind. You are not doing him, yourself, or the department any good by withholding your views.

    b. Offer your advice only if asked for it.

    c. Do nothing. If he wants your opinion he will give it to you.

8. The secretary is making a presentation to the Governor or the Legislature. He just made a factual misstatement. You should:

    a. Speak up immediately and correct him.

    b. Slip him a note telling him he goofed.

    c. Be quiet and tell him afterwards.

(In case you were wondering, the correct answer is "a" to all questions.)

All the preaching about not micromanaging is not to say that there is never a time when you can and should be more directive. Giving people responsibility and then getting out of the way only works if you have very good managers working for you. As stated previously, your ideal agency heads or section leaders are so strong that you do not have much to do. But that is not always going to happen. You must be aware of each staffer's capabilities. Sometimes you cannot get exactly the person you want to head up one of your divisions, so you have to suboptimize the hiring. Or, maybe a hire did not work out as planned. Or, the person in charge of an operation is a merit system employee, not one who serves at your pleasure, and cannot be replaced. Or, the leader may be strong in some areas but weak in others. You still prefer not to micromanage, but some people need more direction than others.

If you have a truly weak director who cannot be fired, or you are in the process of replacing the individual, you will need to jump in with both feet and be very directive. Some **ad hoc managers** (ones who make things up as they go along) practically need a playbook from you. There are also certain non-managerial types you will run into who require more direction and/or supervision. You may have employees who are very technically competent, but lack the best judgment and go "off the reservation." They need to be kept on a short leash. Other employees only work well when being given daily direction. These folks, while frequently both intelligent and good workers, lack the ability to determine what is important and what is unimportant. Left to their own devices, they will spend time on trivial matters while failing to attend to priorities. You or another supervisor have to supply the good judgment that they do not possess. And finally, of course, low performers in general need constant supervision.

There is another time when you must assume direct control: when there is a crisis. Crisis management is one of the subjects of Chapter 7.

In your leadership team, the emphasis should be on the word *team*. You should expect and demand team play from your team. Cooperation, not competition, should always be the order of the day with parties both internal and external. You should have no patience for **turf battles** (disputes about which agency will perform a certain functions), not at your level and not at your subordinates' level. I never feel territorial about any department I run. If some function currently performed by your agency can truly be done better somewhere else, by all means you should let it go. I have done just that when the evidence suggested it. In my initial cabinet assignment, my responsibilities included the Capitol Police force, in a department that was otherwise comprised of support and regulatory functions. Although I very much enjoyed working with them, when a government study commission recommended that they be transferred from my department to the Public Safety department, which contained the rest of the state's law enforcement functions, I saw the move as quite logical and raised no objection. Most managers, unfortunately, have an extreme reluctance to give up anything that is currently in their rice bowl. One of my colleagues reacted very negatively, almost histrionically, to that same commission's proposal to centralize construction management responsibilities in my department. (Ultimately, both the transfer of Capitol Police and the centralization of construction management took place.) You need to make clear to your subordinates that an obstructionist attitude is inappropriate.

Do everything you can to build teamwork among your top aides, because almost all of your department's accomplishments will come from team efforts, even if an eventually successful idea originally comes from a single individual (as they usually do). "Results rarely depend on the work of just one person—they are normally created by groups of employees."[76] When I served as a cabinet secretary, I was always proud of saying that I did not have a single individual accomplishment—but my department had a myriad of accomplishments.

A cooperative working atmosphere among all of your employees does not develop on its own. As noted in Chapter 1, in any group of 10 or more people, two of them are going to actively dislike each other. You will be lucky if three or four don't hate each other. This is true in even the most homogeneous groups. It has been true in every leadership team I have been a part of, even the ones where I handpicked every single member. Start by making clear that working cooperatively is your expectation, but that is only the start, not the finish. Second, treat them like the valuable team members that they are. Make sure they feel that they are a part of your team. Communicate with them often, especially about news regarding what is going on in the department. Let them know about staffing changes, especially changes in the leadership team, before anyone else, inside or outside your agency. E-mail makes such communication extremely easy; there is no excuse not to do it. They should never learn about something major that is going on from anyone but you. It is terrible for morale when ostensibly key leaders learn about changes via the grapevine or read about them in the press. Pass on to them every press release, information sheet, talking points memo, directive, etc. that you get from the Governor's Office, budget office, or personnel department. Your team in turn should distribute selective parts to the rank and file.

Hold regular leadership team meetings and training sessions. Given that other means of communication are readily available, you probably do not have to have a group meeting of your whole team more than once every month or two. But you should have them. The agenda will likely include budget and personnel matters at almost every session. Every team meeting should also include a spin around the table at which time each division reports on major developments going on in their outfits. Also, hold a retreat for your team at least annually, which should include information sessions, strategic planning and **SWOT** (Strengths, Weaknesses, Opportunities, and Threats) exercises, lunches and dinners together, and extensive use of humor. Your team will have a lot of the problems and issues in common, and the best people with whom to discuss solutions are their colleagues.

In addition, I tried to keep things interesting by once or twice a year passing out fake awards, which I labeled "Outstanding/Dubious Achievement Awards" (the recipient and audience had to decide which it was) for a good job done, something amusing or ironic that happened, or a slip-up that we all learned from. They always went over very well.

Years after I have left my cabinet assignments, I still think of the leadership teams of those departments as "my" teams. I will always help them any way I can—with advice or a recommendation if they need it, or maybe just taking a phone call from a team member who wants to discuss something. I expect that this will always be my attitude—and I believe many of them feel the same way.

You need to advise your senior staff that every member of your team has a political job. This may surprise some of them who thought they had merely a policy job or a management job. It should not be surprising, given that the words "politics" and "policy" have the same Greek word, *polites* (citizen) in their etymology. Scholars have recognized since the 1940s that "Public administration is a political process."[77] The fact that they have political jobs does not mean that they have to pass out campaign literature on weekends for the elected executive at the head of your government. But what does it mean?

As one scholar put it, "professionalized public bureaucrats have a capacity to initiate and innovate that is unparalleled in the political system. They are truly political actors, despite any label of neutrality they may give themselves or that others may give them."[78]

Every top manager has to operate in a political environment, something that I have had to explain to many top managers, especially if they are accustomed to doing things their way because they are in charge of a division, section, or branch. In a democracy, we executive branch managers cannot just do what we think is best, even when we are the individuals most knowledgeable about a given subject. The legislature or council, the press, the public, and advocates all have a role and a say. We may or may not agree with all or even any of their views, and we do not necessarily have to do everything they want. We have a great degree of latitude, but we must acknowledge the legitimacy of their opinions. For example, if you are presenting one of your proposals to a legislative committee or group of influential advocates, and the body supports 90 percent of your proposal but wants 10 percent changed or dropped, the appropriate response is to eliminate or modify that 10 percent. Insistence on getting all 100 percent will most likely lead to getting 0 percent. Those of your senior staff who do not grasp this particular point need more coaching on operating in a political atmosphere. The foregoing does not mean that you just roll over and accept unpalatable outcomes, but it does mean that you should pick your political battles.

Even if you have been able to select a high-quality team and clearly set out your expectations, at some point they are going to make decisions that you disagree with. They might make a policy choice you feel is wrong or promote an individual you do not think is sufficiently worthy. Overrule them only in exceptional circumstances. You have hired them; let them do their jobs. Conversely, sometimes they will try to practice **upward delegation**—and the best ones will always be **upwardly managing**. When anyone tries to upward delegate, turn it right back on him. You have selected him to run his operation, and making decisions and getting things done is his responsibility. As for upward management—as long as you recognize that it is being attempted, you have already won the game.

Unfortunately, the day will come when you have to terminate an employee. At your level, it will likely be a member of your leadership team. It is a very difficult thing to do, even when you are ending the employment of someone for a bad act or because they have performed incompetently. Firing someone is unquestionably the aspect of my job that I like least. Still, you need to treat your exempt, top managers like the military in wartime—sometimes they need to be relieved of their command for poor performance. An expert government manager once told me, "My first rule of management is that nobody is indispensable. And my second rule of management is that if somebody is indispensable, don't let them know it." Once you have set clear expectations (again, see "How to Manage Your Employees", above), it is up to your exempt employees to deliver. If they consistently cannot, you should strongly consider replacing them. You can always make a good performer better, but seldom turn someone who is failing into someone who passes (and it is not your job to try). You can teach your managers how to navigate the legislative process, or how to become better at presentations. It is much more difficult to teach someone management or people skills. Obviously, though, you should remove managers for overall poor performance—but never for making a mistake and never to scapegoat someone for being in the wrong post at the wrong time.

You particularly need to adopt the attitude that you will hold your top aides responsible for their performance, because you will make mistakes in hiring or promoting to top jobs; everybody does. As one CEO put it, "We don't have a perfect batting average on hiring. Nobody does, and that's OK."[79] No matter how well recommended someone comes, or how well they have done in previous jobs, sometimes individuals simply do not perform up to expectations. There is no way to know, as the prime example, whether someone who has excelled at the #2 slot will succeed at the #1 position. More than once I have seen a #2 who succeeded at the deputy position because the #1 was there to set priorities, and sand down the #2's rough edges on a daily basis. Once that filter and that guidance were removed, the newly-promoted #2 failed. (It is also true that certain individuals are much better at the top position than the second-ranked one.) Some people are equally good at any position they are put in, while others have their niche and do not necessarily do well outside it—and it is not always obvious who is whom.

I have had to fire people both for specific bad acts (sleeping with a subordinate and criminal justice system involvement, for example), and because they are not up to the job. (Other offenses that should warrant dismissal include ethics violations and lying.) I have also had to replace people because of a change in administration. This particular kind of firing may be your decision as the head of the agency, or it may be the decision of the administration.

Firing someone is never a pleasant task; I never enjoy it even when the employee has misbehaved and richly deserves his discharge. And if it is unpleasant for you as the person doing the firing, imagine how unpleasant, even life-altering, it is for the person being fired. For this reason, you should always handle the dismissal humanely. Your worst enemy deserves nothing less. There are certain ironclad rules for firing someone. First, firing is an act that should only be done in person. Never terminate anyone by telephone, let alone e-mail, fax, or other written communication. I have even heard of a dismissal being announced via an envelope slipped under the door. In one of the more egregious cases I am familiar with, a newly-elected executive let most of the holdover cabinet officials know that their services were no longer required by issuing a press release; their first knowledge that they had been fired came when they read about it in the paper the next day.

Second, if it is your decision to dismiss the individual and the employee reports to you, you do the firing. *Never delegate this task.* Early in George R. R. Martin's bestselling fantasy novel *A Game of Thrones*, Lord Ned Stark has to execute a man for dereliction of duty. He performs the execution himself, unlike the king, whose executions are performed by a "headsman."

He explains to his son that the person ordering the death sentence should carry it out himself; if he cannot bear to look the condemned in the eye, then maybe the man does not deserve the death penalty. You are firing someone, not killing him, but the principle is much the same.

Some management texts (and some of my colleagues) strongly recommend that you never fire anyone except in the presence of a witness. I strongly disagree. Except in the rarest of circumstances, you and the person being dismissed should be the only two people in the room. An exception will occur if there is reason to believe the person being fired will turn violent. (In that case, conduct the meeting not in your office but in a courthouse or other facility with a secure entrance equipped with metal detectors through which visitors must pass.) Never take away an individual's dignity. Being dismissed is a humiliating experience and there is no reason to add to the humiliation by having witnesses to the act. Sometimes the person being fired crumbles before your very eyes. Make sure you have a box of tissues on the table at which the employee will be seated. In your remarks (you should consider using a script), be succinct. If the termination is being done in response to a specific act, identify the act. Otherwise, use a general statement along the lines of moving in a different direction or needing to make a change. This is not the time for a performance evaluation. And never speak publicly of the reason why someone was terminated; speak favorably of the former employee if at all possible. One nationally famous administrator allowed a film crew to tape an unexpected dismissal meeting—a double ambush. The administrator in question disgraced herself. Regardless of whether the dismissed employee deserved his termination, frankly, that kind of self-aggrandizing behavior proved that this particular boss is not good enough to manage a newsstand, let alone a large government enterprise. You do not treat people like that, whatever their faults.

Having made the decision to terminate an exempt employee, the next question to be answered is whether the dismissed employee will get a **hard landing** or a **soft landing**. There is only one kind of hard landing: an immediate dismissal that offers no alternative position for the dismissed individual. For employees being dismissed immediately, hold the termination meeting at the end of the day, so that the employee can clean out his office after hours, without the embarrassment of having to explain the situation to co-workers. A Friday end of the day meeting is even better, if possible, allowing the weekend for removal of personal effects. Even with an immediate dismissal, there is no need to escort the individual from the building; that just adds to his humiliation. He is not going to sabotage his office or commit other mischief if he ever wants to work again. I wholeheartedly agree with the revulsion described by a CEO at situations where employees are "...fired with a security person escorting them out the door. I find that so demeaning and disrespectful. There are times and places for that, like if somebody is intentionally doing something wrong."[80]

There are multiple kinds of soft landings. You might allow the employee to resign or retire, and be allowed to make the announcement himself. If an employee is willing to retire, I generally promise that my boss and I will publicly praise him. You might allow the dismissed employee a fixed or open-ended time period before departure, either to allow the individual to obtain another job or to permit him to earn additional pension credit and/or salary. Alternatively, you can send the employee home, on a sort of leave with pay, for a couple of weeks or a month. I prefer the latter if it allows the replacement to come on board sooner. Any soft landing should be contingent upon the departed employee's agreement not to publicly or privately complain about his former employer. The agreement is unenforceable, of course, but most people will honor it, at least in the short term.

Your jurisdiction may permit individuals to take leaves from its merit system, allowing them to retain merit system protection while holding an exempt position. If the dismissed employee is on such a leave, the decision for a soft landing may already have been made for you.

Generally speaking, I prefer a hard landing when the dismissal is for a specific bad act, although there are exceptions if the employee had an otherwise exemplary record. In a perfect world, I would give almost everybody else a soft landing, although resource constraints will probably prevent it. I particularly favor soft landings if the dismissed employee is being removed for competency reasons, especially if the employee is someone I hired or promoted—obviously, the fault is as much mine as his because I made a poor decision. When a leader is being replaced because of a change in administration, it is more of a judgment call (see Chapter 8). In this case, sometimes you are making the change because the incumbent was a problem or his views antithetical to yours or the new administration's; a hard landing is therefore indicated. But if the previous occupant was a competent manager, strongly consider a soft landing. You and your agency may need her talents later on down the line.

No matter how much an employee may have deserved his firing, no matter how soft a landing you have given that person, do not be surprised if that person resents being terminated and feels no gratitude for the soft landing. Once or twice in my career, a dismissed employee has later said to me, "I realize now that you made the right decision." More often, the individual you removed will shoot at you the first chance he gets.

## PROBLEM EMPLOYEES

The will to confront problem employees and the success in getting rid of them not only separate good managers from poor ones, but top organizations from lesser ones. "The most damaging management failure of all is to accept the unacceptable in employee performance. It follows, then, that the most distinguishing attribute of successful executives and managers is that they reject the unacceptable."[81] "Competent organizations...deal early on with problem employees."[82] One hundred years from now, if public managers are not reading this book, they will be reading one just like it for its chapter covering problem employees. In the "Managing Change in a Bureaucracy" section, below, there is a discussion about change, including the statement that everything changes. But there is one thing that does not change—human nature. Perhaps in 100,000 years, human nature will have evolved, but not in the foreseeable future. Evolution does not move that fast. Employee problems will ever be with us because employees are like all human beings: they are not perfectly rational, but are ruled by emotions.

In the words of one of the best managers who ever worked for me, "People issues are always the toughest." They certainly are the toughest part of the job on any given day. I learned all about personnel systems and collective bargaining in graduate school, but one thing they did not teach me (or talk about in any book I have read, or cover in any training session I have attended) is how much time that, even as a very senior manager, you spend dealing with problem employees. This demand on your time occurs because, as one management consultant put it, "In every organization of size, there are bound to be some people who are crooked or crazy."[83]

By problem employees, I do not mean low performers—below average employees. Every organization has high, medium, and low performers. I am not referring here to employees who are not the hardest workers, or to the ones who trade off-color jokes on office e-mail. The individuals in question are the non-performers, the people who cannot do their jobs, and/or have such toxic behavior that they can fairly be said to be cancers on the organization—organization killers. They deserve special attention. Such individuals are not usually numerous, but they can be found at any level of your agency, from top management to the lowest rank of line employees.

I am also not referring here to exempt employees who serve at your pleasure. As noted under "Whom to Hire," above, if they are not doing their jobs or misbehave, you can call them into your office and terminate them. Instead, I am writing about individuals with merit system and/or union contract protections, who require due process and progressive discipline that make their dismissal cumbersome. Progressive discipline means that, except in extraordinary situations, an employee cannot be terminated until he has been given one or more opportunities to correct his performance; each subsequent failure to improve results in a more serious penalty.

The taxonomy of problem employees includes about half a dozen categories, not mutually exclusive. I classify them as follows.

1. Incompetent employees—individuals who simply do not have the skills, abilities, and/or work ethic to adequately perform their jobs. At lower levels, these employees may lack the appropriate training, may be distracted by personal problems, or they may simply have been brought on board by a poor hiring decision. At supervisory levels, training is not the issue. At these higher levels, frequently you come upon people who at one time may have been adequate if not stellar performers, but because they have been inadequately managed for so long, now completely lack the ability they once had.

2. **Peter principled**[84] **employees**—they were satisfactory at their previous job, but got promoted beyond their level of competence.

3. Employees **retired in place**—veteran employees nearing or past retirement eligibility who are now uninterested or unwilling to do any but the most minimal aspects of their job, and certainly no tasks requiring creativity, problem solving, or, if in management, supervising.

4. **Cowboys and cowgirls**—ostensibly competent employees, these individuals can only do it their way. They are unable to take direction and regard themselves as being the only people qualified and appropriate to determine what they should do on a daily basis. These individuals are disproportionately found in the ranks of regulatory positions, and are particularly harmful in them because those positions typically have a large degree of discretion. Any attempt to manage cowboys and cowgirls is regarded by them as political interference—inappropriate and unethical. They are prone to playing favorites and making arbitrary and inconsistent decisions.

5. Toxic employees—regardless of their competency, these individuals have limited to no people skills and are difficult to work with, work for, or have working for you. These folks have negative personalities. They are not people having bad days; they are employees whose every day is a bad day. There is likely something in their background (recent or from their childhood) causing them to behave the way they do. They are very often unaware of their toxicity.

6. **Political relatives**—these employees were hired through the recommendation or even intervention of an elected official or perhaps the supporter of an elected official (union, contributor, neighbor, fellow church-goer—the list is endless). They may be actual blood relatives or not. Not all employees hired in this fashion are problematic. Those who are not are genuinely grateful to be working in your agency, work

hard, and cause no problems. Unless you were to closely question them, you would never know they are actually a relative or acquaintance of an elected official. At the other extreme are the individuals who believe they are protected by their lineage (literal or figurative) and do not need to worry about their performance. It is likely that they landed the position after failing elsewhere, which is why they required the elected official's patronage in the first place. If you are lucky, these individuals are merely low performers. If not, they may be incompetent or toxic or both, or even, if they are placed highly enough in your organization, cowboys.

Note that there is no category of problem employees comprised of individuals who criticize, disagree, or dissent, no matter how frequently or how loudly.

Now that you have identified and classified your non-performers, what can you do? You really have only three options. One, you can accept the problem—live with it. Two, you can **cubbyhole** the employee—give him minimal to no job duties and otherwise ignore him. Three, you can take action to deal with the problem. Sadly, governments too often limit their options to #1 and #2, due to a combination of inertia, poor management, and cumbersome personnel systems. But in the organizations I run, only #3 is an allowable path forward.

There are several reasons why you must always take action to deal with problem employees. The first and most important is something I learned the very hard way—that with rare exceptions, problem employees never get better, let alone go away. Many managers make the mistake of believing (or hoping) that the employee will improve. But the problem never dissipates. If you wait six months or a year to see if the employee will turn around, the only thing that will likely be different is that you will be very sorry you did not deal with the problem six months or a year ago. The rare exceptions to this rule include 1) if the employee was never given the proper training in the first place, and you now provide him with that training, and 2) a personal or family situation is impacting him and that family/personal situation goes away or is resolved and so it stops impacting him. Note, by the way, that all personal problems, even severe ones, do not impact employee performance. Some employees continue to perform well even in the face of very significant personal difficulties. Sometimes, the island of stability provided by the workday is a tonic for your employee who is otherwise living a chaotic personal life.

Occasionally a "peter principled" employee can regain adequate functionality if returned to his or her previous post. But there are multiple ifs. If the previous post is still available, and if too much time has not elapsed between her elevation and when you have to demote her, and if she has the self-awareness to understand that her current position is not the right fit for her, a return can work. Again, that's a lot of ifs.

The second reason to deal with the problem employee is that other employees are watching to see what you do. They know very well—and usually knew it before you did—that their coworker is nonfunctional. In contrast, "It seems clear that management systematically underestimates the burdens their most troublesome employees create for their best employees."[85] All problem employees cause morale problems among their coworkers and drain their productivity. If you fail to take action, your inaction hurts everything and everybody else. If you do not take action against dysfunctional employee Lee, sooner or later, the employee sitting next to Lee, no matter how dedicated and hardworking, will say to herself, "Why am I working so hard when Lee is doing nothing?" That formerly dedicated employee, having reached what she regards as her limit of tolerance for her problematic coworker, may begin acting out by, among other things, working less hard or even ignoring her responsibilities. You may even lose that coworker completely. But if you do take action, "If you exit those weak links, it's very cathartic for the organization, because the broader population really resents the people who are not carrying their weight...."[86]

Third, your organization does not have the resources to carry dead wood—no organization does. In the current era, there is too much demand for customer service and the restraints on budgets too great for you to allow cubbyholing.

Therefore, the bottom line is as follows: do not try to improve nonfunctional employees. It is a waste of time and effort. Spend any resources you have on trying to improve the performance of low and medium performers instead. That is an achievable goal.

Once you have determined that an employee is problematic, the first step is to make clear to all parties, the employee as well as every level of supervision, that the *status* is no longer *quo*. Some employees, when faced with firm, steady pressure to actually do their jobs, and/or the possibility of future termination proceedings, will depart of their own volition.

In the eventuality that nothing changes, however, there is almost always a lot of hard work necessary to terminate someone. But just because it is hard work—and very time consuming—is no excuse not to do it. The very length of the process is the best reason to take action promptly and not let the situation fester. Having made sure that managers throughout your ranks understand your expectation that they deal firmly with nonfunctional employees, you must also make sure that 1) they have been adequately trained in the discipline and termination process and procedures, and 2) they follow those procedures.

The length and difficulty of the process are also the reasons why management training is vital. Managers from top to bottom need to understand progressive discipline and the necessity of proper documentation. Management has lost many cases by failing to properly document. Unfortunately, some managers will tolerate a poor performer for months or even years and then finally, when their tolerance is at an end, decide that it is time to fire the bad actor. But dismissing an employee does not work that way. The decision to try and rid yourself of a nonperformer is the beginning of the process, not the end.

Because the progressive discipline process is so lengthy, you should never meet privately with an employee who has a pending personnel matter, whether it involves termination or something else. I generally have an open-door policy with staffers, but this type of meeting is an exception. Most employees who request such meetings know they are on the hot seat, and simply want to use them as an additional step in the grievance process, arguing their case to you in the hopes that you will come to a different conclusion than the disciplinary machinery has come to thus far. I have broken my own rule only a few times, and regretted doing so in every instance.

The one time that heavy due process is not required may be during a worker's probationary period. Probationary periods are an extremely effective tool because most employee performance issues will manifest themselves plainly during the twelve, six, or even three months of the typical probationary time. Most personnel systems allow termination during a probationary period at management's discretion. You and your organization should take full advantage of any such latitude. Instruct your human resources section to track probationary periods for every new employee and contact management when each such period is about to end, to make sure that they are completely comfortable with the probationary staffer's performance before the deadline passes. Naturally, the new employee has to have been given proper training and an opportunity to correct any deficiencies spelled out to him. But if performance is still lagging, given the merit-protected, unionized world that many of us live in, do not give probationary employees the benefit of the doubt when it comes time to make the final decision to fish or cut bait.

Government does poorly at weeding out truly bad employees, for multiple reasons. One such reason is that merit systems and personnel offices are, unfortunately, generally part of the problem, not part of the solution. They tend to be better at dealing with clearly illegal behavior (e.g., substance abuse and theft) than poor performance or attitude issues. But in an era when teamwork is more important than ever, how valuable is an employee who, while perhaps technically competent, has limited or no people skills? Human resources offices also tend to be staffed with individuals, up to and including the top person, who can cite every rule, but not help you get where you want to go, whether it is discipline and termination or any other aspect of personnel management. The customer service revolution in government has not penetrated to personnel agencies.

The second reason is that government agencies tend to have weak middle managers, as discussed earlier in this chapter. Agencies often resemble an army that has some good generals and good privates and corporals, but poor sergeants and lieutenants. Many supervisors were initially promoted because they were good line personnel, but do not prove to be good managers. Successive promotions also are often based on program expertise, not management ability. Training for managers often is neither as good nor as strongly emphasized as training for line employees. Weak managers typically do not supervise well; they do not discipline and sometimes do not even confront bad employees, let alone attempt to terminate them. One top executive described this problem: "I call them...adult conversations. People will avoid them. It's something that most of us aren't trained to do. I'm just stunned sometimes with how unwilling people are to bring somebody in the office and say: 'Look, you're a good person. This job is not really working out, and I'm going to have to let you go.' And so they will put people in another position so they don't have to deal with firing them. We don't have the luxury of being able to do that."[87]

A third reason why nonperforming employees linger on the payroll is that middle managers are often reluctant to terminate them during a hiring freeze or period of hiring controls. They are willing to live with the employee because they fear they will not be able to replace him. This approach is self-defeating. Again, we are not speaking of low performers, but the truly awful ones. Eventually the hiring freeze or slowdown will end, but in the mean time the organization killer will have depressed morale and performance even further.

Any discipline, and especially termination, usually must run a gauntlet of procedural steps, including one to three at the agency level, one at the state or locality's central personnel office, perhaps an employee protection board, even a court appeal. The employee only has to win once to dodge the bullet; management has to win at every level. This obstacle course would be bad enough if central personnel agencies did not also frequently take the posture that they should bend over backwards in favor of the employee, rather than be neutral. Every experienced government manager has his or her favorite horror stories about employees whom the central personnel office prevented from being fired. I will cite my two.

One department I headed included the state's psychiatric hospital. Hospital staffers sometimes took patients on field trips. On one occasion, the staff took a group of patients to an aquarium 65 miles away. Upon their return to the hospital—but only upon their return—they discovered that they had left one of the patients behind. Eventually the patient, who was quasi-aphasic, was discovered a dozen miles away from the aquarium by the local police.

Fortunately, he was unharmed. When we terminated the employee whose responsibility this particular patient had been, our dismissal was overturned by the state personnel office. It seems that, in the minds of the state human resources staff, we had insufficient written instructions specifying that the employee was responsible for the patient. To add insult to injury, our dismissal was not just reduced to something less than termination; the personnel office forbade disciplining the employee at all. (This incident caused my wife, a first grade teacher, to comment that "Even I know you have to count the kids when they get back on the bus.")

Another very bad example involved the same hospital. Staffers are required to periodically sign "face check" forms stating that they have eyeballed particular patients at specific times. This procedure is performed for patient safety reasons. We discovered that an employee had falsified a face check form. We discovered it because at the exact time when said employee signed the form supposedly indicating he was visually observing a patient, that particular patient was elsewhere in the hospital, having been left alone in an examination room with a young female intern, whom he proceeded to physically assault. We were able to discipline the staffer whose bad judgment it was to leave the intern alone with the patient. However, when we attempted to terminate the employee for falsifying the face check form, his dismissal was also overturned by the state personnel office. Their stated reason was that our employee manuals did not specifically state that someone could be terminated for falsifying face check documents! I will not go into the other language that, in our minds, gave us ample justification for termination as a result of the incident that occurred. Having that firing voided led me to the one and only shouting match I ever engaged in with a cabinet colleague. I wanted to know how in the world I would explain to the press and the legislature, if the matter ever came to light, that the employee we tried to fire for falsifying patient safety documents was still gainfully employed by our hospital. She had no answer, because we both knew that if the matter ever became public, my department would have to do all the explaining. Surprisingly, the incident never did become public, but for years I worried that it would.

There is a very sad epilogue to the story. That employee's wife worked at the same hospital. She became involved in an extramarital affair with a third worker at the hospital. The first employee discovered the affair and snapped, murdered the paramour, and tried but failed to murder his own wife. This time we did get to fire the employee without a lot of due process, because when someone is spending the rest of his life in prison, he is not coming to work and we can say that he has abandoned his position. I suppose it would be unfair to claim that if we had fired the employee when we originally tried to, things might have turned out differently. But I have always wondered.

Employee termination is seldom a process involving only management, the employee, and your jurisdiction's human resources office. A number of other third parties (unions, lawyers, the media, the legislature, even the courts) may have a role to play.

I have worked in predominantly unionized, partially unionized, and non-unionized environments, with both very aggressive unions and more passive ones. Unions, of course, have a **duty of fair representation**, meaning that they are legally required to advocate for their members in all disciplinary matters, even when they know very well that their member is "guilty." Some union representatives will advocate relentlessly for their members, no matter how bad the member's conduct. Others will trim their sails slightly, or even, ever so subtly, "tank" the case of a particularly bad actor. The union representatives who did not go all out in absolutely every case were the smarter ones, in my view, because they knew "that it is not always in their long-term interest to prevail in the short run."[88] Although they would never say so, publicly or privately, they knew that 1) the truly awful employees make more work for all their other members, and 2) the miscreants ultimately damage the reputation of public employees in general.

In my experience, I have found unions far less problematic than personnel systems and personnel offices. The former are, after all, doing their job by representing the rank and file. Management has lost far more grievances by failing to do its job properly (primarily by not documenting employee misbehavior) than unions have won. In contrast, personnel offices are ostensibly part of management, but as mentioned above, often do not behave as such. The biggest problem with unions occurs when union disciplinary protections overlap or even conflict with merit system ones. In that case, if I had the option, I would prefer to see the union protections (which were probably acquired through collective bargaining) stay and the merit system ones disappear.

As if all this did not provide enough degree of difficulty, dealing with problem employees is often hindered by the actions of the media, the legislature, and the courts, all of whom tend to take the side of the employee far too often, assuming automatically that management is at fault. It would be helpful if these outside parties were not so credulous, but all too frequently they are. The media, which loves a "victim" story, has been known to take an employee's claim—especially if it is a whistleblower claim—at face value. It is not uncommon for a problem employee, aware that he is about to face discipline—or even in the midst of disciplinary action—to verbally or in writing point out to management the problems in the organization. The problems may well be real, although of course everybody in the organization, including management, already knows about them. Then, the employee claims "retaliation" for having pointed out the problems. Says one veteran government administrator, "Often dissent... is the work of one or a few disgruntled employees who are using it to either give their lives meaning or to protect themselves against action for poor performance or behavior problems."[89] The media are not above criticizing an agency for poor performance while simultaneously blasting the same agency for trying to fire a bad employee who contributed to that poor performance.

For a variety of reasons, legislative bodies often give considerable, and undue, weight to the claims of bad employees. A certain amount of this attitude is undoubtedly the result of members of the party opposite from that of your administration desiring to make political hay—but certainly not all of it. Particularly where the bad employee is a constituent of a given legislator, the legislator tends to give the benefit of the doubt to the employee, not management. (I have even had legislators bring up complaints by rank and file employees against managers in my department in budget hearings.)

Those problematic employees who do not depart voluntarily may well fight you to the bitter end. They may exercise each and every one of their rights, stall any and all proceedings, hire lawyers, go to the press and claim victimhood (or whistleblowing), even file suit. It can be a fight to the finish, and you need to be the last one standing.

Terminating a problem employee in the "legislative relatives" category presents a special problem. You will naturally have some trepidation in doing so. As with all other employees, if the individual is merely a low performer, live with her. But if she is a non-performer, I do not recommend an exception. I have had more satisfactory experiences than unsatisfactory outcomes when terminating legislative relatives, but obviously the latter is possible. More than once, the legislator was okay with the situation if I allowed the employee to resign rather than be fired. In another instance, once the employee realized his patron could not protect him, his performance improved dramatically—and then he left within six months. On the other hand, I paid the full price when I dismissed a friend of a state senator. I lost his vote on bills and he badmouthed me repeatedly. I did not get back in his good graces for eight years.

I will use my own department's experience in my first cabinet assignment as a case study in dealing with non-performers. When I took over that relatively small department, and combined my own observations with my division directors' reports, I was shocked to find that about 25 of our slightly more than 250 employees were non-functional—close to one out of ten workers in the entire department! Again, these were not just poor employees; they were incapable of doing their jobs. Some of them had medical issues, while others lacked any work ethic or had major performance issues. The behavior of still others was so bad as to cause disruption and morale problems.

That department had a relatively flat organization; in three of the eight operating divisions, every employee reported directly to the division director, and in the other five, there were only one or two layers of middle management. The department had a large number of production employees performing tasks like carrying internal mail, issuing licenses, handling fleet vehicles, and maintaining buildings. The department's workload had been increasing and was expected to increase even more. Although the state was not in fiscal distress, it was reasonable to assume that the governor and legislature would be assigning any new resources towards direct services to constituents, not support functions like ours.

Partly due to my personal philosophy, partly from past experience, and partly out of necessity, I made the decision to move aggressively to remove those 25 nonperformers. From a philosophical point of view, it is an anathema to me to employ, with tax dollars, somebody who is not working. From my experience, as mentioned above, I expected few if any of those 25 to improve on their own, so we needed to move sooner rather than later. And finally, out of necessity, a small organization like ours, with an increasing workload, could not afford to cubbyhole anyone, let alone 10 percent of our workforce.

I advised my directors of my expectation that everybody had to work, that there was to be no cubbyholing, and that there would be no exceptions. This directive was not greeted with universal enthusiasm. One director was a former social worker who wanted to reform the malingerers, not get rid of them. Others preferred to take the path of least resistance. Many had had unsatisfactory experiences involving not being backed up by upper management and/or being overturned by the state personnel office. I had to assure them that they would be supported by the department's human resources unit and by me personally—then had to make good on that promise. I made it a priority of that same HR unit and made it a priority of our state-assigned lawyers.

In many cases, we had to begin, not continue, the progressive discipline process, because the problem employees had limited to nonexistent documentation regarding their poor performance, even though all the managers knew they were non-functional. Dismissal therefore was not an option at the beginning of this effort. Instead, we engaged in a lengthy, labor-intensive process. We did, indeed, jump through every hoop until there were no more hoops to jump through.

Our results were surprisingly successful. A number of problematic employees got the message that they were now going to have to work a full day and either retired or got a job somewhere else. Three employees, all in the same office, physically could not do their jobs. They were maintenance mechanics who could not perform the most basic physical requirements of the job; they could not climb a stepladder or lift anything weighing five pounds or more. We persuaded all three to take medical disability. Two more individuals had been promoted beyond their level of competence—they were satisfactory mechanics but poor foremen. They accepted voluntary demotions to their former positions, made easier by the fact that they were able to fit into the lower pay scale without a cut in compensation.

As a result of the foregoing, we only needed to fire three employees. We fired two successfully, so that two years after we began the effort to clear out the dead wood, we had removed 24 of the 25 problems. The final employee fought us every step of the way and strung things out the entire eight years of my tenure. But I considered 96 percent a very good success rate.

Had we been in a fiscal crunch, we could have foregone those 24 positions and saved quite a bit of money with, obviously, no negative impact on services because these individuals were not doing anything. But the state was not in financial difficulty and the Governor strongly emphasized customer service, so every time one of those nonperforming employees left his position, we considered reclassifying the post into something that was of greater need to the department. If your personnel system allows it, reclassification of vacant positions can be one of the most powerful management tools at your command. It costs nothing but really produces results. A smaller number of good employees will always out-produce a larger number of uneven quality. Over time, every organization will need to do more of some things and less of others. Needs change, society changes, and workloads change. Reclassifying your positions can re-balance your organization and keep your resources matched with your needs.

Two examples that resulted from our operation to eliminate dysfunctional workers follow. At the start of the process, the fiscal section of one division consisted of a controller and four accountants, with a lot of problems. After our winnowing, the same section consisted of the controller and a single accountant, handling the same workload as before and without any problems. We used two of those slots to beef up other parts of the department and even gave one position to another department. Meanwhile, when I became cabinet secretary, the county maintenance operation of another division consisted of 13 employees, and I heard nothing but complaints. One voluntary demotion, two regular retirements, and three disability retirements later, that section had 10 employees and one less level of supervision—and received nothing but compliments. The department got three positions for use elsewhere.

Sex in the workplace presents a special subset of problem employees with its own dynamic. While it does not happen very often, a romantic relationship between coworkers is problematic. A romantic relationship between a supervisor and a subordinate happens even less often, but can be disastrous to the organization. I am not a prude, and I do recognize that in this day and age, the workplace is often the best place certain people have to meet someone. The rules are obviously different in a small office in the private sector. But in a large government office, sex between a supervisor and a subordinate should result in either the employees being transferred or the supervisor being terminated, provided the personnel rules permit it. Over one seven year period, I had to dismiss four high-ranking individuals (a division director, two deputy division directors, and a hospital director) for such behavior, and would have dismissed a fifth had she not announced her resignation to take another job the day before I was going to terminate her. It is irrelevant, by the way, whether the offenders are married or single and whether it is a gay or straight romance.

A romantic relationship causes problems for at least one and possibly two reasons. First, it is a major distraction, both for the parties involved and for the surrounding coworkers, and the closer in proximity the two individuals involved are, the bigger the distraction. More likely than not, productivity drops for the lovebirds. I remember one situation early in my career, involving two of my subordinates. I had supervisory responsibility, but not, in this case, final hiring/firing authority. These folks were intelligent, hard workers, and very nice people to boot. Nevertheless, once they embarked on their romance, the productivity of both dropped by half, simply because they fell into the habit of performing all tasks jointly, almost all of which could have and should have been done by one person. That staff was small, so essentially their romance cost us 10 percent of our workforce. Eventually I resorted to prefacing every instruction to either of them by saying, "Now I want you to work on this by yourself, not together with Mike (or Cheryl)" [not their real names]. It was only partially successful.

Eventually, they parted company, though fortunately not while they were working in those jobs. If two coworkers in a romantic relationship break up while still in the same office, the situation will only get worse.

Classifying romantic activity between a supervisor and a subordinate as a potential disaster is not exaggerating in the least. While the romance lasts, the supervisor will treat the subordinate unfairly—in a favorable way. The most obvious problem is that it is impossible to objectively evaluate the performance of someone with whom you are romantically involved. The subordinate frequently will take inappropriate liberties, with the explicit or implicit understanding that the supervisor will not hold him or her to account. After all, who is the one person to whom a supervisor cannot say no? The subordinate with whom he or she is in a relationship. In this eventuality, the romance often divides the surrounding office personnel into warring camps—those who like the boss and/or do not really care about his or her behavior versus those who are offended. Most of the latter group will sense that the lover is being treated unfairly, because that is what always happens. If the romance ends, the supervisor will treat the subordinate unfairly—in an unfavorable way. Also, a rogue boss obviously has no moral authority to discipline problematic individuals when he himself is misbehaving.

It is not difficult to spot an office romance. Unless the lovers are very good—professional-level—actors, they cannot keep their feelings a secret.

Interestingly, they themselves often believe that they are successfully concealing what is plain to everyone around them. For this reason, accusations of interoffice canoodling reported to me have proven true 95 percent of the time. Even anonymous accusations are almost always accurate. In contrast, anonymous accusations about virtually any other kind of misconduct are almost never correct.

Examples of workplace romance gone very bad abound. I have previously mentioned the love triangle murder that occurred in my own department. In a sister agency, a supervisor and subordinate were lovers, and a promotion opened up in the same agency but at one level above the supervisor. Both competed for the job and the subordinate got the promotion, becoming the boss of his former supervisor. The unsuccessful candidate and boss-become-subordinate was emotionally devastated and committed suicide shortly thereafter.

The only sensible attitude about workplace romance was once succinctly stated by my secretary: "I don't get my honey where I make my money."

## MAKING YOUR ORGANIZATION'S CULTURE MANAGERIAL

Every organization has its own distinctive culture—"the values, norms, attitudes, and expectations of employees."[90] Usually, an organization has more than one cultural dimension operating simultaneously, or at least multiple dimensions of that culture. Sometimes, different parts of an organization display different cultures. **Organizational culture** does more than influence employee behavior; culture is often stronger than written procedures or regulations, sometimes stronger even than laws. Culture can be challenging to work with because it is usually unwritten—even invisible. Leaders and members of the organization are often unaware of how the organizational culture influences them. In order to truly understand and improve your organization, you need to understand what culture(s) operate therein. Hear one leader on the importance of culture: "If you really want to build something that's going to be around for a very long time and be stable and grow, culture has to be paramount. People have to know how your culture operates and works. Once they get it, they adopt it, and it becomes second nature…. The culture is almost like a religion. People buy into and they believe in it."[91]

Organizations have emotional as well as professional cultures. I have always been more concerned with changing my organization's professional culture—it is more important, but also more difficult.

Among the kinds of cultures I have supervised or observed in government agencies are the regulatory culture, the social work culture, the legal culture, and the scientific culture. Your agency will no doubt have others. In any operation you manage, try to get the agencies to subordinate other characteristics of their culture to a managerial culture. Regardless of whatever other attributes it possesses, a government organization cannot get the most out of its employees, its budget, or any other resources unless a managerial culture is paramount. You do not have to eliminate other aspects of your agency's culture, just bring management to the fore. What you are aiming for is an organization that sets priorities and always tries to get the most out of its resources, whatever level of resources it possesses. A managerial organization always tries to solve problems and continuously improve, which almost always means getting rid of non-functional employees. And finally, a managerial organization works as a team internally and collaborates externally.

Whenever I see an organization chart on which every employee has initials after their names, signifying, usually, their advanced degree(s), I know I am in the presence of a scientific culture. When I ran the state Health and Social Services Department, the public health division exemplified the scientific culture. In this culture, educational attainment is a core value; hiring and promotion are significantly based upon it. Expertise abounds, and you will be constantly impressed by the wealth of knowledge the agency and its troops possess. Scientific cultures stereotypically prefer decision making based on scientific truth, and believe that there is a best answer for every problem. Unfortunately, this belief can clash with the managerial culture. This culture also tends to have trouble understanding the political process, which is, of course, political (in their view, emotional) and not necessarily rational. The scientists are sure they are right because they are scientists. I recall one such manager making a presentation before a legislative committee. The chairman, a very intelligent individual, suggested tweaks to 5 percent of the proposal. When it came time to review the presenter's presentation for the follow-up hearing, instead of making the suggested changes, she had assembled new arguments as to why the questioned 5 percent could not possibly be changed. I had to explain to her that in government, when we get legislative approval for 95 percent of our proposal, we celebrate; we do not try to get the other 5 percent, too. It was a foreign concept to her.

A large portion of that same department, naturally, had a social work culture, including divisions dealing with health care, child support, disabilities, and aging. The social work culture was a huge positive in that our employees genuinely wanted to help people in need of services. The same culture was a negative when it came to dealing with problem employees. Managers tended to want to "save" even the worst employees, believing that if tolerated or worked with, they would improve. In fact, as described previously in this chapter, such improvement rarely happens. Such attitudes elevated the welfare of those problematic staffers above the welfare of the agency and its mission, to the great detriment of the latter. Therefore, these divisions tended to be saddled with a certain number of nonfunctional employees who were drains on the organization. Social work culture was also uncomfortable with budget constraints. "It's just numbers on a page" was a common refrain.

In the same way that legal training does not make for good managers (see "Whom to Hire", above), a legal culture does not make for good management. The emphases in the legal culture are on precedent, advocacy, and process. In managerial culture, creativity, facts, and results are far more important and yield superior outcomes. As stated previously, when faced with a problem, examining precedent is usually the wrong approach, since the way you have been doing things up until now has resulted in your arrival at the current problem state. Similarly, in the information age, you should make as many decisions based on facts as possible, not on the urgings of an advocate whose job it is to see only one side of an issue. And as discussed in "How to Manage Your Employees", above, it is the result that counts, not the manner, path, or process by which the result was achieved. Unfortunately, in the growing clash between legal and managerial cultures, the legal culture, emphasizing advocacy and process rather than facts and outcome, is too often winning. The media in particular seem to be increasingly adopting the perspective of the legal culture when covering government. In any public disagreement, they customarily print or give air time to advocacy positions, but do not participate in the search for facts or the truth.

This book is concerned primarily with the executive branch. But you will almost certainly interact with the legislative branch of government and you may interact with the judicial branch and/or your jurisdiction's Department of Justice or Attorney General's Office. Be aware that each has an aspect to its culture that is distinct from the executive branch. The legislature (see Chapter 10) is primarily an oral culture. They do not write each other memos; they talk to each other (and to others, especially the public). Judges and lawyers, in pointed contrast, have a written culture (in addition to the aforementioned legal culture). Nothing exists unless it is on paper. If you are going to have a meeting with a judge or other court official, prepare talking points, but bring a memo to leave with him. If you are trying to win your case, remember that judges ignore anything that is not written down (see "Lawsuits" in Chapter 12). The executive branch is, of course, a mixture of the written and oral cultures.

Scientists, physicians, lawyers, social workers, and others all embody the values of their professions. But these values are not managerial values. As mentioned earlier, government tends to hire and promote based on expertise, which professionals possess in abundance. "The public sector recognizes and appreciates professional values, but it does not recognize or appreciate managerial values. [But]... government professionals need management."[92]

In addition to making your agency's culture more managerial, you should consider two other cultural changes: making the culture more customer-friendly, and making it less bureaucratic (for the latter, see the next section, "Managing Change in a Bureaucracy"). Attempting to change the culture of any organization is a daunting task, and not one that will be accomplished in a short time frame. "Turning around a culture is very difficult to do because it's based on a series of many, many decisions."[93] Assuming you have concluded that change is necessary, you can seldom accomplish it in a brief period of time. It is one of the reasons why a four-year time frame is the minimum interval you ought to serve in any top position, assuming you have the option (see "Taking and Leaving the Position" in Chapter 9). "Culture strategy requires extraordinary patience.... There are no home runs... only walks and singles, and you will need dozens of them to win the game."[94] When trying to change a culture, a good place to start is with revising guidelines such as policies, practices, and expectations. An even better way to proceed is with training. Training has the potential, over time, to alter the organizational culture and improve the organization. But the best way of all is through new hiring. Each employee new to the organization represents an opportunity to start fresh, because she has not yet been socialized in the existing culture. Turnover in government organizations is generally gradual, however, which is another reason why you need a longer tenure to accomplish your goals. But it all contributes. "Everything matters—everything. You are imprinting decisions, values and memories onto an organization."[95]

## MANAGING CHANGE IN A BUREAUCRACY

Every government organization has a bureaucratic culture to a greater or lesser degree. Bureaucracy is not always a bad thing, although many bureaucrats give it a bad name. Standardizing certain policies and procedures in writing is undoubtedly necessary. In one department I ran we called them Policy Memoranda, or **PM**s for short. The trick is to strike a balance between what needs to be done the same way everywhere and what can be left to managerial discretion. You have to have rules for the situations and actions that occur regularly. Also, where federal laws, state statutes, or regulations require certain things, they need to be spelled out for all to see. But some things occur only occasionally and should be left to a manager's judgment.

Anti-bureaucracy literature has not ended rigid bureaucratic control. In fact, legislators, the press, and auditors sometimes seem to prefer it. But just because other parties favor bureaucratic behavior is no reason why you should.

In my experience, rank-and-file government employees tend to have certain characteristics in common, regardless of agency or jurisdiction. Mostly these characteristics have to do with why they entered government service in the first place. Most top managers are in government because they have an affinity for public policy. But why are accountants and secretaries working for the government instead of, say, Bank of America or General Electric, which also employ accountants and secretaries? I believe that they do so because government jobs disproportionately attract individuals who are seeking certain aspects of employment security that are not available in the private sector. They know that the government will almost never lay them off and is not going to transfer them to another state, and they are willing to trade that security for what is usually a smaller paycheck. Along with their quest for stability, this personality type has certain work characteristics in common. One is that the vast majority of them will give you 40 solid hours a week (or 37½ or 35 if that is the jurisdiction's workweek) and not cause any problems. They are good at carrying out their assignments, but most are less good at thinking of better ways to do those assignments. "Hardworking employees with their chins down," is how one veteran government leader described them."[96] They generally like what they do; whenever I tour an employee worksite, I am always pleased by how many workers say the same thing: "I love my job." Another characteristic of line employees is that if the regularly scheduled quitting time is 4:30 PM, they are out the door at 4:30 PM. No working until the job is done. Finally, and most significantly, they do not like change.

The conservative critique of government bureaucracy as overly liberal is off target. Bureaucracies are not intrinsically liberal; they are inertial. This is because, as stated above, most government employees do not like change. The good news is that if getting them from point A to point B is difficult, even painful, once you get them to B, B becomes the new normal. Now, employees prefer B, and nobody wants to go back to A. The logical implication of this observation is that you can minimize the anguish involved in any change by making the transition from A to B as brief as possible. Pull the bandage off quickly, not slowly.

Overcoming bureaucratic inertia is vital because no organization can be improved unless it is changed. You cannot merely lead your organization; you have to change it. I like the words of the Chinese philosopher Lao Tzu: "If you do not change direction, you might end up where you are heading."[97] Yet in government, organizations and individuals are resistant to change. Even the idea of change is often upsetting to an organization. Administrative agencies are the institutional embodiment of past policy choices. Most policies and procedures were not off base when they were first installed (although some were), but as time marches on and the world changes, they may no longer be the right ones. What was a need-based approach is now a habit, even if the need has lessened or gone away. The current organizational structure was created to implement those policy choices of the past. Once established, bureaucracies develop their own norms and procedures, which become taken for granted and difficult to change or redirect. Individually, the status quo is very comfortable for many people because they understand their roles. Change brings about the possibility that, in a new situation, they will lose something they have or be forced to take on a task they may feel that they will be unable to do. Resistance is based less on the merits of the idea, and more on self-protection. Change therefore is usually neither easy nor fast, and generally occurs because of outside pressure.

However, you need to manage change nonetheless. There are two reasons. First, to make your agency the best, you can never settle for the status quo. Consistently raise the bar of performance, and always insist on higher levels of excellence and productivity. Inspire your team. Second, it is a cliché but true: change is a constant, and the rate of change is accelerating. "In whatever field you work there will be times when existing policies will need to be reconsidered and fought over."[98] Resistance to change is stronger in governmental units than businesses because of the aforementioned personality traits of many rank and file employees. Resistance, unfortunately, leads to stagnation because the world around us is changing rapidly. We live in an era of increasing complexity and change. A mere six years after I was given my first cabinet assignment, not one of my department's over 250 employees was doing the same job in the same way they were doing it when I first took over; not the cabinet secretary, not the maintenance workers, not anybody else. Among other reasons, workload was up across the board, but our resources stayed essentially the same.

Resistance to change causes a variety of bureaucratic behaviors, all of which undermine top management's ability to align the organization behind the goals of the elected official. Many line employees and middle managers fail to grasp the simple fact that (in state government, for example), it is the governor who sets the agenda for the state—because she has been elected to do so. Executives everywhere set agendas. The founding fathers might be a little surprised at how modern government has evolved, because they envisioned the legislative branch of government setting policies and the executive branch carrying them out. But in modern times, since the presidency of Franklin D. Roosevelt during the Great Depression, it is executives who generally initiate, and legislatures that generally react. Once a governor or mayor has set the agenda, it is our job as the executive branch to implement it.

Programs create turf, which must be defended. Middle managers and program managers often believe that it is they, and they alone, who should decide what they will work on and what the department's priorities will be. In their minds, they "own" their programs, regarding them as specialized domains into which other should not interfere. Of course, you *should* interfere, if for no other reason than that programs are not self-correcting. Occasionally I have to remind employees, only half jokingly, that if they disagree with the executive's priorities, they are free to run for the office themselves. Putting elected and appointed officials in charge of bureaucrats is the same principle as having civilians control the military. It is easier to align your top managers, the leadership team described above, because they are usually at-will employees. If all else fails, you can fire them. But middle managers, almost always merit-protected, are a different story. As one top executive puts it, "In any organization, middle management seems to live by its own rules."[99] This maxim is nowhere more true than in government.

Your twin challenges are therefore to fight bureaucratic inertia everywhere you can, and get your organization aligned with your elected chief. If you cannot stop excessively bureaucratic behavior by your sister agencies, you can minimize bureaucracy in your own agency as much as possible. The anti-bureaucratic climate that you foster will also help you attract talent to your agency. I will never forget the exchange I had with an employee who had transferred from another department in state government to ours. Instead of seeing him in his first week on the job as I normally did, scheduling conflicts delayed our meeting until he had been on the job for a month. "Here, everybody wants to do things as soon as possible so that they can get on to more things," he told me. "At [his former department], everybody's attitude was, well, if we don't get it done today, there's always tomorrow." I believe that quotation spoke volumes about our department's culture.

It is a significant challenge to get your entire organization aligned with the executive priorities (and yours, as long as you are keeping the executive's priorities first). It is a difficult thing to do in any large organization, and especially in governmental ones with multiple and varied functions. As with everything else you do, you have to relentlessly communicate your priorities. Communicate your expectation, first to your leadership team, but to everyone else as well, that teamwork is the order of the day. Today, almost every important project is completed by a team. Set an example by working cooperatively with the other departments of your government. Stop any turf battles before they start.

Organizationally, you should do two things to promote alignment. First, do everything you can to streamline your organization. You may not be able to do a lot in this regard, if you are limited by budgetary appropriations, federal funding streams, and/or personnel system strictures that force people and groups into silos—as most of us are. But if you have an opportunity to **de-layer management** (that is, eliminate a layer of middle management) or break up **functional silos**, do so. Whatever your organizational structure, you can always set up cross-divisional work teams for specific projects. Second, although this is somewhat counterintuitive, centralizing common resources does a lot to promote alignment and cooperation, and break down silos and fiefdoms. Decentralized handling of common resources strengthens those silos and fiefdoms, because an entity that does not have to share any resources has not been incentivized to cooperate with anyone. More on resource allocation will be found in Chapter 6, "Money".

Bureaucratic behavior that resists change can take a number of forms. The bureaucratic family tree has at least six prominent members: Carl Can't Be Done, Frank Fed Follower, Sue Standard Procedure, Nan No Time, Trish Technical Expert, and Paul Process Owner. Here they are, and here is how you can handle them.

Carl Can't Be Done might be a line employee, or even a manager. Carl will tell you that something you want done cannot be done. Sometimes he says so because something truly cannot be done, but unfortunately, sometimes he says it cannot be done because, consciously or subconsciously, either he himself does not want to do it, or he does not want it to be done at all. You should never accept no for an answer until the third go around. As with everyone else in your organization, the first two times Carl tells you no, you should do all of the following: ask a lot of detailed questions—politely, of course—about why it is that something cannot be done, request more information, and suggest any and all alternative ways you can think of to do the job. Carl and his brethren are not the most creative of people. When dealing with those individuals who are not, you will need to inject a little creativity.

Where federal funds are involved, you are likely to encounter Frank Fed Follower, who is himself a state or local government employee. Frank likes to **"play the fed card:"** Frank cannot do it (or has to do it) because the federal government forbids it or requires it. Frank and fellow Followers seem to care far more about what the Feds think than what their nominal bosses think. To be sure, there is no shortage of federal mandates. Nonetheless, do not be deterred when Frank plays his fed card. Your automatic response should be: show it to me in writing. Very often there is no such directive in writing. The second-level claim is that a federal official told Frank so, in which case your follow-up questions should be: which official said it, exactly what did he say, and when did he say it? If the matter is important, you or someone high up in your organization may need to speak to the federal official himself. At a minimum, you may need to direct Frank to follow up with said federal official(s)—assuming he has not already done so to produce the opinion he was looking for. Sadly, sometimes the vagueness you are hearing in Frank's voice results from the federal official being vague with Frank in the first place.

Similarly, Sue Standard Procedure will tell you that something requested by a client, customer, or regulated entity cannot be done because it would violate current standard operating procedures. Sue's first cousin is Wendy We've Always Done It That Way, but even Wendy knows that she has a weak case. All you usually have to do to set Wendy's objections aside is to tell her that we are going to try a different way this time.

As for Sue (and as with Frank), you should always ask her to show you those procedures. Very often, not only is there no legal prohibition against the requested act, there is not even a written guideline or regulation covering it. That there is nothing in writing usually means that the denial you have been given is not a standard practice—it is a discretionary practice, and Sue is using her own judgment. Said judgment may be good or bad, but it is almost always inconsistent, not just between Sue and her fellow employees, but exercised inconsistently by Sue from day to day. Despite the fact that one of the ostensible purposes of bureaucracy is to standardize decision making, a lot of it is anything but. You cannot allow Sue and her colleagues to treat the people they deal with in an inconsistent fashion. In the instant case, you should probably permit the requested behavior. Going forward, you should require Sue to put in writing for management review and approval those allegedly standard procedures.

Nan No Time will often say that she is so busy that she does not have the time to do a certain job, even if the request has come from, say, the governor. Nan may be telling the truth, if you proceed from the assumption that everything on her current task list is more important than what you have just asked her to do. Invariably, not everything is. Therefore, your tactic should be to ask to see Nan's work list or priority list. Often the mere fact that you are requesting her list sends a sufficient message that she needs to put your item on her list of things to accomplish. Or, assuming she can produce an actual list, you can reprioritize her list to put your item on it. Nan and her coworkers may actually be grateful in this situation because you have given them some prioritization from which they can benefit, but which they have not previously received. (See Chapter 5 for more on setting priorities.)

Trish Technical Expert presents some unique challenges. Often, Trish will test you, directly or indirectly, about your knowledge, and attempt to use your lack of knowledge to get her own way. You do not need mastery of the subject matter, but you do need to understand most of the jargon and enough substance so that she cannot **BS** you. Do not hesitate to ask her and her compatriots questions whenever they use unfamiliar concepts or terms; that is how you learn. When I was managing engineers, for example, I had to learn that when they talked about a hydrostatic load, they were referring to snow on the roof. Sometimes the dumb questions you ask are not so dumb because they make Trish look at the problem in a new way.

Finally, there is Paul Process Owner. For Paul and other owners, the process is more important than the outcome. In other words, how something is done is more important than achieving a positive result. Paul's approach is exactly the opposite of good management, the object of which is to generate a satisfactory outcome, regardless of the process through which that outcome was obtained. Paul is the quintessential personnel office employee. Paul may or may not have created the process in the first place, but he now owns it and does not want it altered. Obviously, you should never hesitate to adjust or discard any process that is not producing the outcomes you want.

If you get a reputation for not automatically accepting no for an answer from Carl, Frank, Sue, Nan, Trish, and Paul, you will get fewer noes in the future.

Several of the keys to successful change are as follows. First, remember that incremental changes are victories. Half a loaf is truly better than none. Second, communication is vital. Sometimes opposition to change is engendered by lack of information about "the big picture." Lacking any broader context, employees naturally see only their own problem or situation. You should always start by telling all parties why you are making the change in question and how their part fits into the whole. Your message about the changes you are putting into effect should be repeated *ad nauseam*. As one of the governors for whom I worked used to say, "Just when you're starting to get sick of saying something is about the time that most people are starting to pay attention." Another governor used her signature phrase so often that we sometimes counted the number of times she did so during a speech. But we got the message about what was important. A former professor turned university president commented on the difference between academic and managerial communicating. "As a scholar, you don't want to repeat yourself, ever. You're supposed to say it once, publish it, and then it's published and you don't say it again. If someone comes and gives a scholarly paper about something they've already published, that's just terrible. As a...president, you have to say the same thing over and over."[100]

The third key to successful change is to deal effectively with the small group of individuals who lead the charge against change. When a big change is announced, the **"weebees"** come out of the woodwork; weebees as in "We be here before you got here and we be here after you leave." I vividly recall the employees who did their best to sabotage a proposed reorganization even though none of the complainants would have lost their jobs, received a pay cut, or faced added responsibilities. A few of them might have had to change desks. A highly placed leader described his approach in the following way. "Convincing people to give your way a try will work if you neutralize—and sometimes you have to cauterize—the ones who are really against change. They're the kind of person who, if you tell them it's raining outside, they'll fight you tooth and nail. You take them outside in the rain, and they'll say, 'But it wasn't raining five seconds ago.'"[101]

Despite all of your efforts, you will not be able to change everything. "As an agency head, it will be your fate and duty to be defeated from time to time as you push to redirect policies."[102] Just do not ever stop trying.

Many government organizations all over the country have embraced customer service as a positive and necessary change. However, although the bible of the customer service movement, *Reinventing Government*,[103] is now

20 years old, adoption of the customer service ethos is still spotty. Some organizations have made no improvements in this regard, or have deemphasized it as administrations have changed. If your agency does not emphasize customer service, it is something you should consider strongly, even though it is yet another reason why public sector management is more challenging than ever. Before the advent of the customer service movement in public administration, it was enough to do your job well. Once you have adopted a customer service orientation, doing your job well is no longer sufficient. Now, you have to do your job well *and* keep your customers satisfied.

A number of old-style government agencies still emphasize control—it is their job to prevent other parties from doing things, and in preventing them from doing those things, they believe they will save money. Under the new orientation, their job becomes helping customers (be they internal or external) meet their needs, preferably as inexpensively as possible. It is a culture change that requires management commitment, mandatory training for all employees, and universal customer satisfaction surveys for any part of the organization providing services. (Regulatory agencies are a separate case.) Customer service is a never-ending goal; you cannot achieve perfection, and in fact the more you emphasize customer service, the more you raise customer expectations. It is worth the effort nonetheless.

One particular kind of change requires careful consideration before you decide to undertake it, and careful planning if you do—reorganization. Reorganization can be a very helpful thing. Done properly, it can help rationalize a government agency. Times change, circumstances change, the outside environment changes, and your organization must respond to those changes. Programs tend to create fragmented service delivery systems. Programs rarely die; instead, policy reforms often create new programs or agencies. Periodic reorganization is needed to reduce such fragmentation. But make sure that any reorganization is not just change for the sake of change. In addition to reducing fragmentation of services, does a given proposal better align structure with goals, objectives, and priorities?

A federal official described a reorganization that helped to rationalize her agency. "I found that policy was everywhere. We had some policy in the budget office. There were also some policy people in the office of Administrator. The Centers were... very siloed. Policy was very diffuse in the agency so we created a new policy office.... We also moved grants management into finance, so that we had all the money functions in the same place."[104]

One of the collateral effects of major reorganizations is that an actual, or even prospective, realignment freezes many things from the moment it is announced until many months after it takes place. Other than daily responsibilities, not much is accomplished because everyone is focused on bureaucratic issues: who is going to be the cabinet secretary, who will be the division directors, who bosses whom, who will occupy what office space, who gets paid what (is there anybody nearby who is getting paid a dollar more than I am for the same work?)—it can be an absolute nightmare. You may well see a **"J curve"** in employee productivity—it will drop measurably before the positive effects of the reorganization take hold and productivity rises. You will have to spend political capital to reorganize, so make sure that the long-term benefits exceed the short-term costs. Do not attempt to reorganize near the end of your stay in office, or during an election year for your boss.

Finally, management literature talks about making change permanent. It is a worthy goal; you can and should institutionalize as many of your changes as possible. But bear in mind that truly permanent change is unrealistic in a political environment where maximum elected official and top management tenure is likely eight years in all but a few cases. Concentrate instead on doing the best you can with the resources you have, in the time you have available to you.

## NOTES

1. Ransom interview, *New York Times* 1-27-13, Business 2.
2. Weiner interview, *New York Times* 11-11-12, Business 2.
3. Conde interview, *New York Times* 1-17-10, Business 2.
4. Kawasaki interview, *New York Times* 3-21-10, Business 2.
5. Wilson, *Rethinking Public Administration*, 80.
6. Golembiewski and Cohen, *People In Public Service*, 117.
7. Lawrence and Abramson, *What Government Does*, 81.
8. Leahy interview, *New York Times* 2-3-13, Business 2.
9. Dolgin interview, *New York Times* 3-4-12, Business 2.
10. Hicks interview, *New York Times* 6-24-12, Business 2.
11. Ludwig interview, *New York Times* 8-21-11, Business 2.
12. Kuhn, *The Structure of Scientific Revolutions*, 166.
13. See Friesen, Gallas, and Gallas, *Managing the Courts*.
14. Lee interview, *New York Times* 3-28-10, Business 2.
15. Lawrence and Abramson, *What Government Does*, 5.
16. Stern interview, *New York Times* 4-24-11, Business 2.
17. Zambello interview, *New York Times* 4-7-13, Business 2.
18. Hart interview, *New York Times* 1-6-13, Business 2.
19. Albright interview, *New York Times* 10-4-13, B2.
20. Eckert interview, *New York Times* 12-26-10, Business 2.
21. Gutmann interview, *New York Times* 6-19-11, Business 2.
22. Liles interview, *New York Times* 10-28-12, Business 2.
23. Selander interview, *New York Times* 6-27-12, Business 2.
24. Buery interview, *New York Times* 9-12-10, Business 2.
25. Beers interview, *New York Times* 4-1-12, Business 2.
26. Goldsmith interview, *New York Times* 4-22-12, Business 2.
27. Maranto and Wolf, *Good Government is a risky business*.
28. Osborne and Plastrik, *Banishing Bureaucracy*, 12.
29. Sheehan interview, *New York Times* 6-3-12, Business 2.
30. Bryant, *The Corner Office*, 233.
31. Leahy interview, *New York Times* 2-3-13, Business 2.
32. Bryant, *The Corner Office*, 93.

33. Maffei interview, *New York Times* 1-9-11, Business 2.
34. Yamada interview, *New York Times* 2-28-10, Business 2.
35. Schultz interview, *New York Times* 10-10-10, Business 2.
36. Fields interview, *New York Times* 10-2-11, Business 2.
37. Cray, *General of the Army*, 341.
38. Chace, *Acheson*, 160.
39. Cray, *General of the Army*, 88.
40. Bryant, *The Corner Office*, 116.
41. Ibid., 192.
42. Lawrence and Abramson, *What Government Does*, 126.
43. Reimer interview, *New York Times* 7-14-13, Business 2.
44. Canada interview, *New York Times* 12-18-11, Business 2.
45. Hannah interview, *New York Times* 6-16-10, Business 2.
46. LePore interview, *New York Times* 7-1-10, Business 2.
47. Lyne interview, *New York Times* 10-4-09, Business 2.
48. See Halberstam, *The Reckoning*.
49. Maritz interview, *New York Times* 10-3-10, Business 2.
50. Covey, *The 7 Habits of Highly Effective People*, 228.
51. Leahy interview, *New York Times* 2-3-13, Business 2.
52. Bryant, *The Corner Office*, 186.
53. Leahy interview, *New York Times* 2-3-13, Business 2.
54. Hannah interview, *New York Times* 5-16-10, Business 2.
55. Buery interview, *New York Times* 9-12-10, Business 2.
56. Murray interview, *New York Times* 12-23-12, Business 2.
57. Duffy interview, *New York Times* 11-4-12, Business 2.
58. Maritz interview, *New York Times* 10-3-10, Business 2.
59. Behn, *Job Descriptions Often Just Get In the Way,* Governing Magazine, February, 1997, 91.
60. Murray interview, *New York Times* 12-23-12, Business 2.
61. Fields interview, *New York Times* 10-2-11, Business 2.
62. Hicks interview, *New York Times* 6-24-12, Business 2.
63. Faust interview, *New York Times* 11-1-09, Business 2.
64. Hart interview, *New York Times* 1-6-13, Business 2.
65. Hicks interview, *New York Times* 6-24-12, Business 2.
66. The Official Website of General George S. Patton, Jr.
67. Maritz interview, *New York Times* 10-3-10, Business 2.
68. Mathieu interview, *New York Times* 6-20-10, Business 2.
69. Conde interview, *New York Times* 1-17-10, Business 2.
70. Mathieu interview, *New York Times* 6-20-10, Business 2.
71. Lerer interview, *New York Times* 9-9-12, Business 2.
72. Covey, *The 7 Habits of Highly Effective People*, 171.
73. Saunders interview, *New York Times* 5-28-13, B2.
74. Ashworth, *Caught Between the Dog and the Fireplug*, 47.
75. Chase and Reveal, *How to Manage in the Public Sector,* 55.
76. Osborne and Plastrik, *Banishing Bureaucracy*, 147.
77. O'Leary, *The Ethics of Dissent*, 10.
78. Ibid., 12.
79. Goldsmith interview, *New York Times* 4-22-12, Business 2.
80. Lubetzky interview, *New York Times* 9-8-13, Business 2.
81. Wilson, *Rethinking Public Administration*, 135.
82. Ibid., 134.
83. Smit lecture, 4-19-11.
84. See Peter and Hull, *The Peter Principle*.
85. Wilson, *Rethinking Public Administration*, 136.
86. Harford interview, *New York Times* 8-15-14, B2.
87. Canada interview, *New York Times* 12-18-11, Business 2.

88. Wilson, *Rethinking Public Administration*, 175.
89. O'Leary, *The Ethics of Dissent*, 108.
90. Osborne and Plastrik, *Banishing Bureaucracy*, 295.
91. Johnson interview, *New York Times* 11-13-11, Business 2.
92. Wilson, Rethinking Public Administration, 92.
93. Schultz interview, *New York Times* 10-10-10, Business 2.
94. Osborne and Plastrik, *Banishing Bueaucracy*, 295.
95. Schultz interview, *New York Times* 10-10-10, Business 2.
96. Lawrence and Abramson, *What Government Does*, 82.
97. BrainyQuote, http://www.brainyquote.com/quotes/quotes/l/laotzu121075.html.
98. Ashworth, *Caught Between the Dog and the Fireplug*, 92.
99. Bryant, *The Corner Office*, 213.
100. Ibid., 175-176.
101. Canada interview, *New York Times* 12-18-11, Business 2.
102. Ashworth, *Caught Between the Dog and the Fireplug*, 92.
103. See Osborne and Gaebler, *Reinventing Government*.
104. Lawrence and Abramson, *What Government Does*, 17.

## Chapter Five

# Prioritization

### "You Can Do Anything You Want To, But You Can't Do Everything"

Prioritization is vital. Very little that you do is more important. The better you are at setting priorities, the better you are as a manager. In fact, your ability to set and adhere to priorities is one of the most important duties of management at every level, and the second most important ingredient for managerial success, trailing only having the right people on your management team (discussed in "Whom to Hire," Chapter 4). No organization, particularly a government agency, ever has enough resources (people, money, time) to do everything it wants to do. Prioritization, put simply, equals effective resource management. Absent prioritization, low priority items inevitably use up resources that ought to be going towards more important ones. That being the case, where do you place your emphasis? Have you ever heard anyone say, "In our department [division, office] everything is a priority?" This cringe-worthy comment was once uttered by one of my cabinet colleagues, indelibly marking him as someone who did not understand one of the fundamental tenets of management. As an astute observer of government once commented, those departments that have no plans for dealing with their most important priorities will, unfortunately, lurch from problem to problem, crisis to crisis.

This chapter is titled "Prioritization" rather than "Setting Priorities" because the setting of priorities is only the first of three equally important components of prioritization. First, you must identify high versus medium versus low priorities: that is the "setting" of them. Second, you must focus time, resources, and yourself on the highest priorities. Third, you must stick with those priorities and not be tempted into constantly adding to or shifting them.[1] Doing so is called **priority discipline**.

Setting priorities is something that you should do immediately upon assuming the reins of your organization (see Chapter 8), and then revisit regularly thereafter—at least annually. Of course, you first need to know what your agency's code requirements and responsibilities are. You are going to have to carry them out—but almost every agency's legal framework allows for a great deal of discretion. Next, determine what the executive's priorities are for your department—if any. Here too, the elected official for whom you work is likely to give you a lot of room to move, regardless of his personal style. Neither he nor his staff have the time to micromanage you, and while there may be things he wants your department to accomplish, he may not have a lengthy, detailed agenda for you. In return for that autonomy, give top priority to the agenda items he has set out. If one or more of your department's programs are part of the executive's priority (political) agenda, you can probably expect to be at the front of the line for any additional resources that become available, but also to face a higher degree of accountability and the expectation that funding should result in improvements and in the very best execution of that agenda. (See Chapter 9 for further discussion of executives and their priorities.) If you are running a subcabinet agency, a rule of thumb is to allow for one additional priority for each level between you and the very top.

If your department's programs are not part of the executive's agenda, how things are prioritized within your agency will be up to you. You have the autonomy, but also the responsibility. Expect static resources, and to deal with problems, when they arrive, within those resource limitations.

By definition, the number of high priorities you have will be limited. If you have too many, they cannot all be given the attention they deserve. "Most organizations and most executives have too many top priorities.... The more top priorities there are the less coherent and capable the response to each of them will be. Top management has to choose. And it has to tell everyone what its choices are."[2]

Just as your Mayor may not have an identified priority for every one of his departments (again, see Chapter 9), you may not have a list of priorities for all of your operating sections. There is nothing inappropriate about this approach, and nothing wrong with delegating prioritization to the director of the division. It is a variation of **management by exception**. Both departments for which I served as cabinet secretary resembled conglomerates. They mixed production, direct service, regulatory, criminal justice, and other responsibilities. Setting priorities was difficult, but essential. The larger department I ran had 12 divisions, and at any given time I usually only had targeted priorities for six of them. (Some priorities were department-wide.) I did not devote as much time to those other six; I just needed competent leaders in charge who would not cause me problems. Because I did have excellent managers, they were free to prioritize as they saw fit. Within their budgetary appropriation, those directors had the discretion to set priorities, but were also expected to manage problems with existing resources. Even within those six divisions that were involved with targeted priorities, once those priorities were addressed, the directors were free to prioritize thereafter. The smaller department had 11 divisions (later reduced to 8). That was still too many to have a top priority for each division. Again, I gave some directors the complete freedom to prioritize.

You will need to consider the views of any external stakeholders in your department's mission. And you certainly want the input of all of your key staffers from throughout your organization. But at the end of the day, setting priorities is something that only you as the agency leader can do. In the words of a Chief Executive Officer, "A big part of leadership is just being comfortable with the fact that some decisions really are only yours."[3] One of my best aides once asked me, when we were identifying budgetary priorities, if our department were a dictatorship or a democracy. I had to tell him that within the realm of prioritization, we were a dictatorship. Setting priorities is an undemocratic process, and any attempt to lead by consensus will fail. Every division head and program manager can be expected to argue for the needs of his or her own operation. It is only natural that they do so; in fact, you should anticipate nothing else. George C. Marshall called this "localitis"[4]—the propensity of any given commander to believe that his own sector of the war effort was the single most important key to victory. No administrative issue that cuts across the lines of all parts of your organization—priority goals, budgets, legislation, cutbacks—should be put to a vote of your leadership team. It is your job and your job alone. "CEOs... are paid to create order out of chaos, to identify the three or five things employees need to focus on rather than 20 things that will send people off in different directions."[5] If you attempt to satisfy every internal and external stakeholder by agreeing to all of their suggested priorities, you will end up satisfying no one.

What should your specific priorities be? They will almost certainly be unique to your department. As former Michigan Governor John Engler once said, "You can do anything you want to—but you can't do everything." He was addressing an audience of newly elected governors, but his advice is sound for the leadership of any government organization. As the leader, you can select the priorities, but there have to *be* priorities. Pick a small number of clearly defined goals. It is always better, at the end of a year (or any other time frame), to have been able to finish five projects completely than to have ten half-done, or to have made substantial improvements in three areas rather than minimum progress in half a dozen. You will have expended the same effort, but accomplished far more. "I think more about whether something really matters and how it will make a difference, versus thinking that every-thing matters and everything makes a difference."[6]

To identify specific goals, as Stephen Covey said, "Begin with the end in mind."[7] Unless you are in crisis mode (see Chapter 7), it is not where you want to be tomorrow that is important—where do you want your organiza-tion to be next year, or even five years from now? Far-reaching goals are entirely appropriate. What is your vision for your agency? Having a vision for your department is an important part of leadership (and acting on that vision is its corollary). Stated one executive, "Dream, and dream big. What's the world of possibilities for yourself and for your organization? You have to be able to say, 'Here's where I want to get to.' It's not that you'll ever necessarily get there, but if you don't dream, you'll never even get started."[8] Remember which priorities are the most important when setting your goals.

Some examples of (mostly) generic strategic goals are as follows.

—Gaining control of your organization (this is almost always goal #1 when you take over—again, see Chapter 8).
—Getting the budget above water (likely goal #2 in an era of austerity).
—Implementing or improving a specific program that is of importance to the governor or mayor.
—Making your organization's culture more managerial (see that title in Chapter 4).
—Improving employee morale.
—Improving the department's customer service.

When I ran the state health and social services department, the governor's prioritization was textbook. She identified several health-related priorities for us, in the areas of cancer prevention and control, smoking cessation, and infant mortality. Of these, she designated cancer prevention and control as *the* highest priority. When additional resources were available to the state, some of them were allocated to these priority areas. When cutbacks were required, those areas were protected. And she maintained priority discipline; her goals stayed the same for eight years, and we worked on them constantly. At the end of those eight years, our focus had paid off. The state had made huge strides in all three areas. Our Cancer Treatment Program was regarded as the nation's best. Our smoking rates, once among the ten highest states in the country, had fallen to 37th place. And infant mortality was down 10 percent. Had we put our emphasis on a dozen areas instead of three, we would not have made such progress.

Beyond those three priorities, she directed me to manage as I saw fit. With her goals clearly established and placed in the front rank, my vision for the department was to be the best managed department of state government. In accordance with my vision, I wanted us to constantly improve as an organization and make the most out of the resources that we had, whether we were gaining resources, losing them, or staying the same. But that was my vision; you will have your own.

Some careful thought and analysis should go into your determination of specific priorities. Make sure that what you are labeling as most important is, in fact, most important. For example, while in charge of the social services department, I found it interesting that some of my counterparts from around the country appeared to give priority to the **TANF** (Temporary Assistance to Needy Families) program—commonly referred to as welfare. In making my own determination of priorities, I considered the TANF program as well as the **Medicaid** program, the joint federal-state health care program for low income, disabled, and elderly people. The TANF program averaged about 6,000 families in our state, and the numbers shrank during most of my tenure. The Clinton-era federal legislation that established the TANF program, combined with an improved economy, removed many people from the rolls, and during my time in the job enrollment never returned to its previous levels. Medicaid enrollment, in contrast, stood at 100,000 individuals when I first assumed the position and increased significantly every year, regardless of the economic climate. Medicaid consumed over half of my department's budget. TANF policies on the federal level were fairly static, while Medicaid's were dynamic. To me it was a clear choice. Medicaid, rather than TANF, was one of my highest priorities throughout my time as secretary.

In the departments I ran, from top to bottom, at each level we first established an agenda congruent with that of the leader and made sure the organization was aligned with it. In other words, I aligned the department with the Governor's goals. Then, the directors of my divisions aligned those divisions with my goals. Then, the directors set their own priorities for their divisions. Communicate your priorities and goals clearly and repeatedly to everyone in your organization. From the top the bottom, everyone should be clear as to what your priorities are.

In setting those priorities, you will face enormous temptation to focus on policy rather than management. Policy is what you want to do and ought to do. Management is getting it done. Some agency heads spend all their time on policy and leave the management to subordinates. They think that if they get the policy right, that's the end of the job. Good policy, however, fails in the absence of good management. Policy is often more fun; management is almost always more work. You also, by the way, usually have less freedom to make policy changes than management changes. The biggest single failing I have seen among top people in government is to be good at policy but bad at management.

Once you have set goals, make sure that the resources that everyone uses (operating and capital budgets, facilities, personnel, etc.) are prioritized along the same lines. New resources should go predominantly to priority areas, but existing resources should be reevaluated as well. To the extent that your budgeting, accounting, and personnel systems allow for it, give strong consideration to transferring resources from less critical to more critical areas. Even if you have a good staff, are they effectively deployed? Common resources should never be allocated on a "something for everybody" basis. The most resources should always go to the highest priorities. Doing so results in the most effective use of what are always limited means.

After you have set priorities, both internal and external forces will try to pull you and your organization away from those priorities on a daily basis. Internally, the press of daily events (media inquiries, lawsuits, constituent complaints, paperwork, and the like) is omnipresent, and the level of input managers receive from all sources is ever rising. You cannot let routine matters, even if some of them are urgent, leave insufficient time for major initiatives and priorities. "You have a thousand things coming at you each day and you can do 10 of them. So you have to...pick the 10 things that matter."[9] Of course, not getting immersed in urgent matters is easier said than done. The best way to avoid this trap is to manage your time properly, as covered in Chapter 1, so that you have sufficient time to focus on priority matters.

Selective setting of deadlines—and then enforcing them—can be a very effective way of keeping the highest priority items at the top of your staff's lists, in addition to your own. Everything seems to take too long in government, but I am going to pay more attention to how long things take if they are a priority. I am always going to attach a time frame to any top priority item, and I am always going to be looking for the deliverables on the due date. But for jobs of lower importance, I usually do not set deadlines. I want staff to turn around things of high import in a hurry, but work on lower rank items when they can get to them.

Externally, advocates, legislators, and sometimes even the media want to set your priorities for you. In a democracy, obviously you will need to take their views into account, and what they want is often congruent with what you want. Even to the extent that your priorities do not overlap, their requests and demands may well be quite reasonable from a public policy point of view. Usually, however, it will also be the case that available resources will not allow you to devote extra effort to their priority without sacrificing one of yours. Never be unresponsive to outside concerns, but you should strongly though subtly resist efforts to rearrange your priorities, while emphasizing to outside parties your areas of agreement. You cannot accomplish your own goals if you are unable to set priorities and stick to them.

## NOTES

1. Covey, *The 7 Habits of Highly Effective People*, 157.
2. Wilson, *Rethinking Public Administration*, 164.

3. Gayle interview, New York Times 6-23-13, Business 2.
4. Cray, *General of the Army*, 401.
5. Bryant, *The Corner Office*, 56.
6. Hart interview, *New York Times* 1-6-13, Business 2.
7. Covey, *The 7 Habits of Highly Effective People*, 95.
8. Hart interview, *New York Times* 1-6-13, Business 2.
9. Atkins interview, *New York Times* 1-3-14, B2.

# Chapter Six

# Money

"Cutting the Budget Without Cutting Services—That's the Trick"

## INTRODUCTION

Whether you are a budget junkie or not, you should fully understand how much money your agency spends, how it spends it, and why it spends it in the way it does. You need to know all about your operating and capital budgets, for four reasons. First, never forget that you are spending taxpayer dollars. Second, your budgets are your instruments to set priorities and accomplish your goals—and it is impossible to know your department's true capabilities without detailed knowledge of your budget. Third, if there is ever a genuine fiscal problem such as a shortfall or budget overrun, you and your staff should catch it, not have it pointed out to you by your jurisdiction's budget office, auditors, or any other outside party. And fourth, if you are not currently in budget cutback mode, it is only a matter of time during your tenure until you will be. When that happens, your ability to manage cutbacks will have a great deal to do with how well your department is able to carry out its mission in the future.

Understanding your budget includes not just understanding how you spend your money. It also includes having command of the budget process, even improving it, and understanding the exact extent of your budget flexibility.

There is no scientific way to allocate resources via a budget, as political scientist V. O. Key pointed out in his seminal 1940 essay, "The Lack of a Budgetary Theory."[1] Science is absent because, as New York City Mayor John Lindsay stated a third of a century later, "All budgets are political

115

documents."[2] Indeed, it could hardly be otherwise. Every budget decision is
a choice, a policy decision of one kind or another, and a value judgment
about what the government should or should not be spending its money on.
Budgets inspire political battles, not that such battles are necessarily a bad
thing in and of themselves.

Because budgeting is political, to a large degree it possesses the characteristics of a game. To master your budget, you need to figure out how to
play that game. You need to first understand the rules of the game, and then
master them, to win that game.

You must manage your budgetary dollars carefully. You cannot hope to
be an effective government manager without spending time on the money
end of your agency. The reason why budget management is always a high
priority is not that you value dollars over programs, or money more than
results. You should place a high priority on effective budget management
because you and your agency will never have sufficient resources to do
everything you want or need to do. The budget is one of the two basic
resources you have to get your job done (personnel being the other). The only
way your agency can deliver the best services to the most people is if you
maximize your budget's efficiency. Getting more money for your department
may be beyond your reach. In difficult times, even keeping the money you
already have may be beyond your reach. But operating more cost-effectively
is never beyond your reach.

In today's public sector management, success in your job is delivering
positive outcomes within your monetary limits; either one by itself is insufficient. It can be very difficult to do, because sometimes the budget agency
supervising how much money you get seems only to care about the second
part of the equation—yet advocates for your department's programs care
only about the first. If you can move your agency forward even in tough
budgeting times, you will have done very well, even if the press and/or
legislature fail to note that progress.

## THE BUDGET GAME

More than anything else, budgeting resembles a game. You have to know the
rules to play the game. Managing your operating and capital budgets is equal
parts understanding the rules, harnessing the rules, and then using the rules to
accomplish your goals.

Understanding your budgets begins with understanding your responsibilities. 36 of the 50 states have a reference to balancing budgets in their
constitutions, and 13 of the other 14 states have statutory requirements for
balanced budgets[3]. Whether you are the agency head, a high-ranking deputy,
or a line manager, you have to do your part. You have a duty to spend only

within your budgetary limit, even if you have **entitlement programs** or other supposedly "uncontrollable" expenses.

To manage the money you have been given, you need to know how much you are spending. You need regular reports (monthly should do) matching your spending in each operating division and each expenditure category with the appropriations in those divisions and expenditure categories. If your jurisdiction does not already require extensive reporting, institute your own. If the reports are already being generated, pay them close attention. Such reports must include not only how much money has already been spent, but also forecasts of spending for the remainder of the year. Use these forecasts to make whatever adjustments are necessary in your spending to keep your budget in balance. Trend forecasting is not an easy thing to do. It can be difficult to determine whether there is a causal basis for rising or falling numbers or whether the changes are simply random fluctuations; in the words of a crack member of one of my departments' budget staffs, "When is a trend a trend?" But you have to make the effort. Those "uncontrollable" entitlement programs require the most accurate forecasts of all. You should meet with your operating budget director and key staffers weekly or biweekly and your capital budget personnel quarterly. There will be no shortage of issues to discuss with your operating budget staff, especially because the budget process is essentially a year round one. The larger your department, the more issues there will be. Capital projects tend to have lengthy gestation periods; even if you only have a small capital budget, quarterly meetings with those personnel let them know that you want those projects done sooner rather than later. The need to move as expeditiously as possible is a value to inculcate in your capital budget staff, given that delay is endemic to the construction industry.

The next step is to understand what the level of your budget flexibility is. First, can you move money without outside approval within divisions, within programs, within line items, or only within categories inside of line items? Second, what is your ability to reallocate funds, either within a given budget year or from year to year? If you can save money in program A, can you use that money to bolster program B or fund new program C? Alternatively, if you determine that program B is more important than program A, can you downsize program A and use the saved funds to increase the monies you spend on program B?

Third, what is your ability to reclassify positions? Reclassification of vacant positions can be one of the most powerful management tools you have. In an era of constant change, whenever a position becomes vacant, you should examine it and determine if that position should continue as is or whether it should be remade into something different. If you have reorganized, or installed new technology, four clerks may be able to do the work that five did previously. When one of the five clerks departs, you will be able to get the work done with the four remaining ones, freeing up a position which you can change into an engineer, a project manager, a social worker, or whatever you need to deal with increasing workload or responsibilities somewhere else in your organization. Or it may simply be that there is less business over time in a certain area and fewer people are needed to get the job done. In the aggregate, this approach is referred to as "**cutting and investing**," but that is just another way of labeling the reallocation of your budget dollars from lower to higher priorities. There is certainly no reason why you cannot practice it one position at a time. Assuming that you have this ability, or can get the necessary approvals, religiously following the practice of reexamining vacant positions can, over time, help you meet needs and solve problems without having to acquire additional resources.

Now that you understand your budget, it is time to put a harness on it. First, establish a working relationship with your state, county, or city budget department. As an agency head, your most important relationship is the one you have with your boss the elected executive. That relationship is the subject of Chapter 9. But your second most important relationship is likely to be the one you have with the budget director. On a day-to-day basis, it may be *the* most important relationship. After all, your boss can fire you, but only the budget director can help you or hurt you every single day.

Some of my cabinet colleagues fundamentally misunderstood the relationship of the budget director to our mutual boss, the governor. On an organization chart, the budget director might have cabinet rank, as the rest of us do, and budget office box might be parallel to the boxes of our departments. But the budget chief is almost always, at a minimum, first among equals. In tight fiscal times (are there any other times, these days?) the budget director is more than first among equals. In many cases he is virtually the chief operating officer of your jurisdiction.

The ideal budget director is both the keeper of your county or city's purse strings *and* the promoter of the mayor's or county executive's agenda. The bad ones think their job is only the first of those two. I have been very fortunate that some of the smartest and finest public servants I have ever worked with have occupied the budget director's chair. They understood the dual roles of the job. But I have seen others at work, too. When combined with a new governor or mayor, what can happen is that "Chief political executives expect the budget agency head to hold the line; and, especially if they are new and lack management experience, chiefs often do not equate the budget bureau's short-term decisions with the public manager's long-term performance and responsibility."4

You also likely will be working with the budget chief's analysts as well. I cannot say that I have had universally good fortune with them. While they are always bright and possess excellent quantitative skills, they also generally have one weakness—their lack of experience in an operating agency. I tried to convince some of the budget directors I worked with to hire their analysts from elsewhere in government, but my recommendation was usually not heeded. They tended to hire men and women right out of graduate school. Budget analysts cannot know as much about your operation as you do even if they do have operating agency experience, and it is even worse when they are government neophytes. Nevertheless, as with legislative staff (see Chapter 10), treat them with respect and educate them at every opportunity. An informed staff can be strong advocates at times and in places you cannot access.

Whether the budget director is one of your closest allies in government or someone who is problematic, however, your attitude should always be one of cooperation. There are three reasons to adopt this posture. First, it is the right thing to do. It is part of being a team player, and the governor and budget director never need team play more than at budget time, even if you are not in a deficit mode. Managing budgets, and especially managing budget shortfalls and deficits, are keys to a governor's success, both programmatically and electorally. Second, cooperation will always gain you more in return than a confrontational attitude. You might win a battle with a budget head once in a while, but over the long run you will be a big net loser. Third, if you can develop credibility with the budget office, you have the potential to be given flexibility in managing your operations beyond what you might ordinarily have.

To develop that credibility, play the game the way the budget office wants it played. When they give you instructions, follow them to the letter. If you are asked for a cut, give them a real one. Do not suggest reducing services in your biggest and most popular program the first time you are asked for a trim.

Of course, you play the game fairly as long as the budget office is playing it fairly with you. For example, if you suggest a reallocation of your existing budget because you have excess funds in one area but want to create a new program or expand an existing one in another area, the budget office should not hesitate to support you. If they do not, or worse, if they "seize" the money you wanted to reallocate for use elsewhere, don't ever suggest another reallocation. From that point forward, no expansions and no new programs unless you get new money.

With your external relationships squared away, take a look at your internal operation. Start with your internal budget chief and his or her staff. Do you have complete confidence in the knowledge and creativity of your fiscal director? If not, you will need to move to replace the budget chief. If that individual has civil service protection, then you will probably be doing some of that dreaded micromanagement.

If your department does not already have a regularized budget process, put one into place. All budget processes start with a timetable, working

backwards from the date when your budget submission is due to your jurisdiction's budget office. You need sufficient time for each of your divisions to
submit their proposals, for your central budget team to review those proposals, for internal hearings about your divisions' requests, and for your own
review and decision process. The bigger your department, the more likely
that your budget process for the next fiscal year will begin right after the start
of the new fiscal year (in most jurisdictions, this will be in July).

Having a well laid out budget process is important both to control your
spending and to set priorities. When any part of your organization needs or
wants additional funding, their opportunity to do so should only be during the
budget process, not in the middle of the year. You should be clear in your
expectations to your managers that, except in the most extraordinary circumstances truly beyond their control, if they run into a mid-year shortfall, they
need to adjust spending to meet their budget appropriation. The opportunity
to request more money comes with the next budget cycle. The same is true if
a manager wants to start a new program or increase services—the time to and
place to do that is in the regular budget process, except in the rare instance
when no new funding is necessary to do so. The reason why you want new
programs and service increases confined to the regular budget cycle is that
you want to be able to consider all of your department's requests for increases simultaneously, not seriatim. When you have them all in front of you
together, it allows you to rank them in priority order, giving the highest
priority to those requests that you judge to be the most important. Having all
of the managers in your agency cognizant of this rule will force them to do
some planning if they were not already doing it.

Your state's budget bureau may place a dollar or percentage limit on your
requests for new money. If they do, you will probably need to place a similar
limit on your sub-agencies' requests for new funding to keep the process
manageable. If, say, the budget office sets a 1 percent limit on your requested
increase, you might limit your divisions' requests to 2 percent. A larger limit
for them is appropriate, so that you have options from which to choose. You
may want to ask for a 3 percent increase for an important program, while
declining to request new money for a lower-priority one. In really good
budget times, you can allow your divisions to submit unlimited requests for
new money.

Whatever level of money you are seeking, your directors will have to
prioritize, and you will have to prioritize, so everyone should understand that
the items ranked low on the priority list, in good times and bad, have little
chance of being funded. Budget allocation decisions can never be formulaic.
Each and every decision, as stated in the introduction to this chapter, is a
value judgment. As with everything else you do, prioritization is vital. Depending upon how disparate your agency's functions are, setting priorities
may be difficult because nothing is an apples-to-apples comparison. In one

extreme example, I had to choose between the labor relations board's collaborative bargaining initiative and the facilities management division's need for an articulated 4x4 front end loader.

In tight times, of course, you may be told to submit no requests for additional funding or be directed to submit a budget with negative growth; that is the subject of "Cutback Management", the next section.

When you have made your decisions as to which division requests will be included in your department's submission, have a final conversation with each division director. Ask if they wish to make any substitutions; you should generally permit them if requested, as long as their overall budget amount does not change.

When you do have the opportunity to ask for more money, you have to sell your budget request, first to the chief executive and his budget staff, and then to the legislature. Therefore, first, does what you are asking for relate in any way to the governor's or mayor's priorities? Obviously, something that does relate to those priorities will have an easier time clearing the first hurdle than something that is unrelated. It should not be hard to figure out what the governor's priorities are; if she has not spoken about them in a cabinet meeting, she is probably talking about it in her public speeches and remarks. And before that, she probably spoke about them during the campaign. Second, construct a story about why new money is needed, involve stakeholders in your story, and invite decision makers to visit your program. Make contacts in places where the staff can help you. When you construct your narrative, make it a convincing one. Having sat on the budget committee when I was a legislator, I have heard every reason in the world why more money is essential; some are legitimate, but many are not, and transparently so. Specifics of shepherding your budget request through the legislature are covered in Chapter 10, "The Legislative Branch of Government."

If you have successfully harnessed your budget and your budget process, you can put them to work performing your mission.

To the maximum extent possible, give your divisions each a set budget number and then let them manage within that amount. This approach is called the **bucket budget** approach. As long as your directors do not exceed their spending limits, which you will be carefully monitoring via their expenditure reports, allow them to spend whatever they want, however they want. When my daughter got married, my wife and I gave her a bucket budget. Within that sum of money, she was free to have whatever kind of wedding she wanted. If she wanted to have more guests, for example, the per plate cost had to shrink, or the amount set aside for the photographer or for flowers had to be smaller. If she preferred a pricier photographer, the menu choices had to be decreased, or the venue be less fancy. And so on. As long as she stayed within the total budget, the choices were hers. Similarly, I want my directors to be free to spend more money in a certain area and less money in another, as they see fit. The director might spend more money on supplies and less on contractors, or vice versa. Just about anything is okay, as long as their overall spending does not exceed their budget limit—and as long as, of course, their allocations are achieving the desired program results. Another way to conceptualize this tactic is that you are concerning yourself primarily with the 98 percent of your money that will determine whether you are living within your means, and less so the 2 percent that has limited bearing on it. Your directors will greatly appreciate this approach. However, due to restrictions imposed upon you by your jurisdiction, you may not have the ability to offer as much freedom as you would prefer.

Sadly, too much of government does not operate in a flexible fashion. Managers are hamstrung by **line-item appropriations, funding silos**, and strict rules on how much employees can be paid and what they can do. Congress has a far better system. Each Member of the House of Representative is given a **"Member's Representational Allowance"** to pay for staff and all other expenses (with a few exceptions). Almost the only restrictions are that a Congressman can hire no more than 18 full-time and 4 part-time staff, but can have a smaller number; there is also a maximum salary. But otherwise, the Congressman has flexibility. He can employ a larger number of people and pay them less, or vice versa. He can have a bigger office but spend less on supplies. The Senate has a similar system, except that the allowance varies with the size of the Senator's state, and that there are no staff size limitations. Under this system, each elected official can manage in a way that he or she thinks is best; no "one size fits all." For those who are worried about cost controls, Congress has none better. Should a Congressman or Senator exceed his budget in a given year, he must repay the excess personally!

A second approach of the less bureaucratic variety is the pool approach. A given category of expenses, say salaries or minor capital improvements, may be "spread" or appropriated to various parts of your department. But you treat them as one large appropriation or pool of money. Division A may have to exceed its budget but a surplus in Division B makes up for it. Unfortunately, the legislature, auditors, and the media tend to be stuck in the modalities of the past; they do not understand the concept of pool or bucket budgets and are uncomfortable when you employ them.

In good fiscal times and lean ones, always try to solve problems and improve your agency first by reallocating money, and only second by seeking new funding. The easiest thing to say in government is that you cannot solve a problem unless you have more money. Sometimes that is the case, but often it is not. Reallocation is not always possible, but it is possible more often than most managers think it is. The larger your budget, the more opportunity you will have to do so. Of course, you need great command of the details of your budget to reallocate. You also need the greatest possible flexibility. With the credibility that you have developed with the budget office, seek any and all exceptions, waivers, and other flexibility that you can get and then use that flexibility to the maximum extent possible. Use the flexibility carefully and wisely; never abuse it. Get the most out of the money that you have.

There is a simple reason why your focus should always be more on getting maximum efficiency out of existing funds than on getting new funds. Getting additional money is dependent upon many factors not under your control; making the best use of the funding you have is very much under your control. Efficiency and flexibility can become a **virtuous circle**. The more efficiently you operate your agency, the more flexibility and autonomy you will be given, which will in turn allow you to operate more efficiently, and so on.

Budget management is at its most acute when your department is actively engaged in **cutback management**, which is the subject of the next section. But even when you are not actively cutting the budget, the challenge is ever present. These days, it seems that public managers are running ever harder just to stay in place, with very little new money available for initiatives. If you want to move your organization forward, you need to do it with the resources you actually have, not the resources you would prefer to have.

Thus, using your money effectively is not merely about "saving money." It is first of all about maximizing your service output with the money you have. It is also about reducing your costs in one area (while delivering the same services), so that you can use the savings to do more of something in another area.

To that end, always look towards technology to both use your resources more efficiently and improve customer service. In good times, you can redeploy the workforce freed up by technology to higher priorities. In bad times, you can eliminate positions and save money.

In addition to keeping your spending under control, as a manager of taxpayer dollars, you have the further challenge of constantly trying to do your agency's work, whatever it is, better, faster, and cheaper. Your organization should strive, in other words, for continuous improvement. This challenge is not written down in a job description or anywhere else, and it probably was not discussed in your job interview with your governor or county executive. Many agency heads who focus on policy do not see this activity as very important. But for every public manager, the challenge is there. Like much in government, this challenge does not come in the form of a goal that you accomplish and then set aside because you are done with it. It is ongoing. "The managerial way is to continuously attend to performance and cost-effectiveness as a never-ending endeavor. This is the only way to achieve long-term results."[5] The budget is one of your primary tools to handle this challenge.

Meeting this challenge is not only important for the wellbeing of your own agency. Always be conscious of the fact that your organization is part of a large whole—your city, your county, your state, your nation. A dollar you save is a dollar that can be used to help solve another problem elsewhere. There is never a shortage of problems, but there is always a shortage of dollars to solve them.

Getting your work done better, faster, and cheaper is a constant challenge in production agencies, especially those with workloads that generally increase from year to year. Among the improvements we made in the general services department I ran were the following:

—We ran the state printing operation. We made investments in state of the art equipment. We made the investments to better serve our customers, not necessarily to improve our bottom line. But as a result, we cut delivery times, cut our rates, and improved the quality of our products, all of which brought in higher revenue.
—A regulatory agency, by adding just one in-house attorney, cut its outside legal bills by hundreds of thousands of dollars.
—Working with the local power company, we consolidated our 64 separate bills into two, which cut our processing costs and time.
—Our water treatment expenses were not bid through a state contract. When we consolidated them into one bid, we lowered our costs.
—The Postal Service was delivering mail in the state capital to a central location; our department sorted it and delivered it to the various state buildings. We discussed the situation with the Postal Service and they found no reason not to deliver the mail themselves directly to the individual buildings. Eliminating ourselves as the middleman saved positions, which we reallocated.
—We changed delegated signature authority department-wide from $10,000 to $25,000. (In the larger department I headed, with an operating budget of close to $2 billion, the cabinet secretary's signature was required only on million dollar items.) Increasing the signature authority cut processing time. Your approval should be required only on the very largest items, say, those exceeding 1/10th of 1 percent of your budget.

And so on. As with many other aspects of government, you can never rest on your laurels.

You will also have to deal with the press when presenting and defending your budget. Chapter 11, "The Media," will deal with media relations in greater detail. But there are two things to note specifically regarding the media and budgets. First, if there is any area in which journalists stereotypically are weak, it is in budgets and money matters. The press usually regards budgetary matters very simplistically. One of my communications directors, a former reporter herself, urged me to be sympathetic and patient, noting that "It is very tough for a reporter to do a budget story once a year." You should try to display that patience. Multiple explanations of the very basics of budgeting may be required, so spend whatever time is necessary to help any reporter who asks for them.

The second and corollary characteristic of the media and budgets is that they especially do not understand the more progressive concepts of money management, like pool or bucket budgeting. (In this regard, the media are like auditors, the legislature, and almost all parties external to your department.) As an example, I remember my exasperation when one small part of my department took criticism because it had spent more on employee overtime than its nominal budget line for that expense. It was a classic example of everyone ignoring the forest in favor of a tree. Even setting aside the policy and fiscal reasons why overtime spending was necessary in that one agency, it was no use explaining that the department's employee expenditures *as a whole* were well under budget, or that the department ended the year in surplus, or that the department had a history of running surpluses. The press, the auditor, and a few legislators could not get past the fact that the one budget line had been exceeded.

## CUTBACK MANAGEMENT

Although the national economy is no longer in a recession, at least not technically, recovery has been very slow. The state budget outlook is uncertain, to say nothing of the prospects for additional federal funding. My current fiscal year budget is in deficit, which I inherited when I took over my department midway through the fiscal year. It is small enough that I will be able to end the fiscal year in the black, but large enough that I am going to have to manage my finances carefully during the coming months to get there.

A reader of the previous paragraph might think it applies to a job I currently hold. It certainly could. But it actually describes the budget situation I faced in my first cabinet assignment in January of 1993. The only differences between the preceding paragraph and the situation I faced when I took my second cabinet posting in 2001 are that the country was about to enter an actual recession, and the deficit I inherited was much bigger, both in absolute dollars and as a percentage of my budget.

Some would even argue that a fundamental reordering of our economy is now underway, one in which resources available to government will be permanently lower. I am not an economist, but even so it seems premature to state definitively whether our economy is in the midst of a slow recovery, a lost decade, a permanent restructuring, or something else. But be it a softening economy, an economy in recession, an economy struggling to regain its footing after a recession—when it comes to dealing with your budget, it appears that there is a lot of *plus ca change, plus ce la meme chose.*

Just as no educators ever become teachers because they want to administer tests, no public managers ever enter government service because they want to cut budgets. But everybody has to, sooner or later. Economic cycles will ever be with us. The next recession always comes; no president and no Congress have ever succeeded in permanently repealing them. There are only two categories of government administrators: those who are currently cutting their budgets, and those who will be cutting their budgets at some point in the future.

If your department has a budget problem, and/or your state or county or city has a budget problem, it is very likely your number one problem. It may be, in your boss's eyes, your only problem.

A few years ago I had a conversation with a young teacher in which she complained to me that her school district was having a money crunch, but the cuts that were under discussion made no sense. She pointed to a number of areas that would have been more appropriate for cutting as they involved no sacrifices in actually educating the students. I explained to her that there is a science to cutback management and that neither school board members nor school administrators have customarily been trained in that science. Unfortunately, the same situation seems to prevail in many governments throughout the country. The problem is exacerbated because budget crises are often episodic. They occur with regularity, but often at intervals of five to 10 years. Even if they occur regularly, the individuals with the institutional knowledge of how the last crunch was handled may have moved on by the time the next one arrives.

Absolutely no skill is required to cut a budget. Anyone can do it, without the slightest bit of budgetary or governmental knowledge or training. All you need is a pencil and paper. If last year's budget was, say, $10,000 for a certain item, simply write the figure $9,000 on the paper. Congratulations; you have just cut the budget by 10 percent. Unfortunately, to some people, including some people in all three branches of government, cutback management is not any more sophisticated than that.

Cutting the budget without cutting services—that's the trick, and not a trick that very many people seem to have learned. It can almost always be done, but only after a lot of hard work, in-depth analysis, and creativity.

It helps to start by being clear about what cutting the budget actually means. There is an imprecision in the language about budget cuts that should be done away with to the greatest extent possible. A cut should be defined as one of two things:

1.  an actual reduction in next year's budget compared to this year's, or

2. having to give back some money in the current year's budget at some point during that same year.

Not getting what you requested in your budget proposal should not count as a budget cut, nor should getting only some of what you wanted, nor getting an increase that was not a full inflationary increase. Unfortunately, many advocates, legislators, media types, and even some of your own staff (who should know better) incorrectly describe the situation you are in.

That outside parties use incorrect terminology when talking about budget cutbacks is only the beginning of your problems with those parties. When you are cutting the budget, you are very often all alone. No one is your ally.

The second problem is that in many cases the only people who really know whether you can cut the budget without cutting services are you and your staff. Almost no one else possesses knowledge that is sufficiently in depth. With so little information, public budget cutting discussions in the media, nationally and locally, and with advocates and the legislature, are almost always overly simplistic. Lacking specific knowledge, advocates and the media tend to assume that any reduction in your budget will result in a diminution or loss of services—and, as described above, may characterize something that is not really a reduction as a reduction. Your jurisdiction's budget office theoretically should know the score, and sometimes they do. But, as mentioned previously, budget offices are often populated by very smart individuals who have superb quantitative skills, but limited or no operating agency experience. They will make sure that the numbers add up, and that your cuts are genuine ones. However, they will not be in a position to offer suggestions about creative ways to make cuts that have minimal impact on your operations. Unfortunately, sometimes budget directors tend to view their jobs as being done once they have balanced the budget, when in fact they have to balance the budget while at the same time providing services and running the government. There will always be that tension. It may be that you are the only official with two goals, balancing the budget *and* keeping your agency functioning. Should that be the case, you really are all alone.

You should not expect any assistance from the legislature, and you may face active resistance to your proposed cuts. First, they too almost never have the detailed knowledge of budgets that they would need to offer suggestions. As will be discussed in Chapter 10, "The Legislative Branch of Government," this statement is not offered as a criticism, merely as an acknowledgement of the reality. Second, they do not usually view their job as identifying those cuts. They almost always view their role as reactive; they expect you and other executive agency heads to offer suggested reductions, and then they will tell you which ones they approve of and which ones they are rejecting. They will sometimes push back against what in your view are common sense cuts. The good news is that the legislature seldom rejects your proposals arbitrarily. They generally veto them because a) they receive pressure from advocates or the general public not to make a certain cut, and/or b) they view reductions as being too heavily targeted towards their constituents or districts. An example of the latter is any proposal having to do with the closure or merger of government facilities. Managers almost always want to operate one facility at 90 percent of capacity instead of two at 45 percent capacity. As a retired city manager put it, "The application of managerial values to the situation would close the smallest and least-used [facility] in favor of the larger, better-equipped, and much more heavily patronized facilities."[6] It saves money and is easier to administer. But the legislator in whose district the facility proposed for closure is located does not see it that way, nor do the employees at said facility or the public surrounding the facility. Requiring citizens to travel a greater distance to receive a service is not going to be popular with those citizens. That office may be the most tangible government service there is for those members of the public. Even if the general public does not use the services at the facility, it is there, they are used to it, and they are concerned about an abandoned building or buildings and what if anything will replace them. Here is a prime example of the difference between how government and businesses operate. Closing one of those two facilities is an easy business decision to make, but not an easy government decision to make or to stick to. (More about an actual proposal to close a facility shortly.)

Problems result not just from legislators rejecting proposals, but also from how the legislature approaches the proposals they wish to reject. Legislators seldom offer alternatives to the proposals they want to nix. Instead, they expect you to substitute other reductions that they will find less objectionable. When they voice objections to your proposal, you need to do some serious strategizing, and possibly negotiating, which will be discussed below.

Advocates, who will be discussed in greater detail in Chapter 12, are a difficult population to deal with at budget cutting time. First, they are very slow to accept the premise of tight budgetary times. My rule of thumb is always that it will take three consecutive years of austerity before advocates understand both intellectually and emotionally that the budgetary world has changed. Up until that point, they are still arguing about how much new money they want to see added to your budget, not what cuts to accept. The gulf between your reality and their expectations can be very wide indeed. Whether it is the first year of austerity or the last, advocates can be counted on to vigorously object to any budget reductions in their programs. They do not have much ability to distinguish between a reduction in your budget that is simply the result of you operating more efficiently and a reduction that will decrease services. If you hold spending at the current year's level, they will still be complaining that they did not get an increase to address what they see as unmet needs. Partly the unvarying posture of objection occurs because they lack specific detailed knowledge, but part of it results from the emotional nature of advocacy. Most advocates see any reductions in programs they support for any reason as bad, per se. More = good, less = bad, by definition. It is not any more complicated than that. You can spend a tremendous amount of time educating and explaining that your proposed cuts will harm no one—I *have* spent an enormous amount of time educating and explaining—without across the board success.

You may receive suggestions from a different outside group—entities whose payments you have proposed for reduction or might propose to reduce. You might be proposing to give them less work or you might be proposing to pay them less for the services they are providing. By all means, hear them out, but do not enter into the discussions with high expectations. Almost all of these groups want to "help" you by directing cuts elsewhere. Their hope is that if they offer a cut that can be inflicted on someone else, their own reductions will be lightened or eliminated. I do not object to the self-serving nature of their suggestions as much as I am generally disappointed that they have few creative ideas. Typically, they propose cuts which are already on your internal list of proposals; they may also suggest reductions that you have previously determined are not politically feasible. In either case, they propose them because they are not aware of your internal deliberations. If, however, a company or group wants to suggest a way in which the amount of a cutback imposed on them remains the same but is imposed in a different way, you should be all ears.

Do not count on the press to understand budget cutting, either, and report on it accurately. Partly this lack of understanding is a result of *their* dearth of detailed budgetary knowledge (are we detecting a pattern here?) and partly it is a reaction to advocates' claims and complaints. The press loves a victim story, a victim story is an easy one to write, and it is not difficult for advocates to gin up an alleged victim of your proposed cut.

As if the environment in which you are planning and carrying out budget reductions is not difficult enough, with what in a worst case scenario are an unhelpful budget office, unfriendly advocates, an uncooperative legislature, and a skeptical media, you have your own employees to contend with. They may be uncooperative at best and antagonistic at worst. Many employees do not understand why your boss the governor or mayor is not raising taxes, or if he is, why he is not raising them more, to cover any budget shortfall (and a pay increase for them, to boot). As a career public servant, I certainly do not subscribe to the notion that taxes should never be raised. But many of your employees believe that tax increases should be the first resort, regardless of any other considerations. You can also count on employees to object loudly to any reduction that will change their working conditions, even if no monetary penalty is involved. Under the heading of "no stone unturned," offer them the opportunity to suggest their own cutbacks, but do not expect very much in the way of substantive ideas.

You can also expect that they are watching your own expenses, major and minor, very carefully. As with everything else when you are the leader, what you do is as important as if not more important than what you say. In one cabinet assignment, my office's break room had a water cooler. Given the fact that there was no water fountain in my office, the $10-15 a month that it cost did not seem like a unreasonable expense, if I had ever given it a second thought, which I had not. The water cooler was there when I assumed the position, and nothing happened for years. But one year when we were tightening the budgetary screws, a legislative staffer e-mailed us, wanting to know why my office got free water and everybody else in the department had to pay for theirs. It turned out that there were other water coolers in my building, but the employees who used them paid the dollar or two a month per person cost. The difference was that the rest of the building also had built-in water fountains, where the employees could drink free water, while our office did not. Sometime in the past, somebody had made the reasonable decision that since free water was already available to employees, our department was not going to pay twice. In the secretary's office, our department was only paying once because we had no water fountain. Whatever the history, I had no choice but to start having everybody in the office, including me, pay the cost ourselves. No doubt, someone in the finance office of our department had suddenly experienced an "ah ha" moment when paying my office's water bill and either decided to contact the legislature or told someone who did.

Even if you do an excellent job managing the public finances when the economy is poor, the public will give you and your boss the elected official much less credit than you deserve, as will interest groups, advocates, the media, and sometimes your own employees. The public does not tend to understand that a poor economy imposes a much higher degree of difficulty on some elected and appointed officials than on those who hold office in rosier economic times.

When it comes time to cut your budget, as with your regular budget activities, above all you need an orderly process, with decision rules, clear guidance, and a firm timetable. One of my cabinet counterparts from another state once described her approach to cutback management as calling her staff into her office and demanding of them, "All the money you've been holding back, or hiding—show it to me." Unfortunately, it is seldom that simple— even assuming your staff will tell you the answer to that question. You will need something more in depth. Your goal should be to introduce as much objectivity into the process as possible. It should not be an advocacy process. There is a time for advocacy in the budget process, but that time is not now. Advocacy is appropriate for the time when you are seeking new funds, or for when you are making actual *service* cuts. But for now, you are not doing either. Decision rules are also a must, for several reasons. First, especially the first time around, there is probably a lack of institutional memory among your top managers about how to handle budget shortfalls. Second, you need to set parameters. Third, you need to share the thinking of the mayor and her budget director. And finally, there is a lot of technical detail necessary to ensure that the savings you propose are genuine.

Budget cutting is another form of prioritization as described in Chapter 5. As such, the buck stops with you. You need to get everyone's opinion, but as the head of your agency, in the end the final decisions are yours and yours alone. Everyone else can be expected to advocate for their own budget.

Your first task in cutback management is likely to be reorienting the mindset of managers and employees, especially if there has been an extended interval since the most recent budget crunch. Everyone is used to arguing over how much new money they will get, not over how much less money they can get along with. It is not an easy adjustment.

Next, you need a schedule. I do not like **fire drills**, because they inevitably result in poor decisions. The only way to avoid them, even when a very tight time frame has been dictated to you by the budget chief or governor's office, is with proper planning. As with the budget process as a whole, you will have to develop a "work backwards" schedule based on the due date that your administration has undoubtedly given you. In other words, if your deadline for submission is three months hence, you need to decide when you want internal suggestions to be due to your office, when you want to have internal hearings or meetings to discuss the proposals, when you need to have your central budget staff's recommendations to you, and how long you and your top aides will require to study those recommendations, all within that 90-day interval. You need to allow sufficient time for your division heads to come up with their suggestions on where to cut, but you also need adequate time to analyze all proposals, for reasons which will be covered below.

The later you are in the fiscal year, the deeper the budget hole, and the more rounds of cuts you have already been through, the shorter the turnaround time you will likely be given. If you are fortunate, your state's revenue forecasters are telling you that next year will be difficult, and you can incorporate your plans for reductions into your budget presentation for the next fiscal year. Most of the time, though, cutbacks are not part of normal budget cycles. Frequently, cut lists are due in a few months at most, and on one occasion I was required to turn around a multi-million dollar plan for cutbacks in just three weeks. Another important consideration is how far through the current fiscal year you are. If you are halfway through the fiscal year, your department has probably spent about half of your budget already. Your targets of opportunity are fewer, and lead times more of a hindrance.

Having to give back, say, 2 percent of your annual appropriation halfway through the fiscal year is really the equivalent of a 4 percent reduction.

If your county or city is coming off a few "fat" years, you may be able to make a first round of reductions without much consultation with your bureau chiefs. But any subsequent round is going to require detailed suggestions from every one of your internal divisions. You will need to give them a target to hit. If the state's budget director has told your department to make $1 million in reductions, you need to apportion that $1 million among your divisions. One way to do this is to simply assign everyone an across the board quota. Say your agency's budget is $100 million, and your requirement is to identify $1 million in savings. You have to make a 1 percent giveback; therefore, under the across-the-board scenario, every division needs to make a 1 percent reduction. Some observers would say that you should make across the board cuts because they are equitable. But do those cuts minimize the impact on your department's agenda? In my view, if you balance your budget with across the board cuts, you are abdicating one of your most important responsibilities as a manager, which is to determine priorities.

A better way is to ask your directors to assemble a cut list two or three times the size of your eventual target. In other words, if you are required to submit a $1 million cut list, ask your directors for lists that total $2 million or $3 million. There are two reasons why a larger list is in order. First, it will give you the ability to pick and choose among options. You can use the flexibility that options give you. Some proposals will be better or less painful than others. Second, there will undoubtedly be a wide variety of substantive, technical, and/or political reasons why you cannot or do not want to submit a suggested cut, or why a cut does not generate as much in the way of savings as indicated. More on this shortly.

Therefore, if your department's quota is a 1 percent giveback, and you want a 3 percent list of cuts from which to choose, each division should submit a 3 percent cut list. In computing each division's quota, make sure that the 3 percent is computed carefully and fairly. There may be two reasons to exempt parts of a unit's budget from that 3 percent. First, are there any parts of that bureau's operations that are so critical to your department's mission and/or so thinly stretched already that they should be exempted? You probably will designate such exemptions sparingly, if at all, but you may have some. Second, are there parts of a division's budget that are truly not under their control? If so, they should be excluded. I am not referring here to entitlement programs. As discussed below, you should never assume that expenditures of an entitlement program cannot be controlled. Instead, this exemption should cover items like debt service (if it is included in your department's budget) because there is a legal requirement that the money be paid out. Again, the number and amount of such exceptions will be limited, but fairness requires that they be taken into account.

Have the divisions rank their proposals in priority order. You do not necessarily have to adhere to their rankings, but you should consider them carefully. Also, each suggested cut should include a description of the reduction, whether the reduction is a "one-time-only" reduction or an ongoing one, and an analysis of the potential political ramifications, if any. Some proposals will cause you no heartburn with the public, while others most definitely will, and you need to know which are which.

Give your directors as much guidance as you can in terms of what they can and should suggest in the way of cuts versus what they should omit. First, start with any directions you have been given by the budget and/or governor's offices. For example, you may receive a directive that in suggesting cuts, you are not to propose laying off any employees. Next, you should bar any proposals that result only in false savings. For example, absent guidance to the contrary, division directors will sometimes propose cuts that reduce their own budgets, while increasing the costs to another agency. As I explained to the directors, that might solve your problem, but at the cost of exacerbating someone else's. Your cost-shifting proposal has resulted in a net savings of zero to your state or city. Another inappropriate proposal is one that reduces an expenditure, but also reduces the same amount of revenue. Reducing the hours a park is open might enable you to cut your spending, but will probably also reduce the revenue generated by admissions fees, for example. Again, there may be no net savings. A third "cut" to avoid is one that defers expenses until the next year. If you use such a tactic, you will help yourself this year but probably make next year even worse.

Even if you do not receive a directive to refrain from proposing layoffs, by the way, you should go to great lengths to avoid laying off any of your personnel. First, layoffs are a morale destroyer and should be used absolutely as a last resort. (Eliminating currently vacant positions, as discussed below, is another matter.) Second, savings generated by layoffs may be eaten up, at least initially, by required severance payouts (say, for unused sick leave and vacation time) and by the increased costs if laid off employees receive unemployment benefits and/or join the rolls of Medicaid or other programs.

When you receive the recommendations from your bureaus, take a close look at them. If a list is submitted to you with all direct service cuts and no suggested efficiencies, the division in question did not do an honest job. It is time for a special hearing or meeting with them, with some intense questioning regarding budget lines, fund balances, spending patterns, program utilization, and the like. It is probably also time for a new director, if said director is exempt. One of my directors once opined to me that she just did not know how we could possibly cut anything more out of her division's budget. This was after one round of cuts; there were four more during my tenure. I had to tell her politely that she had no business making such a statement since she had very little command of the details of her budget. She did not, in fact, last very much longer in her post.

Samples of memos instructing line agency staffs in how and when to prepare cut lists are shown on the following three pages.

It is now time for the winnowing process to begin. Winnowing is going to occur at three levels. First, there is the department winnowing, i.e., that done by you as the boss. Second, there is going to be winnowing at the budget office/governor's level. And third, your legislative body will do its own winnowing.

At the first two levels, you will have some media/Freedom of Information Act (**FOIA**) considerations to be mindful of. Your goal should be to keep preliminary recommendations confidential to the maximum extent possible. There is a very simple reason for this confidentiality: you want to avoid political fallout for ideas you considered but do not follow through on. You are going to take enough flak for the cuts you do make—why take flak for cuts you do *not* make? If an idea under consideration is disclosed which you or the elected executive would have later rejected, you may end up with the worst possible outcome: you have angered a political constituency for even thinking about cutting them in the first place, but not saved any money. If a preliminary cut list becomes public after you have made your choices, it is still undesirable but not quite the worst case, because those constituencies can at least see that in the end they did not get hurt.

## DELAWARE HEALTH & SOCIAL SERVICES
## BUDGET REDUCTION INSTRUCTIONS
**February 11, 2008**
**FY 2008**

- Please review and close out all unnecessary prior year Purchase Orders by Monday 2/18/08.
- Please submit a revised FY 08 expenditure report for the following programs by Monday 2/25/08: Medicaid, CHIP, Child Care, and TANF.
- Further instructions will be forthcoming on the hiring process.

### FY 2009
**1.** Guidelines

- Every Division must identify a list of GF reductions equal to 6 percent below the Governor's Recommended GF Budget for FY 2009.
- Non-service reductions should be identified prior to implementing service reductions.
- Reallocations are strongly encouraged. Where possible, GF resources should be shifted to ASF/NSF funding sources.
- No reductions are allowed which will result in shifting costs to other Divisions/ Departments, incur increased costs in the following year (FY 2010), and/or result in a reduction in revenue.
- Please give serious consideration to:

  Eliminating or reducing programs with low utilization.
  Creation or expansion of waiting lists for services.
  Consolidating services (provided directly or under contract), where appropriate, to achieve administrative efficiencies.
  Deferral of any new services or planned expansions in FY 2009.

- The following are excluded from consideration: SAMH/DPC and CSE/ DACSES.
- Reduction lists must include a description of the reduction, the amount, whether the reduction is base or one-time, and a description of the potential political ramifications.

**2.** Timetable

- Proposed Division reduction lists due to DMS, Friday 2/29/08
- Internal review with Secretary, Friday 3/7/08
- Final DHSS reduction list due to OMB, Friday 3/14/08

**DELAWARE HEALTH & SOCIAL SERVICES**
**BUDGET REDUCTION INSTRUCTIONS, 2ND ROUND**
**March 18, 2008**
**FY 2009**

1. Guidelines

- Every Division must identify a list of GF reductions equal to 10% below the Governor's Recommended GF Budget for FY 2009, less proposed reductions previously accepted.
- Generally, non-service reductions should be prioritized over service reductions.
- The following are allowable as part of each division's target:

    Anything previously submitted but not taken.
    Eliminating or reducing programs with low utilization.
    Creation or expansion of waiting lists for services.
    Consolidating services (provided directly or under contract), where appropriate, to achieve administrative efficiencies.
    Deferral of any new services or planned expansions in FY 2009.
    Reallocations of GF expenses to ASF/NSF funding sources.
    Estimated savings from the hiring freeze.
    Any other ideas not specifically prohibited.

- The following are allowable but must be in addition to, rather than instead of, each division's target:

    Revenue measures.
    Suggested cost savings in other departments/divisions.
    Reductions which would result in shifting costs to other departments.
    Reductions in SAMH/DPC and CSE/DACSES.

- The following are not allowable:

    Reductions which would incur increased costs in the following year (FY 2010).
    Reductions which would result in a reduction in revenue.

- Reduction lists must include a description of the reduction, the amount, whether the reduction is base or one-time, and a description of the potential political ramifications. They should be ranked in priority order.

2. Timetable

- Proposed Division reduction lists due to DMS, Tuesday 3/25/08
- Initial review with Secretary, Friday 3/28/08
- Internal hearings, Monday 3/31/08, Tuesday 4/1/08, Wednesday 4/2/08

- Revised lists due to DMS (if necessary), Thursday 4/3/08
- Final review with Secretary, Monday 4/7/08
- Final DHSS reduction list due to OMB, Tuesday 4/8/08

\* \* \*

Whether you can maintain confidentiality will depend upon the attitude of the press and your jurisdiction's FOIA laws. The press has varying levels of interest in the details of budget cutbacks, and sometimes may be content to wait for the final version. They do not, of course, care about whether you get into political difficulty, and may well relish the idea of writing about the unhappiness of people potentially or actually impacted by budget reductions. During several rounds of budget reductions, our budget director cleverly had all department heads send their cut lists not to him, but to the Governor directly, thus making them, successfully in the eyes of our lawyers, subject to executive privilege confidentiality.

You now have in your hands a menu of ideas for budget cuts that is two to three times the size of what you need to submit. To help make sense of the large number of proposals, have your budget staff classify them according to how much political pain they will cause, on a scale of zero to three. A zero means that absolutely no one will object to the reduction. A three indicates major political fallout. (This classification could also be done by the divisions that submit the suggested cuts.)

There are both technical and substantive reasons why you will keep some ideas and reject others. Proper instructions at the beginning of the process will go a long way towards reducing the number of suggestions that you have to toss out for technical reasons. Even so, do not be surprised if you still have to reject a fair number due to such problems. In addition to violating one of the aforementioned guidelines, a proposal may be a good one that just cannot be implemented in time. Many possibilities for reductions require a long lead time. Public notice may be required or advisable. Information systems may need to be modified. Personnel may have to be retrained. Taking those actions may require a time interval that puts the desired savings outside of the time frame in which you need the money. Suppose your fiscal year begins in July, and you need money for the fiscal year ending in June. If you propose a reduction in January that takes six months to implement, you will achieve savings, but only for the following year, not the one in which you currently need to revert the money. In any event, the day you propose the reduction is not the day that you can begin any work that precedes the actual reduction— you have to await the governor's and possibly the legislature's approval. To avoid confusion, it is probably advisable to establish a uniform effective date for any proposal suggested by your divisions.

Another important concept to understand is that in the context of cutback management, there are three kinds of savings: outright savings, choosing cheaper alternatives, and cost avoidance. Unfortunately, only the first of those three helps if you have to reduce the absolute number of dollars in your budget, either at mid-year or for a future year. If you can buy an item for $880 next year that cost you $1,000 next year, you can reduce next year's budget by $120. Agency leaders will sometimes choose a cheaper alternative, but not want to see their appropriation reduced. They saved money, but just spent the savings on something else. If you are doing mid-year cutbacks, the budget office will not wait until the end of the fiscal year and expect that you will have made the appropriate savings. They will require you to revert your savings on a fixed due date well in advance of year's end. Cost avoidance, in which you take an action today that will reduce your costs down the road, has its own lead time issues. Cost avoidance is something that is good to do, but will not help you with today's shortfall. You will receive a number of cost avoidance proposals that you will have to put in the discard pile, at least temporarily.

In the early stages of budget cutting, you should try to avoid nickel and dime cuts (but not in the later stages as the budgetary vise gets tighter and tighter). You also may want to reserve some savings for reallocation purposes, but again, the longer the squeeze goes on, the less likely you will be able to afford such maneuvers. Another thing to consider is **leverage**. When you cut a dollar from your budget, does it de-leverage you by taking with that dollar a dollar (or dollars) of federal or other outside funding? If that is the case, you will have saved your budget $1 but reduced your programs by $2 or $3. Entitlement programs with federal matching funds are the prime examples of leveraged dollars. Again, the larger and deeper the downturn, the less likely you will be able to avoid de-leveraging. You should also consider whether funding that you are considering for the cut list will come back at the next upturn or whether, once you give it up, it is likely gone forever. Last but not least, you may judge that something is just not politically doable, due to objections from advocates, the legislature, or the governor's office, and/or negative press.

The last step in your internal process is to rank the proposals in ascending order of undesirability. The easiest cuts are ranked highest and the most problematic the lowest. Your spreadsheet will have a running total, which total will tell you where on the list you have reached your target number. Rank all of the proposals, because you may be required to resubmit "below the line" cuts if "above the line" ones are rejected by your chief executive or legislature.

When your proposals arrive at the budget office/gubernatorial level, they will be winnowed for two primary reasons. First, they may dislike one of your proposed service cuts for programmatic reasons. Second, they may judge a proposal as politically undoable due to predicted objections from advocates or the legislature, and/or negative press. Note that they may have a different take on what is politically undoable than you do. You may or may not be required to resubmit additional reductions from lower on your priority list to make up for the executive-level winnowing.

Finally, your proposals will arrive at the legislature, which will conduct its own winnowing process. They will have the same two reasons for rejecting a proposed cut that the governor and budget director do: dislike of a particular service cut on policy grounds, and judgment that a particular reduction is not politically doable. Again, note that they may have a different take on what is politically undoable than you do, plus, at this point, the cutbacks are public, meaning that it is likely that they are dealing with actual heat from advocates, the public, and/or the press, not just the theoretical criticism you contemplated. The legislature is also virtually guaranteed to have a third reason for rejecting proposals of the administration: the need to assert legislative prerogative. The legislature as a group will almost always reject part of any administration proposal if for no other reason than to remind the chief executive that they are a separate and equal branch of government, one with the final word regarding spending.

As mentioned above, your problem occurs not when they reject some of your proposals, but when they decline to come up with alternatives. How do you react to legislative objections? Do you go lower on your priority list and offer proposals you did not previously submit, or do you argue with them (or both)? You will not be making these decisions by yourself, but in concert with your governor or mayor. It may be that a rejection of your department's offering results in the submission of an additional reduction from another department. Typically, when an impasse is reached, at some point the governor will make the obligatory statement that if the legislature does not like his proposals, they are duty bound to generate their own. But in reality, you and the governor seldom prefer that outcome. First of all, the legislature almost always lacks the ability to identify its own reductions. As stated previously, few legislators have the level of knowledge of government operations to engage in substantive cutback management. Not a criticism; just a fact. Second, the cuts they do come up with might be much more unpalatable to your department than anything you would develop.

In dealing with the legislature, I have always believed that when they give you most of what you want, take what they give you and declare victory. (More on this in Chapter 10.) The path of least resistance may well be to substitute other savings that were not on your original submission. The exception to this tactic would be if substituting other savings would result in cutting services, whereas the original proposals did not. Always have fallbacks ready, but that situation may be one in which to argue a little harder for your preferred path.

I had a very big apple out of that barrel in my second cabinet posting. Our department ran several long-term care facilities that were underutilized, and we proposed that one of them be closed. To us it was a no-brainer. In addition to saving millions of dollars in operating costs, we would have been able to avoid expensive future capital improvements that would certainly be necessary on an aging facility. We had a sister department of government that would have been happy to take over the land and use it to expand parkland. Because the facility proposed for closing was within 25 miles of a similar facility, also underutilized, not only did we not need to lay off any employees, the biggest impact that some of them might face would be an additional 30-minute commute. We spent a great deal of time working with the employee unions to minimize the impact on their members. Emissaries from the governor's office had a successful meeting with the key state senator (of the same party as the Governor) in whose district the targeted facility was located. We rolled out the proposal to all the employees in private meetings on the same day that we announced the closing to the press, so that no one got the word via a third party.

Unfortunately, everything began unraveling the day after we made the announcement. While we anticipated employee unhappiness, we did not anticipate that the key senator would reverse course and oppose the closing. His word was not exactly his bond. In fact, he did not just oppose it; he went all out to block it. He very quickly assembled a working majority of his chamber to oppose the closing.

But the good news for the governor was that as more and more legislators increased their opposition to the closing, they appeared to lose interest in modifying most of the rest of the administration's proposed cutbacks, and were even willing to accede to the governor's proposals for increased revenue—this with one house controlled by the party opposite from the that of the governor. I can still remember the Secretary of Finance calling me and virtually cackling with glee, explaining, "We're going to get everything we wanted except for the hospital closing." My department did not have to offer additional cuts to make up for the hospital remaining open. The hospital closing ended up serving as a highly successful **loss leader** for the administration.

As will be discussed in Chapter 9, "Working For Elected Officials," your job as a cabinet secretary is to be a team player, and I was a team player. The governor and her administration won a huge victory in balancing the budget without cutting services to the residents of our state, which I firmly believe was not just a political victory for her, it was a victory for the state as a whole. But the press portrayed the denouement as a defeat for me personally, and many of the hospital employees bore me animus until the end of my tenure as cabinet secretary. For me, it was somewhat of a bittersweet victory. That facility remains open, and underutilized, to this day.

When the economy goes into a recession and tax revenues fall, often things get worse before they get better. The sour economy leads not just to one round of budget cuts, but multiple rounds of budget cuts. In my second cabinet assignment, we faced three rounds of budget cuts in my first 20 months on the job. Successively, they required more involvement of the operating divisions, necessitated fewer exemptions, needed more precise guidance from me, and took place over shorter time frames. The degree of difficulty, in other words, increased as time went on. The following chart shows that evolution.

| Time | Spring 2001 | Fall 2001 | Fall 2002 |
| --- | --- | --- | --- |
| Ideas generated by | Budget staff | Divisions | Divisions |
| Time frame | None | Verbal | Written |
| Money taken | 3 months | 6 weeks | 3 weeks |
| Division target | No | No | Yes |
| Exemptions | Not applicable | Some divisions | 1 hospital, 1 program |

In the first round of cutbacks, we were able to identify all the needed savings by sitting down with the department's budget staff; we did not need to involve the operating divisions. The question of exemptions did not even come up. By the third round, we had evolved a formal, written process that involved specific targets in every operating division. The exemptions were reduced to almost none. The whole thing was over in three weeks' time.

The deeper you have to cut, the more it will probably be necessary for all of your operating divisions to contribute something. As discussed previously in Chapter 5, resource allocation decisions should usually be made in priority order, not on a something for everybody basis. However, when you have had to make multiple rounds of budget cuts, you may feel that there needs to be shared sacrifice by all parts of your agency. Therefore, you may have to deviate slightly from a strict priority list and make cuts from every division to insure that shared sacrifice.

When you are searching for savings, as with all other decisions you make, do not take no for an answer the first time, do examine all conventional wisdom, and do question existing assumptions. You need the proverbial fine-toothed comb. To that end, you should consider adopting a zero base budget for one year. A zero base budget, in which every single expenditure has to be justified, is too much work for too little gain if used on an annual or regular basis. It is also not going to help you give back money in the middle of the year. But if used on a one-time basis, it should help you analyze your department's spending from a different perspective.

The notion that budgets can be balanced by eliminating waste, fraud, and abuse is nonsense, as any government manager can tell you. That being said, inefficiency is everywhere, and always needs to be minimized. The following are some dos and dont's for when you are assembling your list of cuts.

As stated previously, your goal is to cut the budget without cutting services. How many or how few of the following techniques are going to work will be somewhat dependent upon how many years in a row you have been cutting and how many "fat" years there were before the first reduction.

A hiring freeze is always a tempting notion to save money. Even in a tight economy, there will always be employee turnover. If one employee leaves and you cannot hire another one in her place, you obviously will save that employee's salary and benefits. A hiring freeze is so tempting, and personnel costs such a high percentage of the budgets of many governmental bodies, that one may be imposed on you by your budget office. But if you have the choice, think carefully before you impose one department-wide. A hiring freeze is a very blunt instrument and cannot help but be detrimental to your mission, if not cripple your operational efficiency. You are making cuts based on the happenstance of when and where there is turnover rather than managing by setting priorities. Individual bureaus may put them on their cut lists, but if given the choice, they probably will not propose them. It is even worse if your budget or personnel office imposes a hiring freeze on federally funded positions, as I have seen done. That nonsensical action has zero benefit to the budget and 100 percent harm to your ability to get work done.

Hiring controls are a different matter. In later rounds of cutting, every time a position becomes vacant, it should be carefully evaluated. The bigger your organization, the more likely that, over time, certain jobs, especially in administrative areas, have become less critical than others. In good times, the positions would be prime candidates for reallocation to other, more pressing needs. Now, they can be temporarily de-funded or even permanently eliminated.

Expenditure controls like allotments and purchase order reviews are another effective but highly inefficient means of controlling your budget. If such controls are forced upon you by your budget bureau, you will have to endure them; otherwise, do not impose them on yourself. Insist that your divisions operate within their budgets, but do not unnecessarily restrict how they do so.

Other standard budget cutting techniques that you should avoid include cutting training and employee recognition, deferring maintenance, and other cuts that I refer to as "nickels and dimes." Cutting training and employee recognition are close to managerial malpractice. They might bring short-term gain, but will always result in long-term pain. Reducing maintenance expenditures on your infrastructure (roads, bridges, buildings, etc.) is a similar short-term fix that will cause you problems down the line. In the words of my former chief engineer, whenever you defer maintenance, all you do is "escalate the cost of future actions." Preserving your maintenance budget makes sense even if your agency is one in which facilities are only a small part of your responsibilities.

An early step in cutback management should be to restrict or ban new programs and initiatives. Unless something is being put into place to correct a severe problem, the development of new initiatives should generally take a back seat to maintaining the things you already have. If something you have is less important than something you want to add, either get rid of it or make it less of a priority. Any activities that are not part of your core mission should be reviewed to the maximum extent possible.

Another standard technique is to shift as much of your general fund costs to federal and special funds as possible, keeping in mind that there are always legal limitations on how much cost shifting you can do. Ideally, your department has been doing this all along, but you may discover further opportunities upon close inspection.

Carefully examine all of your agency's contracts with outside vendors. There are likely some which have not been out for bid in a while. If so, you should consider putting them out for bid. Your operating and, to a lesser extent, procurement staffs may not wish to do so; it is a lot more work to put something out for bid than it is to renew a contract. There are not many advantages to a down economy, but one of them generally is that bidders are hungry for work, and may very well sharpen their pencils to obtain or retain a job. There may also be some areas in which you are buying off the shelf when a competitive bid could shave your costs. As a rule, try to bid out everything you can where there are multiple vendors likely to submit proposals. You should also consider renegotiating contracts with vendors. You probably do not have the option to do without the services of some vendors, and there may not be a body of competitors waiting in the wings. If there are not, you might still be able to save money by trading a longer-term contract extension for a lower annual fee.

If your responsibilities include human services, you should also examine the overhead expenses of your providers. Establishing, say, a 15 percent cap on administrative/overhead expenses (something my department did at one point) will probably save you some money, have no impact on services to your clients—and make some providers very unhappy. On the other hand, an across-the-board cut in provider rates may force some providers (most of whom are nonprofits) to operate more efficiently, but in the end it cannot help but force them to cut services. You may have to resort to it, but do not be under any illusions about its likely impact.

If you have any unused assets, like real property, you should put them on the market.

Reviewing your expenditures for savings opportunities should not be confined to a review of projects, but rather, encompass a review of all of your ordinary expenses. It is very seldom that you will not find efficiencies. The words "all of" should be taken literally. Particularly, examine instances where funds are appropriated for one purpose but end up being spent for a different one. Never accept the argument that the budgets of your entitlement programs, if you have them, are not amenable to cutback management. Because of their size, in fact, they are often more amenable than other programs. In the words of a former state budget director, "You should be skeptical about mandates and push to find out how those mandates can be changed."[7]

Cutback time is the time to examine every program and line item balance. It is surprising what leftover money you can find sometimes. It is also the right time to examine the account balances in your capital accounts and compare them to the pace of the projects. Due to the fact that capital projects often take years to be completed, it is very common that there are more funds in the capital appropriation than can be spent in one year (or the rest of the year). If that is the case, there are one-time savings to be had by reverting the funding that is not needed in the next (or current) year. This tactic is especially appropriate in **minor capital improvement (MCI)** lines. If an MCI line is customarily funded at a million new dollars every year, but there are $2 million in the account balance, there is no need to add another million next year if the most you can reasonably spend in one year is about $1 million. Alternatively, $1 million at a minimum can be removed from the current year's appropriation with no diminution in program.

Almost every government agency generates some revenue. Are you doing everything you can to maximize that revenue? Your budget director will generally be just as happy with a dollar of new revenue as he is with a dollar of spending reductions; it may even be considered preferable. I am not referring to maximizing revenue by increasing fees that are paid for your services, although sometimes your chief executive will make a determination that fee increases are more palatable than tax hikes, especially if those fees can be increased by your agency acting on its own, rather than needing the approval of the legislature or council. Instead, I am referring to the process of making sure that all revenue that is due to you is being collected. Are any back fees or charges owed to your agency? What can you do to collect them? You don't want to spend $2.00 to collect a dollar, but you should spend $0.90 extra to collect an extra dollar every time. Also, have you maximized your use of federal and other grant opportunities?

You should never balance your budget via gimmicks, but accounting changes are not necessarily gimmicks, especially if they are used once and not repeatedly. You should never hold bills until the next fiscal year begins. When you hold a month's worth of bills because you are short on cash, you will save money this year, but next year you will have to pay 13 months worth of expenses. If the revenue picture improves next year, you might get away with it. But it is equally likely that you will be pondering holding two months worth of bills next year. That way lies big trouble. On the other hand, for example, if you have a large program that pays its bills on the last day of the month, if you begin paying bills on the first day of the month starting with the next fiscal year, you will only have to pay 11 months worth of bills this year, and 12 (*not* 13) next year. Budget directors sometimes like this idea because it can be used in reverse. In a year when revenue increases but the budget office does not want the extra revenue to be built into the state's base budget, you can move the bill paying date back to the last day of the month and make 13 payments this year, and 12 (not 11) next year. Again, shifting payment dates is a one-time savings. One-time savings work best for mid-year givebacks. If the tough fiscal climate continues—and it almost always does—additional reductions will be necessary the next time around.

It is a given that in a large organization there is programmatic spending that is unneeded or, at a minimum, is of very low priority, but is done anyway because of political factors. Likely, said low priority service was added because it was a pet project of a legislator. If that legislator is still sitting, there is probably nothing you can do. But sometimes such initiatives hang around long after the legislator in question has left the capitol. There is a lot of autopilot spending in government. If anyone in your organization has the institutional memory to recall one of these services, you should strongly consider ending it or targeting it for reallocation.

As stated, service cuts should be your last option, not your first. If you are doing cutback management right, you should be able to endure multiple rounds of cuts before you have to start slashing services. But if you do have to go down that route, the first thing you should look at is any programs or initiatives that have been funded but not yet implemented. People are much less likely to miss (and object to) a service or benefit that they have never had than a benefit or service they already have that is taken away or reduced.

Analyze service levels in low utilization/low priority programs. Installing minimal co-pays and creating waiting lists is probably preferable to reducing services outright. If there is any program that no longer makes sense in the broad scheme of services that you offer, now may be the time to try to end it permanently. Unneeded and outmoded programs and services, unfortunately, often retain their political constituencies past their "expiration dates." A budget crunch may be just the occasion to make a long-overdue change—although it will not often be without a fight of some sort.

If you are in a human services agency, remember the old rule that from a public relations point of view, you should reduce services to adults before you reduce services to children, and reduce services to children before you reduce services to disabled children.

Finally, consider what payments you make to other units of government. If a service is mandatory, do not engage in cost shifting. But if a service is optional, you should consider such payments along with everything else that is on the table. Giving other governmental bodies less money may be a service cut, but on a good government basis, you can justify giving them the responsibility for continuing or ending the service that they were providing (if not paying for).

## NOTES

1. Key, *The Lack of a Budgetary Theory.*
2. *The politics of Mr. Nixon's economics, Life*, 2-13-70.
3. Briffault, *Balancing Acts*, 8.
4. Chase and Reveal, *How to Manage in the Public Sector*, 68.
5. Wilson, *Rethinking Public Administration*, 152.
6. Wilson, *Rethinking Public Administration*, 116.
7. Forsythe, *Memos to the Governor*, 38.

*Chapter Seven*

# Making Decisions and Solving Problems

"Put a Structure on the Problem"

## INTRODUCTION

Leading an organization is more than managing people and money, important as they are. Making decisions is the stock in trade of government managers. You should make only the decisions that *leaders* should make, not the decisions that others can make equally well. Making the right decisions in a timely fashion will leave you time to solve the problems that inevitably come your way. You will also be conducting negotiations on important matters. And unfortunately, the odds are that you and your organization will at some point face a crisis. As with everything else in government, there are useful techniques to make decisions, solve problems, conclude negotiations, and survive crises.

## MAKING DECISIONS

As the head of your agency, you are going to make a very large number of decisions. Making good decisions is equal parts good process and good analysis.

The first part of a good decision process is knowing what decisions you need to make versus what decisions can be delegated to someone else. As discussed in Chapter 1, "Self-Management," you should push as much decision authority to lower levels as you can, reserving your time for matters of the highest importance.

The second part of a good decision process is to make decisions in a timely fashion. Make as many decisions as you can today as opposed to tomorrow or other future date. When faced with matters needing decisions, the first thing to do is make a distinction between what you can and should get off your plate immediately, versus what requires further information, research, and thought. You do not have to be the "clean-desk man—*every* decision was made immediately"[1] that General Douglas MacArthur reportedly was, but do not postpone more than a few of your decisions until another day, because there is a brand new batch of them coming tomorrow. Decisions that you do not delegate, and cannot resolve in short order, pile up on your desk very quickly if you are not careful. Letting that happen will turn you into a bottleneck instead of a manager before long. Getting issues off your desk and onto the appropriate one may lead, counterintutively, to some occasional "last in, first out" processing.

Also, remember that with regard to time sensitive matters and crises (see *Crisis Management*, below), a good decision today is almost always better than a perfect decision next week or even tomorrow. Often you do not even have the option of delay, but must make up your mind very quickly. I can recall many occasions when I was phoned by a state budget director while he or she was in the midst of discussions with legislators regarding my department's budget. A proposal was under discussion, and I had perhaps 10 minutes to agree to a suggested path forward or offer a counterproposal. If I needed a piece of technical information that required staff input, it was difficult to convince my staffers that they did not have the time they wanted to study the issue; they had to give me the best recommendation they could offer within those 10 minutes. On occasion, I had to make a decision in the course of the phone call.

Sometimes the most important thing about a decision is simply that you have made one. What you are doing is confirming a choice someone else would like to make, but does not have the nerve to make the final call and be responsible for it.

As for the analysis, the first fundamental rule is this: get enough information to make the decision, but only enough. You have to be able to identify what the crux of the matter is. Sometimes you may not even need additional information. There is no need (and in fact it is both counterproductive and waste of time) to become an expert on the subject at hand. You are not a lawyer trying to win a case by knowing every last detail. You have experts on staff to provide you with the information you need; it is not your job to become the expert. Let the experts show you their expertise. They'll love you for it, and you will be able to use your time for more important things. Many managers unfortunately fall prey to **paralysis by analysis**, when they cannot decide things for fear that some fact or scrap of information has escaped their attention. Decide, and then turn your attention to the next issue. "I believe that most people want clarity from their boss or their manager, and they want decisiveness. So we don't need to debate something endlessly. Maybe we can talk about it more than once, maybe more than twice, if it's something really important. But let's make a decision and move on."[2] The few occasions when you will make a mistake because you missed a relevant piece of information will be vastly outweighed by the great productivity increase you will experience from making decisions quickly and moving on to make more of them.

For the more complicated matters that require additional information, assemble the individuals and information that you will need. I firmly believe that when it comes to making *major* decisions, multiple heads are better than one. Even if I have a pretty good idea where I want to go, I would like to know what others whose judgment I trust think. If I have the right information and the right people around me, I can make a good decision 95 percent of the time. Echoes one chief executive, "My philosophy of leadership is that four or five of us can come up with a much better decision than just I can alone. And if you follow that philosophy, you'll probably have a very good, talented management group around you."[3] A face-to-face meeting is better than trying to make decisions on line, by the way. My staff always understands that I am going to ask a lot of questions at such meetings. E-mails are great for transmitting information, but are insufficiently interactive for good decision making. The discussion can be 15 minutes long or you can convene a mini-charrette, but for major matters you need the in-person discussion if at all possible.

Which leads to the second fundamental rule: manage with data. Too many of your workers, and too many people in government, manage by gut feelings. And unfortunately, many of the people who do so have an overly high regard for those gut feelings. Sometimes instincts are accurate, but other times they are not. The good news, though, is that most individuals, when confronted with data, will change their approach without any urging on your part. We are living in the information age, and the oceans of data that are now available give us the opportunity to make decisions based on hard facts, not uninformed opinions. Whenever we have to make a decision on a complicated subject, I tell my troops, "facts first, decisions second." Without data, statistics, or other measurement of some sort, public policy is truly blind.[4] For a truly important matter that is not time-sensitive, the analysis and research can be an iterative process—ideally, it is.

Some governments have institutionalized managing with data, variously calling it compstat, citistat, or statestat. Initially it was used by law enforcement agencies, but a few jurisdictions have expanded it to all aspects of their operations. It is the *ne plus ultra* of data management. However, absent a major philosophical and financial commitment from your elected official, it is unlikely that you will be able to accomplish a similar institutionalization.

But that should not stop you from using the data you already have at every opportunity.

You need to ask the right questions to get the information that you require to make the best decision. Very often, if your analytical skills are good and you have the benefit of previous experience, your first impression is going to be the right one—but you still want your staff to offer their thoughts and try to punch holes in your approach. It's called a **reality check**. Remember also that when managing with data, outcomes count more than workload measures, although some pure workload measures can be outcomes: how many individuals are housed, or how many are covered by health insurance, for example. Performance measures are a must. Also, as stated in Chapter 4, trend data is more important than current data. Every program or indicator has its own context and history. Some managers inherit better performing programs than others. For this reason, almost always the better indicator of how any program is doing is what happened previously compared with what will happen in the future. My firm belief is that if you are raising a program's performance over time, you are doing a better job than someone else whose current indicators are better but static.

An example of managing with data occurred when I ran the state health department. The enrollment of the state's Children's Health Insurance Program (**CHIP**)—the **"take-up rate"** in insurance parlance—was consistently less than half of the eligible population. CHIP is a joint federal-state program for children of low-income families, and in my state it requires the payment of a premium. It was therefore generally believed that we should increase our community outreach to make more people aware of CHIP if we wanted to increase enrollment. But when we began to study the program and its data more closely, we discovered that a much higher percentage of eligible children—closer to 80 percent—were actually enrolled at one time or another in any given year. Parents were enrolling their children when they were sick, but then de-enrolling them (or simply stopped paying the premium) when they were well. It became obvious that ignorance of the program was not the problem. Parents of eligible children knew about the program, but could not consistently afford the premium and/or did not understand the concept of insurance as it applied to CHIP. Unfortunately, advocates (and some elected officials) continued to press for more outreach, even pursuing and winning a grant to run their own outreach effort. Predictably, the grant outreach had a very limited impact on enrollment. There was nothing I could do to prevent the advocates' initiative, and I never disparaged it publicly. But I could and did prevent any taxpayer money from being wasted.

Finally, when making decisions, it is wise to make every effort not to become emotionally involved with client cases or issues. Emotional involvement will probably not be a problem if you are working in, say, facilities management or transportation. But when working in human services, it is an occupational hazard. Given many of the truly heart-wrenching situations one encounters in the human needs arena, which could be the subject of an entire book all by itself, it can be a real struggle to maintain your objectivity at times. If you have any compassion at all, you probably will not have a perfect record. You never want to be cold-hearted, but to avoid paralysis, you will have to remain clear-headed.

## SOLVING PROBLEMS

As every good husband knows, when your wife comes home after a hard day and tells you about her problems with work, coworkers, or anything else, your job is to listen sympathetically, *not* try to help solve her problem. In management, it is exactly the opposite. When confronted with a problem in your organization, you don't just listen; your job is to actively manage it. Problems seldom get better or go away on their own.

The best way to solve problems is to prevent them from happening in the first place. In public administration, an ounce of prevention really is worth a pound of cure. By constantly reviewing your agency's operations and performance, you can prevent small problems from becoming big ones. The good news is that it is possible to avoid a lot of problems this way. Some of the best work you will ever do will result from nipping problems in the bud. The bad news is that you will receive no credit for any problems you successfully avoid. Nevertheless, it is certainly better to discover your own problems rather than have the press do it for you. As discussed in the next chapter, "Gaining Control of Your Organization," getting a complete compliance report when you take over the top slot can be very effective in heading off problems.

Unfortunately, you can head off a lot of problems, but you cannot avoid them completely. When confronted with a problem, the first thing to do is to adopt a positive mental attitude. Think of every problem as a challenge, because you can almost always deal with a challenge. Every challenge, in fact, is an opportunity to accomplish something. The next thing to do is, in the words of one of my favorite graduate school professors, "put a structure on the problem."

The first part of your structure is identifying the type of problem you have: simple, complicated, or complex.[5] With simple problems, generally the best way of doing something is either already known or can readily be identified; what has happened is that your employees are not using that best way. Establishing a standard procedure that encompasses the best practice will result in ending most simple problems fairly quickly, as long as everyone follows the new procedure. The keys to success are developing the correct procedure (or maybe even taking a procedure someone has already developed "off the shelf") and then ensuring universal compliance with that procedure. But with a complicated problem, there is probably not a straight-forward formula available for use. It should be possible to develop a solution, but you will need to determine what the key information is that you need, and whether that information is already available or has to be gathered. You also need to decide who are the key players who can provide information and expertise in developing the solution. And finally, you need a process for finding out what will work and then implementing it.

A complex problem is a very real one, and probably a very significant one, but also one that is probably not amenable to "solving" in the traditional sense. Poverty is a very real problem—and a complex one—but your social services department is not going to end it. Instead, your work on complex problems should be both continuous and incremental. Research should be involved. You may need to experiment and proceed by trial and error. Measurement may be difficult. You should always spend time and effort on your complex problems, and you can do a good job or a poor job dealing with them, but they are not the focus of this chapter.

Your problem-solving structure will almost never need to include a history of the problem. How the problem developed is perhaps interesting, but seldom important to the solution. One of my cabinet colleagues always wanted her staff to produce a chronology when facing a problem. Chronologies are worse than useless; they distract you from what is important. How you got to where you are may be worth a glance, but not worthy of study, because it resulted in a bad outcome: the problem state of the present. The key is to identify what is wrong and fix it. The path to here does not count; the path to get you out of here is what counts.

If wrongdoing or criminal activity was involved in creating your problem, let law enforcement search for the culprit. Your own time should be spent more productively on solving the problem and preventing it from recurring, rather than searching for someone to blame. Most problems are systems-related and not caused by a single person. As one of my former colleagues once wisely said, "Fix the problem; don't affix blame."

For certain problems, especially ones that are likely to be the subject of press attention, it is extremely important to convey a sense of urgency to everybody you have working on the matter. Sometimes it becomes a race between when you can fix the problem and when it will become public. The reason why urgency is called for is that it is vastly preferable to be able to tell the media that "we had a problem and here is how we solved it" instead of having to say, "we have a problem and we are considering how to solve it." A day, even an hour or two, can make the difference in what you are able to say. It may also make a difference in the number of times the media covers the problem.

As stated previously, an e-mail exchange is a poor way to make decisions. It is also a poor way to solve all but the most minor problems. When you get an e-mail saying, "here is a problem," your process should be to gather the appropriate staffers around a table (or initiate a conference call) to discuss it. Maybe it will be a 15-minute discussion and maybe it will be a two-hour discussion that will be only the first step in resolving the problem. Unfortunately, in today's era of pervasive e-mails and text messages, many people attempt to solve problems by sending an e-mail to a group of coworkers describing the issue, asking for a few inputs, and then deciding. Unless the matter is very simple, proceeding in this fashion misses a very important part of problem-solving: the interaction of various people who possess different information and can offer alternative perspectives. An interactive exchange in person or on the phone will not only produce better decisions, it will improve communication and help build relationships.

Of course, getting it done takes more than meetings and words. Many organizations spend an enormous amount of time talking about what needs to be done, less time discussing how to attain it, and almost no time doing anything to make it happen. To make sure that discussion flows directly into action, as discussed in Chapter 1, "Self-Management," make sure that every task or follow-up item is assigned either to a specific individual or a team headed by a specific individual, and the responsibility noted on the agenda or your meeting notes.

For any complicated problem, your fix or improvement plan will likely have immediate, medium-term, and long-term components. You will need to address any problem that has garnered outside attention (media or legislative) with at least some improvements that can be put into place quickly, while simultaneously developing other improvements. The immediate can typically include directives (for example, advising everyone that this matter is your number one priority), reprioritization (redirecting resources from other areas), and direct management of the problem area by you and your top staff. Medium term actions can include increased funding for the problem area in your next budget cycle, information technology improvements, and dealing with problem managers, who are often in the merit system and cannot be removed at will. Longer-term solutions may include culture change, facilities improvements, and reorganization.

How you interact with staff when problem solving is important. When in solution mode, closely scrutinize your local conventional wisdom, and always challenge existing assumptions. It is particularly important that you personally do this because career employees, both managers and line workers, tend to question assumptions less than they should. As discussed in "Managing Change in a Bureaucracy" in Chapter 4, never take no for an answer from your employees or managers the first or even second time you hear it. Also, sometimes staff will bring you a good solution, but they want an unacceptably lengthy time period to execute it. Should that occur, never criticize your staff—after all, they have just brought you the answer to your problem. Instead, after praising them for the solution, ask them if they can "improve the timetable" or if absolutely necessary, tell them "we need to improve the timetable." They will almost always be able to do so. Be sure to encourage your staff to bring you the strongest solutions they can identify. If the proposed solutions are too tough, you can easily soften them or water them down to meet internal or external objections, political or otherwise. But if they are too weak, it may not be so easy to strengthen possible courses of action at your level—the specific information that is needed to make alterations will probably reside at the staff level, and it will take them time to go back to the drawing board.

The difficulties that my own department experienced in managing the construction of state facilities during my time as cabinet secretary can provide a useful case study in problem solving.

Early in the administration, the Governor had centralized construction management for most of state government under my department. Due to the building boom during the prosperous economy of the late 1990s, inflation was very high in the construction industry, something the legislature was not attuned to. I commented to the Governor that the boom was good for the state's economy, good for the construction industry, good for the workers, good for everybody except state officials trying to run projects. For the first three years of my tenure, no project had come in over budget, but then over the next few years a series of projects overran their budgets.

Because of the building boom, demand outstripped the supply of quality work by architects, contractors, and construction workers. We saw quality issues emerge first in work done by architects and engineers. They were taking on a higher volume of work, but not staffing up concomitantly. Our only consolation was that for those professions, our selection process operated under the state's professional services selection law, which did not require us to use the lowest cost firm. So, if a firm did poor work, we did not have to use them again. Later we saw the problem appear with contractors. There simply were not enough skilled workers for the volume of construction that was going on. The state's vocational high schools, in fact, had vacancies in their construction trade programs.

State construction projects became increasingly plagued by quality problems, and fewer were completed in a timely fashion. The roof on a new women's prison failed a mere seven years after the facility opened. The contractor repairing the sidewalks around the Governor's House used the wrong mortar, tried to bill us for his bad work, and when we refused to pay him, sued us. On a different prison project, the contractor could not find enough masons, which delayed his work for months. Delays in the masonry work had a cascading effect, and the new prison beds opened a year late.

To a significant extent, these problems occurred because overtaxed contractors gave priority to their private work at the expense of their state work. A contractor simultaneously remodeling the legislative chambers at the state capitol and working on a local mall explained the dynamic clearly when he made the following comment to our director of facilities management. "If I don't do a good job over at the mall, they might not use me again. But the state will always be here." A given contractor might have two good crews but three jobs; the state invariably got the third-best crew. We needed to change that mindset; we either wanted a quality crew working on our job or we did not want that company working for us. Some contractors performed well when they took on a certain level of work, but got in over their heads with a higher level of activity. We were pleased when a particular contractor, whom we regarded as the local quality leader, won the bid for a new juvenile correctional facility. But he had spread himself too thin with multiple jobs. When he was doing one job at a time, as he had customarily done, his attention to detail always yielded satisfied clients. But he was by then trying to do three jobs at the same time, and could not give our project the requisite level of attention. The project endured multiple difficulties. The attitude of many of our contractors was that we worked for them, not the other way around, because we were public servants and they were the public.

State construction bid laws at the time had two major defects. First, contracts were awarded strictly to the lowest bidder. The quality of the work that had been or would be performed by the bidders played no role in determining the awards. Any system based solely on low price inevitably has large problems insuring quality work. A system emphasizing low price might save taxpayer money in the short run, but probably not in the long run. As an architect once told us, "In construction, the three things everybody wants are speed, quality, and low cost. Pick any two." In the state system in which low cost was the only criterion, usually there were problems with either timeliness or quality. In addition, construction quality is not necessarily apparent to the naked eye, and poor quality might not become apparent for 10 to 20 years. Second, the laws were unfortunately slanted towards the interests of contractors, not the owners (in our case, the state). It was tough to prevent a bad actor from bidding, tough to enforce quality provisions, and tough to enforce timelines. A series of unfavorable court decisions made things worse. For example, the state's prequalification statute stated clearly that a contractor could not sue the state to overturn a disqualification; the courts ruled that they could sue anyway. (Prequalification allows the government or other owner to determine, before the bidding process begins, which contractors have the minimum qualifications necessary to do the work.) Judges, lacking experience in construction, were often swayed by obfuscation on the part of counsel for the contractors.

The press was never helpful; they tended to report on problem projects as if the state were the cause of the difficulty, not the nonperforming contractors, or at least took at face value and printed the mumbo-jumbo excuses of contractors.

As we searched for solutions, it became obvious that there was a need for new legislation strengthening the state's hand in supervising projects. Internal staff discussions yielded a number of ideas; my instructions to staff were, first tell me what you would like to see in a perfect world, then I will tell you what we might be able to get passed by the legislature. We began discussions that involved all of the stakeholders: organized labor, the three statewide contracting associations, the Governor, and the Lieutenant Governor. One positive development was that even the contracting associations agreed that there were quality problems on state jobs. The Governor was particularly supportive due to the aforementioned problems renovating the Governor's House. In a fortuitous coincidence, one key legislator, the Senate Majority Leader, was in his day job the head of buildings and grounds for a local school district. Having regularly experienced many of the same problems that we did, he was very supportive and became our lead sponsor.

The bill contained five elements. First, contractors would now be required to use trained and/or experienced workers on state jobs. Second, the prequalification section of the state code was strengthened. Formerly, only financial wherewithal could be taken into account; now, we would be able to consider both performance on previous projects and a firm's legal record, including 1) judgments against it, 2) any track record of violations of laws, including prevailing wage laws, and 3) any fibbing on application forms themselves. Third, and most important, **best value contracting** would be allowed. In best value contracting, we would be allowed to consider, price, time, and quality—not just low bid—in making awards. Best value was not a new concept; other jurisdictions, including the federal government, already had it. Fourth, we would be granted an expanded ability to require forfeiture of **retainages**; previously we could retain them only per court decisions. Finally, for the first time, suspension and **debarment** of contractors would be allowed. We could temporarily or permanently prevent companies with poor track records from bidding on state work.

Next, we began the struggle to get the new law enacted. Notwithstanding what we felt was an obvious need for new statutory authority, prospects were far from guaranteed. Our legislature was divided, the Senate controlled by Democrats (the party of the administration), largely labor-supported, and the House controlled by Republicans, largely business/contractor supported. Organized labor strongly favored the legislation, because they (correctly) saw our push for quality as favoring those contractors for whom they work. Other things being equal, because of their training/apprenticeship programs, union labor is generally of higher quality than non-union labor. This support was helpful because legislators usually pay more attention to the views of interest groups and lobbyists than to those of the administration. (More on this subject in Chapter 11, "The Legislative Branch of Government.") The largest contractors association, composed of both union and non-union contractors, was nominally supportive, but in practice stayed neutral. The small union contracting association was supportive. The non-union contracting association participated in drafting the bill, but then withdrew its support.

The Senate passed the bill thanks in part to a compromise proposed by a senator from the party opposite of the administration, who had no connections with organized labor. He did it for no apparent reason other than that it was, in his view, the right thing to do. His compromise was to drop the "quality" component from the best value construction provision, reasoning that it was viewed by many stakeholders as too subjective. For our part, we were delighted to give way on that provision in return for getting everything else. In passing the bill, we overcame heavy opposition from a coterie of bad actors on state projects. Observing their vociferous efforts against our bill, I was forced to conclude that some companies *wanted* to do lousy work and get paid for it!

Action shifted to the House. The non-union contracting association tried to block the bill in the Republican controlled chamber, but eventually the Republican leadership told them that they were in an untenable position. We helped things along by letting everybody know that we were going to begin parading our problem projects in the media at the rate of one a week until they said uncle, publicizing the flip-flop of that association in the bargain. In return for the leadership's agreement to move the bill forward, we agreed to a **"fig leaf compromise"** of the type described in "Negotiations", below. It was a terrific conclusion.

The new law was a major success, in our department's view. It did not fix the industry-wide problem of demand exceeding supply, but it did enable us to do a better job of seeing that taxpayers got their money's worth. Its first and most successful use was on a new $130 million courthouse. The expanded prequalification provisions in the new law resulted in 20 percent of the prospective bidders being disqualified (mostly they were non-union firms). Equally important, uncounted others stopped submitting bids, understanding that they stood no chance of being awarded work. We saw a lot less of the "usual suspects"—the perennial bad actors—at our prebid meetings. The best value provision did not immediately result in awards to other than the lowest bidder, but did help the department validate work schedules. In a few cases the losing contractors saw that they could have won by shaving a few days off the schedule. The new law was no more costly than the old one, as all remaining bids during my tenure came in at or under budget. Another success was what we referred to as "Senate Bill 204 letters"—communications to nonperforming and slow performing contractors. Sending them letters reminding them that Senate Bill 204, the Quality Construction Act, allows the state to suspend or permanently debar contractors from future state work produced a very good response. The new law was successful enough that subsequent administrations and legislatures have never given a thought to repealing it.

## NEGOTIATIONS

Negotiations are a special kind of decision making and problem solving exercise rolled into one. Negotiations occur regularly in your department, below your level, but on occasion there will be matters in which you will lead the negotiations yourself, because of their monetary value and/or policy importance.

When negotiating items of major importance, whether labor agreements, contracts worth large sums of money, or other major issues, the most important part of the negotiations is what you do before you sit down around the table with your opposite number(s). Do your homework thoroughly before you enter the negotiating room. You need to do four things:

1. identify the team that you want with you on the negotiations,
2. get the ground rules, if any, from your chief executive and any other administration official who has a say in the final outcome,
3. assemble all the numbers and/or other background information you need, and then
4. determine your goals and the strategy for accomplishing them.

Usually you will need three or possibly four types of people on your team. Depending on the nature and complexity of what is being negotiated, one person of each type may suffice, or you may require more than one individual. First, you want a leadership/big picture person, who will customarily be the director of the operating division under which the matter being negotiated falls. Second, if money is involved, you need a numbers cruncher who can cost out various items that will be under discussion. Third, one or more technical people should be on hand to advise you on the details of proposals. There are nuances to many proposals and you need to have someone who can explain them. Fourth, you may also want a lawyer present if the legal language is key to the problem. Sometimes, counsel need not be present because the language of the contract is more **boilerplate** than substantive.

When the time comes to negotiate contracts, the bigger they are, the more you need to have clear guidance from your governor or county executive, her chief of staff, or the budget director, whoever has a say in the matter. Sometimes, you will be given complete autonomy. If not, you will need to be clear on everyone's roles and ground rules, because the first thing the vendor is likely to do is try to end run you. The vendor and/or his lobbyist will try to call and/or meet with all the other people they believe to be players, including legislators. These end runs are not necessarily nefarious; they may occur at least partly because your opposite numbers want to be sure that they are negotiating with the individual who has the final decision. Even if you are the one in the room when the negotiations begin, it is not always clear in government whether you are the person who has the final say. If it is not you, or if you are only one of several people with a vote, they understandably want to make their case directly to whomever it is. By the way, the same goes for you. *Your* first rule of negotiations is to make sure you are negotiating with the individual(s) who have the final say. Avoid negotiating with anyone who has to "take it back to headquarters." Get the decision maker in front of you. I once made the mistake of conducting a lengthy negotiation with an administrator, thinking that he was acting with the proper authority. He was not; his council rejected our deal. I wasted a fair amount of my time; I should have been negotiating with them, not him.

Should a governor wish to conduct a major negotiation herself, that is certainly her prerogative; most chief executives have neither the time nor the inclination to do so. If the governor wants to deputize a different member of her administration to conduct the negotiations instead of you, or make such an individual or individuals part of the negotiating team, that is okay too, although you are likely to believe that they cannot do a better job than you and your staff because they do not have the depth of knowledge that you do. And you will most likely be correct in your opinion. What is not a workable approach is for another member of your administration to claim final approval of a deal when he does not possess it, or be ambiguous about his role. You have been undermined, and you will never be able to get the best deal out of that vendor. The vendor will take the best he can get out of you and run to the other official to improve upon it. Even worse is if (as happened to me once) another administration official directs you to remove your designated negotiator because of complaints from the vendor—which complaints have no other meaning than that they are not getting the terms they want. That official might as well have conducted the negotiations himself from that point forward.

I always requested that anyone in the administration whom I thought might be the recipient of those end-run calls to do the following: meet with them if you want to, take or return all their calls, talk as long as you want, say anything else you want to, as long as you end the conversation with the words, "Vince has the final say." One thing you do want from others, though, is any guidelines the administration wants you to operate under. If the budget director needs to set a guaranteed maximum price that you can pay, that is essential information and you can negotiate accordingly. If the executive office or other parties need to have a contract of specific duration, or certain codicils added, you can work with that. But you need that information up front, not in the middle of the negotiations, let alone after you have reached agreement.

By the same token, if you are delegating the responsibility for negotiations to someone else, tell her clearly what the parameters are, if any, before the negotiations begin. Then, having given her the final word on the matter, never second-guess the deal (or any aspect of the deal) that she has reached, as long as she comes back within those parameters.

It is important to have the ability to quantify proposals in short order when you are negotiating monetary matters. Again, advance preparation is required to cost out any affirmative proposals you will present, plus as many of the likely negotiating scenarios as you can imagine. One numbers cruncher with whom I worked designed some special software to quickly do so for a giant contract we were negotiating. Needless to say, he eventually went on to bigger and better things.

When determining your negotiating strategy, the fundamental thing that you need to understand is how much **leverage** you have and the other side has. Does either side—or both sides—have the ability to walk away from the negotiating table if they cannot reach a satisfactory agreement, or is this contract or agreement something that they must have? If you are negotiating with a current or prospective vendor, do you have the ability to switch to an alternate vendor? Has your boss directed you to reach agreement no matter what (or more problematic, announced an agreement before the details are worked out)? In the latter case, a savvy party on the other side of the table will be able to extract a far better deal from you because he knows you do not have the ability to step away from the table if the terms are not to your liking.

The answers to these questions will determine how aggressive you can be in negotiations. It will seldom be possible to negotiate tough when you do not hold any cards. Bluffing may work in poker, but it will not succeed in negotiations if at the end of the day you have no choice but to get a deal done. Never under any circumstances make a threat during negotiations that you cannot back up. As stated in Chapter 2, you should always do what you say you will do. If you bluff and your bluff is called, there will be negative consequences for you, not just in the instant negotiation, but in your future dealings with this party and other parties. You have been exposed as unreliable, and that is never a label you want attached to yourself.

When you are short of leverage, you can try acting like the other side does not hold all the cards, but it will almost never work. Other parties usually know all too well that they are in a strong bargaining position.

Assuming that there is **symmetric power** at the negotiating table, and that the opposite party has a genuine desire to reach an agreement, the next thing to try and determine is what the other side *has* to have in a final deal. Keep in mind that what they have to have may very well be different from what they want, or at variance even with their stated position. It may not be easy to determine what they have to have. You will have to listen very closely to what the other party says (and does not say) at the table, and perhaps also develop some intelligence through back channels. If you can figure out what the other side must have, though, your strategy should be aimed at reaching an agreement that includes both what they have to have and what you want and need. The path to a successful conclusion can be much shorter in that case. Obey the maxim of one of the best negotiators I have ever dealt with: the deal always has to be good for both sides.

When setting up the negotiating sessions, make sure that there are two rooms available, a larger room to accommodate both sides, and a smaller room that will hold one side, so that the parties can split up and discuss matters privately amongst themselves.

If the other side is amenable, a press blackout is the best way to proceed. But even if the other side is not amenable, never negotiate in the media. Until the agreement has been reached, say as little as you can get away with, other than expressing optimism that a satisfactory conclusion will be reached. Save your public commentary for after the completion of the negotiations.

Your demeanor and that of your team in the actual negotiating sessions is important. No matter how contentious the sessions are, try to keep the tone as light as possible. Casual conversation and a sense of humor are in order before the sessions start, during the sessions, and during breaks. Regardless of how aggressive the other side's positions are, no matter how aggrieved their tone is when presenting them, do not respond in kind. Never negatively characterize the other side's maneuvers and proposals, no matter how unreasonable they are. Instead, when you cannot agree to something, simply say so and say why, in a neutral tone of voice. It always surprises me—but it should not surprise you—how often supposedly hard headed, rational people negotiate emotionally and not intellectually. Yet it is a plain fact that whenever you respond emotionally to the other side's expression of emotion, it increases the likelihood that the opposition will escalate their emotional responses, rather than reexamine them. Always think of the opposite side as your worthy opponents, never your enemies. It may not be easy to adopt studied indifference if your opponents are employing negative, even inflammatory rhetoric in the negotiating sessions or when communicating with the media, but you have to do so.

You may also find, especially when dealing with private sector companies, that they frequently underestimate you, at least initially. Perhaps they underestimate us because they have the customarily biased assumptions about the intellect of anybody working for the government. As they trot out really transparent ploys or ridiculous negotiating positions, it can be incredibly annoying as you wonder, "Do they really think we are that dumb?" But you can never let your annoyance show. Sometimes it can be amusing to see the disappointment on their faces as their ploys fall flat.

Tactically, you need to be very clear from the start of the negotiations that *nothing is agreed to until everything is agreed to*. This simple rule will save you a lot of headaches. Unless you adopt it, the other side may well try to get you to agree on certain aspects of their proposal, decline to agree outright to any aspects of yours, then "compromise" on everything else. Obviously, if they successfully employ this tactic, they will be able to conclude the bargaining much closer to what they want than to what you want. It also prevents another common trick—getting you to agree to a final deal, then trying to add "just one more thing," and that thing may be quite significant. They can keep asking for things, but if they do, you can, too.

There is another tactic that you should religiously employ. When the other side offers a proposal or states a position, listen politely and then ask any questions you or the other members of your team may have. Never offer feedback to the other side or engage in conversation amongst yourselves with the other side present. Save both of those things for when you retire to determine your response. Once you have prepared your response, you or another member of your team can state it when you are back in joint session. I had one employee who simply could not avoid reacting to whatever the other side said, in front of them, agreeing or disagreeing without discussing things with anyone else and without the authority to speak for our side. When counseling failed to correct her behavior, I had to remove her from the negotiations, even though she possessed a wealth of technical knowledge.

No matter how successful you eventually are in the negotiations, remember that you usually will have two goals: reaching an agreement on terms that are as favorable to your department as possible, but also living to fight another day. Most negotiations are not one-offs; contracts and labor negotiations will usually come around again before long. The more you have "won" in a negotiation, the less you should broadcast your triumph. Never deprive your opposite number of dignity and face. In fact, is there any way to offer the other side a "fig leaf compromise"—in other words, a surrender to you that has the appearance of meeting in the middle? If you are getting 90-95 percent of what you want, do not begrudge giving the other side their 5-10 percent.

Fig-leaf compromises can reach ritualistic heights. First, the other side capitulates. Of course, they will signal to you privately that they are doing so, so that you can play your part in the Kabuki dance. The meeting is called, and the two sides engage in what is virtually a **colloquy**. First, the losing side will complain for 15 minutes or so about everything that is wrong, but then, because they are civic-minded, good citizens, propose a "compromise" in which you get almost all of what you want. Your job is to reply, with a straight face, that you can live with it in the spirit of compromise. All parties then announce this "good faith compromise" to the press, public, and legislature. You cannot say that 1) you won, 2) they surrendered, or especially, 3) you kicked their butts. This process can work extremely well if both sides are willing to play. Remember that there is almost always another negotiation, when the shoe may be on the other foot.

Some entities like to reach agreement, shake hands, have legal documents prepared, and then tell you that they want something else. There are two schools of thought on how to approach this development. One is that you should never agree to any such changes, once an agreement has been reached, unless you can get something in return; this approach may be necessary in a very contentious environment, or if the other side makes a habit of it. The other is to allow the change if it is more technical than substantive. You will have to decide which approach is best if and when it happens.

## CRISIS MANAGEMENT

The worst kind of problem to deal with is, of course, the crisis. You are virtually guaranteed to face one if your stay as a department head lasts more than a couple of years. There are things you can do to prevent problems from arising, but in the end, "It is impossible for any public manager to prevent all wrongdoing, incompetence, or fiscal irresponsibility."[6] Eventually, some of that wrongdoing, incompetence, fiscal irresponsibility or other unforeseen event is going to put you and your agency in a crisis mode. And no matter how far beneath you in the organization that misfeasance, malfeasance, or nonfeasance occurred, as head of the organization, you own it.

When you are experiencing a crisis, you have one overarching goal. Logic might suggest that your first priority is to fix the problem that caused the crisis. You certainly do have to address the problem, but that is not your first priority. Nor is your goal is to avoid negative press, legislative criticism, or an unfavorable regulatory finding, even a sanction or penalty, not that they aren't all messes. You cannot prevent any of them; you may not even be able to prevent all of them from occurring consecutively or even simultaneously. Instead, your primary goal is to avoid having a garden variety crisis degenerate into what I am going to call a **hypercrisis**. A hypercrisis is the worst case scenario of a (pick your imagery) witches' brew, perfect storm, or death spiral in which media, legislative, regulatory, and possibly even law enforcement criticism and investigations become so intense, and feed on and reinforce each other so much, that the whole thing achieves critical mass and explodes. When you are in a hypercrisis, bad news just follows in a cascade. The media will not be covering you, or even criticizing you. They will simply be attacking you.

This kind of disaster does not happen often, but if it does, you will be in a situation, one of the few there are, which is truly and completely unmanageable. If it happens, you are playing a rigged game; you cannot win. In addition to calling for your head, outsiders will be driving your agenda and wrecking morale in your agency to boot; recruiting new personnel to join the agency under fire will become difficult precisely at a time when you might most need fresh blood. You are in for some nightmarish months, or even a year or two, and that is if you survive. Improperly handling a crisis that spirals into a media/investigative feeding frenzy can be a career ender, or at least a tenure-ender. Unfortunately, even handling it properly can yield the same result. "Many an official's public career has been halted, sometimes very unfairly, by the media's characterization of the official's views or decisions. While clean hands are obviously the best defense, they are many times not enough; the reach of the media is just too great."[7]

The good news is that:

1. there are things you can do to limit the number of crises you face,
2. not every crisis turns into a hypercrisis, and
3. while there is little you can do once that critical mass has been reached, there is a lot you can do to prevent it from reaching that point.

As discussed in previous sections, proactive reviews of your agency's operations will prevent many problems from turning into crises. There is no magic formula, just a lot hard work and remembering to spend time on what is truly important.

One additional thing you can and should do to reduce the likelihood of entering crisis mode is to pay close attention to regulators who have responsibility for any part of your agency's operations. Treat them as if they are important, because not only are they important, they know they are. When they want to meet with you, you should jump at the chance to tell them how important their work is, and how important you think the problems they have pointed out are. Unlike auditors (see Chapter 12), regulators almost always point out legitimate issues that need to be addressed. Never give them a reason to focus on you; they cannot be everywhere, and so they go where they think the biggest problems are. Federal regulators, especially, will be wary if they see a pattern of non-compliance or "yo-yo compliance," and will likely place you in the bull's-eye. Let them form the opinion, correctly, that the biggest problems are not in your shop.

The first thing to do as a leader in a crisis is to remain calm. It is awfully easy to lose your **emotional intelligence** when you are under attack. It will be difficult to do given the enormous pressure that you will be under, but you must do it. If you are calm, it is likely that others will be, too. If you are hysterical, others will be, too. Everybody will take their cues from you, so be the voice of reason. Your job will be to reassure subordinates when they are losing their cool. While maintaining your calm, always try to retain your sense of humor—another difficult trick.

At the same time as you are projecting calm, you also need to 1) assume direct control of the situation and 2) instill in everyone a sense of urgency about the problems you are facing. No matter how able the staffers are who are running the part of your department that is under fire, you need to involve yourself directly in everything that is going on. Here is one of the few occasions when micromanagement may be called for. Getting your organization to feel a sense of urgency about the problem may be more difficult than you might assume. Many individuals in the organization under fire will be very slow to appreciate what is going on, and thus not understand the need for urgency. Eventually most will catch on, but your response cannot wait for universal comprehension of the situation to unfold on its own. Not just the unit's top management, but everyone, including the rank and file employees, needs to understand that time is of the essence as you try to remedy the problem(s) and avoid the worst case scenario described above. Sometimes a day makes a huge difference; sometimes even an hour makes a big difference in how effectively you are able to respond to a new development. As mentioned in "Making Decisions", above, in a crisis environment, a good decision or improvement today is vastly superior to a perfect one next week.

When people in leadership positions during a crisis want to resign, politely walk them to the door and wish them well; never try to talk them out of quitting, no matter how good a job you think they are doing. You do not want them in the post any longer than necessary because they are not emotionally equipped for the crisis environment they have been thrust into. Wanting to leave does not make them bad employees by any stretch of the imagination, just the wrong ones for the current circumstances. Few people get into government, or even take leadership positions in government, expecting to face crises, and even fewer have any experience in dealing with them. As for you, never quit in the middle of a crisis. Doing so would, at a minimum, be abandoning your team during the middle of the game. Just as you would do in any other part of your life—when life knocks you down, there is one and only one possible response: get back up off the floor and get on with it. You may sometimes be down, but never out.

As for actual remedies, in fixing the problem that caused the crisis, you will not have 15 different options available to you. Virtually everything you might do to improve your situation will fall into one of only three general categories, not mutually exclusive. First, you can change top managers. This approach is perhaps the most obvious, and the one the media, bloggers, and your political opponents may most want to see, but it may or may not be warranted. Even if it is warranted, the trick is usually to be surgical. Do not clean house unless it is truly necessary. The most likely scenario in which cleaning house would help is if the problem is partly or wholly related to the organization's culture. (The current Veterans Administration hospital problems are obviously at least partly cultural in nature.) Due to merit system protections, cleaning house is seldom an option in any event.

Second, you can provide additional resources. If you have internal funds that are available, now is obviously the time to deploy them. You may also be provided with additional funds from the governor or legislature. There is only ever one benefit from being in a crisis, and being the recipient of additional resources is it. Third, you can make management changes in procedures, training, and/or oversight. Almost always, management changes can help, even if they do not completely solve the problem. Once in a while, only more money will do the job, but not often. Generally, you should try improving management before making other changes. If you are dealing only with civil service employees, and if more resources just are not in the cards, this approach may be the only one available to you.

Take a flexible approach to management improvements. Most crises come from out of left field. The odds are you were dealing with other issues and this one hit you cold, or else you would have been working on it already. Plus, plans can be overtaken by events as the crisis unfolds. Also, make sure you are getting reliable information and seeing things for yourself. It is not always easy to get accurate information, as other managers were likely caught unawares, too. Now is the time, if you were not already doing it, to get information from throughout your ranks, not just the supervisory level. You may have to resort to doing some of your own detective work in a crisis—you have to know the full extent of the problem on your hands. Ask a lot of pointed questions; make announced and unannounced visits. But your investigation and your time should focus on what is going on now, not how things got the way they are. At a national association meeting, I was disappointed to hear a presentation from a counterpart in another state, who went into great detail about how she personally took charge of the investigation into the origins of the crisis her department was experiencing. She had nothing to say about improvements she was trying to make that would avoid a recurrence of the problem; it was all looking backward, not forward. It did not surprise me when she did not survive her particular crisis.

The standard rules of management, as described in Chapter 5, "Prioritization," and Chapter 4's "Managing Change in a Bureaucracy," among others, apply doubly during a crisis. Prioritization is vital, because time is of the essence and you need to complete improvements as rapidly as possible. Better to have some improvements done right away than twice as many done months from now. You will also need to work hard to overcome bureaucratic inertia by not taking no for an answer. There is a staggering amount of inertia in government. As stated previously, when you ask if something can be changed or improved, and someone tells you no, never accept that response at face value. Only by pushing do changes get made.

During a crisis, you will undoubtedly find out 1) what your boss really thinks of you, and 2) how he feels about concepts like loyalty and scapegoating. The chief executive is likely to want to wade in personally (just as you do), but also likely to want you to intercept the flak; these two attitudes, while not mutually exclusive, are difficult to balance. But whatever the executive's level of loyalty to you, he wants the problem to disappear, for several reasons. First, he genuinely wants the problem fixed. Second, any crisis does him political damage to a greater or lesser extent. And third, it is a distraction from the things he wants to accomplish. He cannot talk about the progress he wants to make or is making in a policy area X when all the media wants to do is focus on the crisis area. It will not matter how important policy area X is to the chief executive himself or even the general public; the press has a way of concentrating on what *they* want to.

Assuming that the chief does not fire you, he may want a symbolic firing of someone else in your organization. If you are not in agreement that someone deserves to be fired, you will have to consider whether to resign on principle. I have never been asked to remove someone who did not deserve it, but it does happen; I have fired plenty of people, but only for legitimate reasons.

Your chief executive may also feel that, for political reasons, he must convene his own outside investigative panel to look into your operation. Make no mistake, any time your agency has to be examined by outsiders, it is a negative public statement about your organization, even if an unavoidable one. A governor or mayor establishing his own investigation may or may not solve the administration's political problem, but it will not head off other investigations (see below). It may even be used by the media and the legislature as an additional cudgel to beat you with. It is also likely to end up being no more objective than other, outside, investigations. Individuals named to the panel, whether friend, neutral, or foe, are under both external and self-generated pressure to develop negative findings. If everyone else is criticizing your department, it is very unlikely that this body will do anything except the same. But if one is convened, you have no choice but to cooperate, and then take your lumps when the report is issued.

Outside investigations are even worse. There are two problems. First, there is the political nature of many of them. "Investigations with their media attraction are likely to be politically rather than substantively oriented."[8] Outsiders have the motive—and the investigation provides the opportunity— to find things wrong. The second problem is identical to that of your own administration's review panel. Special investigations, once created, will find things wrong—they need to, to justify themselves. For this reason, the conclusions are foregone as soon as the investigation is announced. After all,

"Given enough time and enough people, almost anybody can find something wrong in any public agency."[9] No matter if the investigating body cannot find proof or evidence of what they were originally convened to investigate, they will simply shift their focus to examine something else. Also, investigations often find that there are no standard procedures for dealing with the specific situation that just occurred. The lack of standard procedures will be taken as a significant indicator that things are out of control at your agency. In fact, though, your department (like departments everywhere) very likely has rules for things that recur, the repetitive actions and situations. No one has rules for things that occur occasionally or rarely—that is what managerial judgment is for. But the media, auditors, and legislators will demand to know why no formalized procedure was ever created. And no one will believe anything contrary to what is contained in the report, because it fits everyone's worst stereotype of government.

Your daily dealings with the media are covered in Chapter 11. All of the rules covered in that chapter apply here, plus there are some additional ones.

As stated above, your overall goal in managing a crisis is to avoid having all the criticism and investigations achieve critical mass. In dealing with the media, primarily you want to have the media not contribute to that intensification, to the extent that it's possible. Secondarily, you want to avoid having the media **"frame"** you and/or your organization. The media frequently establishes a frame of reference for individuals, organizations, and situations that they cover. A very prominent example was the media's tendency, during the 2000 presidential campaign, to characterize the election as a contest between Al Gore's untrustworthiness and George Bush's lack of knowledge. Neither portrayal was accurate, but the ultimate truth or fairness of those characterizations was irrelevant; once they were established, much of the media tended to fit subsequent stories within those characterizations or frames.[10] The media tend to adopt and then keep frames both because they make reporting easier and because, to a greater or lesser extent, they believe them. The problem with frames is that, once established, they are practically permanent. Unless you are a celebrity or an individual of independent means, and public managers are neither, you have no way of jettisoning a frame. So you have to avoid having the media frame you and/or your organization as, say, incompetent, uncaring, dishonest, out of touch, or all of the above.

One thing to understand about the media and crises is that some things get labeled by the media as crises even though they are not, by objective standards, actually crises. Alternatively, a crisis may be generated by the confluence of the media and your political opposition. For example, although the Ebola virus is certainly something to be taken with the utmost seriousness, it is hard to attach the label crisis to something that has resulted (as of this writing) in 12 reported cases and one fatality in the United States. Even in Africa, Ebola ranks well down the list of leading causes of death. Nonetheless, no matter how inaccurate the label, such situations become de facto crises anyway and you have to deal with them accordingly.

The first standard rule in dealing with the media is never to lie or mislead them. As with much else that you should not do as an agency head, not only is it wrong, you will not get away with it. The second rule is that, to the extent you know exactly what your situation is, you should announce it to the media yourself. "Get all the facts out, good and bad, often, and in context." [11] It is a basic rule of damage control to put out all the facts, not just the ones that help your argument. There are three reasons to follow the second rule. First, it's a certainty that everything is going to come out anyway. Second, if you can get all the bad news out at once, the story has nowhere to go. Of course, it may not be possible to reveal everything, because in the initial stages of a crisis, you yourself may not be privy to all the information. You may therefore have to do some of your own investigating, as discussed above. Third, when dealing with the media (and this applies just as much in non-crisis situations as in crises), you have to place things in context for them. Releasing information yourself allows you to provide the context right alongside the facts. For example, if a program of yours has a 50 percent success rate, the context might be that last year your success rate was 25 percent. Maybe 50 percent remains too low, but you are making a lot of progress. Unfortunately, the media may not be interested in the context if it interferes with their chosen story line, but you still have to provide it.

The third rule is that the statement, "Everybody does it," even if completely accurate, never works as a defense. No one believes it, and no one cares.

Additional basic rules of damage control include the following:

1. do not put anything out to the press without reviewing it and trying to anticipate the questions the media will be asking,
2. if you make a mistake and can correct it early, do so,
3. denying the obvious never works—it just motivates the press to prove you wrong, and
4. you cannot change facts, so use them as friends, not enemies. [12]

The very first media story about your crisis is extremely important, for three reasons. First, it sets the tone for future coverage. Second, it will be repeated and rehashed by the original media outlet, picked up by other outlets, and copied on line by media aggregators. It will greatly contribute to establishing a negative frame for your organization that you very much want to avoid. If the story will have a negative slant, as they almost always do, what facts and context can you supply to ameliorate that slant? The press, lacking specific knowledge or background regarding just about everything you do, is very susceptible to negative spin supplied by a political rival, a disgruntled em-

ployee, or an unhappy constituent. You must counteract that spin by supplying context. In damage control, the press is overwhelmingly ignorant of facts,
details, and information—just like the general public. Third, you want to get
as much of the bad stuff in the initial story as possible. "If you let the story
dribble out in pieces...there'll be ten bad stories, each half right and incom-
plete, rather than one bad story." [13]

You should provide good spin—"surrounding bad facts with context,
with good facts (if there are any), and, if possible, with a credible, favorable
(or less damaging) interpretation of those facts." [14] You should never provide
bad spin—pretending that bad news does not exist or trying to turn it into
good news.

Unfortunately, following these rules is no guarantee that you will receive
fair coverage. Press/media headlines and lead paragraphs, if not the entire
article, will always favor the attacker (whoever he may be). Maybe your side
of things will be covered further down in the article. But be under no illusion
that you will emerge unscathed. You may be reported on by "a scandal-press
corps that focuses more on innuendo than on substance and the facts." [15]

At the same time as you are undergoing media scrutiny, you may also be
subjected to public hearings. Investigative hearings convened by the legislature are also a no-win situation for you. Your friends do not conduct such
hearings—they would not hold them if they were your friends, and if they did
hold them they would not be your friends. You might have allies sitting on a
panel and trying to help, but there is a very limited amount they are willing or
able to do. These panels are convened at best by neutral parties, and much
more likely by your adversaries, even your enemies. It seems that during a
crisis, your enemies will come out of the woodwork. In one extreme case, a
legislative hearing on my agency was convened and conducted by an individual whom I had demoted years before when he was working for me. He had
no committee chairmanship or even committee membership that warranted
an investigation, nor had he displayed any previous interest in the agency
under investigation. As with most politicians, however, he did have a long
memory. The best I could do was make sure that all of my friends and neutral
parties knew of our history. It made his "when did you stop beating your
wife" questions somewhat less credible in their eyes. In the words of another
legislator, letting your allies know of such personality conflicts that go beyond policy disagreements "devalues these types of oppositional moments."
That knowledge did not, however, alter any press coverage, even when he
made a complete fool of himself at one of the hearings. The fact that I had
once demoted the legislator was never mentioned in print; the press knew of
it, but that fact did not fit their narrative.

Just about everybody who has a multi-year tenure gets his turn in the
dunking stool at some point, and you will have yours. As with any legislative
hearing (see Chapter 10 for further detail), the only sensible approach is to

prepare carefully. "Legislative investigations are war; you have to organize your defense."[16] Hold one or more dress rehearsals to practice your testimony and responses. At the hearings themselves, do not lose your cool or allow yourself to be baited into raising your voice. Do not act defensive or petulant, which of course is easy to say and tougher to do. If things are bad, and often they are, acknowledge the same and then go into detail on what you have done and/or what you are doing about it. This is where a sense of urgency is vital. By the time the hearings are held, you need to be able to explain in detail what actions are already being taken. It is even better if you can explain what actions have already been completed. Your response will be much stronger if you can talk about what you have already done than if you talk about what you are planning to do. But even talking about what you are going to do is far superior to having to say that you are still working on solutions.

Even if you maintain your composure, you will not emerge unscathed. As one experienced manager summarized the prospects, "The public manager is unlikely to come out of these episodes looking better than when he or she went in."[17] Investigative hearings are not searches for facts. They are **political theater**, and pretty nasty examples of it. Panelists will always have the last word. They can of course decide what questions to ask and how to ask them, and they can launch into speeches that may or may not contain questions for you to respond to. They can determine who will and will not testify, so do not expect anyone favorable to your side to be testifying. No one, in fact, will testify that your agency's services are satisfactory. Even your strongest allies and most satisfied clients generally know enough and have a sufficiently well developed sense of self-preservation so that they will not interpose themselves between you and legislators (or the media) in attack mode. And even if you do well, press coverage will emphasize the allegations and criticisms. A legislative leader attended one such hearing at which the testimony of the witnesses criticizing my agency was, shall we say, less than completely credible, but the next day's newspaper coverage did not reflect that fact. He said to me, "I must have attended a different hearing."

On top of everything else, there may be lawsuits to add to the maelstrom, but that is one the subjects of Chapter 12.

If your first goal is to avoid the crisis achieving critical mass, and your second is to fix the problem that caused the crisis, your third goal is to do all of the foregoing *and* not neglect the rest of your agency. You cannot neglect the problems elsewhere in the department and you cannot neglect the continuous improvement process.

In summary, notes one perceptive observer, "The political and journalistic focus on scandals, and the willingness of politicians to take advantage of the destructive power of that focus for their political advantage, are now deeply imbedded within the body politic.... Democrats and Republicans, journalists and lawyers, not to mention a public ready to assume the worst about politicians—have combined to produce rot, horrible rot."[18]

If at the end of your crisis, you are still in charge of your agency, and you have avoided outside governance of any kind (monitors, oversight committees, etc.) being placed on your agency, score the game as a victory for you, regardless of the media beating you might have taken.

## NOTES

1.  Manchester, *American Caesar*, 131 (emphasis added).
2.  Black interview, *New York Times* 12-19-10, Business 2.
3.  Subramaniam interview, *New York Times* 11-14-10, Business 2.
4.  Paraphrased from Deaton, *The Great Escape*, 16.
5.  Gawande, *The Checklist Manifesto*, 49.
6.  Chase and Reveal, *How to Manage in the Public Sector*, 101.
7.  Ibid., 149.
8.  Ibid., 112.
9.  Ibid., 98.
10. See Jamieson and Waldman, *The Press Effect*.
11. Davis, *Truth to Tell*, 37.
12. Ibid., 100-101.
13. Ibid., 43.
14. Ibid., 41.
15. Ibid., 205.
16. Chase and Reveal, *How to Manage in the Public Sector*, 112.
17. Ibid, 113.
18. Davis, *Truth to Tell*, 255.

## Chapter Eight

# Gaining Control of Your Organization

"Whom Do You Trust?"

### INTRODUCTION

Gaining control of your organization should be one of your top strategic goals, if not your single most important one, because you cannot accomplish any other goals you have unless and until you have accomplished that one. Do not think that just because you are head of your agency that you have control of it. Some agency heads do and some do not. The larger your organization, the more the tendency is for everybody to be doing her own thing. You never want to resemble the old joke about the man who runs the cemetery—lots of people under you, but nobody listens. If you are ascending from the ranks of your organization to the top spot, or worked there previously, you may know the lay of the land; whether gaining control will be difficult or easy will depend to some extent on the situation you inherit. This chapter primarily describes what you should do when taking over an agency without having worked there previously (something I did twice), or worked there some time ago.

Collaborative, delegated, decentralized, push-the-decisions-to-the-lowest-level-possible management should always be the order of the day in your operation, with a few exceptions. One is if your department is in crisis, which was the subject of "Crisis Management" in Chapter 7. The other occasion is when you have just assumed the reins of your agency. Gaining control of an organization calls for, *on a temporary basis*, some special techniques. Many of these techniques are contrary to what is normally sound management practice, so you should employ them only at the start of your tenure. How long you use them will depend upon how quickly you can assert the control you need. Some things you are going to speed up, and some things you are going to slow down.

The first days of your time in the job can be a tricky period. People may try to pull a fast one or two on you, test you to figure out what you know and do not know, and try to make things happen that they could not quite get done under the previous leader. Some matters presented to you for approval and described as strictly routine will be exactly that, while others will be anything but routine. Take your time; almost nothing that will be placed on your desk of this nature is urgent.

For the first few months of your tenure, you should gather the administrative apparatus of the department closely around you, including but not limited to hiring, all resource allocations (especially budgetary), and all policy decisions. Then, as you become more familiar with your environment and figure out who among your staff has good judgment and whom you can trust with certain activities, you can begin to let go. Take it in at first, but then gradually let it out. Although there may be a few land mines awaiting you, the time immediately after you start your leadership assignment can also be very fertile. It is the time to ask as many questions about everything that you can. Because you are looking at things with a fresh set of eyes, without the preconceived notions of someone who has spent many years in the agency, your observations may be very keen. This is the time when you will have some of the best insights that you will have during your entire stay in the position. It may not be the best time to make every change you want to make, but it is certainly a great time to be thinking about such changes. Conversely, as will be discussed in Chapter 9, if you are fortunate enough to enjoy a long tenure in the top job, after you have been doing it for seven or eight years, it is time to for you to think about moving on. Your observations are not as fresh; inevitably, the status quo is getting comfortable, and it is approaching the time for someone else to come in with a fresh perspective and review the decisions you have made, just as you examined everything when you came on board.

## CONTROL—WHAT IT IS AND WHO NEEDS TO KNOW

The definition of control is a simple one: the elected executive at the head of your jurisdiction (governor, mayor, county executive, or other official) is in charge, and you are her agent. There is only one agenda: your agenda, and your agenda is the mayor's agenda. Why does the mayor set the agenda? For a very simple reason: we live in a democracy and in a democracy, elections are held to decide who our leaders are. The charter or constitution of your jurisdiction clearly spells out who is head of the executive branch, and it is the mayor, not any employee of your agency, no matter how knowledgeable he may be. If there is any doubt about the absolute veracity of either one of the first two sentences of this paragraph as they apply to your department, then you are not yet in complete control of your organization.

Having control of your organization emphatically does not mean that you will make every decision, avoid delegation, or micromanage your employees. Nor will you ignore the opinions, whether congruent or contrary to your own, of your staff. Nor does it mean that you will ever act contrary to the laws of your jurisdiction as they apply to your organization. It does mean that when it comes to certain personnel decisions and major policy issues, no department employee is a free agent.

Gaining control is part of the broader process of alignment—getting every employee of your organization going in the same direction, not a lot of individual directions. As discussed in previous chapters, there are a number of components to alignment, including but not limited to proper leadership, good hiring, training, streamlining and de-layering management, centralized resource allocation, and most important of all, communication. But there is a necessary element of control as well.

Why is control so important? When an organization is not under the control of its leader, one or more of the following are bound to occur:

1. rogue hiring,
2. different parts of the organization operating at cross-purposes, or even making budget and policy end runs, and
3. ignoring programmatic and management priorities of the administration.

There are two prime types of rogue hiring. One kind is any hiring of exempt ("at the pleasure of") positions without your express approval (and/or the approval of your executive's office, if she requires such approval). It is likely that your agency has a limited number of positions you can hire and fire at your discretion, so every one is very important. Very early during one of my cabinet positions, a division director called to tell me that her deputy was retiring, and named the individual whom she had told would be promoted to the deputy slot. The deputy position was exempt, and I had to tell her to rescind the appointment because it was not hers to make. (And I made clear at the initial leadership team meeting—I had not yet convened one—that all exempt appointments were mine to make.) I was sorry to have to do that to the individual who had been told he had been promoted, but on the other hand, it was a good opportunity to demonstrate who was in control. (Eventually, when I made my own choice for the job, I picked the same individual.) Later in my tenure, when deputy vacancies occurred, I often let directors pick their replacements. But I was not going to allow that flexibility until I had a better sense of who my directors were and what their capabilities were.

One of my cabinet colleagues once stated that it was the "tradition" in his department that the directors never changed when the secretary changed, or even when the administration changed. That probably explained why his department had the reputation of being one where policy was not made at the gubernatorial level or even the secretary's level, but by the program managers.

A second type of rogue hiring is the hiring or promotion of individuals in contravention of your hiring priorities. If promotions are being made strictly on seniority rather than merit, if policy experts (instead of good managers) are being hired for management positions, if the individuals doing the hiring are ignoring diversity considerations, or if they are hiring relatives and friends, you need to work with your directors and your human resources office to straighten things out. Ending these practices will be a tougher nut to crack than assuming control of exempt hiring, but no less important.

Another sign of an out of control agency is different parts operating at cross purposes to each other. There will be much less improvement unless each part of your organization operates as a team and not separately. "A major stumbling block to innovation in government is the tendency of each governmental unit to do 'its own thing,' independently of the others."[1] Separatists may even make "end runs" to the legislature or advocates. These end runs are appeals for a third party to block your governor's or your initiatives, or to advance the policy preferences of a lower rank employee. You probably cannot stop managers or line employees from making such end runs if they disagree with your decisions. But you can stop them from succeeding. If you cannot block all such end runs, or almost all, from succeeding, you do not yet have control.

Unless you have control of your organization, it will not be giving the most attention to the priorities you and your executive have identified for the department; in extreme cases, they might be ignored completely. No organization ever has sufficient resources to do everything, let alone do everything well. As discussed in Chapter 5, not everything can be a priority. If the governor has identified, say, diversity in hiring and increased customer service as his priorities, you cannot have your department make no progress in either area. If the leadership and rank and file operate at cross purposes, it is likely that progress will not be made on anyone's priorities—yours or theirs.

Who needs to know who is in control? Most important, all of your employees, management as well as rank and file, need to know that there is a new sheriff in town. But the Mayor and Mayor's Office, the legislative body, other agencies, and all the stakeholders in your department's activities need to know, too. To sum up, everybody internally and externally needs to know.

## ASSESSING YOUR ORGANIZATION

You need to gain control of your department, and quickly. Explains a former agency head, "I know you only have a certain period of time in these jobs so I didn't want to waste a single day. I wanted to get a running start and hit the ground running."[2] However, you do not want to proceed in a "Ready, fire, aim" fashion. Therefore, first assess your organization, quickly but thoroughly. If your designation by the chief executive to head a department has been made during a transition period following an election, you may be fortunate enough to have a period of time in which to research the organization of which you are going to assume command. This transition time period could be as short as a few weeks or, as is increasingly the case on the federal level, a period of months. And ideally, the assessment process is done or close to done by the time you take the reins of the agency. But in the case of a shorter time period, your assessment may overlap with your time on the job.

For your research, read everything about your new organization you can get your hands on, including as much of your agency's statutes and strategic plan (if they have one) as you can make time for. Take any previous occupants of your position for whom you have contact information to lunch, including your immediate predecessor. If they do not have any insights, they will at least empathize with you. Talk to as many stakeholders as you can. Ask them their opinion about any and all key personnel that they are familiar with. Ask them also about policy, and the following question, too: "What are the five biggest problems and challenges facing the agency?" This question should also be asked of all internal personnel you talk to. Even if you know absolutely nothing about the agency you are about to take over, you will soon discern patterns in the responses. As you digest all of these inputs, begin to mentally formulate your own strategic plan.

You should not make any personnel changes or embark on any policy initiatives until you have received your Senate or Council confirmation, if one is required. In most cases, you will not assume your position until that confirmation has taken place. In one of my cabinet assignments, however, I took the position on an acting basis and was not confirmed for a few weeks. I made no personnel or policy moves during that pre-confirmation interval. If you are placed in a similar situation, the Senate may regard any changes you make prior to their confirmation vote as extremely premature and discourteous to them. If you should have any time on the job pre-confirmation, it is ideal for assessment purposes.

If you do not have the luxury of a transition period, though, you should still get as much information from outside parties about your agency as possible, including legislators, advocates, and others, after you take office.

## GAINING CONTROL OF YOUR PERSONNEL

Once you have formally taken the reins and been confirmed, your first task should be to closely examine the list of top personnel to see which positions are vacant, and which employees serve at the pleasure of the governor or other top executive, versus which have civil service protection. (This information may have already have been provided to you during the transition period.) Your exempt positions plus your vacancies equal the universe of positions you will need to consider. Next, you need to review hiring ground rules with the Governor's Office. Does she want to make the decisions on at-will employees herself, be consulted, require final approval, have veto authority, determine the pool of applicants, be completely hands off, or delegate any of the foregoing to her chief of staff or other governor's office official? I have seen most of these operational modes. You can work with any of them, but you need to be very clear as to what they are. She also may give you either specific instructions to dismiss or retain a particular individual, or express preferences about such choices, while leaving the final say to you. She may have a particular individual in mind for one of your positions. You should obey all of her directives, and see if you can accommodate her preferences. Some of the ground rules may be a function of when in the life cycle of your boss's administration you take the reins, as discussed in Chapter 4. If your assume your post 18 months before the governor's term of office ends, you will likely have different options available to you than if you are entering at the start of an administration.

If you have been given the authority to pick most or all of your top management team, selecting your team should become your highest priority. It was job one in both of my cabinet assignments. You should make your decisions as rapidly as possible so that you can begin managing your team and moving your department forward. In my initial cabinet assignment, I spent the entire first week interviewing for every position and made all my choices at the end of that week. My second assignment was a much larger department, and I was not able to achieve that ambitious a schedule. But it was still the item that I spent the most time on until my team was in place.

If you are in a situation where you cannot change most of your top management team (in extreme cases, your jurisdiction's rules may allow no "at-will" hiring among your top ranks) evaluate your top personnel anyway, both during the assessment period and thereafter. You will be working very closely with them and need to know as much about their skills and abilities (or lack thereof) as you can. But admittedly, "It is hard to run an agency effectively if your immediate deputies are not of your own choosing."[3] They are simply not going to be as responsive if they know (or think they know) that they do not owe their job to the administration.

Why should appointing your leadership team be at or near the top of your to-do list? Change, while necessary and inevitable, is unsettling to government organizations, as discussed in "Managing Change in a Bureaucracy" in Chapter 4. Nothing is a bigger change to an agency than change in its leadership. As one high ranking veteran civil service employee likes to tell me almost every time he sees me, "Have I told you how much I hate transitions?" You can minimize the disruption by making the transition period as short as possible. Get your team in place, then get on about the business of improving your agency.

This approach is not the only possible one, of course. One of my cabinet colleagues took his first year to work on policy, and only then turned his attention to determining his team. Ultimately, though, I am convinced that picking your team should be your first order of business. There are two reasons for making it job one. First, trying to work change through individuals whom you might or might not retain cannot help but prove cumbersome. Second, if key personnel are left in limbo for an extended period of time, the uncertainty may drive them to seek employment elsewhere. You might lose a valuable asset that you would have retained.

You should also ask for an additional piece of information from your department's human resources office. Get a list of all personnel hirings, transfers, and promotions that occurred within the last six months to a year prior to your arrival. It is interesting information in any event, but what you are especially looking for is previously exempt employees who have been given merit system jobs. In other words, who used to be a political appointee who now has civil service protection? Such moves will most probably occur at the end of an administration, when it is either highly likely or a certainty that a new governor or county executive will arrive. They will occur even if the successor is of the same party as the previous occupant.

You should have a relaxed attitude about this maneuvering, for two reasons. First, there is nothing unusual or even, in my opinion, untoward about placing people in civil service jobs who were formerly political appointees, provided of course that they are qualified to do the work. I have seen it occur during every transition I have been apart of, incoming or outgoing. An elected official might act shocked—shocked!—that said hiring is occurring, but they will have to put on a good act to do so. Sometimes, the individuals hired in this manner are overqualified for their new positions; they are simply willing to trade salary for security. Second, there is nothing you can do about it anyway. If you attempt to dismiss any such employee in the merit system who is doing satisfactory work, you will likely subject yourself to a lawsuit, and likely lose it, because you will be dismissing a civil service employee for political reasons.

What you can do and should do is be aware of who these individuals are. Most of them will want to keep their heads down, do their jobs and not attract any attention, and the last thing they are going to do is throw grenades at you. But there are exceptions, of course, so be on your guard. Also, just as there may be overqualified individuals in these jobs, there may also be some who should not have gotten their positions because they do not have the ability do them adequately. Any employee in that category should be watched closely. Be aware of their probationary period, and if they truly cannot do the job they have been hired to do, then you can consider dismissing them. But make sure that the agency in charge of the employee, your human resources department, and your lawyers unanimously agree that the employee is completely unsatisfactory, and that their due process and paperwork are ironclad. As with any other employee, just being a low performer should not be grounds for dismissal (as discussed in Chapter 4 under "Problem Employees"). Given that they may try to assert that they are being fired for political reasons, you need an open and shut case.

Armed with this information, and your list of exempt employees and vacancies, and having been confirmed, it is time to pick your team.

My first decision rule is not to change competent support personnel, if any of them hold exempt positions, even your own secretary if you have one. The only exceptions would be if they display serious issues of disloyalty or incompetence, or if they were patronage hires of the opposite political party. Generally, support personnel have valuable institutional memory, and if given the opportunity, will display fierce loyalty to you and the administration.

Key leadership positions are a different story. Here there should be no presumption of retention. The most important thing that you need to do is *make it your team.* When I gave a presentation on gaining control of one's organization to my national association, I used the acronym **BIYOT**, for Bring In Your Own Team. Bringing in my own team was highly successful for me. There are many advantages to bringing in your own team, and very few disadvantages. People you bring on board are going to owe their first loyalty to you and your governor. Equally important, they will almost always bring a fresh perspective and fresh ideas to the job. (Shortly after one transition, I would go to meetings during which, if I closed my eyes and listened, it was easy to tell which employees were new to the administration and which were holdovers. The contrast between the ones who saw opportunities for change and improvement and the ones who had the mentality that "it can't be done" was very obvious.) The disadvantage is that new leaders are going to have a learning curve. But the benefits of fresh approaches outweigh the drawbacks of learning curves almost every time.

There may also be a situation or two where a section of your agency is so damaged and so in need of change that you must consider only outsiders to lead them, regardless of the competence of the incumbent(s).

To make it your team, you do not need to make change just for the sake of change. You *can* retain incumbents *if* they meet all of the criteria below.

Sometimes a fair number of your incumbents will pass the test. Sometimes few will pass. Are your incumbents tops in competence, loyal to you and your elected executive, creative, and (if occupying a management position), managerial and not just a program expert or technically competent? Apply all the considerations in hiring discussed in "Whom to Hire" and "Your Leadership Team" in Chapter 4, above all in hiring managers for managerial positions. If you make your selection between an incumbent and a non-incumbent on the basis of knowledge of the position, the incumbent will win every time. That is the last thing you should want.

In considering the incumbents, you should place them mentally in one of three categories:

1. individuals you are sure you are going to retain,
2. individuals you will consider for retention, and
3. individuals you are sure you will not retain.

It may well be that everybody is in the middle category. Next, you should bring each of them into your office, one by one, for a private meeting at which you advise them of their status. The one-on-one meeting is important even if you are retaining a person, because it is part of the process of making sure that his first loyalty is to the current secretary and the current administration. The message you are sending is that "you are being retained *because the Mayor and I have decided* to retain you." Indeed, you should say so in exactly those words: "The Mayor and I have decided to retain you." Even if you are retaining every single person, do not call a meeting of all concerned and announce to them as a group that they are all being kept. *That* message tells them that they are too good to be fired, and says nothing about the requirement that they be part of the new (your) team. For those individuals who are being allowed to compete, be very clear that they will be given fair consideration, but that other people will be interviewed as well.

For those who will not be retained, I do not believe in putting them through a process that is not genuine just to salve their feelings. As with any other dismissal (see "Your Leadership Team" in Chapter 4), treat them courteously and professionally, but do not offer a lengthy explanation. Tell them you are making a change and that there will not be room for them in the new administration. Discuss transition arrangements with them: when exactly will be their last day, whether they wish to resign or retire rather than be terminated (always offer them that opportunity if they desire it), and what, if any, opportunity they will given to compete for a different position. Again, "soft landing" considerations were discussed in Chapter 4.

As you consider the group of incumbents, whom do you trust? Is there one individual who has been on the inside in whom you have confidence? (The role could also be filled by a high ranking civil service employee.) It can be a big help to you to have a holdover—you really only need one—to advise you on the strengths and weaknesses of other department employees, to tell you some of the history of how things got to where they are, and to let you know where some of the bodies are buried.

Some incoming agency heads do not, as a matter of policy, advise any incumbents of their status, even if they have made a determination to replace them, until they can announce their replacement. They allow the process to stretch out for weeks, months, even a year or more. Proceeding in such a fashion is inappropriate because it is both inhumane and disorderly. As stated, I never hesitate to replace someone, especially when administrations change, but I am going to be up front with him if I am doing so. In addition, employees in limbo are unlikely to be candid with you if they disagree with you. You may therefore be deprived of their best advice at a time when you most need it.

With everyone's status clarified, it is time to move to the interview stage. In addition to your personal interviews, now is the time to consider the opinions of the stakeholders you interviewed during the transition. They do not have to be determining, although you should probably think twice before retaining someone who is universally panned. On the other hand, you might well be just as wary of someone who does not have a single person criticizing him. To do any job properly in public service, at some point one has to make tough decisions that people will not be happy with. Somebody who has never made anybody unhappy probably has not made very many difficult decisions.

Every top manager needs to be mindful of diversity—and I do mean every, regardless of your party or your own ethnicity. If the only African-American president this country has ever had is subject to criticism for appointing too many white males, it is hard to believe that there is anybody else who would not be. An additional advantage of hiring your team all at the same time is that it is easier to take diversity considerations into account. To maximize your flexibility, evaluate your group *as* a group, not just as individuals. It may be better to delay making final decisions on any of your personnel until you have all or almost all of them set, lest you put yourself in the position of having announced some non-diverse appointments and having to hit diversity bull's-eyes with your remaining opening(s).

Once you have made your selections, it is time for another private one-on-one meeting with incumbents who were in the "fair consideration" category. If you are retaining them, this meeting is an additional step in reminding them who is now in charge. If the incumbent is deficient in one or more areas, and you are absolutely convinced that you do not have anybody better, bring the incumbent in and advise her that you are retaining her, but that you expect improvement in areas A and B. If you are not retaining the individual, the same rules apply as discussed above and in previous chapters. A third option is available, but you should use it sparingly. You may reappoint an individual to his job, but let him them know he is continuing on a trial basis while you evaluate him further. The problem with those ground rules is that they are very awkward for the person living under them, and for you too. Most people in that situation will immediately begin searching for a new position, and the job search is going to be their focus, not doing the best at their current job. If I believe that I am eventually going to replace someone, I much prefer letting him know sooner rather than later. If you do not have a replacement ready, the incumbent can hold over if he wishes to, or you can appoint an acting director. The straightforward approach is the best one, in my view.

The quality of your appointments will go a long way toward setting the tone for your time in office. But the timing and manner of the announcements of those appointments are important, too, in signaling that you are going to be crisp and professional in going about your business. First, of course, pre-arrange with the executive office of your boss as to who will make the announcements, the executive or you. Next, carefully schedule the timing of those announcements. All of your choices, whether holdovers or newly appointed, should be instructed to tell no one except for their spouses or significant others that they got or have kept the job. On the day that you or the county executive announce the appointments, appointees can tell anyone they want to. Think carefully about who needs to be given personal notice of any new appointment (key legislators or advocates, for example). Such individuals should receive a phone call or e-mail prior to your announcement, although generally not too far in advance—the day before at most, or even earlier in the day of the announcement, provided that is logistically possible. Immediately after the public announcement, mass e-mails should go to, first, your leadership team members, and second, to the employees of the affected division, advising them of the situation. At the start of your tenure, the mass e-mails should come from you personally. It is another way of making clear that you are in control. Later on, they can come from a subordinate or even the appointee himself or herself. Finally, all unsuccessful applicants for any position being filled should be so advised prior to any public announcement.

There are two goals of this somewhat elaborate but very necessary notification process. The first is that both successful and unsuccessful aspirants get the news the way they should get the news, and from the person they should get it from, not via the grapevine, or worse, the media. The second is to maximize the benefit of any favorable publicity from appointments or reappointments.

The one aspect of timing that you cannot control, and probably should not attempt to control, is notification that an incumbent will not be retained. It is only human for such individuals to tell, at a minimum, the co-workers to whom they are closest that they will be departing. And once they tell a few employees, everyone in their bureau will quickly find out.

No matter how thorough your appointment process is, you will not make the right call every time—not every time with incumbent retention and not every time with new people you bring into the organization. The important thing is that, if you eventually determine that you have made a mistake, you move as expeditiously as possible to correct that mistake by making a change. Never adopt the attitude that you should live with a poor performer because you would be embarrassed to admit a mistake, or because you feel that you need to settle for less than top performance.

In addition to making your leadership appointments, there are a few other things you should do regarding personnel. You should do your best to visit as many worksites under your umbrella as possible, and greet as many of your employees as you can. Depending upon the size of your jurisdiction, it may not be possible. But you should try. (As an alternative, greet employees at the start of their day by shaking hands in front of worksites.) In the larger department I ran, it took me two years, but I got around to every single worksite and met every single one of my almost 5,000 employees, if they were on site the day I visited. If you are new to your agency but know any employees personally, sit down with all of them individually regardless of the level at which they serve. If there are too many, meet with a cross section of them from different levels. Ask them about the department. What do they like, what do they dislike, what would they do differently, what would their priorities be if they were in your shoes, etc. Take some notes. You can learn a great deal from even a few such meetings.

At least initially, you should slow down your agency's civil service hiring process. You should exercise your authority to give final approval to each and every hiring, in terms of both authorization to fill the position and the final hiring choice. Get a thorough briefing from your human resources folks as to what the current policies are (centralized vs. decentralized approach, final signoff of how positions are posted, how hiring plays into your budget limitations, etc.) Ask for justification for each position being filled. Check to see if current at-will employees are about to be hired into merit positions. Once you have your preferred human resources chief on board, and you have received satisfactory answers to these questions, you can loosen or abandon your restrictions. Too much of government operates on autopilot, and so you want to put manual controls on the engine for a while.

If you encounter resistance from your human resources staff—if, for example, some or all of them are process owners instead of problem solvers (as discussed in Chapter 4), use your organizational structure as a tool for achieving compliance. Depending on who the problematic individuals are and where they are organizationally located can determine whether you change your system to a centralized or decentralized one. If the personnel deployed to your component bureaus are more flexible than your central office, consider decentralized personnel operations. If, on the other hand, the main office displays more flexibility than the hinterlands, it might be advisable to centralize as much as you can.

Once you have gained control of your personnel by establishing who is in charge, then you can resume (or begin) normal management. The more of your own team you have been able to bring on board, and the more you trust them and have schooled them in your agenda, the more you can delegate authority.

## GAINING CONTROL OF YOUR AGENDA

You need to control your agenda for the same reason that you need to control your personnel. This imperative is not about your power or your ego; it is about who sets the agenda. Unless there are good reasons for checks and balances, and a truly good reason for independent actors, your agency should have a single agenda, as articulated by the elected official for whom you work. After all, in our democratic society that is why we have elections—to determine who will make the decisions. Mostly, gaining control of your agenda will follow from gaining control of your personnel. But there are some additional considerations.

The press (and the opposition party) love "independent" agencies, independent parts of agencies, and independent employees. For some reason, it is believed that these independent actors are free from political influence. In reality, they can be no less political; they simply have a different agenda. In addition, the more independent an employee or agency is, the less accountable they are to anyone—managers, elected officials, even the public itself. If the opposition party wins an election and becomes the administration, they usually lose their love for independence. As you try to push through the governor's and your agenda, you will not love independent folks either.

The best way to keep your employees "on the reservation" is to, first, make sure they have an opportunity to express their opinions to you (and to other managers), and second, clearly explain your rationale for the decisions you make. Stifling contrary voices, acting arbitrarily, and failing to articulate your reasons for taking positions will cause staff resentment; they will push back, up to and including engaging in **guerrilla government**. "Staff have figured out that if they don't like the decision a manager makes, they can go to the press, or Congress, or to an...interest group. When that happens, you've got a real big problem."[4] Chapters 4 and 7 have already identified multiple reasons to listen to your staffers, and not feel unhappy or threatened should they disagree with you. Here is another: most employees will not feel the need to secretly contact parties outside your agency if they can openly contact managers (or even better, are contacted *by* managers) inside your agency to air their views.

Most employees, in fact, will align themselves with you and the administration, provided that you communicate your goals and priorities clearly and repeatedly. And to the extent that they disagree, they may differ only to a slight degree or not at all.

As soon as you assume your new position, there is additional information you should gather. First, ask for a compliance report from each of your operating divisions. The compliance report should indicate all programs or aspects of your operation that are out of compliance with any federal, state, or local laws and regulations. Then, depending upon what you find, take appropriate action to bring your department into compliance if at all possible. Anything that is out of compliance is a future negative press clipping, legislative hearing, and/or federal/state sanction waiting to happen. Second, if possible, ask for a complete audit of your operations. If that is not an option, examine the latest comprehensive audit report for any major issues. Third, request a **backlog** report for all areas of your agency, being sure to accurately define backlog. A backlog is not just cases that are open or pending; every process has pending items. A backlog is an accumulation of cases that cannot be processed in a reasonable time frame. If $x$ cases came into the system in a month, is the number of cases completed in a month greater than, equal to, or less than $x$? If the number of cases completed in a month is consistently less than $x$, it is a sure sign of a problem. For a limited time period, you can proceed to fix the problems you uncover without being held responsible for causing them.

Again, get the ground rules specified for policy initiatives; to what degree does the executive office want to review them before you go forward? How rapidly you move on your initiatives will be at least partly dependent upon what fires you need to put out as a result of the compliance report and audit(s) you ordered and the general state of the agency you inherited.

The legislature is one of the groups of people to whom it is most important to signal that you have control of your agenda. In my first cabinet assignment, I went to my initial legislative budget hearing virtually solo (only my chief budget officer accompanied me). It occurred only a month into my tenure and I wanted to send a message both to the legislature and to my department that I was in charge. Of course, I prepared for the hearing within an inch of my life. I never did it again; subsequently, I always brought my division directors, their assistants, and many other staffers with me. That same year, I rewrote my department's entire capital budget request (with the permission of the Budget Office). Every other department was using the previous administration's request, but I wanted to put my own stamp in things right then and not wait a year.

I also established new ground rules for the department: no bills could be submitted to the legislature for introduction without my approval, and all legislative contacts had to be reported to me. It was not my intent to stop legislators from contacting my line employees, which I could not have done even had I tried, but I did want to know about such contacts. That department was small, and for that reason, I served as my own legislative liaison (I was also a former state representative). I performed the task out of necessity, but it had the added virtue of letting the legislators know that they were going to have to deal with me one way or another. Being aware of legislative concerns will also help you at budget hearing time (see Chapter 11).

As soon as you have completed your appointments, meet with every direct report, whether new to the organization or not. This is the time to go over ground rules and lay out any priorities you have developed for each section, as previously discussed in Chapter 5. If you do not have any specific ones, communicate to the director that her first priority is to keep her organization out of trouble and out of the headlines, while you focus on priorities elsewhere. After she has accomplished that, she can set her own priorities.

Finally, you should centralize your press operation. At least initially, you should review every substantive press release before it goes out. Again, once you have determined that you have confidence in your media relations staff, you can ease off that requirement. If your press office has determined that the response to a reporter's queries should come from a line agency, make sure that the employee(s) who will be doing the talking are briefed first. If the line agency took the initial call, they should not be commenting to the press until they have spoken with your communications office. More on this subject will be covered in Chapter 11.

## NOTES

1. Lawrence and Abramson, *What Government Does*, 29.
2. Ibid., 13.
3. Chase and Reveal, *How to Manage in the Public Sector*, 41.
4. O'Leary, *The Ethics of Dissent*, 93.

*Part III*

# Your Environment: Managing Externally

No matter how well your organization works internally, you do not operate in a vacuum. You have to deal with many external parties—advocates, the media, the legislature, elected officials, and others. You have to interact with all of them, sometimes all at once; you cannot specialize. Some outside parties have direct power over you and some indirect; all can either help you or hurt you. You have to deal with them when they are happy with you and when they are calling for your head. Like the rest of humanity, they may be fair or unfair, professional or unprofessional, pleasant or disagreeable, grateful or perpetually dissatisfied, broad-minded or parochial. I periodically have to remind certain aides, when they are grousing about one of the aforementioned parties, that if the only people we had to deal with were the people we liked, we would all have very easy jobs.

Interacting with multiple parties is especially challenging because you will have to make tough decisions that do not please everybody. Often, decisions you make please one party at the expense of another. Each of the outside parties has its own interests and agendas. You will be lucky if, occasionally, their priorities and yours intersect.

The four chapters of "Part III: Your Environment" cover working for and with people and organizations external to your department. Chapter 9 describes what it is like "Working for Elected Officials." Topics include "Taking and Leaving the Position," "Understanding the Boss," "Elected Officials and Management," "Helping Them Do Their Jobs," "The Executive Office Staff," and "Telling Them No." Chapter 10 covers "The Legislative Branch of Government" "Legislative Culture," "Legislative Relations," "What Legislators Want From You," "Legislative Hearings," and "Legislative Strategy." Chapter 11 deals with "The Media," with sections on "A Different Value System," "Understanding the Media," and "Media Strategy." Chapter 12, "...And More," rounds things out with a variety of other subjects, including "Interest Groups;" "Agencies That Should Always Help You—And Sometimes Do;" "Privatization, Vendors, and Contracts;" "Lawsuits;" and "A Few Last Random Thoughts."

*Chapter Nine*

# Working for Elected Officials

"They Are All Human Beings"

## INTRODUCTION

Of all the relationships external to your organization, your relationship with your boss, the elected governor, county executive, or mayor, is the most important. You need to understand that relationship, and understand why he behaves as he does. And you need to understand that if that relationship fails, no other successful relationship with parties inside or outside your agency will matter. I was privileged to enjoy an excellent relationship with each of the governors and county executive for whom I worked. They were smart, hardworking, funny, and, what I admired most about them, willing to make tough decisions. There was also mutual respect (I hope). Those positive relationships were keys to any success I had. I have a difficult time imagining how it could have worked otherwise. A cabinet counterpart of mine from another state once stunned me by saying that he had never had a one-on-one meeting with his nationally famous governor in seven years (and only three cabinet meetings). I could access my bosses any time I wanted to, although I made sure that I did not abuse the privilege.

## TAKING AND LEAVING THE POSITION

But before you understand that relationship, should you take the job working for an elected official in the first place? Not many people interested in public service are inclined to turn down the opportunity to work for a governor or a mayor. But sometimes, maybe you should. If you have previously worked for the executive who offers you a position, you probably already have a good idea of what it will be like working in the new post. If not, you owe it to yourself to look before you leap. These days, it is not hard to find out what kind of person you will be working for. Although it might seem counterintuitive, not every elected official is a people person. Not every elected official views loyalty as a two-way street. Beware of certain early warning signs. Did the job description change between the interview and your first day on the job? Does the official act as critic-in-chief? Does he or she like to identify scapegoats and throw people under the bus? Does he or she use staff for personal errands? Constant turnover in top staff almost always indicates an individual who is difficult to work for.

Another pre-employment consideration is that you have a responsibility to be candid with anyone you work for, even if it means disagreeing with them, just as your staff should always be the same with you (see "How to Manage Your Employees" in Chapter 4). With every elected official I work for, I let them know before taking the job—if they do not know it about me already—that I am always going to tell them what I think. If what I think is critical of a contemplated action of theirs, so be it. (Of course, once the final decision has been made, it is my job to execute, not continue to argue the point.) You should have a similar understanding with your executive before you take the job.

Never be deterred from taking over an organization that is not doing well or is in crisis. (In the words of Chicago Mayor Rahm Emanuel, "You never want a serious crisis to go to waste.")[1] When your prospective agency is at the bottom, there is usually nowhere to go but up! Sometimes, that is the best time to assume a leadership position. The barriers to needed change, both internal and external, may be at their lowest during a crisis.

Deciding how long to stay and when to leave your job is one of the more important decisions you will have to make. How long you hold office may, of course, be limited by the electoral cycles of your jurisdiction. If you take office with two years remaining in the final term of a term-limited governor, you should not be surprised if that is exactly how long you remain in office. Every elected executive has the right to install his or her own team upon election, as they should. Do not be surprised, and do not take it personally, if the new governor has someone else in mind—even if the new Governor is of the same political party as her predecessor.

But if you have any say in the matter, avoid a short-term stay. You cannot make your organization into a continuously improving one if you do not supply some continuity yourself. Apparently the average stay in federally appointed positions is 18 months to two years. (Some of this rapid turnover is undoubtedly the result of non-managerial types being appointed to managerial positions and realizing or being told that they are ill-suited for their posts.) You need a longer tenure than that to improve an organization. "It's hard to turn the Queen Mary on a dime....the larger the organization is, the longer it will take to transform the... culture and the leadership."[2] At a minimum, if you have the opportunity, you should stay in an organization's top position for four years to make an impact and see your changes through. Some things, like reorganizations, modifications to the laws governing your agency, structural reform, and culture change, need time to be accomplished—and then you will want at least some time to take advantage of improvements after you have made them. A longer time on the job will also allow you to make a series of incremental improvements rather than having to try for a big change all at once. Implementing a series of small changes is almost always easier to accomplish than one big change, but you may get just as far if not farther in the end with the former approach.

Equally important, if at all possible you do not want your employees to have the impression that you will be leaving soon. They are all too aware that you are appointed, while they enjoy civil service protection. As a change in administration nears, those employees who are not aligned with your goals may begin to adopt the mindset that they should await your departure rather than cooperate with your initiatives. You cannot avoid some of your personnel from following that inclination, but you can minimize their number with a lengthier tenure.

I tend to view with disdain those individuals who voluntarily leave after shorter periods on the job. They are the "ticket punchers," the ones who stay only until they can get what they feel is a better job elsewhere, and not a day longer. One CEO offers this advice: "Never chase the next job. Just do the job that you're doing today the best you can, and be selfless and do the right thing for the people you are managing and leading."[3] The only reason to take the leadership position is so that you can make a difference and improve an agency, and you cannot do very much of that high level management in a short time frame.

On the other hand, in my opinion, your stay in the top slot should not exceed six to eight years. (Others whose judgment I value insist that five to six years should be the limit.) After that length of time, you are no longer looking at your agency with the fresh eyes that allowed you to suggest improvements and question conventional wisdom when you first took the job. Your organization will benefit from a new perspective, and so will you. I was privileged to serve both of my cabinet assignments for the full eight years of the governors' terms in office, but in each case, even had an additional period in office been offered, it was best for the organization and best for me that there be a change.

## UNDERSTANDING THE BOSS

Once you have taken the job, the first and most important thing to understand about your boss the elected official is that he had the good judgment and keen intelligence to hire you in the first place. Unless you are the *rara avis* whose management skills are so great that you are in demand to manage agencies all across the country, your appointment may be the only such opportunity you will ever have. It is certainly one that is envied by many government professionals who will never have the same chance. At the very least, that hiring decision ought to earn your chief a significant measure of your loyalty. Loyalty seems to be a forgotten value these days, but it is an important one. Never be the kind of aides who seem increasingly to populate the White House, regardless of which party is charge. When something goes south, they are very quick to tell reporters—anonymously, of course—how they urged the President to take a different course of action. (They will not call reporters to tell them when the President's action proved successful over their objections, of course.) In other words, it is all about the aide. If you disagree with your boss over something really fundamental, say, a matter of principle, you should resign, not try to undermine him.

Elected executives as a group are intelligent, hardworking, dedicated, personable, driven, tough, and focused. They are especially blessed with political skills far beyond what you will ever have, or they would not have been elected. But their superior ability in this arena makes them no less human. And that is the second most important thing to understand about elected officials, once you have taken the job: they are all human beings. No matter how high their office, no matter how charismatic they may be, no matter what their reputations are, they are still human beings. They sometimes make mistakes, they react negatively to criticism (even legitimate criticism), they occasionally lose their temper, they might make decisions based on emotion rather than reason or that you simply disagree with. Their personal lives may be messy, or at least imperfect. Their private personas may be quite different from their public ones. And, they behave like the politicians they are when the occasion requires it (which will certainly not be all of the time). So, do not be surprised when they display their humanity. More than once in my career I have had to explain to a younger staffer that the official they have just seen act all too human is exactly that. You should not require such an explanation.

In a certain sense, I have an advantage over most of the other folks who work for elected officials along side of me. As an experienced colleague of mine once pointed out, almost everybody who ever works for an elected official, at one time or another, wonders if he couldn't do the job better. In fact, I have seen some colleagues make the very bad mistake of thinking that they are smarter than their boss. Before I ever worked for an elected official, however, I was one myself. That experience mostly disabused me of two notions, 1) that I wanted to be one, and 2) that I was particularly good at being one.

## ELECTED OFFICIALS AND MANAGEMENT

Everyone is accustomed to thinking of elected executives as political leaders. Equally important, however, is that they also occupy high-level management positions. They are in charge of millions if not billions of dollars, and thousands, perhaps hundreds of thousands, of employees. Nevertheless, many officeholders, even veteran, have limited to no previous management experience. Most have backgrounds which were not managerial in nature. This may be true even if they have held office for a number of years, if the office or offices are legislative.

The legislature is not a great training ground for executives because the time horizons and scope of responsibility, among other things, are so different. Legislative experience prepares a governor or mayor for some of the policy aspects of the job, but almost none of the managerial aspects of the job. A direct transition from legislative office to executive office can be jarring. In the legislative world, a legislator may have weeks, months, even years from the time he learns about an issue until he has to cast a vote on it. In the interim, a legislator may read his mail on the subject, talk to experts, and communicate with constituents in order to formulate his views. If in the course of formulating his position, he gets off track, he has plenty of time to get back on track by fine-tuning his thoughts. In contrast, an executive may have only hours between when he learns of a problem and when he has to do something about it—or at least talk intelligently about it. For the same reason, former legislators who assume executive positions can sometimes be slow to articulate agendas; in the legislature, a member is often reactive except for the handful of bills she might introduce. It is not a coincidence that of the country's last six presidents, only the current president did not serve as a governor, or head a large agency, prior to becoming president. Governors have had to manage budgets, problems, and issues and produce results in ways that senators and representatives have not.

Despite the public's view of businessmen as bottom-line managers, executives with business backgrounds may not possess well-developed management skills, particularly if their experience was primarily in marketing or finance. As a management consultant once said to me, "Finance guys who become chief executives focus on the bottom line, but in running an organization there are so many other lines that are important."

Because most of them lack managerial experience, elected executives are going to be learning on the job. Most are very intelligent and will learn, sooner or later, the importance of good management. Ultimately, what will count with them are delivering results, avoiding as many problems as you can, and solving the ones you are guaranteed to encounter. But along the road, there will be many bumps; your task is to cause as few of those bumps yourself as humanly possible.

Elected executives have had to win electoral contest(s) to achieve their offices. A common assumption is that a successful candidate has at least managed his campaign for office. In fact, winning candidates generally have devoted their scarce time on the campaign trail to those activities that are best done by the candidate (as opposed to a staffer)—meeting voters and raising money. The actual administrative details of the campaign have been delegated to a campaign manager and/or other consultant. One of the most common blunders committed by unsuccessful candidates, in fact, is attempting to manage their own campaigns.

It is also the case that few American politicians have gotten elected because of their management track records or because of their promises to improve the management of agencies. It is easy to build a track record in some government positions—prosecutor, police chief, or legislator, for example. As this book is being written, the governors of four of the five states geographically closest to my own are former United States Attorneys or attorneys general; the executive of the county in which I live and the mayor of the nearest big city are both former high ranking police officers. Legislators vote on legislation, introduce bills, and get laws passed. Law enforcement types can put the bad guys away. In contrast to law enforcement and the legislature, it is less easy to build a track record as a manager, even a public manager. And even if a manager is successful, it is unlikely that the media will be aware of or interested in that success.

The voting public has very different expectations of executives and legislators: executives are expected to deliver results, whereas what matters to the voters about legislators is how they stand on the issues. Legislators can run on what they say, but executives have to run on what they do. Yet even elections for executive positions seldom focus on which candidate possesses the management skills necessary to achieve those results.

The other significant difficulty the elected executives have in managing is the time constraint. You already know how difficult it is to run an agency, and you have all day long to do it. Imagine trying to run the whole state or county on a part-time basis. Even if an executive is interested in management, his time demands are overwhelming. Every elected official for whom I have worked has had a seven-day-a-week schedule, year round (and I had one myself when I was a legislator). Executives have a huge volume of activities that are only tangentially related or completely unrelated to management, and which they cannot delegate: public speaking, meetings with individuals and groups of constituents, and ceremonial events, not to mention political activity including but not limited to fundraising. It would not be difficult to entirely fill any elected executive's schedule with non-managerial events.

If the elected official for whom you work lacks management experience, there are multiple implications. First, an executive lacking management experience may not, at least initially, be able to distinguish between good and bad management. "Managers cannot expect from their chiefs the kind of understanding of the manager's problems that grows out of personal experience."[4] Second, inexperienced managers do not identify priorities. They do not necessarily know what they want, or if they do, they may not clearly articulate it. Third, they and their staffs sometimes display a media-centric view of government: if the problem is in the press, it's a real problem; if it is not in the press, it does not exist. That attitude will come back to bite them in the long run, because management problems do not get better on their own.

Fourth, they may make poor personnel choices—hopefully, you are not one of them. Whereas the non-manager may previously have had to select only a handful of key staffers, none of whose jobs required managerial skills, now he has to hire an entire cabinet and administration, including dozens more key personnel. As one veteran public servant presciently advised a governor-elect, "You'll be surprised at how many smart people it takes to run a government." Intuitively one might think that at the cabinet level, given the pay and prestige that go with such positions, the elected official would be choosing from among a lot of really good people and it would be hard to go wrong. But that does not seem to be the case.

Elected executives generally have three options when selecting individuals for cabinet posts. They probably do not conceptualize their options in these terms, but the choices are these nonetheless. They can choose:

1. managers,
2. technical and policy experts, or
3. individuals with political constituencies.

Nobody is all three, a very few individuals are two, and most people are only one.

The category of those with political constituencies includes activists and advocates, plus political allies and individuals for whom the appointment was in payment of a political debt. Unfortunately, few advocates have any training in management and fewer see management as their primary responsibility. And if hiring is done to satisfy a political constituency, "Performance is not the primary criterion for the appointment, in some cases [it is] not a criterion at all."[5] Presidents, governors, and other executives, especially if they are inexperienced, tend to pick people with political constituencies or experts, but not managers. Most of those hired come into their jobs without any specific training and are never given it; it is therefore no surprise that at the end of their time in office, they can point to very few tangible accomplishments.

Nevertheless, do not expect to train chief executives—not in management and not in anything else. They have been successful and are customarily unmotivated (with good reason) to change what has worked well for them. The higher the office held by the executive, generally speaking the longer their successful track record, and the greater degree of reluctance to change their basic approach to government and politics. The successful elected official stands at the apex of a human pyramid of unsuccessful aspirants for that same job. The bottom rows of the pyramid are populated by the individuals who wanted the job but never formally sought it, and the higher rows by the people who sought it unsuccessfully. Along the way, your boss has had many experiences and made judgments and come to conclusions about why he was successful when so many others were not. More than a few legislators with below average political skills gain office because of their good fortune (an opponent's scandal, an unexpected retirement or death, or when riding a "wave" election, in which one party wins many contests beyond their normal rate of success). But the same seldom happens with elected executives. They rarely succeed by accident.

Instead of trying to train your boss, it is your job to adapt your style to the executive's. Your job is always to manage your agency well, but if you are working for an inexperienced manager and/or alongside colleagues with limited managerial experience, all the more reason to properly manage your department and not cause your boss and his executive staff to have to spend time trying to fix problems therein.

Most chief executives have readily identifiable philosophies of governing, not to mention party labels, from which you can take cues. But do not be surprised if the elected official does not, at least initially, have a specific priority list for your agency. There are two reasons he may not. First, the public dialogue of political campaigns such as the one your boss had to win is by definition thematic. Indeed, political consultants will have urged the successful candidate to speak in simple messages, constantly repeated, rather than in detailed policy prescriptions. As former New York governor Mario Cuomo once said, "You campaign in poetry. You govern in prose."[6] A gubernatorial candidate once spoke to me about the "bubble" the gubernatorial race seemed to be in that year. Despite the fact that the state in question was facing a significant budget deficit, the media coverage of the campaign was aspirational in every way: all things were possible, money was no object, and no hard choices needed to be made. (A staffer from the same campaign, but working for a different candidate, commented, once she joined the government, that the campaign had been much easier. "We just had to figure out what we ought to do and then say so. Now we actually have to get it done.")

The second reason has to do with the operational capacity of executive offices. One astute academic who spent a sabbatical on assignment in a governor's office made the observation that the governor's office only had time to work on the five major priorities of the governor, deal with the legislature and the crisis of the day, and handle the media (coverage by which often centered on the crisis of the day). In my own observation, most executive offices operate similarly. Some executive offices are large and powerful, like those of the governors of New York and Michigan and the mayors of Chicago and New York City. They are exceptions to the rule. But no matter how many resources they have, no office has enough hours in the day to micromanage all of the government. If yours is a high profile agency (say, education, criminal justice, or economic development), it may be the focus of one or more of the executive's priorities. In that case, obviously those are the issues that you yourself should emphasize. If you have a lower profile agency, the executive may have no priorities for you at all. After you have devoted the appropriate time, energy, and resources toward the executive's priorities (if any), you will still need to prioritize the rest of your department's agenda yourself (see Chapter 5).

The foregoing assumes that the executive communicates his or her priorities. One of the foremost rules of management is to communicate clear expectations to your subordinates, as discussed in Chapter 4. Some executives are good at this, but many are not if they do not have management backgrounds or experience. They may know what they want, but they do not always proactively communicate their wants to their staffs and cabinets. Sometimes even elementary things like securing an executive's signature on documents requiring it (grant applications, statutorily mandated reports, and others) are not spelled out in terms of which staffer or staffers have the responsibility, how the documents get transmitted, and who must pre-approve the signature before it is affixed by the executive.

## HELPING THEM DO THEIR JOBS

Voters vote for elected officials, of course; no one votes for or against appointed officials like you. To that end, your boss the executive should always have the opportunity to announce good news emanating from your department. In contrast, your job is to:

1. handle problems,
2. explain why something went wrong, and
3. tell people no.

You are the lightning rod for criticism that may come your department's way. Insulating your boss, while never pleasant, is an essential part of your job.

Good news is always offered first to the Executive Office for announcement purposes. The good news could be routine or momentous, anything from a constituent who has been helped by a program your department runs (and is willing to speak publicly about it), to successful regulatory/audit reports, to appointments, to budgetary achievements. Only if the executive passes on the opportunity does the department make the announcement. When bad news happens, as it inevitably will, your department does the explaining. The governor or mayor will have to comment in the event of a truly major problem, but your agency should do the bulk of the talking. In addition, the Governor or Mayor should be invited to all of your department's events even if no major public announcement is involved; he or she can choose which ones to attend.

Of course, one of the most important things you can do for your boss is to avoid as many bad headlines as possible. As the physicians say, "first, do no harm." This is not always possible—negative developments will come your way anyway because some things are truly out of any manager's control. But by hiring the best managers you can, and proactively managing your department as described in other chapters, you can prevent a large number of problems from happening in the first place. Some of the best accomplishments in the departments I ran took the form of identifying organizational weaknesses and strengthening those weak spots before problems got out of hand and resulted in unflattering media coverage. Unfortunately, in American government, credit rarely if ever accrues to an official for preventing a problem from occurring in the first place, or even for preventing a problem from escalating to the point where media attention is warranted. The best you can hope for is that a perceptive executive, executive staff member, or legislator will comment on the absence of problems in your neck of the woods. When a key legislator once told me that he was amazed at how seldom he received constituent complaints about my department, I considered it to be the highest form of praise. News that an agency in state A has a particular problem, or even that identical agencies in states A, B, C, and D have the same problem has never, to my knowledge, inspired a journalist to write that the same agency in state E does not have the same problem because it is well managed.

I was always amused when friends who do not have a lot of familiarity with government thought that because I was a cabinet secretary and therefore a close advisor to the Governor, he and I spent a lot of time together. When in a truthful mood, I told them that I generally saw the Governor only once or twice a month. In reality, if a Governor or County Executive is spending a lot of time worrying about your department, one of the two of you is not doing your job right. Either you are screwing up badly enough that the Governor has had to step in, or the Governor is not spending sufficient time on his priorities (see Chapter 5). The Governor should be spending his time on his highest priorities and the major issues affecting life for all the state's citizens. If some of them fall within your department, fine; otherwise, his time should be spent elsewhere.

There are a number of other things you can affirmatively do to aid your elected boss. As will be described in Chapter 11, start by searching for opportunities to generate positive media coverage. Virtually every government agency that provides services to the public has positive stories to tell every single day.

If the executive office shares the chief's schedule with the cabinet (some do and some do not), or you otherwise become aware of scheduled meetings with an outside party, don't ever let the chief be blindsided. If you have any information about that outside party that they should know about, make sure that they do. If the visitor recently had a negative (or positive) interaction with your department, for example, make sure that the executive office is aware of it.

It is very likely that your boss will have communicated an expectation to you to be responsive to legislative inquiries, but you should be responsive to legislators whether you have been specifically instructed to do so or not (see Chapter 10). However, said cooperation should never include making a side deal about a budget, policy, or personnel matter with a legislator without the knowledge and approval of your boss or her staff.

There is also likely to be an expectation, explicit or implicit, that you will work cooperatively with other departments. Said cooperation includes but is not limited to the following imperatives:

1. communicate,
2. do not blame your colleagues, and
3. align your media responses.

You have a duty to communicate with your sister departments on matters of mutual concern. Also, never publicly criticize or scapegoat another agency. When a problem develops in an area where there is joint responsibility, it is likely that there are joint sources of the problem. But even in areas where your own operation is blameless and the other department caused the difficulty, blame assignment does not solve the problem. Removing the onus from your agency while it remains on another agency does not remove any of the onus from the elected official to whom both agencies report. Finally, make sure that different departments always make identical comments to the public, the press, and the legislative branch. Nothing looks worse for an elected official than to have his appointees contradicting each other publicly.

I have been fortunate to work for bosses who genuinely viewed their teams as teams. But not every team member feels that way. Just as you should have no patience for turf battles amongst your senior staff, so should you go out of your way to avoid engaging in them with your compatriots. Work things out amongst yourselves. Do not force the elected executive to intervene in an interagency dispute. When you are in a meeting with your boss and one or more of your colleagues about a problem or issue, you should feel free to speak your mind and disagree with your colleagues (or your boss). But never, ever bring a disagreement between you and a cabinet colleague about a low priority policy area or an administrative matter to the Governor to referee. If you have to do so, your management performance on this issue has been an abject failure. Also, it should be the rarest of occasions when you bring the boss and her staff a problem without bringing a solution (or multiple options, all of which would result in a solution). The only reason to present your boss with a problem but no solution is if the elected official or key aide has more detailed information about an area than you do—an unlikely eventuality. If it can be said of you that you never bring problems without bringing solutions, you have done very well. It was a badge of honor for me not to bring such matters to the boss; I would rather take the hit.

Unfortunately, I have seen colleagues trade on the fact that most elected executives are not quick to dismiss their cabinet officials. As elections near, officeholders may not be willing to risk the negative media coverage that a cabinet shakeup may engender. With that knowledge, the appointees sometimes skirt standard operating procedures, or even make unilateral decisions. This should never be your approach.

In addition, you have the duty to spend within your budget limit, in good fiscal times and bad, which was the subject of Chapter 6.

Keep the executive and his staff informed of press issues, brewing crises, and major problems, especially if they are likely to become known to legislators and the media. If you are required to submit a regular written report to the elected official for whom you work, do it yourself; do not pass this responsibility off to a subordinate. Focus the report on key issues, special projects, and political concerns, and use it, as previously mentioned, to convey advance intelligence. Include updates on any assignments you have been given by the boss. Write it in the form of a narrative, tell stories, and make it personal. Remember that this report may be the basic, sometimes the only source of information about what you and your agency are doing on a daily basis. While I am not a fan of self-promotion, there is nothing wrong with letting folks know the amount of work that went into a project, an initiative, or solving or avoiding a problem. Your reports give you the opportunity to convey such information to an audience that may hear about it in no other way. I discovered the effectiveness of reports by accident when I learned that no one else wrote them as I did. They were a major time commitment on my part, often done long after hours, but they were worth it because I was able to get my messages to the governor.

Sometimes you will want to fix a problem or take on an issue important to you but less so (or not at all) to the executive for whom you work. If said course of action is likely to require a political price to be paid, consider it carefully before you proceed. Elected officials are willing to spend **political capital** on issues that are important to them; they are unwilling to (and you should avoid to the maximum extent possible having them to) spend it on issues that are unimportant to them. Even the most popular elected official has a limited supply of political capital. They have to spend it every day to get things done that they *have* to get done. Do not force them to draw on their account for something important only to you. Stated more broadly, you should attempt to be an exporter of political capital, not an importer. Judging what is or will be well or poorly received by the public (and thus might result in the expenditure of political capital) is one area in which you should always defer to the judgment of elected officials (both executive and legislative). They talk to the public far more often than you do, and they "read the street" very well (or they do not last very long in their jobs).

At times, you will have to brief your boss. Depending on your job, you may have to do so regularly or only occasionally. In either case, be sensitive to whether your boss is an auditory or a visual learner, and structure your briefing accordingly. "You simply must find out, early on, how your boss likes to receive information."[7] One of my former colleagues always wanted to hand our boss a memo, when what he wanted was to hear her *talk* about the issue or situation. Most briefings are updates; if so make them executive-level briefings, mindful that such officials have a lot of demands on their time. Remember that the word for what you are doing is "brief." The presentation should be crisp, heavier on bottom line considerations like how much something will cost and how long it will take, and lighter on the fine details, unless it is an area the elected official has a particular interest in, or a part of your presentation that the official has previously asked a lot of questions about. "Your bosses don't want a long dissertation from you. They want their answer. Make sure you can deliver the message in a page or two, rather than giving a long presentation. Otherwise, you'll lose them."[8] I vividly recall the disastrous presentation one of my aides gave to the governor. My aide ignored repeated signals from the boss that the details were unimportant, and continued to plunge on. It was, frankly, embarrassing, and that was the last time I failed to review an important presentation in advance.

A longer briefing is called for if you are recommending the adoption of a particular policy position. Make sure alternate approaches and dissenting opinions are acknowledged and explained, including the possible consequences of what you are recommending. You should do the presentations yourself, but have anyone with you that you might need to answer technical questions or fill in details. And remember the aphorism of one of my former colleagues: "It doesn't get any better than yes." Many presenters do not stop talking after they have been told yes. You cannot improve upon it. If you keep on talking, by definition, anything that changes from then on is bad.

On policy matters relating to your department, chiefs may consult, listen to, and even employ people other than you—other elected officials, outside experts, and of course his executive staff. Some of those outsiders may be the elected official's political allies and personal friends. Make sure you are courteous and cooperative to them all. Don't sweat it; it is part of the democratic process. Whether your boss is an experienced manager or not, the more you deliver (and the fewer problems you cause), the more autonomy you will eventually get. Once you have established your record, the chief and his executive office will be too busy elsewhere to interfere with your smoothly running operations.

Be aware that the time horizons of elected officials may be different (and shorter) than yours. Part of your job is to translate the elected official's time frames, which are tied to electoral and budgetary cycles, into language the bureaucracy understands. The bureaucracy, left to its own devices, almost inevitably is insensitive to everyone else's time horizons. You therefore must be attuned to the cycles important to the executive. Also be aware, and be sure your department's leadership team is aware, that in an election year, things like routine problems and difficulties that are not typically headline-worthy suddenly become very much so. What is the routine business of government in an odd-numbered year may become grist for your boss's opponent in an even-numbered one, as he or his legislative surrogates try to construct narratives faulting the incumbent administration.

Finally, executives do not like to believe, as least initially, that someone will come into their office, look them in the eye, and flat out lie to them. Yet it happens all too often. This disbelief is not a function of your boss's ego; it is that they find it hard to fathom that someone meeting with, say, the governor will have so little respect for that office that he or she will try to deceive it. So be on guard for this eventuality (which you may or may not be on hand to witness personally), try to make the boss aware of it, but do not be surprised if the executive has to learn this particular lesson the hard way.

## THE EXECUTIVE OFFICE STAFF

In addition to working for your elected official, you will be dealing with her executive staff on a regular, if not daily, basis. The exact nature of your working relationship will depend upon how the elected official arranges her administration. Some workers from the executive's successful campaign will be appointed to agency posts, but more likely individuals with that background will appear in the executive office positions, up to and including the chief of staff. Most executive office staffers are capable and intelligent. Some are immature, but with experience and age, they will get better or they will not last. In contrast to elected officials, you can and should try to "train" executive office staffers, ever so subtly, in what constitutes good management.

George Reedy, press secretary to President Lyndon Johnson, once said that "There should be a flat rule that no one be permitted to enter the gates of the White House until he is at least 40 years of age and has suffered major disappointments in his life."[9] A Governor's or County Executive's office, even a large one, is not quite the White House, so perhaps that bit of advice should be modified to refer to individuals under 30 years of age. Anybody under 30 is likely to have some deficits. They will probably not have read Chapter 4 of this book. Among other mistakes, they may be poor communicators. I'm just glad I was not given that level of responsibility at age 28. I might have had the intellect for the job, but certainly not the necessary maturity.

Notwithstanding **Reedy's dictum**, you will be dealing with executive staffers of varying levels of experience and skills. Treat them all respectfully, regardless of the different backgrounds you may have, and whether or not they match you in age and maturity. They have the same interests as you do; for this reason, you should genuinely want them to succeed. Recognize also that their jobs are very different from yours (and hopefully they understand that the reverse is true as well). They do the "care and feeding" of the elected official, in terms of her schedule, meetings, transportation, speeches, etc. They also have to manage her politics and the big policy issues.

When the Governor's chief of staff or communications director calls, you should react the same way that you would react if the Governor herself were calling. Work cooperatively with them by being a team player. If the Governor's expectation is that his key staff, say, review your proposed hiring of senior aides, let them do so. If a request from the executive staff is anything that you can reasonably accommodate, do it. Never take the attitude that you work for the Governor and only the Governor can give you orders. When you work for an executive, you work with her team as well. Keep the Governor's Office informed of press issues, brewing crises, and any other major problems likely to become known to legislators and the press. E-mail makes this easier than ever, or the regular report you may be required to submit is the perfect vehicle. Do not insist that all contacts between the executive office and your department be run through you. Just make sure that you know about them from your team.

Interacting with the executive office can have advantages. They can provide perspective on a problem or issue that you, down in the weeds, may lack. They can be very supportive when you most need it. There can also be disadvantages. They can play petty power games and they can meddle. Some governor's offices display an **ignore-micromanage polarity** with nothing in between—depending on the issue, either they pay you no mind or they breathe down your neck. The biggest problem of all, however, can be if they attempt to limit your contacts with the boss. Any such restriction is trouble. In that case, it is more important than ever to use your regular reports as communications tools. You should have unfettered access, but never abuse the privilege if you do.

## TELLING THEM NO

Some psychology and management texts will tell you that you should regularly stroke the boss's ego, because he has a big one. Even if elected officials do have big egos, I have never found that I need to do any stroking. I worked for one very arrogant elected official, but otherwise I have been very fortunate to work for elected officials who do not require ego stroking. I *am* always happy to tell them when they have hit a home run, because 1) I do not hesitate to speak up when they strike out, and 2) just as I like to praise my colleagues and my subordinates when they do well, it is no different with my bosses.

But having been an elected official myself, I know that there is seldom a shortage of people to tell you that you are great. A few of those people who do so may actually mean it. What elected officials really need, though, are people to tell them when they are wrong.

Elected officials are human, so you will at some point have to do what almost nobody likes to do: tell the elected official no. This is not the same thing as disagreeing with a proposed course of action or policy decision. It is an order of magnitude more significant—preventing a disaster from happening. Delivering the "no" generally comes in two forms: telling them that they have to do something they do not want to do, or more commonly, telling them that they cannot do something that they very much want to do. You will not need to perform this task regularly, and you may need to do it only rarely. But inevitably, you will need to do it.

Elected officials must have people around them who have the strength of character to say no to them on occasion, even though the person they are saying no to is someone who holds their job in his or her hands. Even officials who have a high tolerance for disagreement do not generally like to be told no. As discussed previously in this chapter, they are almost always strong if not outsized personalities and have been successful, and so trust their own judgment. Do not be surprised if many of your colleagues are very reluctant to perform this task or simply will not do it at all. When the time comes, you must therefore do so whether you have known your boss for years or only a short while. Be assured that you are doing an elected official no good by failing to advise him that a particular course of action on which he is about to embark will end badly.

No book is big enough to describe every possible misstep that requires telling the boss no, but some of the more common are the following. Probably the single most common is the executive wanting to go forward with a policy decision or appointment that will be received with overwhelming negativity by the press, public, and/or legislature. Generally the official's political skills enable him to avoid this pitfall, but everybody misses a call once in a while. The elected official may be contemplating a course of action that is illegal, but not be aware of its illegality. (Of course, if the elected official is contemplating a course of action that he *knows* is illegal, or ignores you when you point out illegality, you should absent yourself from his employment as soon as possible.) You may need to prevent the elected official from saying or doing something publicly because he has been angered and is ready to take action during his angry mood, when you know that he would later regret it. In this case, counseling a cooling off period may temporarily delay or permanently remove the need to tell the boss no. You may also need to curtail an elected official's refusal to deal with someone who is perpetual critic, because it is now necessary or advantageous for your boss to do so.

## NOTES

1. Seib, *In Crisis, Opportunity for Obama, Wall Street Journal* 11-19-08, 1.
2. Cooper interview, *New York Times* 12-13-13, B2.
3. Saunders interview, *New York Times* 6-28-13, B2.
4. Chase and Reveal, *How to Manage in the Public Sector*, 25.
5. Ibid., 29.
6. Keyes, *The Quote Verifier*, 21.
7. Chase and Reveal, *How to Manage in the Public Sector*, 53.
8. Schwartz interview, *New York Times*, 6-15-14, Business 2.
9. Herbers, *The Spokes of Power, New York Times* 5-18-73, 20.

*Chapter Ten*

# The Legislative Branch of Government

"There Are Three Levels of Legislator Questioning"

## INTRODUCTION

Whenever you have a particularly bad day dealing with the legislative body in your jurisdiction, repeat the following like a mantra: "the legislature is a separate, equal branch of government." When they refuse to consider your proposal or even defeat it, when they will not give you the appropriation you need, when they try to micromanage parts of your department, remember that they are doing exactly what the writers of your constitution or charter contemplated.

I served in a state legislature, albeit briefly. I know the tricks of the trade.

All of the following apply whatever your legislative body is—state, county, city, or other.

## LEGISLATIVE CULTURE

Every legislative body has its own culture. You need to understand that culture, because when you are in the state capitol or council chambers, you are going to play by their rules, not the other way around. The most important rule to understand is that legislatures embody democracy itself. Even at its smoothest, the legislature can be chaotic. "By its nature, legislative decision making is an unruly process."[1] Or as the old saying goes, two things you do not want to see how they are made are laws and sausages.

Even in this day of e-mails and text messages, legislatures are oral cultures, not written cultures. Their oral culture probably derives from two factors. First, public speaking—to individuals and groups—is a legislator's stock in trade. Second, speaking is how legislators interact with each other in the capitol, whether it is in the hallway, in committee, or on the floor. For this reason, it is always better to talk to legislators rather than write to them. (This mode of operation is in complete contrast to the judicial branch of government, which is a written culture.) While serving in the legislature, I once foolishly sent a memo to my leadership urging them to support a particular measure. They were appalled, not about the content, but about its method of delivery. As they patiently (or perhaps not so patiently) explained to me, "Sending that memo makes it look like we can't talk to each other." Whatever point you want to make, whatever you want from them, whatever questions you have to answer for them, speak to them if you have the option. Personally is better than over the phone, which is better than e-mail.

All legislatures have dichotomies. Party affiliation is certainly one of them, but it is never the only one, and especially in jurisdictions dominated by one party, it is not even the most important one. Upstate/downstate, east/west, or urban/rural dichotomies may exist, as may ideological divides within parties (conservatives or liberals versus moderates), ins versus outs, or supporters of the chamber's leadership versus non-supporters. In a bicameral legislature, the House and Senate may have very different ways of doing business. Whatever the dichotomies are, you need to be aware of them and know which members belong to which ones.

Once upon a time, the **favor bank** was a controlling principle of legislative politics. Notwithstanding one's party affiliation, you could count on subsequent support for something from a given legislator if you helped that legislator with a problem or issue. Unfortunately or fortunately, in many jurisdictions the favor bank is on life support if not completely dead. Similarly, legislators' words were once their bonds, but that too is no longer a universally held principle. What was agreed to on Monday may no longer hold on Tuesday, let alone next week. A deal, in other words, is no longer always a deal. A colleague of mine once reached agreement with a legislator at an afternoon meeting in the capitol, only to receive a letter from that legislator the very next day reneging on the bargain. Obviously, for the letter to have arrived the following day, the legislator must have written it immediately after my colleague left her office! Just as some legislators are more amenable to compromise and less driven by ideology than others, so are some legislative bodies. With all of these dimensions, understand how they operate and conduct your legislative business accordingly.

Look carefully at the role legislative staff plays in legislative business. There is a wide continuum—sometimes staffers virtually run the body and sometimes they are irrelevant, with everything in between. Those legislative bodies that do not effectively use staff or have weak staffs place themselves at a great disadvantage compared to the executive branch. Sadly, these bodies use their staffs as patronage and not as an opportunity to surround themselves with talent. This attitude drove me crazy when I was a legislator. It bothered me less in the executive branch. Whether or not this is best for democracy, it may be very helpful to you that you and your colleagues control the information and have the ability to formulate proposals and solutions that the legislature lacks. Of course, regardless of the overall posture of the legislature *vis-à-vis* legislative staff, there may be individual exceptions—the legislator who has identified and makes good use of a staffer or staffers in a body that collectively does not, or a "lone wolf" legislator in a well-staffed chamber.

Some legislative staffers merit your professional respect, and some do not. Perhaps the most annoying staffers are those who, impressed with their proximity to elected officials, display legislative ego without the corresponding legislative power and ability to get things done. Nevertheless, there is no reason for you and your staff not to be cordial to all legislative staff and try to help them if you can.

Legislatures and legislators are not particularly constant in their approaches to governance, over time or even contemporaneously. Therefore, do not expect such consistency, regardless of party or ideology. Their attitudes may vary with the day's headlines or the phone calls they receive. Among many examples, they may want an agency to be independent from political control when that agency's officials take a position congruent with the legislature's views but contrary to the executive's. They may want that same agency firmly within a command structure if they fear it is taking positions contrary to their views. Today they may support privatizing, tomorrow the same task must be done by government employees.

Very few legislators have a broad perspective. What matters to them are their districts and their constituents. Most are provincial, and with good reason. We live in a representative democracy; it is the job of legislators to represent their own constituents, not those in anybody else's district. In political science terms, this is the **delegate model of representation**, and is practiced by almost all legislators. Once in a while, a legislator can afford to follow the **trustee model of representation**, as formulated by 18th century British Member of Parliament Edmund Burke; such a legislator would take a broader view (statewide or even nationwide) and use his own judgment, not merely channel the views of his constituents. But only legislators in very safe districts and/or who are veterans who have "secured" their seats fall into this category. (Burke, as every sophomore political science student knows, lost his next election after espousing the trustee viewpoint.)

Legislatures differ in their degrees of gender, racial, even political diversity. But every legislature's members are widely diverse in their personalities. In that sense, they really are a microcosm of society. Regardless of your party or performance, some legislators will treat you politely, others with disdain. Every legislative body has individuals whose view of the world is that you are either with them 100 percent of the time or you are not with them at all. As one of my colleagues once said of such a legislator, "Senator A is very easy to get along with as long as you are doing exactly what he wants you to." Other problem types are the ones who are never satisfied, no matter what you do. For this type, once I have identified them as such, I will always try to help them, but I will not make any special effort. If you know you can never satisfy someone, it is foolish to keep trying. The good news is that such personalities are uncommon. Overall, not only is a legislator favorably treating you not necessarily correlated with being in the party of your administration, some days you will swear it is inversely correlated.

Most legislatures also, unfortunately, have one or more powerful bullies. I can offer no proven formula for dealing with this archetype, only the reminder that these individuals can always smell fear, so be careful never to display it even if you feel it. Certainly, you should not give them any unnecessary reason to pick a fight with you, but inevitably there will be disagreement, even conflict. And as with bullies everywhere else in society, you have to stand up to them. Usually these individuals understand power. As an agency head, you have power, and sooner or later, the bully will probably want or need something from you. When that happens, be sure you have something you want to get in return. On one occasion I recall, a legislator whom I had assisted on many occasions would not release some bills I wanted from his committee, after promising to do so. The session came and went and the bills went nowhere. It turned out that he was angry with a legislator from the other chamber, coincidentally the sponsor of my department's bills, and had decided that his need to punish the object of his unhappiness by blocking all of the other legislator's bills outweighed his own previous commitment to me to pass some of them. Sure enough, a month later he asked that my department do something. I instructed my department not to do so. I seldom take action of this kind, preferring to help people if I can and expecting that eventually I will be helped in return. But there is a time and a place for everything. As soon as that legislator found out that I had declined to assist him, he was on the phone, which of course was my objective. I explained that I was unhappy that my bills had been bottled up, and would be willing to help him with his issue, but I expected those bills to be released as soon as the legislature reconvened. I could almost hear the smile in his voice. He agreed to do so without argument or complaint. As a regular player of the game, he understood when it was played on him.

You should understand that not every legislator runs for office because he has an interest in public policy. In my personal experience, I have not found that even a majority of them do so. Some legislators are ideological, but many are not. Some love the politics but are not too interested in the governing. Others enjoy the power of being in office but have no fixed philosophy of governance. Still others want to help constituents with problems but seldom legislate. And there are those who run simply because winning makes them a prominent person in their community. Regardless of any reason an elected official may have for running for office, knowing which legislators are in office for which reasons is another important thing to understand when it comes time to deal with them.

Finally, note that when the public is in a bad mood regarding the economy and/or the direction that they perceive the country is moving in, legislators can and do criticize, even campaign against, not just the government that they are part of, but the legislative body or even chamber that they are a part of. Candidates for legislative office do this, but so do incumbents. You are obviously part of the government, too, but legislators do not usually consider themselves part of the same team.

## LEGISLATIVE RELATIONS

"If you are serious about public management, you will be serious about legislative relations."[2] Every high level manager must have positive legislative relations, because 1) they have ultimate control over your resources, and 2) they have ultimate control over the laws that affect you. Legislative relations are something you need to personally spend time on.

To a great degree, your relationship with the legislature or council is a function of their relationship with your boss. It is difficult, though not impossible, to have a better relationship with the legislature than your boss does. It is easy for you to have a worse one, though.

One of the reasons why legislators behave the way they do is that being a legislator can be a frustrating experience for anyone trying to accomplish something. More than once I had occasion to compare my situation as a cabinet secretary with that of a typical legislator. Even in the Delaware General Assembly, the second smallest state legislature in the nation, any legislator's idea requires a vote of 61 other individuals. Any legislature has limited staff, and not all of them are competent. Most legislators do not have a single personal staff member. The legislature collectively has the power of the purse, but few individual legislators have discretionary funds to spend. In contrast, as a cabinet secretary I made decisions every day on my own. I had the ability to handpick almost my entire senior staff, all of whom were highly competent, and had almost 5,000 employees who would do anything legal I asked them to do. Plus, my budget amounted to nearly two billion dollars with which to carry out our department's responsibilities. "Legislators cannot deliver services—only managers can."[3]

As a callow freshman state representative, I once engaged in a speculative conversation with an experienced state senator about the relative merits of being in the legislative branch of government versus the executive branch.

Although neither of us had any experience on which to base our analysis of what it would be like on the other side, we decided we liked it better as legislators. Little did I know.

There are certain standard rules you should obey when dealing with legislators, whether Congressmen, state legislators, or county or city councilors. They are as follows.

1. Communicate frequently. Do not overestimate their knowledge or information, especially if you are in a jurisdiction with term limits. Like elected executives (as discussed in the previous chapter), most legislators do not have management backgrounds and, with a few exceptions, are more concerned with policy than management. Most legislators serve part-time. Even those who do serve full-time have to specialize in a small number of areas, perhaps only a single area, and the odds are it is not yours. Legislators are among the last generalists operating in all of society. Explanations—often very basic ones—are almost always going to be required when communicating with them, due to their unfamiliarity with your operations. You are the interface between the professionals of your organization and the legislature, and as such, you will be doing a lot of translating (in both directions).

2. At the same time as you are being careful not to overestimate their information, never underestimate their intelligence. Do not mistake a lack of formal education for a lack of intelligence, or for that matter, a high level of education for a high level of common sense.

3. Never lie, not to your enemies and not to your friends. It is both wrong and easily found out.

4. Never provide bad information. Legislators must believe and trust you. This rule needs to be observed by both you and all your staff. Making mistakes is not fatal, but providing bad information is, because it erodes or even erases the trust a legislator may have had in you. You cannot always do what they want, and many legislators understand that, but they do expect that you will give them correct information. One state senator called to ask me about something in one of my divisions, and I responded based on what was conveyed to me by my director. The senator later called again, asking the same question, stating that he did not think I was correct. Again I sought out my director, and again I responded based on the information I was provided. Later on, the senator discovered an internal document that contradicted what I had twice told him. That senator served for many more years after that incident, dying in office, and I do not believe he ever trusted me thereafter. I feel so strongly about giving correct information that I have standing instructions to my staff that if I ever

misstate a fact at a legislative hearing, they should correct me on the spot.

5. If there is bad news, try to let them hear it from you first.
6. Answer their queries as rapidly as possible (see next section). Consider designating a staffer whose primary or sole responsibility, depending on volume, is responding to legislative requests. My goal is always to exceed their expectations for responsiveness, whatever those expectations are. Even a yes that is too long in coming has a tendency to look like a no to a legislator.
7. Never lose your cool or become argumentative with a legislator, no matter how impolite, condescending, and/or confrontational they are with you—in public *or* private. The legislator verbally abusing you probably will not take note of your calm demeanor, but his or her colleagues will.

In addition to these rules, there are also simple matters of protocol. Legislators are owed the deference and respect that comes from being that separate and equal branch of government. In any public setting or in front of staffers or aides, always address a senator as Senator Johnson, never as Bob, even if you helped get him elected, which I sometimes did. All legislators are on my phone interrupt list and are welcome to my cell phone number—I will almost always interrupt a meeting or other activity to take their calls. They should be welcome to call you personally even on low level matters; some will take advantage of this offer and some will not. If at any point they want to see you, go see them as soon as you can, and stay as long as they want you to. If anything special in your agency is going on in their districts, let them know about it. If there is an event, make sure they are invited, whether they are members of your party or not. Sharing credit and glory, if it is even the slightest bit deserved, should be the order of the day. Including them in photo opportunities and press releases regarding new laws and projects go a long way toward building political capital with them.

All of the above go toward your credibility and responsiveness, which is what you need when you lobby the legislators for things you want and need. If you have that credibility, you can get a huge amount done, sometimes easily. One year I needed to execute a multi-year, $300 million per year contract without following the letter of the state procurement law, and obtained a waiver of the procurement law from the legislature allowing our department to do so. The legislature had confidence that we would make a solid decision, and we did. On another occasion, we amended the state's construction laws via a budget bill rider, without dissent.

To maximize the effectiveness of your lobbying, either you or an aide should be in the capitol or City Hall every day the legislature or council meets. They like to see you sometimes when you do not need anything. If your staff size allows it, one person should be given the responsibility of legislative liaison (or the title, if the volume of work indicates it). Even if you are your own legislative liaison, consider having an aide with you to keep track of requests. The aide might be able to go off and begin chasing down the problem or issue while you are doing further communicating.

The key to lobbying is that if you do not ask, you will not get. As one experienced cabinet secretary put it, "No one is waiting around to solve your problem." If you are lobbying on behalf of one of your programs, if at all possible try to get legislators to "touch" that program—perhaps with a site visit, a tour, or a review of program activities in their districts. Try to understand how the legislator you are lobbying thinks, and how the world looks to her. Remember that the issue you are interested in is one of many that she must deal with.

Try to develop a personal relationship with as many legislators as possible. Relationships are important because "lawmaking is fundamentally a personal, interactive affair."[4] If your legislative body is as hyperpartisan as Congress has become, developing relationships may be difficult. But not every legislative chamber is, and you should make the effort nonetheless. Try to develop some intelligence on individual legislators beyond the basics of districts and politics. What are they interested in, what special interests control or greatly influence them, even what do they like in terms of passions or hobbies? As one representative who became a great friend, even though we were of opposite parties, advised, "Always good to bring up the Yankees with Senator A, Senator B's granddaughter, national energy issues with Senator C, history stuff with me, high school sports with Representative D, NASCAR with Representative E, etc., etc." I dealt with a small legislature and an even smaller County Council, so I did, in fact, know them all personally. But certainly you need to know, at a minimum, all the leaders, all the members of the appropriations and budget committees, and all the members of the jurisdictional committees covering your department. Those relationships will help you play both offense and defense—and you will be playing both. You will not have only friends and no enemies. Some days you will swear that the truest aphorism ever stated is, "Friends come and go, but enemies accumulate."

Understand that when you are being attacked by a legislator, no matter how unfairly—and everyone gets his turn—even your legislative friends are unlikely to challenge the attacker personally. This passivity occurs because 1) they view it as every legislator's prerogative to behave that way, even if they themselves do not, and 2) they need to reserve their disagreements with their legislative colleagues for when something is involved that they want or need. Maintaining your blood pressure at an appropriate level is not among those needs. Most legislators will recognize it if you are always truthful with them, keep your word, and keep your cool. They just are not going to necessarily reward you for it.

But even with enemies, if you cannot make them friends, you can manage them. If you can turn down the volume of their anger and obstreperousness, that is worth a lot. As a friendly state senator once explained to me about another senator in leadership who was notoriously difficult to deal with, "There's Senator X voting against you, and there's Senator X working against you—and there's a world of difference between the two."

## WHAT LEGISLATORS WANT FROM YOU

Virtually every legislative request will fall into one of three categories. First, they may ask you to take a certain policy position. Second, they may ask for a personnel decision. And third, they may ask for help with a constituent issue.

Whatever category into which it falls, every legislative request should go to the top of your list of things to do. You cannot hope to have good relations with the legislative branch if you are not responsive (as stated in the previous section). Having said that, regardless of the request, if it is made to me directly, in person or over the phone, I almost never respond with a yes or no immediately, even if I am virtually certain what my decision will be, or certain as to whether the rules do or do not allow what is being requested. If I know the answer is going to be no, I want them to think that I took their request seriously and gave it due consideration. If I know the answer is going to be yes, I still do not want them to think that their request is too easy to accomplish—I want them to believe that I went a little bit out of my way to help them. In either case, though, I do not delay the decision more than a business day or two.

Because almost every policy matter is different, it is difficult to offer advice that is universally applicable. Keep in mind that while some legislative urgings on issues are ideologically driven, more often legislative complaints and positions arise from their constituents' complaints and positions. You are not going to convince them that your position is the better one if their constituents think otherwise. Sometimes, your response on a given issue will be dictated by the office of your governor or county executive. Most legislators whose political affiliation is opposite from that of your administration are not going to waste their time or yours trying to convince you to adopt an idea that they know you are philosophically opposed to. Therefore, when they do come to you with a proposal, if there is a win-win or middle ground, give it fair consideration. Also, as a courtesy, my departments were always willing to draft bills for legislators even if we opposed the measures, so that there were no technical problems (and so that there were no hidden surprises).

In the ideal world, the legislature acts as a board of directors, setting broad policy. They can and should make decisions on what functions government should carry out to the exclusion of others. In the real world, however, the legislative branch occasionally wants to micromanage executive departments—even to run specific parts of your operation. Be ready for it. If a legislator wishes to micromanage a small corner of your organization, try to understand what motivates him. Maybe he formerly worked there, maybe he has constituents, friends, political allies, or even family who work there, maybe he has constituents who advocate for that section. Or maybe he simply is interested in that program. Any such interest should not necessarily change your decisions, but it should cause you to monitor events in that section closely, through more frequent oral or written reports than you might otherwise call for. You never want to know less about a part of your enterprise than a given legislator does.

Congressmen are forbidden by statute from offering recommendations for federal Civil Service jobs. State and local legislators are under no such restrictions, and will often recommend individuals for positions. You should consider them all on the merits, remembering from Chapter 4 that you always want to hire the best. Keep in mind that having positive relations with the legislature does not mean that you have to employ their cronies. I had a rule of thumb about such recommendations. The ability of the applicant to actually do the job for which he was being recommended appeared to be inversely correlated to how high up in the organization the position was. For the highest level, especially exempt positions, I cannot recall a single suggestion that resulted in me hiring the recommendee. Unfortunately, some of those recommended were laughably unqualified. Separate from the qualifications issue, I would have been reluctant to hire someone for a leadership position who knows she owes her job to her patron, not to you, and therefore likely behave as such when it comes to organizational alignment and the sharing of confidential information. In contrast, many individuals suggested for entry-level jobs were highly competent and motivated—although sometimes they have failed elsewhere and hence, they will fail for you, too.

For this reason and two others, I am much more amenable to hiring entry-level personnel based on legislative recommendations. Often, there are many equally qualified applicants for entry-level jobs, so much so that the difference between the very best and others is negligible. You can still generally hire the best *and* hire based on the recommendation at the same time. Also, most personnel systems are biased in favor of people already in the system. I do not mind helping somebody enter the system so that they can then succeed or fail on their own. Such hiring depends on your personnel rules—some systems I have worked in allow hiring for entry-level jobs without the standard merit process. If such a person was hired, my follow-up rules are, a) once they get the job, they have to keep the job on their own merits, and b) all further advancement has to be on their own merits.

For positions above entry level but below the top levels, it is a mixed bag, some good and others not, so everything is done on the merits.

Irrespective of the level of the position being sought, I try to determine how serious the recommendation is. Generally, a letter of recommendation, absent any other contact, means that the recommendation is perfunctory. In these cases, I always reply to the legislator, copying the constituent, stating that I have received the letter of recommendation from the legislator and will give it careful consideration, adding as much information about the process and timetable as is available. If a legislator calls with a suggestion, or even seeks me out personally to hand me a resume, it means that they are genuinely trying to get the recommendee a job. Given personnel system restrictions, sometimes there is little you can do even if you want to. But in any event, try to give the legislator as much information as possible about the process and the timing. If there is any way to get the applicant past the initial screening and into an interview, I do so. In either case, I communicate the status to the legislator personally. This seems to satisfy most legislators.

Legislators will also sometimes want you to retain someone you are about to fire or have already fired. You should never do that, but you *can* allow the employee to resign in lieu of being terminated, as long as he will not be applying for a different position elsewhere in your organization. This outcome can be a win-win-win; it allows the legislator to tell his friend or constituent that he did the best he could, while the employee can put "resigned" on his resume rather than "terminated." You still get rid of the bad employee without the usual personnel system rigmarole.

You should be wary of legislative requests to intervene in personnel matters, even when they do not involve disciplinary action. Typically, a legislator will contact you and claim that his constituent, your employee, is being treated unfairly by management. In all my years in government, I have yet to encounter a single instance where such a claim proved to be true. Undoubtedly it does occur, but I have never seen it. Rather, in every single situation, the employee in question deserved his discipline. Often, the employee was a chronic problem who at long last was being called into account; he had now decided that a legislative appeal was yet another way to try and avoid being held accountable for his or her performance.

The third category of legislative requests is the request for programmatic or other assistance for one of their constituents. You should start by understanding that to remain in office, legislators must be responsive to their constituents. Legislators the world over view helping their constituents as a major part of their jobs. So help them help their constituents if you can. Good casework has the potential to turn legislative negatives into positives. Even if

the favor bank mentioned above is dead in the formal sense, telling legislators yes or helping them with their casework puts money in that bank for the
day—it always comes—when you have to tell them no or cannot be of
assistance.

Sometimes, the job of helping the constituent is easy. The constituent and
the legislator do not know what services are or are not available, and your job
is simply to match them with the resources in question.

More difficult is when your agency has already denied the request or
placed the individual on a waiting list, and the legislator is basically asking
you to act as a court of appeal from your bureaucracy's ruling. If the constituent was denied the service because they do not meet fixed eligibility criteria,
be wary of setting aside those criteria. Even if there are not firm federal,
state, or local laws and regulations, and the criteria are set administratively
by your department, do not make the individual in question eligible unless
you are prepared to adhere to that change consistently going forward. If the
threshold of eligibility for a given service is, say, a maximum income of
$10,000, it can be very difficult to deny a person with $10,050 of income.
But rest assured that if you offer the service to that person, you have effectively changed your threshold of eligibility to $10,050 for all future appli-
cants. And at the new threshold, there are going to be plenty of individuals
who are just a little bit over that limit because they make $10,100. It can be a
slippery slope.

Similarly, legislators may seek help for a constituent needing a service
you do not offer. They may want, say, an abandoned cemetery in their district
cleaned up using your agency's resources. You may well be able to do this
cleanup one time, without too much difficulty. But consider carefully the
precedent you are setting. One-time requests generally become recurring
ones. How many other abandoned cemeteries are there in your jurisdiction
that you will be asked to clean up, and how will you say no? In this era of cell
phone cameras and near-universal internet access, you should never assume
you will be doing the cleanup without everyone eventually knowing about it.

When *do* you bend the rules? Generally speaking, do not change your
policies unless there is a compelling case for doing so. On the other hand, I
have been known to advance an individual's place in a queue, if the situation
is worthy. I might do so if the waiting list is structured on a first come, first
served basis, and involves a wait of days or weeks, because the individuals
who might be passed over temporarily will still get the resources eventually.
But if the resource to demand ratio is so unfavorable that citizens have to
wait many months or even years, you should not allow the constituent to
jump the line. More important, if the waiting list is structured according to
need, never alter it to serve a less-worthy client instead of a more deserving
one.

As mentioned previously, use your constituent relations staffer, if you have one, to the maximum extent possible. The best one I ever had on my staff employed a simple technique that won her universal acclaim from legislators. As soon as she received the case from me or from anyone other than the legislator, she sent an acknowledgement to the constituent and the legislator. This elementary device assured both the legislator and constituent that someone was, in fact, working on their case, and they did not have to worry that the request had gotten lost. Otherwise, a week might elapse and, having heard nothing, they do not know if it has even been received.

The use of a full-time constituent relations staffer, or at least a designated staffer for whom response to legislative requests is a high priority, serves to reduce response time to the minimum possible. That is always the goal. Just as justice delayed is justice denied, so too constituent service delayed is frequently constituent service denied. You cannot always say yes; in fact, often there is an expectation that you are going to have to say no. But in the words of one of my governors, "Sometimes it's all about how you say no." If you are saying no, make sure there is a plain English explanation of why a service cannot be provided or a problem solved, both for the constituent and the legislator. Needless to say, if there has been a denial of service, there need to be firm grounds.

By the way, when you or your staff are inquiring on behalf of a legislator (or anyone else, for that matter), be sure that your line personnel know that you are merely making an inquiry and not issuing a directive. While over-responsive bureaucrats are not a pervasive problem, sometimes your employees will jump the gun when a question is asked and change their action or decision when you are simply seeking information and not requesting any alteration.

## LEGISLATIVE HEARINGS

The most important presentations you do will be legislative presentations. (However, for presentations to your executive or to budget officials, the majority of the same rules apply.)

As with much else in government, there are some standard procedures that you should follow. In general, advance preparation is the key. To that end, the most important of these standard procedures is that every presentation should be preceded by a dress rehearsal. At the hearing itself, as much of your presentation as possible should be scripted. I even devised a seating chart for legislative budget hearings in order to have key staffers close at hand to answer questions. The dress rehearsal should be sufficiently rigorous that the actual presentation or hearing will seem easy by comparison. And the dress rehearsal should be sufficiently far in advance that the presentation can be improved—missing answers to likely questions can be compiled, the re-marks or power point presentation made clearer and tighter, and the like. A dress rehearsal the morning of your afternoon hearing usually does not allow time for loose ends to be nailed down.

In a large department that I ran, we had 12 operating divisions. At our legislative budget hearing, as cabinet secretary I gave overall remarks, as did each of the division directors. Therefore, we had 12 separate dress rehearsals. In each case, a draft of the introductory remarks was due one week in ad-vance of the dress rehearsal. I was present at every rehearsal, as were the department's central budget and policy staffers. Each director brought his or her deputy, the division's top financial officer, and such other program man-agers as might be necessary to answer questions.

At the rehearsal, first, the directors read their remarks aloud, exactly as if they were reading them to the appropriations committee. Our instructions were that these remarks were to be short (10 minutes maximum) and were to address the big picture—progress since the last budget hearing (in particular, use of new funding granted by the legislature in the most recent budget, if any), workload trends, and a brief description of any new funds requested. Then, the entire audience critiqued the speech. The director took the various suggested improvements and was required to submit revised remarks in ad-vance of the legislative hearing, so that we could check to see that the necessary upgrades had been made.

The second part of the dress rehearsal consisted of all the non-division staff asking the division personnel questions, using as a guide a list of likely questions prepared in advance by the department's budget team. Their term for the questions was the **"land mine list."** Most of the possible questions were never asked in the hearing, but that was precisely the goal—to be overprepared. Certain legislators have pet projects or customary areas of interest. They were not a secret, so we prepared for them by having at the ready the latest developments or statistics for when asked about those pro-jects. Also, some of the "land mine" questions were devoted to these areas. As discussed in Chapter 4, you should be aware of all legislative contacts that have occurred in your department. Any such contacts that involve money issues should cause you to anticipate some budget hearing questions in those areas.

When staffers are asking questions of their colleagues, and those folks are answering, there is a natural tendency to ask and answer differently than one would if addressing a legislator. The questions and answers are more infor-mal and likely assume a certain amount of background knowledge that your staff possesses but legislators do not. To make the rehearsal as realistic as possible, I insisted that questioners pose their inquiries exactly as legislators would ask them—sometimes in clear ways, but sometimes in confused wording or in badgering, sarcastic, or accusatory tones of voice. I reminded them that there are three levels of legislative questioning:

Level 1—The legislator genuinely does not know the answer to the question and would like to know the answer.

Level 2—The legislator knows the answer to the question and wants to see if you know the answer.

Level 3—The answer is irrelevant. The question is being asked for the purpose of embarrassing or criticizing the agency.

I advised my team to be ready for all three levels. One can often judge the success of a hearing by counting how many Level 1 questions were asked compared with how few Level 2 and especially Level 3 questions were asked.

Answering questions as you would answer the legislator was a hard habit to adopt for some of my directors, even the best ones. I had to constantly harp on it. But it is the best way to replicate battlefield conditions.

There are certain ironclad rules to employ when answering legislative questions. The first and most important is what I term **the Ross Rule**, named for Pete Ross, a former state budget director and himself a longtime top legislative aide, who first articulated it. The Ross Rule states that when answering a legislator's question, you need to reply with enough information to answer the question, but not so much information that it invites further questions. In the years before he taught me that maxim, I watched responder after responder get into trouble by giving excessively lengthy answers. Getting into the weeds with expansive answers usually clouds rather than clarifies the issue.

This lesson is a difficult one to master, especially for individuals who are experts at what they do, which is most of your directors. They almost always know the subject far better than the legislator asking the question—who, of course, is a generalist. They have a natural tendency to be quite detailed in their responses. It is a mistake, and you need to wean them away from the practice. In addition to relentless badgering in the rehearsals, I went so far as to make up mock "awards" for most succinct and least succinct answers, to be presented at the next directors' meeting or legislative hearing "post-mortem" session. It took many years, but I eventually got all of my directors to give succinct answers just about 100 percent of the time. I was highly pleased when my former worst offender won the award for most succinct answer one year. Instead of expounding at length in response to one legislative soliloquy, she simply responded, "I would agree." (Another year, my award winner had this to say in response to a long statement from a budget committee member that may or may not have included an actual question: "I'm going to incorporate your comments into my future thinking on this subject.")

The second cardinal rule is never to give an answer unless it is accurate. If you do not know the answer, simply say you do not know, but you will get back to them. This answer (unless it is given to every question) is virtually always acceptable. Then, of course, be sure you do get back to them. To that end, have one aide assigned the task of writing down every question to which "I'll get back to you" was the response, to make sure that the answers are provided in a timely fashion. As one CEO put it, "If you don't know the answer, say you do not know the answer. People will accept that you don't know the answer. But what they cannot accept is if you tell them something that's wrong, because they are going to act on that. And then if you have to come back later with a different answer, you will lose credibility. And the other thing is, get back.... If you say you're going to get back...make sure you get back."[5] If you give or anyone else gives an incorrect answer and staffers present are aware of it, have them correct you on the spot. Do not worry about whether you look bad. If you discover the mistake later on, correct yourself to the audience before which you misspoke via the earliest possible communication. In the hearing itself, do not hesitate to turn to staff for a fact or an answer that you do not know. The correct answer is important, not who provides it.

In the course of preparing your agency for budgetary hearings, make sure your team is aware of other characteristics of these hearings. One is that at budget hearings, the majority of questions will probably not be budget-related, but program- or policy-related. Prepare your "land mine list" accordingly. Also, do not be surprised if the amount of time spent at a budget hearing is inversely proportional to the sum of money involved. The Chief Financial Officer at one agency I worked in explained the dynamic. "Most legislators don't really understand what $10 million is, but they do understand what $10,000 is." As if in proof of that explanation, one year not a single legislative question was asked about my department's largest individual program by far, the $600 million Medicaid appropriation. The next year, questioning was closer; six inquiries, or as I joked to the division director, one question for every $100 million in her budget.

At hearings, you can expect questions about aspects of your department that are not running well. Every agency has them, and they are probably not a secret to the legislature. If you are in the midst of a crisis, detailed responses are definitely called for (see "Crisis Management" in Chapter 7). Otherwise, in responding to questions about your problem areas, you should acknowledge the problem, and then follow the advice Peter Boyle gave to Robert Redford in the 1972 movie *The Candidate*. (Ostensibly a satire, within 10 years it had unfortunately become an extremely accurate depiction of modern American political campaigns.) In the movie, campaign manager Boyle is engaged in debate preparation with United States Senate candidate Redford. Boyle doesn't give Redford a lengthy briefing on crime policy; he commandeers the airplane cockpit after the campaign plane lands and hands Redford a five point anti-crime program, telling him to use it if the subject comes up in debate. Redford does, successfully.

Your agency's response should be much the same. Take the four or five things you are doing to address the problem (real things, not imaginary ones, of course) and succinctly describe them. No long explanation of how the problem began—it's irrelevant.

A final cardinal rule is that at budget hearings, it is your job not just to support the executive's budget proposal, but to defend it. Defending the executive's proposal can be a delicate dance to perform when a legislator wants to add money to your budget where the executive did not. For this reason, some of your dress rehearsal mock questions should cover this ground. It generally will not be difficult to anticipate where such questions will be asked.

Even when a legislative body is seeking a routine update on one of your programs or initiatives, careful planning is the key. Some employees, often technical employees with great expertise in their subject matter, just do not have very good presentation skills. People who are not good presenters generally have faults that include but are not limited to the following. First, their presentation manner may be poor because they are excessively nervous. Many, many individuals fear public speaking. After all, surveys frequently show that people fear public speaking more than they fear death! Second, they may not be good at identifying what is the crux of the matter. They cannot put together a concise listing of background material, facts, and conclusions. Third, they may have difficulty in answering pointed questions, either because they are not good at thinking on their feet or because they have difficulty following the Ross Rule (see above). Being a poor presenter does not make anyone a bad employee, simply one who requires a lot of coaching. Alternatively, a better presenter may have to take the lead at show time even if she is not the program expert. One agency with which I worked always required four versions of their power point presentations before I was satisfied. Very often these folks have a positive story to tell, but do not know the best way to tell it.

## LEGISLATIVE STRATEGY

Thus far we have discussed primarily legislative tactics. But in addition to tactics, there is legislative strategy—how you get your agenda passed and how you can successfully block legislation inimical to your organization.

The first strategic principle, as with almost every other aspect of government administration, is to prioritize. Like your boss, you have a limited amount of political capital. Expend it only on the highest priorities.

You are going to be playing both offense and defense in the capitol building. Sometimes playing defense is easier than offense in American democracy. Whenever I teach political science, one of the key concepts that I try to get my students to understand is that the founding fathers set up this country's governance structure so that it is hard to change things, not easy. It is true on the federal level and equally true on the state and local levels. With checks and balances and separation of powers, it is by design easier to stop something than to get something done. A bill can be killed in subcommittee or committee level, or on the chamber floor, or sometimes by the leadership alone—and that's in each house. Because bills can fail at multiple levels, you do not have to take firm stands and alienate legislators about bills that are going to die anyway. Let the legislature itself say no so that you do not have to. The overwhelming majority of bills introduced are never enacted. Use your judgment. Look carefully at who the sponsors are, how vigorously the sponsors are trying to move a bill, what outside groups support or oppose it, etc.

But keep in mind that legislating is, after all, the business of legislators. When playing defense, give way on the little things and concentrate your energies on major items. Legislators know how to install earmarks, attach mandates to legislation, and add specific instructions on how to spend money to appropriations bills. If the sums of money are small in the cosmic scheme of things or the instructions not overly burdensome, mostly you should just grin and bear it. A phrase you can use very often is, "we can live with it." Even on major matters, a better strategy than simply trying to defeat legislators' bills is in many cases to engage them and make their proposals palatable. This strategy is all the more important when you are dealing with proposals that you dislike but which are coming from a legislator who is generally an ally and/or of the same party as your administration.

Similarly, you should be prepared to compromise or modify your own legislative proposals if necessary. Do not compromise on principle, but is there any way to reach accommodation with legislators without giving major things away? If your proposal is before a legislative committee and they support 90 percent of it, but want 10 percent changed or dropped, by all means modify or abandon that 10 percent because you are about to win a big victory. As the old saying goes, do not let the perfect be the enemy of the good. Half a loaf is better than none; as stated in an earlier chapter, incremental changes are victories. And 90 percent of a loaf is just about perfect.

With your own initiatives, picking the right sponsor is important. Generally speaking, protocol dictates that any legislation should be offered to the chairs of your department's jurisdictional committees first. If you have a good relationship with them, they should be willing to carry all of your technical legislation, whether they are of your party or not, and most if not all of your substantive legislation. (If you do not have a good relationship with them, you probably need to improve those relationships before you do anything else.) This sponsorship is called "carrying your water," and if you have the productive relationships that you need, it can go on year after year on bill after bill. If there are bills that the appropriate committee chairs do not want to sponsor, for whatever reason, they will tell you so and you are then free to identify alternate sponsors.

Timing is important. You should have your staff prepare your legislative package of bills during the months of the off-session. The bills should be completely ready to go on the first day of the session so that you can meet with the likely sponsors and get the bills introduced sooner rather than later. The more time there is for bills to go through the legislative process, the less time there is for opponents to kill them not by overtly opposing them, but by slowing down their passage through the system until time runs out. It's a standard technique. Then, you either have to wait until next year's session to resume your efforts, or, if it is an election year, start all over again when the new legislature is sworn in.

Whether pushing through your preferred legislation or stopping undesirable bills, enlisting third party support is of paramount importance. There are two reasons that third party support is vital. First, many legislators do not tend to know the details of even major pieces of legislation; usually, they do not even read the bills. But they all know which interest groups and other outside parties are for or against those bills. You can fill them in on the details, but they want to know what others think of your proposal. The facts behind most legislation are important, but not as important as who supports or opposes it. Second, all of your understanding of legislative culture, all of the personal relationships you have built up, and all of the constituent work you have done for them is likely to be necessary but not sufficient to get a truly major legislative initiative passed. You need additional help from individuals and groups who want to see your bill passed or a bad bill blocked. Sometimes these groups come forward on their own, but often you have to spend time and energy persuading them and organizing their supportive efforts. You may have to meet with them, provide them with talking points, and coordinate their scheduled visits to the capitol. There is no such thing as too much support for your bill or too many groups lining up behind you. The only limit should be how much time you have available to organize them.

You should be generally familiar with which legislators are the most responsive to which outside groups. You should also try to generate support for your proposal from individuals and groups within any undecided legislator's district. While most legislators will not completely ignore contacts from non-constituents, they are all going to give their highest priority to contacts from their own constituents. Any lobbying effort should therefore begin by having all of your supporters contact their own legislators first. This approach goes for you and your aides as well.

Third party support can also come in the form of legislative allies friendly to your cause. If you do not have a strong relationship with legislator A, maybe legislator B, who is supporting your bill, does, and is willing to make an approach to legislator A on your behalf. You should play the party label card to enlist legislators whose party is that of the administration to support any administration initiatives. Another point to note is that legislative alliances can be bill-specific. A legislator may well support you on Senate Bill No. 100, but oppose you on Senate Bill No. 200. Never take it personally; there is always another issue coming up soon.

Ironically, sometimes routine, technical, or housekeeping bills take as much or more time and energy to get passed as major bills, because there are no outside parties to help you push them through.

If something is not moving according to your preferred timetable, remember that any deadlines you might have are meaningless to the legislature. They only have one deadline that matters: the end of the legislative session. So measure your success by what you have gotten done by the end of the session, not at any interim point in time. Also, be aware that sometimes the legislature has only one card to play: the delay card. They play the delay card because (even if they will not say so aloud) they know they are eventually going to approve your proposal or otherwise say yes to you. So let them play that card.

Whether you are playing offense or defense, always keep in mind the positions of your boss the governor or county executive. It is not unusual for a given legislator's position on something to more closely resemble yours than your boss's. If that ever happens, do not let it show. Your first loyalty is always to your governor or mayor. Make sure that the closest a legislator can come to agreeing with her and not your boss is along the lines of the comment a state senator once made, that left everybody laughing, about one of my cabinet colleagues: "His lips said no, but his eyes said yes."

## NOTES

1. Forsythe, *Memos to the Governor*, 48.
2. Chase and Reveal, *How to Manage in the Public Sector*, 115.
3. Ibid., 109.
4. Ibid, 110.
5. Gumz interview, *New York Times* 2-13-11, Business 2.

## Chapter Eleven

# The Media

"The Only Unaccountable Institution in America"

### INTRODUCTION

An unfettered media may be second only to free elections as an essential element of a successful democracy, so important that it is enshrined in our national constitution and the constitutions of all 50 states. The media has two primary roles, that of gatekeeper and that of watchdog, both equally vital. In its gatekeeper role, the media devotes column inches, broadcast time, and megabytes to certain issues, conveying information to the public about what news is essential (and by omission, what is not). Many of those issues will be governmental. In its watchdog role, the media sheds light on problems and exposes corruption; again, much but not all of the problems and corruption will involve government. Without the media, it would be impossible for the public to know whether the government is doing its job properly.

For this reason, regardless of any criticism that can be put on the media, you have no choice but to work with it. And in addition to a free press being an essential element of democracy, it is also the most important—though no longer the only—vehicle through which you can convey messages about your department and your issues to the public.

### A DIFFERENT VALUE SYSTEM

A significant reason why media relations present one of the most difficult challenges that a public manager faces is that the media's value system appears to be so different from ours. We value facts and try to make decisions based on them; they publish assertions, typically with no concern for the veracity or lack thereof of said assertions. We try to manage conflict and resolve it; they encourage it for its circulation or ratings (and entertainment) value. We value success and recognize it at every opportunity; they report on failure. We want to fix problems; they want to identify scapegoats. We have to make decisions in real time; they can investigate us at their leisure.

I made one of my more accurate predictions when I became a cabinet secretary for the first time. I had just finished being campaign manager and media spokesman for a successful gubernatorial campaign; I was in the media regularly. I said to my wife, "From now on, if you see my name in the paper, it is probably because something bad happened." Not a bad description of media relations while running a government agency. It is hard to get a good headline, but easy to get a bad one.

A considerable number of media outlets no longer expend much effort to sort out the truth. They make little attempt to ascertain the facts in any dispute, considering their job done if they quote both sides. As the joke goes, an assertion by the Flat Earth Society that the world is, in fact, flat and not spherical would be met by the headline, "Shape of earth: opinions differ." Combining the media's preference for drama, conflict, and scandal with its disinclination to sort things out has obvious implications both for you and for anybody who wants to take a shot at you: expect allegations about you and your department to be given ample coverage, no matter how specious they are. If someone calls for your resignation, it is virtually a guaranteed story. Although many people who take their complaints to the press lack any credibility at all, they nonetheless often know exactly how to manipulate the media; indeed, that may be their only goal and expectation. In many a dispute with a private party that garners media attention, you are presumed to be wrong and the private party right, regardless of how little evidence there is to their claim. At best, you can expect a full airing of the alleged grievance, with you allowed to respond—on the inside of the paper, of course, or later in the on-air segment.

If a free press is the price you pay for a democracy, as a government administrator you may nevertheless feel that you are too often the victim of price gouging. When I gathered my leadership team around me in the midst of a difficult circumstance (not necessarily media-related), I sometimes began the meeting by inviting everyone to vent. Letting everybody expel their negative energy for a few minutes allowed us to get it off our chests and then move on to productively work on the problem at hand. I am going to avail myself of a similar opportunity to vent my feelings for a few pages, then move to the instructive part of the chapter.

Like most educated Americans, I don't believe everything I read in the paper, see on television, or view on the internet. Unlike most educated Americans, some of what I don't believe is about me. The old saying is that newspapers should "print the truth and raise hell." The media seems to be terrific at the latter, but somewhat spotty at the former. It is a strange media landscape indeed that exalts reality television stars and trashes public servants who are, for the most part, just trying to do their jobs. Criticism comes with the job, and that certainly includes press criticism, but most of us would like to be quoted accurately, completely, and in context when we speak to the media. It does not seem to occur with regularity.

Dissatisfaction with the media is as old as the republic. The same founding fathers who so wisely wrote the soaring, magisterial language of the First Amendment to the Constitution in 1789 passed the Alien and Sedition Acts less than 10 years later (in 1798), restricting press freedom. They used the new laws to arrest 25 journalists, one of whom was also a Congressman, and convicted 10 of them for criticizing the government. A typical example of the "seditious" language that got a journalist arrested criticized the incumbent administration for "ridiculous pomp, foolish adulation, and selfish avarice."[1] Media relations in the 21st century would be a lot less stressful if that were as bad as it got. As one college government textbook puts it, "Today it is hard to imagine what anyone might write about any politician that would get its writer in trouble with the law."[2]

More than 200 years later, arresting journalists is not an option, but sometimes when specific reporters, or outlets, or even the entire media are doing nothing but attacking you, arrest seems like too mild a solution. The media can vilify you, questioning your decisions, motives, and character. Most of us do not object to the first of those three, but we take strong exception to the second and third. A media attack on you has all the elements of a political campaign in which your opponent is spending large sums of money to run negative ads against you. In a political campaign, however, you can raise money to counter those negative ads with your own ads. In fact, you have no choice but to do so, because it is a fundamental rule of politics that a charge that goes unanswered for long enough is assumed by the public to be true. But in your public manager's job, you cannot go raise money to mount a counterattack. Worse, the public has more of an inclination to believe media attacks on you than political attacks, coming from ostensibly objective journalists. Whether it is biased reporting, inaccurate analysis, or unsubstantiated personal attacks, it is difficult for public officials to offer counterarguments.

Everyone in public life has his or her choice media head scratcher stories. Here are a few of mine. I am not bothering with any of the large number of times I was misquoted, paraphrased using a more inflammatory term than the one I actually used, quoted today using something I said a year ago, or was not called for a response when someone trashed me. The 12 times the same reporter told us he had to have something because he was on deadline, only to have the story appear days or a week later—the dog has eaten a lot of that reporter's homework, but it did not make the list. When the paper ran the most unflattering photo of me they could find in preference to others, it just seemed like business as usual. The journalist who critiqued our department one day and called the next day wanting us to look into a personal matter for him—not worth further ink. Looking back, I mostly find the following comical—but they did not seem quite so amusing at the time.

A daily newspaper once published, over a several month time period, the salaries of every single state employee. Not just the salaries of the elected officials and the high ranking administrators, but every single employee, down to and including clerks, custodians, and typists. As a cabinet official, I was accustomed to having my salary published. But should the custodians, who were being paid barely above minimum wage, have been fair game?

On another occasion, a newspaper decided that they would not speak with any media personnel (some of whom had been hired from that paper's staff), only with department heads, because we were "the decision makers." The policy reached its nadir when a young reporter called me at home (my phone number has always been listed, and this call occurred before I carried a cell phone) to get my reaction to something that had occurred earlier in the day. I explained that I had just arrived home because I had spent the last few hours at the doctor's office with my daughter, who had broken her foot. I suggested he call the department's communications director, who I was sure would have knowledge of the situation. He of course refused to do this, because his paper was not talking to media relations staffers, nor did he allow me the time to make a call myself to get the necessary background. Instead, his story the next day reported that I had refused to comment, omitting any explanation of my situation. (In this one case, cosmic justice eventually prevailed when the reporter in question joined a subsequent administration. He could be observed from time to time pacing the halls of the governor's office, complaining out loud about the unfairness of certain reporters.)

One of my personal favorites occurred when a reporter, unanimously and deservedly regarded as a hatchet man, called me for comment about a story he was writing. In fact, as the conversation revealed, he had written the story already, with the exception of the space he had left for my reaction to his allegations. When I attempted to offer assorted facts that would add some context to his story line, he explained that he was uninterested. "It's going to be a negative story," he growled. There would be more such stories from that character. Perhaps I should have credited him for his honesty, but a straightforward hatchet man is still a hatchet man.

Sadly, that practice has become a standard for some reporters and some media outlets. They first develop a story line, and second, gather facts. Facts that bolster the story line are included; facts that contradict or simply are not in alignment with the story line are discarded. It is intellectually dishonest and just plain dishonest—and all too common. Explains a veteran of many media jousts, "The...danger is inherent in the investigative process itself.

Once a news organization or reporter chooses a subject for investigation, it becomes difficult to avoid trying to prove a predisposed hypothesis. This is done, sometimes unconsciously, through choices in researching, writing, editing, and headline writing—and by omitting or downplaying evidence that tends to undermine the hypothesis."[3]

A fair amount of the trouble with newspapers in particular is that most of them are monopolies, and unregulated monopolies at that. If I am unhappy with my haircut, I can go to another barber. If my car is not satisfactory, I will buy a different make and model next time. But if I don't like my local newspaper, I can't cancel my subscription and buy the other newspaper, because there isn't one. Unregulated monopolies are not, of course, accountable to anyone except themselves. For most of my government career, I have served at the pleasure of elected officials, who could dismiss me at a moment's notice. The elected officials themselves are subject to regular elections (and if they lost, I was out of a job, regardless of how well I was doing it). If my employees misbehave, I can discipline or even fire them. But a monopoly media outlet is the only unaccountable institution in America. Or as a veteran administrator, writing about the media in general, put it more gently, "Its quality controls are almost exclusively internal, and it is an enterprise beyond regulation."[4] That is how it has to be, of course, in a democratic society. But with freedom and power come responsibility, a notion to which some in the media might do well to give additional thought. Like the citizens who do not like to vote, pay taxes, fill out a census form, or serve on jury duty, some in the media appear to be more concerned with their rights than their responsibilities.

## UNDERSTANDING THE MEDIA

But as Katharine Hepburn said in the movie *The African Queen*, "Nevertheless." Like everything else in a public manager's environment, you have no say in whether you deal with the media—it is a requirement. The press is very powerful; people's opinions about government are formed not just by personal experience, but also because of media coverage. As that is the case, try to understand the media and base your dealings with it on that understanding. You should try to understand both the media as an institution and reporters as a class. Unfortunately, as you try to understand their world, do not expect them always to try to understand yours.

It is no secret that the media landscape has changed dramatically in recent years and seems headed for even bigger change in the years to come. Change is now coming at such a fast pace that this chapter may already be out of date by the time this book is published. First and foremost, we are well into the ubiquitous 24/7 news cycle that requires no further explanation.

Second, the media has fragmented. Television's three major networks (and three nightly news broadcasts), each with huge viewerships, have long since been supplanted by 500 channels or more. Some of those channels are devoted exclusively to news, but all of those channels individually have smaller audiences. Instead of a few daily newspapers in your vicinity, there is likely only one local newspaper, but hundreds or thousands of blogs and websites.

The third development is that the (print) newspaper industry is in a steep and apparently inexorable decline. Circulation and advertising revenue at almost every newspaper throughout the country have shrunk. At your city's one surviving newspaper, there are fewer reporters and editors, fewer pages, a smaller physical size, and a smaller news hole. Some newspapers have now begun to cut back print editions to three days a week.

For the past ten years, whenever I have been in front of a group of students, I have always asked if anyone reads a daily newspaper. In those ten years, only one student has raised her hand. Ten or 15 years from now, will there be any daily newspapers in America except for *The New York Times*, *The Washington Post*, *USA Today*, and *The Wall Street Journal*? In the interim, many newspapers have made the conscious decision to increase coverage of local government at the expense of state or national coverage. They apparently believe that this will help circulation. The result is a bizarre situation in which, for example, local zoning matters affecting a relatively small number of citizens may have as much ink devoted to them as state or national policies affecting millions. Precise statistics on viewership of newspapers online are not easy to come by, but evidence suggests that online consumption of newspapers is both less frequent and less in-depth than consumption of the print editions.

As a lifelong and avid reader of newspapers—I still have two delivered to my home daily—I do not view any of these developments positively. The gatekeeper role of the media, in particular, is generally far better served by newspapers than by television or other media.

Eighteenth and 19th century journalism was heavily partisan. Only in the middle of the 20th century did the concept of objective, neutral reporting take hold. In the 21st century, we are returning to our roots. All media are not yet partisan, but two of the television network news operations (Fox and MSNBC) are unabashedly so, as is almost all of talk radio, much of the digital media and, increasingly, newspapers. The age of objective journalism may be drawing to a close. "If you pull back a few thousand feet, you can see newspapers coming full circle. Before World War II, newspapers were mostly owned by political and business interests who used them to push an agenda. People like William Randolph Hearst and Robert McCormick wielded their newspapers as cudgels to get their way. It was only when newspapers began making all kinds of money in the postwar era that they were professionalized and infused with editorial standards. 'We are going back to a form of ownership that dominated in an earlier era,' said Alan D. Mutter, a newspaper and technology consultant. 'As newspapers become less impressive businesses, people are going to buy them as trophies or bully pulpits or some other form of personal expression.' "[5]

This "back to the future" trend is troublesome enough in and of itself, especially for those who believe that objective journalism is good for the body politic. The old saying that "everyone is entitled to their own opinion, but not their own facts" has given way. Now, everyone is apparently entitled to his own facts, too. On top of that, non-objective journalism by a daily newspaper often sets the tone for the smaller media outlets. Smaller outlets may not have a single reporter available for investigating; lacking the wherewithal to do their own investigations, they play follow-the-leader, and if the newspaper is off base, they will be, too. Many media outlets continue to self-identify, against all evidence, as adherents to journalistic neutrality, even as their coverage increasingly slants toward the partisan and polemical. The old rubric of opinion in editorials and facts in stories appears to be receding in the rear view mirror as editorials masking as coverage increasingly show up in the news sections of the paper.

The fourth development is that you have to ask yourself, "What exactly is the media?" The decline of newspapers is a discouraging development, because what will replace them? Other types of media are not exactly filling the gap. Local television and radio news, even in major media markets, are often little more than headline services, with a heavy emphasis on fires and murders. Broadcast journalists often know less about government than print reporters—although this ignorance can sometimes be a blessing as it comes without the attitude of certain print reporters. Broadcasters also focus less on substantive matters. Talk radio is more entertainment than news.

Political and government-oriented web sites and blogs are a major part of today's mix. The majority of them are of two types, aggregators and opinion-based sites. Aggregators collect material originally developed elsewhere; they are a positive development for newshounds, but do not have much general readership. Because they lack such general readership, they cannot perform the gatekeeper role that newspapers do. The opinion-based sites generally have even less knowledge of government and fewer quality controls than the traditional media. The vast majority of them fit the description on the clever t-shirt I once saw: "More people have seen this t-shirt than have read your blog."

Public opinion surveys indicate that per capita "news consumption," as measured by how much time the average person spends reading, watching, or listening to news, is actually on the rise. The fragmenting of the media has created more opportunities to consume news. More people are getting at least some news and most people are consuming more news than 10 years ago.

But what is the quality of the news they are getting? The positive role of newspapers in providing a baseline of information and news to Americans has fallen by the wayside. As newspapers decline and are replaced by digital media, and as the media more and more conflate news and entertainment, it is hard not to conclude that the quality of news that Americans are getting is on a downward trend. In a country where interest in politics and government has always ranked well down on the list of things that are important to most citizens, the media trends described above are not encouraging signs for the future of our democracy.

Public opinion polls show something else: the media are not very well regarded by the American public: "U.S. Distrust in Media Hits New High"[6] is a typical summary. Only 21% of Americans have a great deal of confidence in television news, with 25% indicating a lot of confidence in newspapers, according to 2012 polls.[7] Americans these days do not have a lot of faith in many of our major institutions, governmental included, and the media are not bucking the trend. As a public servant, you may not be particularly well regarded, but unless you are a member of Congress, you are probably held in higher esteem than the average journalist.

Media businesses, at bottom, are like all businesses. To survive, they have to make money: sell newspapers, get ratings, and sell advertising. In their view, controversy, scandal, and negativity sell (in their words, as the old saying goes, if it bleeds, it leads). Does negativity really sell better than a more balanced approach? There would not seem to be a great deal of scientific evidence on that subject. Certainly, in the case of newspapers, with almost all of them losing circulation and advertising, it can be pretty safely said that the current approach is not working. If I had the opportunity to sit down with a group of newspaper publishers, the question I would probably not be able to resist asking them would be, "How is the emphasis on negativity working out for you?" Whether a different approach would work better will probably remain an unknowable question. But at any rate, in most media, but especially newspapers, small problems rate coverage over large successes. "It is unfortunate but inevitable that the prevailing view of government institutions will to a large extent be based on those worst cases. Things done right are not newsworthy."[8]

All of the foregoing does not add up to a happy time for journalism and journalists. If you think you and your troops are underpaid, try journalism. Supply and demand, not to mention shrinking newspaper readership and ad revenue, have made journalism a buyers' market. Media outlets do not need to pay well to fill their ranks, and they do not. Job security is nonexistent. It is hard not to ascribe some of the general negativity regarding public employee salaries and benefits, and a lot of the specific negativity, to simple jealousy on the part of reporters and editors trapped in a shrinking industry, with limited chances for advancement. Why are there so many reporters who seem to relish writing negative stories and only negative stories? Admittedly, some negative stories (in addition to being entirely appropriate) are more interesting. Still, when I spot a reporter who appears to be nothing more than a hatchet man, the amateur psychologist in me speculates about his personality and about the psychic income (or lack thereof) he gets from his job. Does expelling all that negativity make him feel better about himself?

Journalists are skeptical by nature, an attitude that in general is probably healthy. It can be very frustrating to have so much of what you do looked at with a jaundiced eye, however. Some journalists with whom I have interacted are so jaded that they simply cannot distinguish between what is genuinely bad versus what is alleged to be bad by one's political opponents or others with agendas. Reporting nearly everything in government in a negative light cannot help but contribute to a culture of mistrust that seems to be more and more prevalent in American society.

Another important characteristic of journalists is that although they themselves make their living as critics, many of them do not like to be corrected, let alone criticized. It is ironic that many individuals in the most critical of professions are so uncomfortable with being subjected to the same. They love to dish it out, but they do not like to take it. Recall the media's reaction to the media watchdog magazine *Brill's Content*, which was published from 1998 to 2001. Some of the outrage with which its targets reacted bordered on the hilarious. I believe that hypersensitivity to criticism is a characteristic of other professions as well; it is certainly true in politics. The more critical a person is, the less likely he is to be tolerant of criticism. Worse than the intolerance is the tendency of some reporters and editors to retaliate. Criticize or even disagree with them, and you have guaranteed that the next story (or stories) will either reemphasize their initial viewpoint or launch a fresh line of attack. As will be discussed in the next section, the level of insensitivity to criticism that the media displays will play a role in determining what your response will be when you are on the firing line.

Because of the press cutbacks mentioned above, news reporters are spread too thin; they no longer have the time or inclination to "cover the waterfront." And the space cutbacks prevent blanket coverage in any event. These developments have multiple implications.

First, your agency may be covered by a single reporter. Obviously, then, your relationship with this reporter will be very important. Second, because of its resource limits, once a given media outlet seizes upon a story, it will rehash and follow up that particular story, seemingly ad infinitum. It is easier to work a single story line repeatedly than to develop, research, and write multiple ones. Coupling the tendency to repeat story lines with the well-known herd mentality of the media means that it is vitally important to get the first story as right as possible because it will be repeated, rehashed, and copied by others in the press (as was discussed in Chapter 7).

Third, while normally the smaller media outlets track the larger ones, the reverse can be true as well. Old and new media seemingly trade the lead role periodically. Because they are stretched thin (or maybe because some of them are just lazy) print and broadcast reporters will read blogs for story ideas. One newspaper columnist in a local paper was notorious for writing like clockwork about a subject three days after a local blogger posted on that topic. Many blogs have microscopic readership, but if the reporter who has your beat is one of those readers (it will very quickly be apparent if she is), it will be incumbent upon your media staff to read the relevant blogs so you know where the reporter will be heading.

A fourth implication is that reporters who lack information are looking for easy stories to write, so you will get calls like this one: a reporter has just read a report by an "independent" group located somewhere far from where you are, evaluating your department's efforts in some area. The independent group is very likely an advocacy organization or is funded by parties that are hardly disinterested, like businesses. In the course of compiling their report, they have not talked to anyone you know, and they have cherry-picked statistical measures to bolster their arguments. Their grading is not done on a curve, so, say, 40 of the 50 states are rated D or F. To write the story, all the reporter has to do is take highlights from the document and get your reaction. More than once I have been called after hours by a reporter working on such a story, wanting me to drop whatever I am doing, read a report I have not heard of and do not care about, and give him my reaction in 60 minutes. It can be a real head-shaker.

Reporters, even experienced ones, often do not understand much about government in general or your department in particular. In this regard they are not very different from legislators or the general public—but the ones who cover you may not have the excuse of being generalists like legislators are. This lack of understanding does not just mean lack of understanding about government policy; it extends to the basic mechanics of your operation. This can be problematic when they assume, for example, that the information they want is available at the touch of a button; it usually is not. With no background in government, most reporters and editors are unfamiliar with any up-to-date concepts of public administration. All of which means that you will be spending a lot of time trying to explain how things work, and that is assuming you get the chance to explain. And add journalists to the list of people who do not really understand management; lacking understanding of what it is, naturally they cannot distinguish between good and bad management. It is quite ironic that journalists are so judgmental about your performance despite often lacking even elementary knowledge of government, management, or the substantive area they are writing about. When (as happened to me) a new reporter who has a very limited understanding of what you do decides that his next story will detail how you are handling something all wrong, you will swear you are living in the *Dilbert* cartoon where the eponymous character says, "Now let's open the floor to suggestions from people who are unqualified to do their own jobs, much less mine."[9]

But the dirtiest little secret about reporters' psychology is that they do not really see you—or anybody else they are writing about—as people. Instead, you are material to them. Lest you think this is a harsh appraisal, it is one that most journalists themselves will admit to in unguarded moments. In fact, I watched a communications director, a former reporter, explain exactly that dynamic to an elected official when prepping him for media interviews. This fact has obvious implications for the futility of trying to befriend them or even establish a truly professional relationship with them.

## MEDIA STRATEGY

The fundamental rules for dealing with people who are your coworkers have not changed all that much in the last 40 years (see Chapter 4), and they probably will not change much over the next 40—or the next 400. But dealing with the media has. You have to work within the media environment as it exists today, and as it will exist tomorrow.

There is no such thing as a perfect formula for dealing with the media, because 1) everybody fumbles the ball now and then, and 2) the press generally views itself has having an adversarial relationship with the government rather than a neutral or observational one. For the most part, regardless of your performance, they view it as their job to knock you around periodically. As the head of a government agency, your competency will be questioned daily and your integrity periodically (which leads to the one of the essential elements of your media strategy, below).

The six basic elements of your general media strategy should be:

1. don't argue with people who buy ink by the barrel,
2. never lie to or mislead the press,
3. develop a very thick skin,
4. understand that how the media covers you bears on your ability to manage,
5. do your research on the media types with whom you interact, and
6. get as much positive media coverage as you can for your organization.

As mentioned, the basics of how you and your department respond to media inquiries have changed. But something that has not changed is the oldest and most important rule: avoid getting into an argument with the media—especially with the aforementioned critics who do not themselves like to be criticized. The more unfair they are, the more you will need to resist the temptation. But they will always have the last word, and will often go out of their way to have it.

As stated in *Crisis Management* in Chapter 7, you should never lie to or mislead the media. Do not mislead either by commission or omission. It is both wrong and stupid. In addition to not lying or misleading, try to be as open and transparent as you can be.

The third and perhaps most obvious element of your general strategy is that you should develop a very thick skin. Following this advice is another one of those things easier said than done. It is awfully hard not to be defensive when you are being attacked. I have noticed that, when I am under heavy attack, those people counseling me to turn the other cheek, who make light of the criticism, who even disdain me for not keeping my cool—not only are they not under attack themselves, they may be in positions or professions that do not expose them to public criticism. They have no real idea what it is like to be under fire. Most of the few people who are advising me to chill out and who *have* been under similar attack, I have also noticed, were not so sanguine when they were in a similar situation. And the same goes for me: it is very easy for me to assure a colleague that the slings and arrows he is facing are nothing to worry about when they are aimed at someone besides me. Is there really anybody with a thick enough skin? Everybody takes it to heart, at least partly because we take our jobs seriously even if we do not take ourselves too seriously. So do not feel that you are flawed if you do take it to heart on occasion. I once watched television sportscaster Charles Barkley comment that while people in the public eye like to pretend that they ignore unfavorable press, "We read the papers."

When you have just received a beating in the press, take consolation in the words of Theodore Roosevelt about critics (which apply especially to media critics) from more than a century ago:

> It is not the critic who counts: not the man who points out how the strong man stumbles or where the doer of deeds could have done better. The credit belongs to the man who is actually in the arena, whose face is marred by dust and sweat and blood, who strives valiantly, who errs and comes up short again and again, because there is no effort without error or shortcoming, but who knows the great enthusiasms, the great devotions, who spends himself for a worthy cause; who, at the best, knows, in the end, the triumph of high achievement, and who, at the worst, if he fails, at least he fails while daring greatly, so that his place shall never be with those cold and timid souls who knew neither victory nor defeat. [10]

The key implication for the foregoing is that when dealing with media criticism, because you are naturally defensive, it is insufficient for you to rely on your own instincts, regardless of how well honed you believe them to be. Third party perspectives from your media team and from individuals outside your organization are extremely important, because it is so difficult to maintain objectivity about yourself.

The fourth element of your general strategy is simply to understand that how the media covers you does bear on your ability to manage. In politics and government, as the old saying goes, appearance is reality. How you and your department appear in the media, regardless of the accuracy of that appearance, becomes the reality not just to the general public but also to the individuals and organizations with whom you work. "A sensitivity to the media implications of any management decision—internal or external—is essential to the skillful public manager."[11] To that end, perform your job well. Good performance will not prevent you from being shot at, but you do not need to make it easy for journalists by running a slipshod operation.

The fifth element is to do your research on the reporters, editors, and editorial writers with whom you are going to work. Get to know (primarily by observation) their values, rules, work habits, ability, and professionalism. As an example, a reporter covering one of the agencies in which I worked had a lengthy daily commute and did not like to work past 5:00 P.M., so he was writing his story at 3:00 or 4:00 at the latest. We therefore had a shorter amount of time chase down answers to his queries than we did with other media. Which reporters will honor your request to keep something off the record and which ones will not (see below)? Which ones will retaliate if you complain to them or to their higher-ups about their coverage? Some media types are very susceptible to flattery; oddly, there are those who expect to savage you on Monday and be told they are doing a great job on Tuesday. You may have a greater or lesser stomach for kissing the posteriors of certain individuals, but the sad fact is that it can be effective all too often. Which editors expect to drive your agenda with their coverage and will continue to write about something until you react?

The sixth and final element of a good media strategy is to try to get as much good press as you can for your organization, so that you have some good will to draw on when you are criticized. You do not necessarily have to see your own name in print—ever, for that matter—but your agency probably does good things every day, many of which are newsworthy.

Your communications director should spend a large percentage of his time trying to get positive stories about your agency into the media. In this regard, do not forget that **op-ed pieces** can be used to talk about good things happening, in addition to rebutting negative editorials or news articles. Your department, if it works directly with the public, probably does good things every day. Catch a bad guy, improve a program, build something, do more of something else, provide a service to someone who needs it—all are fodder for press stories. Understand, of course, that not every proposed story will get coverage. Some approaches will work and some will not. And be sure to include each and every one of the smaller media outlets (radio stations, weekly newspapers, and any or all websites) in your outreach.

To improve your outreach, you need to instruct and re-instruct your directors to feed good stories to your communications team. Most members of your team are managers who are focused on doing their jobs and not used to thinking about public relations. It is always easier to get positive stories about your agency into the media than to prevent negative stories from happening. If you have a positive story, do not hold onto it, lest your good news be overtaken by events or swamped by a national news event. I recall an argument about when to release the news of a program we were starting to help mortgage foreclosure victims. We released it, it got headlines, and a national news story on the same subject broke the next day. Had we waited 24 hours, our program would never have received coverage.

Make sure that everyone in your operation understands that the truly good stuff is reserved for the chief executive of your jurisdiction. The simple rule, as was articulated in Chapter 9, is that the governor or county executive gets the good news and you get the bad news. It is amazing how many high-level administration officials do not quite get this one. Never get into a competition with the executive office over a good story; remember, your boss has to run for reelection and you do not. When the governor is announcing something, it may be the perfect time to display your "passion for anonymity." [12] In any case, if the governor is announcing something good in your department, does that not reflect well on you?

There is a reason why your media specialist is now called a director of communications and not a press secretary. While dealing with the traditional media is still her prime responsibility, there are other ways to communicate with the public. You should take full advantage of them. Do not ignore social media; it should be a mandatory part of your communications efforts. In addition, software now allows you to send mass e-mails to interested parties and track, for example, whether they are opened and read. You can and should send as much information as possible directly to the public. Some legwork is required to assemble a list of e-mails and set things up, but it will pay dividends. Social media and e-mail software will allow you to bypass the traditional media by sending out a communications pieces regularly and send targeted messages to give "your side of the story" when needed. It is a way of leveling the playing field somewhat.

Setting up your office properly can contribute to an effective media strategy. You should do all of the following:

1. employ a media professional,
2. fully integrate your media office into your daily operations,
3. have the media officer act as traffic controller for all media contacts in your department, and

4. establish a department-wide media policy.

If your agency is small and/or has a low media profile, you may be doing most of the media yourself. But any larger organization that has a media profile should have a media specialist if at all possible, and more than one if the volume of inquiries warrants it. One job of that specialist is to gather the intelligence about the media personalities as mentioned. Your lead press staffer (communications director) should prepare a media log at the end of every workday. A media log details all of the contacts your department has had that day with the media and either what the story prognosis is or links to the actual stories if online; it should be distributed to you, your leadership team, and the executive office of the elected official for whom you work. You do not want to be surprised by anything you read online, or in the paper the next day. I never want to read an employee of my department quoted in the press about a non-routine matter if I do not know about it first. Also, your director of communications should act as the chief spokesperson for your department.

Fully integrate your press team into your operations. Your communications director should always be an integral part of your leadership team. You should have no secrets from her. When discussing strategy, have your communications director in the room, both to advise you on the media implications of your decisions and to hear the background, context, and nuances of what is going on. She can do her job a lot better if she can hear the discussion firsthand, as opposed to having someone tell her what the decision is and then expect her to explain it to the outside world.

Especially when something bad is happening, the press always wants to push things to the highest level. They want the governor or mayor to comment in preference to you, and for you to comment in preference to anyone else in your department. In some jurisdictions, it is expected that the chief will comment on everything, and some executives like it that way. Absent that understanding, your job, and the job of your communications director, is to direct things to the lowest appropriate level possible. There are two reasons for this approach. First, the person with the most knowledge should do the talking, and that person is seldom you or the governor. Second, you are attempting to give the matter the attention you believe it deserves, which is not necessarily the attention that the press believes it deserves. When you speak about something instead of the communications director, you are elevating it in importance, so make sure the issue is important enough to warrant your participation. Of course, the key word here is appropriate. If something genuinely bad has happened in your agency, it is foolish for you to try to avoid talking about it. But unfortunately, many in the media believe that they and they alone should determine who will speak for your department on any matter, period. This insistence is no more appropriate than you getting to pick which reporters will cover you or which editors will pen the editorials concerning your department, but at some point you will have to deal with it.

All of the above assumes that if you assign spokesperson's duties for a given story to someone at a lower level, he can handle the job; he needs to be sufficiently articulate and not get stage fright or flustered if asked a difficult question. It is your communication team's responsibility to make sure that is so, providing media training if necessary and substituting another individual if warranted.

To that end, you need a media policy for your entire department, formally designating your director of communications as the department's chief spokesperson and requiring all individuals to check in with her before talking to the media. You need this policy because some members of the media will not hesitate to call your department's employees directly, without going through your media office. Also, while ideally your middle managers and your rank and file employees know what department policy is on an issue that the press will be covering, sometimes they do not. Employees at the rank-and-file level, and sometimes at the middle management level, are not at the level of responsibility to make policy—but sometimes they see a media contact as an opportunity to announce their own policy. You cannot prevent your employees from talking to the press, but you can insist that you know about it, and you can make it clear both to your employees and to the media what your policies are and who determines them. As with every employee policy, make sure it is clearly communicated to everyone, including the staffers who answer the phones.

Line employees seldom understand how they might be used (in both senses of the word) by the news media. When the health department I led banned smoking on the grounds of all of our office campuses (state law already prohibited indoor smoking), the local paper rushed over to the nearest campus to interview some of the smokers for their reaction. The coverage was about what we expected: an emphasis on the negative reaction of the smokers (as opposed to the positive reaction of the vast majority of employees), along with speculation as to the ulterior motives for the ban—as if we were something other than the health department. But the reaction of the employees who had been interviewed was interesting, if predictable. They were shocked that they had been quoted and photographed and landed on the front page. They were just having a conversation, not trying to make a statement, in their view. We did not doubt that the reporters had identified themselves or that their photographers had taken the photos in plain view. Rather, our employees simply were unsophisticated in their understanding of how the press operates. We assured the employees that there were no hard feelings, but it would have been nice to have had a chance to educate them in how the media works before they spoke.

You are going to be interviewed, so you should be aware of and use standard "best practice" interview techniques, most of which have not changed over the years. If you have not already received media training, schedule yourself for some, have your media staff train you, and/or read a good book on the subject.[13] You need not undergo weeks of training. One day should do it; just make sure that one of the topics covered is how to field difficult questions from difficult reporters. Media training is one area where the basic rules are pretty much the same for the public and private sectors.

In addition, the following are a few items that go beyond the basics.

You can read any number of media training materials about the supposedly inviolable ground rules for talking "off the record," "on background," or "on deep background." There are two problems with these rules: first, no two reporters seem to interpret the terms in exactly the same way, and second, certain reporters simply do not honor them, occasionally or usually. And even if they do honor the arrangement themselves, they can always be overruled by their editors. You therefore need to have a discussion with each reporter if you want to say something and not have it appear in print or on air with your name attached. And they have to agree to it, up front, before you proceed. Alternatively, do not say anything to a reporter that you would not mind reading in the paper, hearing on the radio, or watching on television. The latter is certainly the safer policy, although it may deprive you of the ability to provide some context that you cannot say publicly. In any event, your media staff should know which reporters will honor confidentiality and which will not.

Once upon a time, you could give a presentation to a large group (of either employees or the public) and be assured of its confidentiality by asking, at the start of your remarks, if any reporters were present. Those days are over. Asking the question is no longer sufficient now that everyone has a cell phone camera to record your every utterance and post it on YouTube if the mood strikes. A better policy is to remember the maxim that the camera is always on and the mike is always live.

Another media relations practice that has gone the way of the horse and buggy is that of "dumping" bad news on a Friday or right before a holiday, hoping that the timing of the release would get it less coverage than otherwise. Unfortunately, this approach does not work as well in a monopoly newspaper town, which is almost everywhere these days. They do not worry as much about anybody scooping them, so they may simply hold the story until they can give it more prominent play.

Another defect of the one-newspaper town is that you cannot play competitive reporters off one another. You cannot give access to some and shun others and you cannot go around a given reporter to give the story to another; they are sitting at adjacent desks in the newsroom. If you are dealing with the national press or a very large media market, you may have that weapon at your disposal.

All too frequently the media will respond to accusations by an employee or (if your department has people in institutional care) by someone who was in your care, or by the family of someone who was in your care, that you have mistreated them in some way. In my experience, most individuals and families who have legitimate complaints—and there certainly are those— seldom go the press. They want the situation corrected, maybe they want an apology, and in some cases they may want to know what you will do so that the problem will not recur. As long as you respond to their complaints, they neither need nor want publicity. Sadly, very often the employees, patients, and families who do go public are unreasonable, irrational, and/or have ulterior motives. The employee is likely trying to avoid discipline, and the family may be considering litigation to collect a damage payment.

You may face a significant issue in properly responding to an untrue accusation because of personnel or patient confidentiality rules, something that the complainants probably know all too well. They like it just fine that they can trash you and you are unable to respond. To prepare for this eventuality, have a confidentiality waiver form available, prepared by your lawyers, which you can give to the complainant and the media. Insist that the complainant sign it, and make public to the media that you have provided one to the complainant. Seldom if ever will the complainant sign, and he will usually cry foul that you asked. But in reply to the media you can say the following. "We would be most happy to provide all records and discuss the case in detail because we have done nothing that would not pass public scrutiny. At the very least, you will find that there are two sides to the story." In case of an extreme but unwarranted allegation, you can add that "You may find that the complainant has omitted key facts. When a complainant refuses to sign a privacy waiver, you can rest assured that it is because he does not want the facts revealed." Harsh language indeed, but it is 1) the truth, and 2) sometimes the only way to end the matter. Demanding that a privacy waiver be signed will not prevent initial press accounts of the allegations, but once the complainant refuses to sign, the media will catch on and that will generally be the end of the story (although nothing already in print or on air will be retracted or corrected). One thing that you can count on with the media—any time there is something that they cannot see, they get suspicious. This time, the suspicion will be directed at the complainant.

All of the foregoing similarly applies if the complaint is directed at the legislature instead of or in addition to the media.

If you get an "ambush" phone call and do not know what the reporter is talking about, or need time to reflect on a possible answer, it is perfectly acceptable to say, "Let me call you back." Of course, the return phone call has to be made before the reporter's deadline (not *at* the deadline), so inquire as to whether there is one and when it is.

Responding to e-mail is a little trickier. One the one hand, e-mail makes it more difficult to delay responding to a reporter if you need more time to prepare your response. Even if you are out of your office, assume that the press has your e-mail address and will not hesitate to use it. For their part, they will assume that you are monitoring your e-mail off hours—which you probably are. On the other hand, you can use e-mail to your advantage because you can respond quickly with information if that is all that is being sought, or take a little time to shape your answer if the question or questions being asked are difficult.

When in an actual interview, whatever the question, the key is to verbally pivot from *their answer* to *your answer* as quickly and as smoothly as possible. *Their answer* is the literal answer to their question, while *your answer* consists of the information you want to impart. As they say in political campaigns, whatever the question, always give them your answer. Your answer should always contain a **message**. A message is a short statement, usually 25 words or less, that expresses the essence of the point that you want to get across. The message is about what you are doing, but should be stated so that it will be of interest to your viewership, listenership, or readership. Political campaigns are conducted using messages (think "It's the economy, stupid" from the 1992 Clinton presidential campaign, for example), as is commercial advertising. Messages are sufficiently powerful that, other things being equal (like party registration totals and campaign fundraising), the campaign with the better message will almost always win. The elected official for whom you work will have effectively used messages in her successful campaign. Messages work in political campaigns and they work in everyday media relations.

Sometimes you will not be able to give their answer because you actually do not know. Should that be the case, your response should be different from how you respond to the legislature in the same situation (as discussed in Chapter 10). To legislators you almost always simply say that you do not know, and then respond to them as soon as you obtain the information. But with the media, never say you do not know and leave it at that. Say you do not have that information (their answer), but then provide some information you do have at hand that bolsters your argument (your answer). Even when you do know the answer to the question, you want to answer the question (their answer) but then append your message (your answer). At other times, the question will be phrased in an unfriendly way, often in a deliberate attempt to catch you off guard. You do not need to accept the premise of the question. As one communications director stated, "Once I figured out that I don't need to answer every question, this became an easy job." You can say that you do not agree with the premise of the question (their answer), and again, verbally pivot to adding the information that makes your case (your answer).

If you have watched any political debates, the best politicians are very good at this process. Whatever questions they get, they execute a quick verbal pivot to the point or points they want to make. This technique is referred to in political circles as "staying on message."

You can seldom persuade reporters that such-and-such is not news-worthy, because they have probably already made that determination prior to contacting you. As stated previously, reporters all too frequently have their story fleshed out mentally, if not already half-written, before they call you. But you can always put things in context for journalists—even if they are not interested because the facts interfere with their chosen story lines.

Naturally, to do a good job of providing your answers, you need some advance preparation. The more important the interview, the broader the audience, obviously the more preparation you should put into it. Interview preparation is equal parts anticipating questions and formulating not just answers, but *your* answers. You may not be able to correctly forecast every question you will be asked, but with a little thought, you and your communications director can probably anticipate about eight out of every 10. Think about what the two or three most important things you want to get across are—not details, but themes. Being able to give *your* answers is helpful when you are playing offense (explaining a new program, for example) but vital when you are playing defense (explaining why something went wrong and what you are going to do about it). Bolster those important points by marshaling facts, statistics, arguments, talking points and anecdotes. They are not the answers in and of themselves, but they can aid in illustrating your answers. As for your delivery technique, the media training should help you in that regard.

Regardless of how bad or unfair the questions are, do not zing a reporter in response. As stated earlier, the old saying is, never get into an argument with someone who buys ink by the barrel. In the digital age of today, the saying is, do not argue with someone who has thousands of Twitter followers. An extremely popular elected official can, once in a while, get into a public battle with a journalist or a media outlet; he will not win, but maybe he can get out of it with a draw. You, however, cannot, no matter what your level of professionalism or previous accomplishments.

The following is a comment and a story about corrections. Is there anything more worthless than a correction of a newspaper story error? No matter how grievous the mistake, no matter how prominently displayed, even if in a front page article, it will be corrected—if you can get a correction—in the fine print buried inside the paper where no one reads it. If you doubt the preceding, consider the following. My local paper once incorrectly stated my compensation, to the tune of about $30,000 annually, in an unflattering news story given prominent coverage. Instead of asking me what I was paid, the paper had apparently put two and two together and got 22. If it had been $300 or even $3,000, I would not have bothered, but I thought that $30,000 was an error sufficiently large to warrant correction. The correct figure ran in their semi-hidden corrections box. Shortly thereafter, I prepared an op ed piece rebutting the article. In the article I made humorous reference to my compensation not being what had been reported in the paper. The editor to whom I submitted my piece quickly shot back an e-mail asking me why did I not simply reveal what I was actually being paid. I replied that I had, and his paper had run the correction. His response: "I guess I missed that."

If a paper's own editors do not read the corrections, what are the odds that the average newspaper reader will? Certainly the bloggers do not, because they faithfully repeated the original error. I guess I should not complain; the paper did print my op ed. I can only laugh. In terms of strategy, you might try a phone call to the reporter and/or editor pointing out the error and asking them not to repeat it. Obviously, this approach will only work with a factual error.

But beyond the fact that a lot of journalism is not good for your digestion, negative media coverage has negative impacts on your organization. You should be aware of those impacts and try to manage them as best you can.

When I was a cabinet secretary, my philosophy regarding negative press was that my position amply rewarded me in terms of salary, prestige, and ability to accomplish things, and in return I had to expect that the press would hammer me periodically. I was paid to take the heat, but I did not feel the same way about my subordinates, and I especially did not feel that way about the rank and file employees of my department. Bad press, especially when untrue or only partially true, can depress morale, cause internal dissension, and even inhibit recruiting. I saw all three of those negative consequences at close range. As one communications director pointed out, "It's simple cause and effect."

The media, of course, does not view any of that as its concern even as it exacerbates what problems there really are. The head of the children's services division in one of my sister departments once graphed the departure rate of his social workers against newspaper criticism of his department and found, unsurprisingly, that there was a spike in resignations right after each spate of newspaper criticism. He himself did not last that long in the job, either.

There are limits to what you can do to combat such criticism, and what makes it worse is that your rank and file employees are generally at a disadvantage compared to politicians or corporations under attack. Elected officials and companies can fight back; government employees cannot. Assuming that you have terminated or are moving to terminate any bad actors, and that you are doing everything you can to fix whatever problems there actually are, what you can also do is remind your troops that they are good people, doing good work in a good agency. As detailed in Chapter 4, praising your employees and employee recognition are very important, and never more so than when a department is being subjected to severe criticism in the media.

## NOTES

1. Rosenfeld, *American Aurora*, 527.
2. Wilson, *American Government*, 38.
3. Davis, *Truth to Tell*, 138.
4. Chase and Reveal, *How to Manage in the Public Sector*, 146.
5. Carr, *Newspaper Barons Resurface*, New York Times 4-9-12, B8.
6. Morales, *U.S. Distrust in Media Hits New High*, Gallup Politics 9-21-12.
7. Ibid.
8. Wilson, *Rethinking Public Administration*, 139.
9. Adams, *This Is the Part Where You Pretend to Add Value*, 124.
10. http://www.theodore-roosevelt.com/trsorbonnespeech.html.
11. Chase and Reveal, *How to Manage in the Public Sector*, 151.
12. Brownlow, *A Passion For Anonymity: The Autobiography of Louis Brownlow*.
13. See, for example, Phillips, *The Media Training Bible*.

*Chapter Twelve*

# . . . And More

## "You Don't Always Get What You Pay For"

### INTEREST GROUPS

Interest groups have replaced political parties as the prime outside movers of public policy in this country. Almost anywhere you are in government, you will have to deal with them. They can be a significant challenge to you because both their goals and their frame of reference are usually very different than yours are as a manager.

A taxonomy of interest groups would consist of the following categories: good government groups, advocates, **NIMBY**s (NIMBY being the acronym for "Not In My Back Yard"), and economic interests. All of these types of groups have certain characteristics in common. There are also some universal approaches to take, whatever group you are dealing with.

The first and most obvious characteristic of interest groups is that, by their nature, they are not objective. They want what they want; that is their *raison d'etre*. Given that your goal is to make as many objective decisions as you can, it is inevitable that you will frequently disagree with them, if not clash. There is nothing inappropriate with them doing what they do; after all, when they contact you and your colleagues, they are exercising their First Amendment right to petition the government.

The first fundamental rule to obey when dealing with interest groups is never to ignore them, whether they are reasonable or unreasonable, and whether they are quiet or noisy. You have both a managerial and a democratic requirement to be responsive to them. Third parties (your boss, legislators, other elected officials, and the media) are always observing and evaluating your interactions with interest groups. They may display some understanding of your behavior if you disagree with these groups, but they will be completely unsympathetic if you ignore the groups or are otherwise unresponsive. Words you never want to hear at a meeting or read in print are, "We contacted them and never got an answer." A corollary of this rule is to remember that almost every group is composed of citizens who are constituents of your chief elected official. The second rule is to know what interest groups want. Whatever action you are taking, be sure to be familiar with which groups will be interested, and anticipate their reaction. There is no reason to be blindsided.

In making decisions regarding matters likely to be of concern to interest groups, consider a few things. First, to what extent do your boss, legislators, and the media listen to them? They have varying degrees of influence. With regard to your boss, while all groups are comprised of the citizenry, some are bound to be more important to her than others. If the Governor's Office does not tell you specifically, try to figure it out anyway. It should not be too difficult to determine which groups have political or other longstanding ties to her. When you do have to tell them you cannot do what they want, I repeat the maxim stated in Chapter 9 by of one of the governors for whom I worked: "Sometimes it's all about how you say no." A straightforward but gentle response beats a brusque one every time.

I want to add parenthetically that your approach with individual constituents should be identical. You and your staff should always be responsive and treat them courteously. Many constituents have no hesitation at telling you when to head in, differing only in how abrasive they are in doing so. The irate letter or e-mail (**"nasty-gram"**) from a citizen is a staple of government service. Always take the high road and respond professionally. You may be pleased at how often a courteous response to an impolite missive will surprise a constituent into reasonableness. They wanted to vent their anger, and having done so, your response will be just what they needed to calm down.

On the other hand, do not insist that your staff take verbal abuse. A disagreeable or even obstreperous citizen is one thing, but if a constituent is screaming and/or cursing at them, it is perfectly okay for staff to say, "Sir, if you continue screaming I am going to have to hang up and wait for you to call back when you have stopped." If that does not do the trick, they should be allowed to hang up. It does not happen often, but staff should be able to deal with such behavior appropriately.

Good government groups are perhaps the easiest interest groups to deal with, because they are generally well behaved and because they are not particularly influential with the media or legislators. In many places they are now virtually defunct. Such groups tend to have a limited understanding of how government actually works, which is why some of their proposals are so unrealistic. (Disclosure: I once served on the board of one such group.) Good government interests can be of almost no assistance to you; whether they can hurt you will depend upon how frequently or infrequently they are quoted in the local media. Your recipe for dealing with them is identical to dealing with other groups: be polite and responsive.

Advocates are an entirely different kettle of fish. Advocates have some characteristics that are very much in their favor and a few that will try your patience on occasion. The first characteristic that you should never forget is that advocates are generally advocating for someone else (even if that someone else is a family member) and not for themselves. That is all to their credit. This orientation is in contrast to that of other groups, like economic interests and NIMBYs, who want something for themselves. Second, they are mostly advocating for society's less fortunate. To that extent, they truly are on the side of the angels.

Perhaps fortunately for society, but unfortunately for you as a manager with limited resources, it is not the nature of advocacy to be satisfied, especially in the area of human services, where you are dealing with societal problems the permanent solutions for which are beyond the scope of your agency, or any agency, at least in any near time frame. No matter what your agency did yesterday, advocates will invariably see something new and more necessary today. From your point of view, this lack of satisfaction would be easier to deal with if your action yesterday had been met with a thank you from the advocate. But too often, the advocate takes what he received today and inserts it into his pocket; then, as if spring loaded, his hand returns to the beseeching position without any mention of what just went in to the pocket. For this reason, advocates might have easier jobs than yours—advocacy, after all, carries with it no responsibilities—but not more satisfying ones.

Even legislators often find advocates' behavior disconcerting. Legislators like very much to keep interest groups happy, but when they pass a bill or add to an appropriation and find that their actions are met with further requests more so than thanks, it is not what they are accustomed to.

Because of their passionate but limited focus, advocates do not understand your job and do not understand the environment in which you operate, and efforts to increase their understanding will probably meet with mixed success. Advocates have upbraided me after budget hearings, saying, "You have to be an advocate for more money for [name of program]." Sometimes, advocates think that you should be arguing against your governor and against your budget office, and in public at that! They do not understand that you are not in your job to advocate; you are in your job to make difficult decisions.

This lack of comprehension is most acute in difficult fiscal times. Advocates have little stomach for budget realities. Talking about resource constraints to advocates is generally like talking in a foreign language. What is highly important to you—perhaps the dominant element of your managerial day—is largely irrelevant to them. They will give you limited credit for preserving their programs in a cutback era. In their view, services should always be expanding and if they are not, you are partly or mostly to blame. I stated in an earlier chapter that my rule of thumb is that it takes three consecutive years of fiscal difficulty in your jurisdiction before advocates will begin to acknowledge that you, your department, and your city or state as a whole are constrained by money difficulties. This mindset was summed up by an advocate who urged me to allocate additional money to her nonprofit agency. I explained that our department not only had no additional resources for her operation, worthy though it was, we were actively cutting things back and I was trying to preserve the services we offered. My explanation should not have been necessary, as the facts were easy to ascertain for anybody who read a newspaper once in a while. Instead, she replied, "Well, that's not my reality," and renewed her entreaties. It was pleasant for her that she, by her own admission, lived in her own reality, but we managers do not possess a similar ability.

Advocates for the disabled (and some other groups) are a particularly sticky wicket. They see services for the disabled as civil rights issues; they are immune to any discussion of budgetary limitations, and such conversation talks past them.

Whereas you, in your dealing with always-limited resources, have to prioritize every day of the week, advocates do not. Engaging them in a discussion about where your limited additional resources should be placed (if more resources are actually available), or what vital services should be maintained if you are making cutbacks, is usually an unproductive exercise. They cannot prioritize, and they do not want to. Everything that they want is, in their view, essential. More than once I have advised groups of advocates to unite behind a few items and devote all their energies to seeking those items, rather than trying for everything, every year, but my advice has seldom been taken. They could be both more effective for themselves and more helpful to you if they would prioritize more often, but such is seldom the way of the world.

Because the foregoing characteristics are so pervasive, when you find advocates who are reasonable, go out of your way to befriend them. Give them as much access as they want, listen more closely to their requests than those of the less reasonable advocates, and put them on the advisory councils and other boards and commissions that may orbit your agency. Unfortunately, the more reasonable advocates tend to be heavily outnumbered by the less reasonable ones. But with all advocates, whatever their degree of reasonableness, the number one rule of thumb is to engage, engage, engage. Take their phone calls. Meet with them whenever they request it. You should be on a first name basis with the leaders of any major advocacy group. When your goals and those of advocates do line up, make sure that you go out of your way to communicate that alignment to them.

Two things advocates always do are try to get more money for you and request reorganizations of your agency. Advocates will constantly make proposals to legislators, on their own, seeking additional funding beyond what you asked for or the governor recommended for you. Sometimes, such efforts will succeed and you will have additional money to put towards a program or programs. Usually this is helpful to your department, although it may mean that some other agency did not get what they wanted or needed. Advocates also like to propose reorganizations that always have the same goal: concentrating the programs they favor into a (generally) smaller agency that focuses only on their area of interest. The desire for reorganization is a typical advocacy response, based on a fundamental misunderstanding of the political process. Because advocates believe so fervently in the rightness of their cause, if they are not getting what they want, in their view it is obviously because the structure of the government is inhibiting them. Advocates are always convinced that if their program or programs stood by themselves, they would not have to compete against everybody else and they would get more money as a result. They want to "capture" that new agency and have it do their bidding. In reality, of course, regardless of any program's place organizationally, there is always competition for resources, another thing that advocates do not understand. Such reorganization proposals are seldom adopted, but you may end up spending more time than you would prefer to explaining that the move is not indicated, because it would almost always end up fragmenting services.

Advocates' narrow focus also means that, when you are taking heat for a program they are concerned about, they are not likely to come to your defense. An action like that is simply too far outside of their customary operating parameters.

As passionate as advocates are in favor of something, NIMBYs are equally passionate, if not more so, against something. Typically the NIMBYs (pronounced NIM bees) are against the construction of something (a road, a new development, a new building, low income housing, or other) or the location of a special population (the mentally ill, the developmentally disabled, ex-inmates in halfway houses, recovering substance abusers, and the like) in or near their communities. NIMBYs are probably the most problematic of all outside entities with which you will have to deal, for a simple reason: their issues are not generally amenable to compromise. The objectionable (to them) construction or population is either going to be located in their community or it is not. There is no middle ground.

The most important rule to live by when dealing with NIMBYs is to be very, very thorough every step of the way. Follow all statutory requirements, cut no corners, and do not deviate from any standard procedure or regulation. Nobody does hypertechnical review like NIMBYs. They will place every facet of your decision process under an electron microscope and use the slightest abnormality as a basis for their protest, up to and including legal action. Such individuals will often advance what they believe to be sound policy arguments, in considerable detail, against your facility. But in reality, they have no interest in programs and policies, generally or specifically. Their only interest is in policies as they may pertain to the facility in question. They never previously expressed such policy views, and they will never subsequently express them.

I have the most familiarity with NIMBYs protesting the location of special populations in their neighborhoods, so I will write primarily about them. I have seen this issue from almost every angle except for having a facility located next door to me personally. As a civic association president, at the behest of my neighborhood I lobbied against an apartment complex being located in our single-family home community. When I was a legislator, I exposed a department doing something to the patients of a hospital that department ran that they should not have been doing, then wrote a law restricting them from doing it again. Within a few months, a high profile group home was installed in my district by that department. I am sure it was just a coincidence. I worked for an elected official whose spouse objected to a facility proposed for location near her home. And as a cabinet secretary, I spent a lot of time getting funding for and then supporting the siting of residential treatment facilities for needy populations.

It is futile to advance high-minded arguments in favor of treatment for people with disabilities (people recovering from addictions/people trying to reenter society). Opponents of your facility do not care. NIMBY objections to locating a special population in their neighborhood revolve around two types of fears: fear that the population will do something untoward and fear that having them live nearby will depress property values. That neither of these things is likely to happen is beside the point. Many people believe them to be true and there is nothing you can do to convince them otherwise. If you hold a community meeting and, say, 100 people show up, as you give them information, you will be able to allay the worst fears of some of those 100. You can tell that this is happening because those individuals who have received answers to their questions will leave when they are satisfied. That is not to say that those who are satisfied are happy to have the facility in their neighborhood; if given the choice, they would not opt for its location in their community. But they have been satisfied to the point that they are going to withdraw from active efforts to block the facility. However, even after that cadre departs, you are always going to be left with an irreducible minimum of people who remain unhappy and strongly opposed to your facility. For these individuals, the one and only thing that will remove their concerns is the passage of time. After a year or so goes by and nothing bad happens, the opponents will consciously or subconsciously realize that, in fact, nothing bad *has* occurred, and they can live with the special population in their midst.

Do not expect to ever hear them acknowledging that their fears were over-blown, however.

Complicating your dealings with NIMBYs is that they will often have the support of local legislators. The legislators may in fact know, based on previous experience, that the facility being sited is no danger to the community or its property values, but it is a rare legislator who will stand up to an angry crowd and tell them they have nothing to be worried about. Too, legislators often have longstanding ties to the civic activists who become the leading NIMBYs. Sometimes they will try to have it both ways by being supportive of such facilities in general while attacking your process for locating one in their community. Which is, in fact, the origin of the term NIMBY and an accurate description of one. Many NIMBYs will make what they think is a sophisticated argument against your siting decision by stating that such a facility is much needed—just not where you are proposing to locate it.

In addition to the "just not right here" line of attack, other arguments against your facility will be so numerous that you can only admire the NIM-BYs' creativity and tenacity. Many of them will put you in a "damned if you do, damned if you don't" conundrum. If your facility is located in a more affluent community, residents will demand to know why you are not saving taxpayer money by locating all facilities in neighborhoods where property purchase and remodeling costs are cheaper. Individuals in less affluent neighborhoods want to know why all the homes are located in their communities; a typical question will be, "Is there one in *your* neighborhood?"

While openness in government is usually a good thing, it is much less so when siting residential treatment facilities. The less attention that you can draw to your location decisions, the better. Given that the passage of time is the only way in which certain community residents will stop fearing that something bad will happen as the result of a new facility being located nearby, the more you can do to let that time pass without incident, the better. You should not make your siting decisions a secret, but there is no reason to trumpet them publicly, either. You should make every effort to portray the installation of a group home or other facility as completely routine, especially if your department has others already up and running. For this reason, you as the organization's head generally should not attend community meetings. You do not skip the meetings to avoid taking fire; instead, your absence is an effort to send the signal that nothing extraordinary is taking place. I have not always followed my own advice in this regard, and often regretted not doing so.

If the protest reaches critical mass, you will probably have to have a public meeting and take questions from the NIMBYs. How the meeting will go in large measure is dependent upon how the legislator or civic leader who runs the meeting introduces things, sets the tone, and conducts the proceedings. You can be faced with the civic leader who opens things up by stating,

"Maybe they'll explain to us why they lied." (The leader who actually made this statement in a meeting I attended eventually realized that he had made a mistake, but he had already fed the audience red meat, and it was too late.) Or perhaps you will be fortunate enough to have the civic leader state that "These gentlemen are our guests and we will treat them as our guests." Whenever a friendly legislator conducts the meeting, I do not ask him to defend us; I just ask him to set the proper tone of the meeting up front. We can handle anything that comes afterward.

It is very important to avoid procedural mistakes. As soon as you have to admit that your agency has made one or more, you have lost the moral high ground and your task of dealing with the NIMBYs becomes much more difficult. Your department might have failed to follow its own procedures for notification, there might be a construction mishap, you might not have properly vetted your providers—whatever you have done incorrectly, the NIMBYs will find out because they are looking very closely for any misstep. Making mistakes confirms every NIMBYs belief that your agency is incompetent and makes bad decisions, the worst of which is locating the facility in their neighborhood. Now you *do* have to attend the community meeting personally and apologize to the group for your agency's mistake(s).

The worst NIMBY situation I ever experienced was when a local newspaper, which was in the midst of bashing our department, decided to put the news of a group home on the front page. It was probably one of the more irresponsible journalistic acts I have ever seen. It was at that community meeting that the civic leader opened the session by hoping that we would explain our lies. The paper then decided to join the NIMBY review of our process. In our system, a group home usually involved two providers, one who owned the home and another who provided the services to the residents. The reporter covering the story discovered that the provider who owned the residence was also the owner of adult bookstores in an adjacent state. Although that ownership really had no bearing on the matter at hand, it represented a substantial **"ick factor."** I felt like the John Travolta character in the movie *Primary Colors*, slamming his fist against the locker, complaining, "I just can't catch a break, can I?"

Even if your agency has made mistakes, you cannot deviate from the placement of the treatment house in the location you have chosen. You want to be able to say, in the future and truthfully, that you never reverse course on a siting decision because then you would be reversing course repeatedly. I have made the statement to angry groups of NIMBYs that from my point of view, it does me no good to exchange one group of upset citizens for another. They do not like it, but it might be the only thing I say which they completely understand. If you do change direction, you are greatly increasing the likelihood that the next community will insist on the same thing—if not every community thereafter.

Anti-development activism produces a slightly different kind of NIMBY. I have little experience working with them, so I will not offer recommendations. I will observe that some anti-development activists are so strident that they should more properly be labeled not as NIMBYs but as **BANANAs**, as in Build Absolutely Nothing Anywhere Near Anybody.

The final kind of interest group is the economic interest. Their interest is in your agency's spending—they want to see it directed towards their businesses. Examples are construction companies and building trade unions who want to see government spending on infrastructure, and pharmaceutical companies that want to see government health care spending on drugs. Insofar as economic interests want spending directed to general categories, their efforts are mostly benign. You may disagree (or may have to defend your boss's allocation), but it is just an argument over priorities. Occasionally, economic interest groups can, through their lobbying efforts, get you more resources in, say, your jurisdiction's capital budget.

What is more problematic occurs when they want spending directed in very specific ways, to very specific companies. The worst of them are the pharmaceutical companies, which do not want any kind of cost controls put on drug spending. They will engage in very sophisticated tactics, from lobbying to lawsuits, to prevent such cost controls from being put into place. They will send consultants to your doorstep to explain ways in which you can save money—which ways will exclude any mention of medication costs. They will introduce bills in the legislature to thwart your efforts. After they do, you may encounter one of their lobbyists in the capitol, as I did, who will tell you that "we're doing this for good government," in which case it will be all you can do not to laugh in her face. They will enlist advocacy groups and persuade them—perhaps with a nice grant to their organization—that they should complain that cost controls will hurt the health of their members.

I cannot offer any tactics that guarantee success, only the encouragement to keep fighting, because you represent the public interest, while they represent only their own corporate profits.

## AGENCIES THAT SHOULD ALWAYS HELP YOU—AND SOMETIMES DO

"So you think you are going to run a health department and spend all your time making people healthy? Wrong."[1] Why is that statement incorrect? Because if you are in charge of an operating or line department, you are going to spend as much if not more time on budget and personnel issues as on program issues, and because you cannot deliver services without enough money, enough people who can do the job, facilities that are adequate, and the right information systems.

Interagency cooperation is vitally important, whatever agency you are in. No agency is an island. That being said, there is a dynamic tension between overhead or central agencies on the one hand and line or operating agencies on the other. If you are on the operating side of the fence, in an agency with responsibilities for health, social services, transportation, correction, agriculture, commerce, or labor, you tend to use the term "overhead agency" to refer to the departments on the other side. If you are on the central side of the fence, in a budget office, personnel or human resources office, administrative or general services department, or finance or revenue department, you tend to use the term "line agency" when speaking of those on the other side. But both sides need each other. In my first cabinet assignment I ran a central agency, and in my second cabinet posting I ran an operating department, so I have seen things from both perspectives. If you run a line agency, your relations with central agencies like the budget, personnel, accounting, facilities, and information technology departments are key. States one private sector chief executive, "You need to get X done, and you need these other three departments to give you X amount of time in order to succeed at that. The people who truly succeed... are the ones who actually have figured out how to mobilize people who are not their direct reports. Everyone can get their direct reports to work for them, but getting people who do not have to give you their time to engage and to support you and to want you to succeed is something that is sorely missing from...school courses."[2] A veteran city manager put it in these terms: "It is not nearly enough to assemble a staff of competent and achieving managers inside one's department; one must find and enlist such people in... other departments as well if one wants to accomplish anything."[3]

But the shoe needs to be on the other foot, too. If you run one of those central support/control agencies, your mission is simpler, if not easier. You need to help the line agencies get their jobs done while doing your own. You need to have the attitude stated by one of my directors, who made this comment about the other agencies with which he worked: "They like me because I help them succeed." If your agency does not have a customer service orientation, it needs to adopt one. Do everything you can to avoid petty bureaucratic behavior, and keep the lines of communication open not just at your level, but also at every level below. Never insist on the protocol that a line employee once told me prevailed in his department. At an interdepartmental meeting, I told a mid-level staffer from another department to phone me if he needed further information. He explained that he could not do so; he would have to send his request up the chain of command in his department until it reached the secretary's level; that secretary (who was not present at our meeting) could then forward it to me. Hearing that, I was surprised that the employee had been allowed to attend my meeting unescorted.

When you have your own internal decision to make as to whether a function or an activity will be centralized or decentralized, by the way, the key dimensions to consider are how specialized the activities are, how regularly or episodically they are performed, and how sizeable the existing infrastructure is to handle the problem. The less often an activity occurs and the greater degree of specialized expertise that is required, the greater the argument for centralization. For example, management of construction projects is very complicated, and the projects themselves do not occur very often in a given agency, which means that most agencies do not have anyone on board whose job it is to run a project. Centralization is therefore indicated.

As a cabinet secretary running an operating department, I tended to understand the job of and sympathize with the budget director, relations with whom were described in Chapter 6. Every unit of government has as part of its responsibilities to carefully manage tax dollars, including but not limited to a balanced budget requirement. Because I always tried to make my departments more efficient, I related well to the budget office, which had the same goal. I was much less sympathetic to the personnel office or other central agencies because, in my view, they did not have responsibilities of their own in the way that the budget office did. Their job should simply be to support other agencies. I especially viewed them unfavorably if they displayed poor customer service. It is all the more exasperating because whatever the staffing issues you have (problem employees you cannot get rid of, shortages of particular skills, inadequate training, or whatever) you are going to take the criticism when those problems contribute to poor performance, not the central human resources office. You have the responsibility, but they have a lot of the authority.

Of all the central agencies, by far the worst tend to be the personnel or human resources operations. One veteran manager and wit described them as "neither civil nor service."[4] Of the federal personnel system, the recent "A New Civil Service Framework" report issued by the Partnership for Public Service had this to say: "The American federal civil service system, the foundation for effective government, is in crisis...stuck in the past, serving as a barrier rather than an aid to attracting, hiring, and retaining highly skilled and educated employees needed to respond to today's...challenges.[5] The chief problems of government personnel systems tend to be the hiring process and the disciplinary process. Working with the discipline and especially the termination process was covered in Chapter 4. As for hiring, "More often than not the hiring process involves an interminable number of steps and a great amount of time."[6] At one jurisdiction in which I worked, the hiring process averaged over 270 days—nine months! Gestational analogies aside, the personnel folks did not view the length of time it took to hire someone as any kind of crisis; the system was what it was. At least they had the data; many personnel offices cannot even tell you how long it takes to bring a new employee on board. The customer service ethos of many human resources offices is encapsulated by the credo of one human resources middle manager, as follows: "You start by saying no to the request."[7]

Another systemic problem of personnel systems is their bias towards people already within the system—in other words, preferences for tenure and hiring from within over even lateral transfers, let alone individuals from completely outside the governmental body. Sometimes the bias is overt, sometimes not.

Another common criticism of civil service is the system's inability to reward top performers. While said inability is pervasive, it will probably present less of a problem to you, because many government employees are not as strongly motivated by money as employees working for corporations. As described in Chapter 4, many public sector employees are in government because they are willing to trade a little less compensation for a little more security. They will still complain if they do not get a raise, but they are less likely to leave because of it. You would certainly prefer to be able to reward your employees for top performance, but not having that particular tool in your toolkit just does not cause you as many difficulties as other personnel system defects. Also, there are other ways to reward employees, chiefly with praise and recognition.

Despite my fondness for almost every budget director with whom I have worked, if in your jurisdiction human resources is rolled into an Office of Management and Budget structure or a Finance and Administration department instead of standing alone, the situation may be worse and not better. If the two functions are combined, you will almost always see a numbers person at the head of the outfit. You will have a numbers person in charge of the people function, never a people person in charge of the numbers function. The result, unfortunately, is that personnel may be seen as a cost center rather than a vital support function, exacerbating the lack of customer service. This is all the more true when your jurisdiction is experiencing difficult fiscal times. Human resources will be used as a cost control mechanism, to the detriment of operating departments. In one jurisdiction where I worked, the merger of budget and personnel into an OMB office resulted, when times got tough, in the budget director's elimination of the ability to reclassify positions. As discussed in Chapter 6, reclassification of positions is an extremely powerful management tool that allows agencies to adapt their organizations to changing times, needs, and workloads. While some positions require upward classification and greater expense, just as many reclassifications downgrade a position into something less costly. Properly done, the reclassification process need not cost any additional money. And even if it did, managers should be allowed to reclassify positions if corresponding cuts are made elsewhere. But that ability was lost. Later, that office ended all expenditures for employee recognition, a very penny wise but pound foolish decision.

Arguments among departments are not confined to central agency vs. line agency issues. Line agencies can also argue amongst themselves. Some arguments are set up by design, e.g., prosecutors and pubic defenders. But other arguments come about because jurisdictions overlap and laws are unclear or ambiguous.

Personnel systems cannot be changed unless the elected executive—who almost always has bigger fish to fry—makes it a priority or hires a customer-friendly human resources director. In either case, the decision will not be yours to make. "Most managers can't change the governing system within which they work."[8] You can complain, but more importantly, you need some coping strategies.

The first and most important coping strategy is to focus on what you can do that is internal to your own organization. You are going to spend a lot of staff time trying to tweak the personnel system (and, to a lesser extent, other systems) so hire a good tweaker as your personnel or administration director. Good ones can be worth their weight in gold. Second, master the administrative rules of personnel, procurement, facilities, budget, and information technology. Ideally, your administration chief can take the lead, but you and your immediate staff should know a lot, too. Your directors also need to understand the rules. Train them, orient them, explain things to them. Your leadership team meetings will probably never lack for agenda items because there are always budget, personnel, and other overhead rules and procedures to discuss—in other words, learning how to play the game.

In dealing with any overhead system, make your case on the merits. Take the time to justify your requests, and jump through all the hoops. Present your arguments professionally at all times. Scream amongst yourselves if need be, but smile to everybody else. When middle managers deny you unreasonably, go to their bosses. Often that will produce results. Almost the only bureaucrats you will never be able to work with are those who have no boss or whose boss is unwilling to manage them.

Of course, sometimes the merits alone will not get things done, as in dealing with problem employees. When that happens, it is time to be persistent. Persistence pays off. You should not hesitate to make repeated requests; the squeaky wheel gets the grease. When denied, repeat your request at every opportunity. They can deny you every time, but they are going to keep hearing from you in the future. "The stamina and resourcefulness of the administrator are what count."[9]

Try to play by the rules, but all rules are not created equal. First, do not wait for permission to do something not specifically prohibited by the rules; do it if it will help get the job done. In other words, be entrepreneurial. One of my departments constructed a building to provide some space we desperately needed, using our own employee labor, plus leftover funds we had on hand. We did not get a specific legislative appropriation because we did not need it. A few years later, the auditors did not like it, but had to admit there was nothing that legally prevented us from doing what we did.

Second, almost every rule or procedure has flexibility. Identify all the flexibility you have and then "max out" on it. Third, almost all rules have exceptions or waiver mechanisms. Look for every opportunity to acquire as many of them as you can and then use them. Appropriations measures frequently have explanatory text attached to them, which can provide a perfect vehicle to obtain exceptions for your agency. If any other department has been granted an exemption, try to get it for yours as well; it should be easier because the precedent has already been set. For example, when we noticed that regular merit system hiring procedures had been waived for certain difficult-to-find employees in other departments, we sought and received permission to hire doctors and nurses in our department without the normal personnel rigmarole. The Department of Transportation was given permission to waive overtime pay rules during certain weather-related emergencies; we got the same waiver for our facilities staff who also worked during those emergencies.

Fourth, get permission to do a "test" or "pilot" project as a way of proving that something will work. Our department wanted to replace newspaper classified advertisements with internet classifieds. Our belief was that it would save money but not restrict the number of bidders. Instead of trying to pass a law converting all of state government, we sought and received an exemption for our department. Ultimately we were proven correct; we saved advertising expenses and, in today's world of e-commerce, did not lose any bidders. Finally, if there is any way to get any part of your operation set up to operate exclusively via special or enterprise funds and not general funds, do so. The flexibility special funds offer will be a great boon to your agency.

As much as you try for a collegial working atmosphere with your cabinet colleagues, and try to work out your differences at your level and not the governor's, unfortunately not everyone will have the same attitude. Some of them will not be using the same rules of team play, especially those who are more worried about their own image than that of their boss. These individuals are easy to spot; they will often occupy their positions only as long as it takes to get a better, higher-paying job somewhere else. As mentioned in Chapter 9, they are the ticket-punchers. One thing to bear in mind is that Memoranda of Understanding (**MOU**s), those documents beloved by bureaucrats, are valueless. If people in the two agencies have a cooperative spirit, a memorandum is unneeded. If the staffers have a confrontational approach, no MOU can force them into cooperating. Sadly, once in a while, what does work is acting like a jerk. If you never behave badly, sometimes your bad behavior will force an uncooperative counterpart into action. I discovered this by accident. When confronted with an e-mail offering the latest excuse for why his department could not do something for us, I composed a very nasty, heated e-mail to forward to one of my staffers bitching, frankly, about my colleague. But I made the classic e-mail *faux pas* and hit the "reply" button instead of the "forward" one. Because the e-mail was addressed to someone else, my colleague may have thought I did not realize I had sent it to him. I never received a reply, but the job I had been requesting be done in vain for months was completed forthwith. I tried the same tactic, this time on purpose, on one other occasion, and it worked then, too!

## PRIVATIZATION, VENDORS, AND CONTRACTS

To privatize or not is one of the key management questions that you may face from time to time. Depending on the length of your tenure and your budget situation, you may be stuck with the status quo (government employee provided services or privatized ones), because the transition costs and implementation time required make a change both mechanically and politically undoable. But if you are fortunate enough to be implementing a new or expanded service, or if fiscal exigencies force you into an examination of whether you could save money by privatizing one or more of your activities, you will be at a key decision point. You will need to make your decision very carefully. Unfortunately, a lot of the advice you may be given is more simplistic or even ideological than practical. I have attended conferences where the superiority of privatization was taken as a given. I have read a great deal of literature extolling the benefits of privatization. I have heard the advice given by a well-known privatization expert and former elected official, who suggested that any service that could be found in the yellow pages (when there was such a thing) is a service that should be privatized. The ideological approach to the problem is the wrong one, however. Instead, privatization decisions should always be made on a case-by-case basis. The decisions are complicated ones. You have to be very careful when you privatize a government service, because "You don't always get what you pay for."[10]

Privatization has two major benefits that are hard to ignore. First, it is attractive from a media point of view. A public-private partnership sounds good, and implies the best of both worlds. In fact, it may deliver them. Second, contractors are free of the personnel restrictions, procurement rules, and budgetary micromanagement that often bedevil you. In theory, free of the bureaucracy, they should be able to move more nimbly than a group of government employees carrying out the same activities. On the other hand, your managers probably fear the loss of control and the ability to be responsive once services become privatized, and with good reason. It is never guaranteed that you will be able to maintain the appropriate level of quality in service, and save money over the long haul, merely by privatizing.

Three questions must be answered before anything is privatized. The first, threshold question is whether the service is appropriate for privatization. Second, will your department have sufficient resources to monitor and supervise the contractor or contractors who will be performing the service? How good will your agency be at "steering rather than rowing"?[11] Third, and most important, is there sufficient competition in the marketplace to provide you with a product that is equal to or better than what you could deliver with government employees, and at a cheaper price?

You should not place policy-making functions, or regulatory and compliance functions, in private hands under any circumstances. Public safety functions, judicial activities, and revenue collection theoretically can be privatized, but the public is likely to be nervous when they are, and you can expect quality issues somewhere down the line.

Some literature portrays good oversight as the key to the success of your privatization. It most emphatically is not. You can have all the oversight you want, but it is having viable alternatives that gives you leverage and protects you against the downside risks of privatization: poor performance, and the possibility that you will generate savings in the short term but incur higher expenses in the long run. It is competition that lowers prices, not privatization per se.

It is not enough to be able to bid out a service. A competitive bidding system, by itself, is insufficient to guarantee either an adequate product or service at a reasonable price. The key question, instead, is whether there is a genuinely competitive market for what you are buying. Will there truly be multiple bidders—bidders with a demonstrated track record of delivering the specific service well, for other governmental bodies? Will there be multiple bidders not just the first time you bid, but every time? Further, once you have selected a given company, can you terminate the contract? Not just, do you have the legal ability to terminate the contract, but do you also have the practical ability to bring in a new provider if the original vendor's performance is unsatisfactory, not just six months into the contract, but six years down the line? It will probably have to be a substitute provider, because privatization is usually a one-way door. Once you exit, there may be no re-entry. If you give up your employees and assets when you privatize, and a few years down the line you want to go back to delivering the service in-house, you will almost certainly have lost your ability to do so. You need to either perform a very thorough analysis before you privatize, or else retain some capacity to perform the work yourself.

That analysis, by the way, should either be performed in-house, or if contracted out, never by a firm which wants to provide the service being studied. Segregate the analysis of whether to buy something from the buying of it; allow a firm to bid on the study or on the subsequent work, but not both.

Otherwise, there is a huge potential for a biased analysis in favor of outsourcing.

There are various reasons why a bidding process by itself may not produce the competition you are seeking. Many American industries—everything from telecommunications to prison health care—either have already devolved into oligopolies as the large vendors buy the smaller ones, or are trending in that direction. The oligopolistic or even monopolistic nature of certain sectors will hinder your ability to control costs, as they charge you (and all of their other customers) what economists refer to as **rents**. More important, it will diminish competition for privatized services. In one department I ran, we issued a very large bid and received five qualified respondents. We needed to hire two qualified vendors, and we were pleased to be able to do so. But by the time the service was next out for bid three years later, two of the five original companies had bought out two of the others. We were down to just three likely respondents when we needed two—not much of a margin for error.

It may also be the case that the industry is operating at or near capacity. Should this be the situation, you may not get competitive prices or adequate quality the first time out. The private sector eventually responds to increased demand with increased capacity, but "eventually" may be problematic for you in the interim.

Exactly what constitutes a sufficient number of bidders should be considered carefully. One bidder is obviously insufficient—and governmental bodies on occasion do put out contracts for bid and do receive only one bidder (or even no bidders). Half a dozen *qualified* bidders give you more of a comfort level. Privatization usually succeeds when there is a large volume of providers. But any number between two and five should make you nervous, if not immediately, then over time.

As discussed in Chapter 7, in one department I ran, we handled a service that is probably privatized in 100 percent of the jurisdictions across the country—construction of government facilities. Would I change that arrangement were it within my power? No, but as indicated, it was hardly without a series of problems. Other privatization efforts throughout the country have either not saved money, or achieved notoriety due to quality problems, or both.[12] A Massachusetts state auditor's report in 1995 debunked that state's highway department claim of savings from privatizing road maintenance.[13] A 2001 Bureau of Justice Assistance study of prison privatization concluded that the projected large cost savings had not appeared.[14] In 2012, New Jersey's privatized halfway houses became embroiled in scandal due to performance issues.[15] In 2014, Idaho's privately run prisons were under investigation.[16] Closer to home, I insisted that a department over which I had jurisdiction bid out a weekend service which was being provided by our in-house employees on overtime. I was convinced that an outside firm could do the job cheaper. The *low* bid came in at triple what it was costing us. Fortunately, in that case it was a simple matter to reject the bids and go on as before.

Whether you add any privatized services or not, you will be dealing on an ongoing basis with contractors, vendors, and providers who are already performing those services for your agency. Those interactions will include but not be limited to the following: hearing them out when they have ideas on how things should be run, inviting bids for their services, and negotiating contracts with them. Each of these areas presents challenges.

As also mentioned in Chapter 7, vendors, if they are resident in your jurisdiction, sometimes forget that although their contracts are with officials like you, they really are working for the public. Because they themselves are members of the public, while you are government officials, they have a tendency to think that you work for them. When it comes to insuring that you are getting quality work, you may have to gently or not so gently remind them that *you* represent the citizens and taxpayers.

Prospective vendors like to present ideas to your agency about new and different ways you can hire them. You will sit through a few such sales pitches yourself. Some of them may come from supporters of your boss the elected official. Some of the ideas may be good and others not so good, but in any event, no matter how attractive the idea, and regardless of the fact that company X was the first to bring you the idea, you should always issue an request for proposals and see who else wants to sell their services to you besides company X. If company X genuinely has the best product, they will prevail in a fair procurement process.

As discussed above, you need analysis before privatizing. Sometimes, even after performing the analysis and having it come back favorably, you will face additional obstacles. "Any willing provider" regulations or laws—which require you to set a price and allow any provider willing to accept that price to deliver the service—are an obstacle to saving money. Dispense with them if you have the option; of course, you may have no say in the matter.

Opposition to bidding for services maybe even come from your own employees. If you have dedicated procurement staff, they do not usually object to rebidding services, because writing bids is what they do. However, frequently some or all of your procurement work is performed by line agency staff. Be aware that line staff are often reluctant to go out to bid. They generally prefer to renew existing contracts as opposed to issuing a new request for proposals. For one thing, it is far less work, and for these line employees, a new bid is often an additional task for individuals for whom procurement is just one part of their responsibilities. Your staffers also have an unfortunate tendency to develop relationships with vendors—not necessarily anything inappropriate—that prevent them from seeing the potential advantages of a fresh approach or an opportunity to save money with a lower price. You can also expect that vendors who have enjoyed long-term contractual relationships with your agency prefer things just the way they are, and will lobby you, your boss, and the legislature to keep them that way. I recall more than one borderline obnoxious phone call from a board member of a vendor vociferously arguing for a no-bid renewal of his agency's contract. "We're the only ones who can do that job," he asserted. He was not happy with *my* assertion that if that were the case, it would be plainly revealed by an invitation to bid. As discussed in "Interest Groups" earlier in this chapter, pharmaceutical companies did everything they could to prevent my health department from moving drug buying into any kind of competitive process. Sometimes, ostensible proponents of a free market system are not so keen to compete in the marketplace they claim to revere.

A good way to look at any prospective or current vendor is to examine their clientele. Does the vendor sell to multiple clients, preferably both public and private, or do they have only a few clients, all government agencies? More problematic is the current vendor who has only one client and you are it. It is a good bet that you could deliver those services in house, better and cheaper, but reconstituting the capacity to do so may not be an option if one of your predecessors dismantled it to save money.

As mentioned previously, adequate reporting and monitoring systems are not the most important ingredient in the success or failure of a privatization effort. But they are nonetheless essential if you have any contractors working for you. Good monitoring efforts can save you a lot of embarrassment at the hands of auditors, legislators, and the media. If a vendor is not performing well, you certainly want to know it before anybody else knows it, so that you can take corrective action.

Unfortunately, any bidding system that awards contracts based solely on lowest price is not going to give you the best quality. Low-bid contracting is bad for human services, bad for professional services like architecture and engineering, and even bad for construction, although it is almost universally used therein. It is okay for commodities, where the vendors are all selling the same things. Make sure you know exactly what you are purchasing. "Proposals to provide 'drug treatment' are quite different from proposals to provide methadone maintenance to a specified number of addicts."[17] Performance contracting is the way to go. What is it that you need delivered, and how much? Do not tie the vendors up with "how;" specify the "what." Expect them to make a profit; there is certainly nothing wrong with businesses making money. If they do make money, as Economics 101 tells us, that fact will attract more bidders the next time you go out to bid. If they do not, they will not be bidding the next time around.

The basic principles of negotiations, including negotiating contracts, were covered in Chapter 7.

## LAWSUITS

As the head of a government agency, you will be sued regularly. The bigger your agency, the more litigation you will face. Get used to it. Although I never made an exact count, I estimate that my departments were sued about once a month, every month, for 16 years in a row. When you are working with your legislature, some days you are playing offense and some days you are playing defense. Unfortunately, with litigation you almost always get to play only defense. Some lawsuits named only my department as the defendant, some named my department and me, and in some I was the only defendant. Individuals, businesses, and advocacy groups sued for all manner of reasons.

Some suits will be substantive and contract, policy, or employment oriented, some will be eligibility oriented, and some will be frivolous. Frivolous lawsuits may well outnumber all the other kinds of suits put together. In the frivolous category, my personal favorite had to be the time that a very overweight individual sat down in a chair in the waiting room of an agency the offices of which were in a building my department maintained, and the chair collapsed underneath him. He sued. To make matters more amusing, the agency in question, the Department of Justice, supplied the attorneys who represented our department in almost all legal matters, including this one. They succeeded in getting the case dismissed; they did not, I noticed, provide any clarification to the court or the defendant that the furniture in question, like all office furniture, was purchased and maintained, if maintenance applied in that case, by the Department of Justice, not our department.

Organizations and people who sue you do so for a variety of reasons. Sometimes they want to win the case, but just as often they want to embarrass you and/or want to achieve through the adverse publicity of a lawsuit what they cannot achieve through negotiations. In extreme cases, they can resemble terrorist attacks—they know they cannot win, but they hope they can disrupt you and make you fearful. In the course of one cabinet assignment, I came upon an unusual situation involving a service to individuals with disabilities that, primarily due to its expense, could not be offered to everyone who wanted it. A waiting list had been established. I discovered that, instead of the list being either strictly first come/first serve or alternatively, greatest need first, certain wealthy individuals were being allowed to make a kind of co-payment and jump to the head of the line. I was appalled; it was one of the most unsettling things I had ever seen in all my years of government service. I immediately halted the practice, and from that point forward, the waiting list was based solely on greatest need. I expected to pay a political price, and sure enough, when the advocacy group representing them could not get me to change, they filed suit. The group's press release and subsequent commentary trashed our department thoroughly, although they did not speak of the new policy that did not like. Eventually, we did settle that particular suit, but I am proud to say that we did not alter the "neediest first" policy.

Lawsuits should not bother you because you are thin-skinned or because they often result in negative publicity (see above and below); they should bother you because so many of them are frivolous, political in nature, weak attempts at extortion, and/or enormous time wasters.

One thing to understand is that many individuals and groups will threaten to sue you even if they have no intention of suing. If you back down every time a suit is threatened, you will be emasculated very quickly. I do not care about threats; my question to my attorneys is always, can you defend me? Never be afraid of a threatened lawsuit, even when you get a nasty letter like the one I once received from a leading member of the "sue the government" bar in our state. That 19-page, single-spaced epistle, written on behalf of one of my employees, threatened me and two other administrators at great length and in colorful verbiage with all manner of professional, personal, and financial ruin. As the employee on whose behalf the letter was written had never been disciplined beyond receiving a verbal counseling, let alone been subjected to the horrendous acts we were accused of, I was not too worried. Beyond turning over the letter to our counsel, and making sure that we documented all further dealings with that employee, we did not modify our behavior. No lawsuit ever was filed, and the employee left for a different job before the year was out. I am reasonably certain that the original conversation between the client and the attorney took something like the following form. The lawyer told the employee that she had no case, but for $1,000 or some other sum, he would write the nastiest letter imaginable and see if that produced any results. After all, nobody can bloviate like a lawyer in high dudgeon. When the letter brought about no change, that was the end of the matter.

Never be afraid of an actual lawsuit, either. As stated, it comes with the job. Being sued can be a terrifying experience to someone who has never been sued (and to someone who has never been threatened with a lawsuit). Part of your job is to reassure your staffers who are named as defendants or threatened with litigation that the end of the world is not nigh.

Of course, such reassurance should be offered after you make a careful assessment of the quality of your lawyers. I have been in situations where I have had to use lawyers who were not chosen by and did not report to me. On other occasions, I have been able to choose my own outside counsel. At still other times I have worked with in-house counsel but have been able to select them myself. Be aware that your counsel, especially if you have no role in selecting them, may not be of first quality. I have been represented by highly competent in-house lawyers and by below average ones, including the gentleman who assured us the case was in the bag right up until the day we lost a million dollar damages verdict. How vigorously you contest a case is unfortunately going to be determined as much by the quality of your counsel as it is by the merits of the case.

In a major case, by the way, you should generally opt for outside counsel if you have the choice. As a wise head once stated, "It's nice once in a while not to have to go up against guys in $1,500 suits with guys in $150 suits." But there may be an exception. It is sometimes helpful to know (and know that your adversary knows) that your legal costs are zero while your opponent's legal meter is running. If you are in that kind of situation, consider having your attorneys string the case out by filing some extra motions to run up your opponents' bills. It may well have an impact on their will (or even their ability) to pursue the case.

In the course of working in the judicial branch of government for eight years, in addition to being a regular defendant for 16 years, I have learned a few things about how to handle being sued. The most important thing that I have learned is that you need to be a client who actively manages any litigation in which your agency is involved. Never leave the decisions about case management and strategy solely to your lawyers, no matter how competent they are, lest they fall back on certain lawyerly habits. Some lawyers will resist your efforts to make the final decisions, because they think the judicial process is their bailiwick and you should defer to them. This is especially true when the lawyers are not your department's employees. As one frustrated colleague of mine lamented, "I had to draw them a diagram showing that I'm the client and they're the lawyers who work for me." Always consider their advice carefully, but make your own decisions, because 1) it is your name and/or your department's name in the **caption**, not your attorney's, and 2) every decision you make sets a precedent. You should not let attorneys make decisions that have management implications without your supervision, any more than you would let other technical personnel make management decisions by themselves.

In my observation, lawyers love to settle cases. Many think that they have done their job when they have "mediated" (in their minds) the disagreement so that you compromise somewhere in the middle between your position and that of your adversary. And, of course, they no longer have to prepare for a trial. I seldom need lawyers for that because I can negotiate things myself, or deploy one of my trusted aides to do it for me. I need my lawyer to advocate for me, something she has been trained to do, and which I am not allowed to do in court myself because my advanced degree is in public administration, not law. And I never want to settle a case when I believe my department is clearly in the right.

Lawyers also like to give you policy advice in the guise of legal advice. Make sure you are getting the latter and not the former. This recommendation applies to lawsuits and it applies even more to other times when you are consulting them. Finally, be sensitive to lawyers who are more concerned with what the judge wants than what you want.

Lawyers always advise you to have no comment when you are sued, but that is one piece of advice you should rarely adhere to. When you are sued, plaintiff's lawyers often use the following tactic. They file the suit in court very late in the workday and send a statement to the press. What they are hoping for is that the press will print their allegations and that you will decline to comment because you "have not seen the suit." Or, as the lawyers like you to say, "We don't comment on lawsuits" or "In view of the pending litigation, it would be inappropriate to comment." Should that occur, the plaintiffs have accomplished their goal: gotten their side of the story into the media without the public hearing your side. If nothing else, unless you truly have no idea what the suit is about, you should have your spokesperson say that there is absolutely no truth to the allegations and that you will defend yourselves vigorously. As in politics, if you let attacks go unanswered, you risk having the public believe what is being said by the other side. Even better is to issue a detailed refutation. If you have gotten wind of a possible lawsuit, prepare your talking points in advance. If you are taken by surprise, assuming the suit is not available on line, if necessary have a press aide drive to the courthouse and get a copy of the complaint.

The press handles litigation as they handle many other things. The allegation by itself is generally news, regardless of its merit, and at best you will get to offer a refutation. There is no attempt by the media to discern the truth. Weeks or months later, when many lawsuits are dismissed as baseless, the media is nowhere to be found.

Knowing the status of every case you have on the books is part of effectively managing your litigation. Your directors should be required to give you an update on every single item of pending litigation in their weekly or biweekly reports. Unless every case is listed on every report, it is too easy to lose track of cases and have counsel tell you something that happened after it happened. You need to know, of course, that a case has been filed in the first place, and the report should include all developments in the case, including motions, depositions, discussions your staff has had with counsel, trial progress, verdict, etc. Naturally, the update may (and frequently will) consist of the words "no new developments since the last report." For major cases, and for all cases heading to the mediation, settlement negotiation, or trial phases, make sure you get a briefing on the case, and give your lawyers parameters within which to work. Because I was sued all the time, and most other staffers are sued only occasionally, this area is one where I was careful about delegating my decision making authority. (Despite the size of my agencies, I never had a general counsel on staff. If you have one, delegation is appropriate.)

Your lawyers, if they are competent, should be able to get rid of most of the frivolous lawsuits. But occasionally one will advance farther, and you will have to consider whether to settle. Many public and private sector entities believe that you should settle cases to avoid headaches and the possibility, even if remote, of a bad verdict. I disagree strongly. Every settlement, but especially a settlement in an unworthy case, increases the likelihood of future lawsuits and settlements. Settlements create the expectation on the part of litigants and lawyers alike that your jurisdiction will automatically pay money to get rid of a lawsuit. As one government lawyer put it, "You're sort of feeding the monster, if you will."[18] Most jurisdictions now have a "sue the government" bar whose practice consists of suing public officials and governmental bodies. Be aware that the members of this bar talk to each other and trade case files. There is no possibility that your "confidential" settlement will remain so in terms of other counsel—although it may keep the result out of the press.

Beware of end runs by plaintiffs. While you are sticking to your guns, they may be talking to your fellow cabinet secretaries, legislators, the mayor's office, the mayor's supporters, even the mayor himself, to generate pressure on you to settle the case in their favor—giving only their side of the story, of course. The good news is that if they are trying to go around you and force you into settlement discussions that you are not willing to hold, it is a pretty good indication that they suspect they are unlikely to prevail in court.

The one exception to this general rule is in the area of employee litigation. If such litigation is being brought by a dismissed employee trying to get his job back, your calculus should shift. As discussed at length in Chapter 4 under *Problem Employees*, it is very important to get rid of bad employees, and once they are gone, even more important to keep them gone. If you have won at every stage—and there are always many stages you have to win before you get to court—you do not want to lose at the very last step and have to welcome the bad actor back into your department. In this type of lawsuit, unlike other litigation, your most important goal is not to avoid paying out taxpayer dollars unnecessarily, but to keep the dismissed employee out of your organization. If the cost is not too great, *and* if the settlement terms include the employee remaining fired, *and* if those terms insure that the fired employee will not be trying to get any other job in your jurisdiction, consider a settlement. To put it a little more colloquially, pay the two bucks before you have to eat the employee.

Cases in which your agency has truly done something wrong call for a different approach. You should not only settle the case, you should issue an apology, which should be made by you personally, to the offended party. It is your agency's responsibility as a public organization to apologize, and your responsibility as the captain of the ship to issue the apology, simple as that. You should do so even if the suing party exaggerates his injury or the extent of the damages, which they very often do. It is easy to tell when that is going on because the litigants run to court before they have even complained to upper management; they smell a payday. Nevertheless, wrong is wrong and that is all there is to it. Again, my favorite example: the family who sued because one of our employees purposely disclosed personal health information about their child to a third party. They sued, alleging that the violation of privacy was unconscionable. The violation of their privacy *was* unacceptable; we disciplined the offending employee, apologized, and settled. But I did find it ironic that the disclosure of private health information to one person was so awful that it merited disclosing that same information, via public court documents, to the entire world.

Just because I do not like settling cases does not mean I like or have confidence in the judicial process. Litigation and court cases are a terrible way to decide anything. Judges know nothing about your business, and that lack of knowledge frequently shows up in their rulings. Many of the substantive lawsuits you will face are economic in nature, but, as a couple of scholars put it, litigation "addresses matters that are economic in substance, but it must deal with them through a complex legal process."[19] These scholars were referring to antitrust matters, but might as well be talking about any technical matter you deal with. The legal process is also cumbersome, lengthy, and inadequate. In a court of law, process, unfortunately, is more important than substance. The courts recognize these defects on some level, because they frequently mandate mediation before any trial. Unfortunately, the mediation process is not much of an improvement, especially if you believe you have a strong case. The mediator's job is to persuade or hector you into a settlement. They care not for the merits of the case; their goal is to get you to split the difference. As stated, if I have a strong case, I am disinclined to meet in the middle.

Your attorneys, if they are good ones, are going to tell you how risky trial is, and they are correct. Trials are risky because you never know what a judge or jury will do. They are also risky if you do not have complete confidence in your counsel (and sometimes even if you do). Remember that in the legal process, the only thing that counts is what is in writing. If it is not written down, to a judge it does not exist. You may have said something verbally 100 times, and it may be everyone's understanding of standard procedure, but it does not count if there is no piece of paper. To a layman, therefore, it seems that the side with the biggest pile of paper is going to win most of the time. Also bear in mind that certain judges never seem to rule in favor of the government, whether your opponent is an individual, group, or company.

How you deal with litigants and potential litigants may increase or decrease the likelihood of future lawsuits. One firm rule you should always employ is not to engage in discussions with any organization or individual who is suing you, outside of the legal process. I am always surprised when an organization asks for a meeting or meetings to discuss an issue, does not immediately get what they want, and then sues me. Then, they want to come in and have some more discussions. Sorry, you can sue me or you can talk to me, but not both. Use the ongoing litigation as the rationale to avoid dealing with the organization in other areas. There has to be a negative consequence for litigating. One lawyer had the nerve to depose me and then, as soon as the deposition was concluded, ask for a private meeting on the spot to discuss the case. I sent him on his way. Another firm rule comes into play when a party with whom you are having a dispute, but who has not yet taken legal action, asks for a meeting. Schedule the meeting, but if the other side shows up with their attorney, the meeting is over. Meet with them on another occasion with your counsel present, too. They are simply gathering evidence for their upcoming lawsuit.

## A FEW LAST RANDOM THOUGHTS

Information technology is not only vital to your operation, it gets more vital every year. You cannot function without it. In the current information age, your department's information systems should be a constant priority. Even when I was in charge of building maintenance, one of their main priorities was first acquiring and then improving their scheduling software. Better information technology both allows your agency to be more productive (doing more of the tasks that you have) and increases your capabilities to perform additional tasks. Most of the major initiatives in my cabinet assignments could not have been accomplished with adequate **IT**. Governments should generally spend more money on information systems, not less. Unfortunately, governments are often reluctant to commit funds to upgrade IT, spooked by systems projects gone wrong or gone way over budget, or both, if not in their jurisdiction, then in a nearby one or on the national level.

Most such projects have failed because they have been poorly managed. Every jurisdiction needs a cadre of good systems project managers, but many governments do not have sufficient numbers of such managers, if they have them at all. Agency management of IT projects is like agency management of construction projects. Most agencies embark on such projects sporadically rather than regularly, and therefore have no infrastructure in place for such management. Even when agency personnel gain experience from participating in or managing a systems project, by the time the next one comes around, those experienced personnel may have moved on to other positions. As a result, departments often have neither the ability to select the best contractors nor the experience to supervise them. If your agency lacks adequate project management staff, either get such managers on board before you embark on major systems improvements, or turn project management over to a central agency that has them.

Projects have also failed because they bit off more than they could chew. Incremental improvements are usually the way to go, not enterprise-wide solutions.

The well-publicized difficulties with the information systems of the Affordable Care Act, both on the federal level and in some states, has thrown a spotlight on this area, but in reality these types of problems are nothing new.

If your agency has regulatory responsibilities, you should be aware that legislative and public attitudes towards regulation demonstrate a high degree of volatility. Such attitudes shift with the political winds, and wax and wane depending upon the latest headline involving the regulated entity or industry. Your challenge is therefore to maintain as great a degree of consistency, both from case to case and over time, as possible. Keep an even keel and strive always for fairness. Also, regulatory jobs have an unfortunate tendency to attract people with punitive personalities. As discussed in Chapter 4, here is where you are likely to find cowboys and cowgirls. They will be a difficult challenge to manage and, hopefully, terminate.

As for a philosophy of regulation, your first goal should always be bring people or organizations into compliance. Punishment, in the form of monetary penalties and sanctions for non-compliance (not to mention shutdowns), should be regarded as tools to achieve your ultimate goal of compliance, not ends in and of themselves. There are many advocates, not to mention the media on occasion, who are convinced that the imposition of punitive measures is the only appropriate course of action. In severe cases, punishment is required. But educating the staffs of regulated entities about compliance requirements, creating incentives for compliance (not just consequences for being out of compliance), and providing services that facilitate compliance will very often achieve better performance by regulated entities, along with less disruption and cost to those entities. This approach has been called "winning compliance."[20]

Finally, elected officials with executive responsibilities (other than your boss the chief executive), such as attorneys general, auditors, comptrollers, and cabinet officers in some states, can cause problems for you and your chief if they are of the opposite political party—and sometimes even if they are of the same political party. Ditto legislators and legislative staffs of sunset committees charged with reviewing your agency. They all have both the motive and the opportunity to publicly criticize you and your department. If they are not bold enough to take a swing directly at your boss, you make a convenient alternative target. At their worst, these officials "second guess your decisions...have perfect hindsight...[and] claim to see the big picture, but get bogged down in trivia and minutiae."[21]

Among the worst of these characters I have dealt with are those of limited intelligence, the investigators who continually shift the focus of their investigations until they find <u>something</u>, and especially, the shameless self-promoters. Of course, not all such officials are so bad; many are very professional. Few cause you constant, as opposed to occasional, problems. Regardless, your strategy in dealing with the bad actors should always be to act as though take them as seriously as they take themselves.

In my mind, auditors typify these officials. In more than 30 years of reviewing audit reports, I have seen exactly one that identified a significant issue that we in management were not already aware of, and one other audit that made a good recommendation on how to improve our operations. Instead, overwhelmingly, audits focus on how well organized your paperwork is. But there have been a lot more than two negative newspaper headlines generated by those audits over that same 30-year time frame. Fortunately, because the audits generally lacked substance, the newspaper accounts were one-day stories.

## NOTES

1. Chase and Reveal, *How to Manage in the Public Sector*, 82.
2. Lyne interview, *New York Times* 10-4-09, Business 2.
3. Wilson, *Rethinking Public Administration*, 77.
4. Chase and Reveal, *How to Manage in the Public Sector*, 69.
5. Partnership for Public Service, *Building the Enterprise: A New Civil Service Framework*, 7.
6. Chase and Reveal, *How to Manage in the Public Sector*, 69.
7. Ibid, 73.
8. Osborne and Plastrik, *Banishing Bureaucracy*, 51.
9. Chase and Reveal, *How to Manage in the Public Sector*, 75.
10. Sclar, *You Don't Always Get What You Pay For*, iii.
11. Osborne and Gaebler, *Reinventing Government*, 25.
12. See General Accounting Office, *Private and Public Prisons*, for example.
13. Sclar, *You Don't Always Get What You Pay For*, 39.
14. See Bureau of Justice Assistance, *Emerging Issues on Privatized Prisons*.
15. Dolnick, *As Escapees Stream Out, a Penal Business Thrives, New York Times* 6-16-12, A1.
16. Associated Press, *Idaho: F.B.I. Enters Investigation Into Prison Operator, New York Times* 3-8-14, A12.
17. Chase and Reveal, *How to Manage in the Public Sector*, 87.
18. Weiser, *To Curtail Lawsuits, City Decides It's Time to Fight, New York Times* 2-26-13, A19.
19. Adams and Brock, *The Bigness Complex*, 103.
20. Osborne and Plastrik, *Banishing Bureaucracy*, 199.
21. Ashworth, *Caught Between the Dog and the Fireplug*, 126.

# Acknowledgments

Writing a book is similar to managing a government agency in that it is a team effort, even if the people who help you with the book do not necessarily know they are helping you. Some people help you get the book published, others assist you with the writing of it, and still others teach you, advise you, correct you, mentor you, and share their knowledge with you so that after 40 years or so you possess enough knowledge yourself that you can attempt a work like this one. Some individuals helped me in more than one category, so you will see their names more than once.

Ted Harpham and Honey Meconi, published authors themselves, gave me encouragement and excellent advice on how to get published, and my only mistake was to take most of their advice rather than all of it. The staff of Bernan Press were a pleasure to work with, especially the perpetually cheerful Mary Meghan Ryan.

As for the writing, I'll start by thanking my wife, Sharon. When I said I was going to take a year off from salaried employment to write a book, she neither questioned my sanity nor, since she was going to be the only one earning income for a while, demanded to make all the financial decisions for the family. That year came to a close, I took a new job, and it eventually took four years to write the book, but she was still nothing but supportive. She also served as first reader and ace proofreader.

Some individuals read drafts and provided extraordinary help. Pete Ross critiqued my original outline and rough drafts and provided raw material in the form of his own lecture notes and prepared remarks. Then he read the entire draft and provided even more good suggestions. Mark Brainard is the individual described in the introduction who gave me the idea for the book in the first place. He, Jim Grant, and Wayne Smith provided incisive commentary in their areas of expertise. Carolee Kunz calls her reviews hypercritical, but they are also hyper-helpful. Harry Hill read every word and kept me going with his feedback. The book is so much better for their input.

Thanks to Attorney General Matt Denn, Steve Groff, and Leah Jones Woodall for supplying institutional memory in areas where I did not follow my own standard procedure and failed to write it down, and to Madge Farooq and Doug Gramiak for providing needed information. Also, thanks to Mary Kate McLaughlin and Albert Shields for their moral support.

Now the teaching, etc. end of things. As I look back on my career, three people stand out as having taught me the most about human nature, politics, and government: Lowell Groundland, Ed Freel, and Pete Ross. They have been and continue to be endless sources of wisdom. They have been my mentors, whether they knew it or not. My hope is that somewhere along the line, I have helped others the way these three have helped me.

When I first sat down to write this book, I was going to call it, *What They Didn't Teach Me In Grad School*, but as I kept recalling things to add to the book that the **MPA** faculty at the University of Delaware taught me, I realized that title was completely off base. The teachings of Jeff Raffel on problem solving, Dan Rich on organizational dynamics, Jerome Lewis on personnel, George Hale on budgeting, Paul Solano on financial management, Bill Boyer on comparative government, Bill Rives on statistics, and Rick Sylves on intergovernmental relations, among others, remain with me to this day.

The University of Notre Dame's government department also taught me very well as an undergraduate. John Roos and the late Paul Bartholomew in particular stand out.

My siblings and I laughed endlessly at our dad's P3s ("Policies/Practices/Procedures") that he used to manage everything in his life, from his architectural practice to his July 4th cookouts, but there was a lot of wisdom in what he had to say, and he had a checklist for everything long before people were writing books about them. Those siblings (Honey, Kevin, and Mike) and I, despite the fact that we work in four completely different fields of endeavor, all ended up in management of one form or another—and found a great deal of commonality in our managerial efforts.

I have drawn material from a multitude of interesting biographies and books on history, government, and management. I particularly want to tip my cap to Gordon Chase and Elizabeth Reveal's *How To Manage In the Public Sector*, Kenneth Ashworth's *Caught Between the Dog and the Fireplug, Or How To Survive Public Service*, and Richard Clay Wilson, Jr.'s *Rethinking Public Administration: The Case for Management*. I have never met the authors, but I know that their understanding of and appreciation for management makes them kindred spirits. Some very good book and newspaper interviews of public and private sector managers also provided me with a ready supply of quotations to illustrate points I wanted to make, especially Adam Bryant's *Corner Office* column in the *New York Times*.

The backbone of this book, however, comes from what I have learned throughout my career from bosses, colleagues, and coworkers. It is not too strong to say that I have loved almost all of the people I've worked with over the years. Because of my coworkers, there has scarcely been a day in my life that I didn't look forward to going to work. And almost every week of my professional career, somebody offered a new (at least, new to me) aphorism or insight that perfectly described something or captured the way something should be managed. It is surprising how many I remember, but I can't remember the provenance of all of them. You may recognize something in this book that you said to me but that I did not give you public credit for. If so, I apologize and assure you that I am no less grateful for the insight you provided.

I do remember specific things said by former bosses Senator Tom Carper, County Executive Paul Clark, Attorney General Matt Denn, and Governor Ruth Ann Minner; former cabinet colleagues State Senator Brian Bushweller, Congressman John Carney, Judge Carl Danberg, J.J. Davis, Ed Freel, Dave Mitchell, Pete Ross, Tom Sharp, and Stan Taylor; former members of my various leadership teams Elaine Archangelo, Lynn Beaty (who gave me the lead quotation for Chapter 4), Ollie Edwards, Carol Ellis, Renata Henry, Harry Hill, Gloria Homer, Paul Ignudo, Michael Kelleher, Allison Taylor Levine, Jay Lynch, Karryl McManus, Bob McWilliams, and Kathi Weiss; former colleagues and coworkers Angie Basiouny, Mark Brainard, Jeff Bullock, Dana Rohrbough Garber, Jim Grant, Steve Groff, Lowell Groundland, Marcus Henry, Mike Houghton, Larry Lewis, Terry Martin, Janet Huber Mason, Tom McGonigle, the late Bob McMahon, Wayne Merritt, Greg Patterson, Joe Schoell, Brian Selander, the late Paula Shulak, Chief Justice Leo Strine, Dawn Thompson, and Sherry Woodruff; legislators I served with or worked with: State Senators Nancy Cook and Dave Sokola, and three Speakers of the House, Lonnie George, Bob Gilligan, and Pete Schwartzkopf; consultants T.J. Brown and Ruth Hallenbeck; and assorted friends, acquaintances, relatives, and teachers, including the late Alda Burrows, Bob Byrd, Ed Crumlish, Scott Douglas, Lucy Frontera, Scott Green, Bill Holloway, Mike Meconi, Ed Menzel, Jeff Raffel (who gave me the lead quotation for Chapter 7), Dan Rich, the late Jim Soles, and Jill Taylor.

And last but not least, thanks to The Best Management Team Ever Assembled In the State of Delaware. You know who you are, you know what you did, and you know how much I enjoyed every single day I worked with you. We put on a show that I wish had never ended.

# Glossary of Terms and Abbreviations

**Adding value**: reviewing a document for content rather than signing it perfunctorily

**Ad hoc manager**: a manager who directs operations using no fixed philosophy or norms, but makes it up as he goes along

**Alignment**: employee congruence with the goals of your department and/or the elected official to whom you report

**Asymptotic relationship**: approaching closer and closer to a goal but never reaching it

**Backlog**: an accumulation of cases that cannot be processed in a reasonable time frame

**BANANA**: an acronym for "build absolutely nothing anywhere near anybody;" refers to an individual strongly opposed to almost all types of land development

**Best value contracting**: a bidding system in which an agency is allowed to consider factors other than just price, including speed and quality, when selecting construction contractors

**BIYOT**: an acronym for "bring in your own team"

**Boilerplate**: standard contract language dealing with technical details rather than major provisions

**BS**: cattle excrement

**Bucket budget**: a budget in which the agency and its leadership are responsible and accountable for spending within the overall total rather than within each specific line item

**Caption**: the heading of a legal document containing the names of the parties (e.g., Smith v. Johnson), plus the court name and case number

**CEO**: Chief Executive Officer

**CHIP**: Children's Health Insurance Program, a government health care program for low-income children, jointly funded by the federal and state governments

**Colloquy**: a scripted public dialogue

**Conflict of interest**: a situation in which a government employee has an outside interest that has the potential to interfere with his judgment in a government matter over which he has authority

**COO**: Chief Operating Officer

**Courtesy interview**: an interview conducted to fulfill the request of a job applicant or someone recommending that applicant, but that is not expected by the interviewer(s) to result in a job offer

**Cowboys and cowgirls**: ostensibly competent employees who are nevertheless unable to take direction and regard themselves as being the only people qualified and appropriate to determine what they should do on a daily basis

**Cubbyhole**: assign a problem employee minimal or no duties and otherwise ignore him

**Cutback management**: reduction of expenditures, ideally in a manner that minimizes or avoids reductions in services

**Cutting and investing**: reallocating an agency's spending from lower to higher priority items

**Debarment**: prohibition against a contractor bidding on future work

**De-layer management**: eliminate a layer of middle management

**Delegate model of representation**: the philosophy that a legislator should base his votes on the views of his constituents, even if they conflict with his own judgment; converse of trustee model of representation

**Duty of fair representation**: the legal obligation of a labor union to represent all of its members in collective bargaining and disciplinary matters fairly and in good faith

**EAs**: executive assistants

**Emotional intelligence**: the ability to control one's own emotions and assess and understand the emotions of others

**Entitlement programs**: government programs that distribute benefits based upon fixed eligibility criteria; individuals meeting those criteria are automatically entitled to those benefits

**Exception report**: a report that documents only what is abnormal

**Exempt position**: a position that is exempt from merit system hiring and firing rules and serves at the pleasure of the agency head and/or the elected executive

**Faculty room admonition**: a directive by a supervisor to modify certain behavior, communicated to an entire group of employees verbally or via e-mail, when only one or two of the employees have engaged in the behavior that needs correcting

**Favor bank**: interactions with the legislature in which assistance one individual renders to another invariably results in reciprocal assistance at a future date

**Fig leaf compromise**: a compromise that is announced by both parties as reaching a middle ground, but which in reality greatly favors only one of the two sides; the minor provision(s) that favor the other side constitute the fig leaf

**Fire drills**: processes that are rushed, chaotic, and confusing

**Fiscal year**: an organization's budget year, which is usually different from the calendar year; the federal government's fiscal year runs October 1 through September 30, and the fiscal years of many states and localities run July 1 through June 30

**FOIA**: an acronym for Freedom of Information Act; pronounced FOY uh

**Frame**: a media description of a government official or organization that is both overarching and stereotypical; it is likely neither fully accurate nor complete

**Functional silos**: organizational sub-units whose employees typically display more loyalty to their unit than to the organization as a whole; also known as functional stovepipes

**Funding silo**: the money appropriated to a governmental sub-agency or program that cannot be used or reallocated for any other purpose

**FYI**: for your information

**Game of Old Maid**: when a sister agency highly recommends a poorly performing employee of theirs in the hopes that you will hire them

**GPRA**: Government Performance and Results Act

**Guerrilla government**: employees of an agency advocating, publicly or privately, for policies contrary to those of higher management

**Hard landing**: an employee dismissal that takes effect immediately after the employee is so advised, and which offers no other position to the dismissed individual

**HR**: human resources

**Hypercrisis**: a crisis in which media, legislative, regulatory, and/or law enforcement criticism and investigations become so intense that they achieve critical mass and explode

**Ick factor**: disgusting or disreputable aspect of something

**Idiot-proofed**: a document prepared for signature on which the place(s) to be signed are indicated by highly visible, easily removable markers reading "sign here"

**Ignore-micromanage polarity**: a supervisory style of the executive office of an elected official in which they either completely ignore or try to micromanage the different aspects of what is going on in your department, but nothing in between

**IQ**: intelligence quotient

**IT**: information technology

**J curve**: an indicator that gets worse before getting better than it was at the starting point; so named because if graphed, the trend line resembles an italicized capital J

**The John Q. Citizen rule**: never ask for or accept special treatment because of your position as the leader of a government organization

**Land mine list**: a list of questions that might be asked of you at a legislative hearing

**Leadership team**: an agency's highest ranking managers and the key professionals in the office of the agency head, with whom the department leader runs the agency

**Leverage (1)**: an expenditure of an agency's funds that generates additional funding in the form of a grant from another government agency or other outside entity

**Leverage (2)**: when negotiating, the amount of power either side has to force an agreement favorable to its own interests

**Life cycle of the administration**: the phases of the term of office of an elected executive and his appointed officials, focusing on the time elapsed from the most recent election of the executive and the time remaining until the next election for the executive position

**Line-item appropriation**: a budgetary appropriation for a specific category of expenditures in an agency, such as personnel, travel, supplies, or contractual services

**Loss leader**: in retailing, an item deliberately sold at an unprofitable price, designed to induce customers to purchase more profitable items; in government, a deliberately or accidentally unpopular part of a broader proposal that becomes the focus of negativity, resulting in the other parts of the broader proposal gaining approval

**Management by exception**: a style of management that focuses on identifying and fixing problems

**Managing upward**: a subordinate adjusting her style to fit that of her boss

**Medicaid**: a government health care program for low income, elderly, and disabled individuals; jointly funded by the federal and state governments

**Member's Representational Allowance**: the sum of money budgeted to each Member of Congress for office, staff, and other administrative expenses

**Message:** a brief statement, usually 25 words or less, that succinctly expresses the point that you want to get across

**Minor capital improvement (MCI)**: a smaller construction project; may be defined as a project not exceeding a fixed dollar amount, or as one that does not require the use of professional design services

**MOU**: memorandum of understanding; a written, interagency agreement

**MPA**: Master's degree in Public Administration

**Nasty-gram**: an e-mail harshly critical of something you or your staff has said or done

**NIMBY**: an acronym for "not in my back yard;" refers to an individual protesting the proposed location of a facility in or near his community

**Op ed piece**: a relatively brief essay written by an outside source and printed on the page opposite the editorial page of a newspaper

**Organizational culture**: the values, norms, attitudes, and expectations of employees of your agency (or other organization)

**Overtaken by events**: when your planned course of action is rendered less optimal or even moot by rapidly changing circumstances

**Paralysis by analysis**: reluctance or inability to make a decision for fear that some salient information has escaped the attention of the would-be decision maker

**Pareto principle**: the concept that 80 percent of one's results derive from 20 percent of one's activities; first articulated by Vilfredo Pareto in the early 20th century

**Peter principled employees**: employees promoted beyond their level of competence; from the book of the same name

**Phone interrupt list**: a list of potential callers for whom you have instructed your staff to always interrupt your activity to take the call; by implication, your activity should not be interrupted for calls from individuals not on the list

**Playing the fed card**: when a state or local government employee insists (sometimes accurately and sometimes inaccurately) that the federal government prohibits or requires a certain action

**PM**: policy memorandum; standard operating procedures for your agency

**Political capital**: the amount of influence an elected official possesses to further her agenda; distinguished from the amount of power an elected official possesses

**Political relative**: an employee who gained employment with your agency through the support of an elected official or someone close to an elected official; may or may not be an actual blood relative

**Political theater**: an event that is intended to promote an advocacy position or embarrass the opposition rather than objectively search for information or solutions

**Priority discipline**: sticking with your priorities, notwithstanding the many temptations to alter them

**Progressive discipline**: an aspect of personnel management in which management responds to negative employee behavior by escalating responses designed to improve the employee's performance; in most cases employees cannot be terminated until they have moved through several stages of such discipline

**Psychic income**: the mental and emotional wellbeing generated when a government administrator helps other people and/or makes society function a little better

**Put the donkey ears on**: publicly admit to your staff that you have made a mistake

**Reality check**: a critical evaluation of your proposed course of action by your aides, or vice versa

**Reedy's dictum**: the recommendation that no one be allowed to work on the White House staff until age 40; first stated by George Reedy, former Presidential Press Secretary

**Rents**: the excess profits businesses can extract from their customers when they face little or no competition

**Retainage**: the portion of the construction contract price deliberately withheld by the owner until the project is substantially complete, to assure that the contractor or subcontractor satisfactorily completes their work

**Retired in place**: an employee nearing or past retirement eligibility who is uninterested or unwilling to do any but the most minimal aspects of his job, and no tasks requiring creativity, problem solving, or, if in management, supervising

**Revolving door laws**: statutory restrictions covering former government officials employed by the private sector, designed to prevent conflicts of interest

**The Ross Rule**: the maxim that the best way to answer a question at a legislative hearing is to provide enough information to answer the question, but not so much information that your answer invites additional questions; originated by Pete Ross, former Delaware State Budget Director

**Scientific management**: a management theory that seeks to optimize workflows; originated by Frederick Taylor in the 19th century

**Soft landing**: an employee termination in which the dismissed employee is allowed to resign or retire rather than be fired, is placed in a different position, or is given a fixed or open-ended time interval to remain on the job prior to his removal

**Stakeholder**: a group or organization that, or an individual who, affects or is affected by an agency's actions, policies, and/or services

**Stare decisis**: the policy of judges and courts to abide by principles established in earlier cases (precedents)

**SWOT**: Strengths, Weaknesses, Opportunities, and Threats

**Symmetric power**: when each side in a negotiation has equivalent leverage

**Take-up rate**: a percentage equal to the number of persons enrolled in a government program divided by the number of persons eligible for that program

**TANF**: Temporary Assistance to Needy Families; pronounced TAN if

**360 degree evaluation**: the process of evaluating an employee not just by her supervisor but by her peers and subordinates as well; may refer to an employee evaluation in which a supervisor is evaluated by all of the individuals who directly report to her.

**Toxic employees**: regardless of their competency, these workers have limited to no people skills and are difficult to work with, work for, or have working for you

**Trustee model of representation**: the philosophy that a legislator should base his votes on his own judgment, even if they conflict with the views of his constituents; converse of delegate model of representation

**Turf battle**: a dispute between government officials about which agency will perform a function and possess the resources dedicated to carrying out that function

**Upward delegation**: when a subordinate attempts to assign to a superior a task that should properly be performed by the subordinate

**URL**: uniform resource locator, the formal name for an website address

**Virtuous circle**: a type of improvement in which positive changes in one area lead to positive changes in a second area, which in turn lead to more positive changes in the first area, *ad infinitum*; antonym of vicious circle

**Weebees**: tenured or civil service employees who do not change with a change in the administration (and, presumably, a change in the organization's appointed leader), as in "We be here before you got here and we be here after you leave"

# References

## MANAGING GOVERNMENT AGENCIES

### Books

Ashworth, Kenneth, *Caught Between the Dog and the Fireplug, or How to Survive Public Service*, Washington, D.C., Georgetown University Press, 2001

Bartholomew, Paul C., *Public Administration, Third Ed.*, Totowa, New Jersey, Littlefield, Adams & Co., 1972

Chase, Gordon and Elizabeth C. Reveal, *How to Manage in the Public Sector*, New York, McGraw-Hill, Inc., 1983

Lawrence, Paul R. and Mark A. Abramson, *What Government Does: How Political Executives Manage*, Lanham, Maryland, Rowman & Littlefield Publishers, Inc., 2014

Mosher, Frederick C., Ed., *American Public Administration: Past, Present, Future*, University, Alabama, The University of Alabama Press, 1975

Osborne, David and Ted Gaebler, *Reinventing Government: How the Entrepreneurial Spirit is Transforming the Public Sector*, Reading, Massachusetts, Addison-Wesley Publishing Company, Inc., 1992

_____, and Peter Hutchinson, *The Price of Government: Getting the Results We Need In an Age of Permanent Fiscal Crisis*, New York, Basic Books, 2004

_____, and Peter Plastrik, *Banishing Bureaucracy: The Five Strategies for Reinventing Government*, Reading, Massachusetts, Addision-Wesley Publishing Company, Inc., 1997

Wilson, Richard Clay Jr., *Rethinking Public Administration: The Case for Management*, Minneapolis, Minnesota, Mill City Press, 2013

## INTRODUCTION

### Books

Frank, Thomas, *The Wrecking Crew: How Conservatives Ruined Government, Enriched Themselves, and Beggared the Nation*, New York, Henry Holt and Company, 2008

# CHAPTER 1

## Books

Covey, Stephen R., *The 7 Habits of Highly Effective People*, New York, Free Press, 1989
_____, *Living the 7 Habits: Stories of Courage and Inspiration*, New York, Simon & Schuster, 1999
Gawande, Atul, *The Checklist Manifesto: How to Get Things Right*, New York, Metropolitan Books, 2009
Peck, M. Scott, *The Road Less Traveled*, New York, Simon & Schuster, 1978
Rath, Tom and Donald O. Clifton, *How Full Is Your Bucket? Positive Strategies For Work and Life*, New York, Gallup Press, 2004
Shipley, David and Will Schwalbe, *Send: The Essential Guide to Email for Office and Home*, New York, Alfred A. Knopf, 2007

# CHAPTER 2

## Books

Harvey, Eric, David Cottrell, Al Lucia, and Mike Hourigan, *The Leadership Secrets of Santa Claus: How to Get Things Done In YOUR "Workshop"...All Year Long*, Dallas, Walk the Talk Company, 2003
Jami, Criss, *Venus In Arms*, Lexington, Kentucky, CreateSpace Independent Publishing Platform, 2012
Sandys, Celia and Jonathan Littman, *We Shall Not Fail: The Inspiring Leadership of Winston Churchill*, New York, Portfolio, 2003

## Newspapers

Bryant, Adam, *Corner Office: Bill Flemming, New York Times*, Business p. 2, August 12, 2012
_____, *Corner Office: F. Mark Gumz, New York Times*, Business p. 2, February 13, 2011
_____, *Corner Office: G. J. Hart, New York Times*, Business p. 2, January 6, 2013
_____, *Corner Office: Joel Babbit, New York Times*, Business p. 2, July 8, 2012
_____, *Corner Office: Mike Sheehan, New York Times*, Business p. 2, June 3, 2012

## Online

US Government Printing Office, http://www.gpo.gov/fdsys/pkg/BILLS-111hr2142enr/pdf/BILLS-111hr2142enr.pdf

# CHAPTER 3

## Books

Cooper, Terry, *The Responsible Administrator: An Approach to Ethics for the Administrative Role, Sixth Ed.*, San Francisco, Jossey-Bass, 2012
Fleischman, J. L., "Self-Interest and Public Integrity" in *Public Duties: The Moral Obligation of Government Officials*, ed. Joel L. Fleischmann and Mark Moore, Cambridge, Massachusetts, Harvard University Press, 1981
O'Leary, Rosemary, *The Ethics of Dissent: Managing Guerrilla Government*, Washington, D.C., CQ Press, 2006

# Online

American Society for Public Administration Code of Ethics, http://www.aspanet.org/public/ASPA/Resources/Code_of_Ethics/ASPA/Resources/Code%20of%20Ethics1.aspx?hkey=acd40318-a945-4ffc-ba7b-18e037b1a858


# CHAPTER 4


## Books

Blake, Robert R. and Jane S. Mouton, *The Managerial Grid: Key Orientations for Achieving Production Through People*, Houston, Gulf Publishing Company, 1964

Blanchard, Kenneth and Spencer Johnson, *The One Minute Manager*, New York, Berkley Books, 1982

Bryant, Adam, *The Corner Office: Indispensable and Unexpected Lessons From CEOs On How To Lead and Succeed*, New York, Times Books, 2011

Calzada, Laurie, *180 Ways to Effectively Deal With Change*, Dallas, Walk the Talk Company, 2006

Friesen, Ernest C. Jr., Edward C. Gallas, and Nesta M. Gallas, *Managing the Courts*, Indianapolis, The Bobbs-Merrill Company, Inc., 1971

Goleman, Daniel, *Emotional Intelligence*, New York, Bantam Books, 1995

_____, *Working With Emotional Intelligence*, New York, Bantam Books, 1998

Golembiewski, Robert T., and Michael Cohen, *People In Public Service: A Reader In Public Personnel Administration, Second Ed.*, Itasca, Illinois, F. E. Peacock Publishers, Inc., 1976

Halberstam, Dave, *The Reckoning*, New York, William Morrow and Company, Inc., 1986

Kuhn, Thomas S., *The Structure of Scientific Revolutions, Third Ed.*, Chicago, The University of Chicago Press, 1996

Nigro, Felix A. and Lloyd G. Nigro, *The New Public Personnel Administration*, Itasca, Illinois, F. E. Peacock Publishers, Inc., 1976

Perrow, Charles, *Complex Organizations: A Critical Essay*, Glenview, Illinois, Scott, Foresman and Company, 1972

Peter, Lawrence J. and Raymond Hill, *The Peter Principle*, New York, William Morrow & Company, Inc., 1969

Pugh, D. S., Ed., *Organization Theory*, Middlesex, United Kingdom, Penguin Education, 1971

Rutter, Peter, *Sex in the Forbidden Zone: When Men in Power — Therapists, Doctors, Clergy, Teachers, and Others—Betray Women's Trust*, New York, Fawcett Columbine, 1989

Schein, Edgar H., *Organizational Psychology, Second Ed.*, Englewood Cliffs, New Jersey, Prentice-Hall, Inc., 1970

Schon, Donald A., *Beyond the Stable State*, New York, W. W. Norton & Company, Inc., 1971

Telford, Fred, *The Principles of Public Personnel Administration*, Newark, Delaware, University of Delaware, 1976


## Monographs

Partnership for Public Service and Booz Allen Hamilton, *Building the Enterprise: A New Civil Service Framework*, April, 2014


## Periodicals

Behn, Robert D., *Job Descriptions Often Just Get In the Way*, Governing Magazine, February, 1997, p. 91

## Newspapers

Bryant, Adam, *Corner Office: Amy Gutmann, New York Times*, Business p. 2, June 19, 2011
_____, *Corner Office: Angie Hicks, New York Times*, Business p. 2, June 24, 2012
_____, *Corner Office: At His Company, It's 'Ready, Fire, Aim': Tom Erickson, New York Times*, Business p. 2, March 30, 2014
_____, *Corner Office: Ben Lerer, New York Times*, Business p. 2, September 9, 2012
_____, *Corner Office: Caryl M. Stern, New York Times*, Business p. 2, April 24, 2011
_____, *Corner Office: Charlotte Beers, New York Times*, Business p. 2, April 1, 2012
_____, *Corner Office: Cristobal Conde, New York Times*, Business p. 2, January 17, 2010
_____, *Corner Office: Daniel Lubetzky, New York Times*, Business p. 2, September 8, 2013
_____, *Corner Office: Dan Rosensweig, New York Times*, Business p. 2, July 11, 2010
_____, *Corner Office: David Reimer, New York Times*, Business p. 2, July 14, 2013
_____, *Corner Office: Dawn Lepore, New York Times*, Business p. 2, July 18, 2010
_____, *Corner Office: Debra L. Lee, New York Times*, Business p. 2, March 28, 2010
_____, *Corner Office: Drew Gilpin Faust, New York Times*, Business p. 2, November 1, 2009
_____, *Corner Office: Finding a Team That Fits to a 'T': Barney Harford, New York Times*, B2, August 15, 2014
_____, *Corner Office: Francesca Zambello, New York Times*, Business p. 2, April 7, 2013
_____, *Corner Office: Geoffrey Canada, New York Times*, Business p. 2, December 18, 2011
_____, *Corner Office: Gregory B. Maffei, New York Times*, Business p. 2, January 9, 2011
_____, *Corner Office: Guy Kawasaki, New York Times*, Business p. 2, March 21, 2010
_____, *Corner Office: Howard Schultz, New York Times*, Business p. 2, October 10, 2010
_____, *Corner Office: John Duffy, New York Times*, Business p. 2, November 4, 2012
_____, *Corner Office: Jeff Weiner, New York Times*, Business p. 2, November 11, 2012
_____, *Corner Office: Kevin Liles, New York Times*, Business p. 2, October 28, 2012
_____, *Corner Office: Lars Albright, New York Times*, p. B2, October 4, 2013
_____, *Corner Office: Michael Mathieu, New York Times*, Business p. 2, June 20, 2010
_____, *Corner Office: Pamela Fields, New York Times*, Business p. 2, October 2, 2011
_____, *Corner Office: Paul Maritz, New York Times*, Business p. 2, October 3, 2010
_____, *Corner Office: Richard R. Buery Jr., New York Times*, Business p. 2, September 12, 2010
_____, *Corner Office: Robert Eckert, New York Times*, Business p. 2, December 26, 2010
_____, *Corner Office: Robert J. Murray, New York Times*, Business p. 2, December 23, 2012
_____, *Corner Office: Robert L. Johnson, New York Times*, Business p. 2, November 13, 2011
_____, *Corner Office: Robert W. Selander, New York Times*, Business p. 2, June 27, 2010
_____, *Corner Office: Russell Goldsmith, New York Times*, Business p. 2, April 22, 2012
_____, *Corner Office: Steve Hannah, New York Times*, Business p. 2, May 16, 2010
_____, *Corner Office: Tachi Yamada, New York Times*, Business p. 2, February 28, 2010
_____, *Corner Office: Terri Ludwig, New York Times*, Business p. 2, August 21, 2011
_____, *Corner Office: Terry Leahy, New York Times*, Business p. 2, February 3, 2013
_____, *Corner Office: Tracy Dolgin, New York Times*, Business p. 2, March 4, 2012
_____, *Corner Office: Victoria Ransom, New York Times*, Business p. 2, January 27, 2013
Herbers, John, *The Spokes of Power, New York Times*, p. 20, May 18, 1973

## Online

BrainyQuote, http://www.brainyquote.com/quotes/quotes/l/laotzu121075.html
Maranto, Robert and Patrick J. Wolf, *Good government is a risky business: Few competent public officials go unpunished*, philly.com, December 1, 2010
The Official Website of General George S. Patton, Jr., http://www.generalpatton.com/quotes/index3.html

## Misccellaneous

Smit, Gary, lecture April 19, 2011

## CHAPTER 5

## Newspapers

Bryant, Adam, *Corner Office: Helene D. Gayle*, New York Times, Business p. 2, June 23, 2013
_____, *Corner Office: Shanti Atkins*, New York Times, B2, January 3, 2014

## CHAPTER 6

## Books

Aronson, J. Richard and Eli Schwartz, Eds., *Management Policies in Local Government Finance*, Washington, The International City Management Association, 1975
Briffault, Richard, *Balancing Acts: The Reality Behind State Balanced Budget Amendments*, New York, The Twentieth Century Fund Press, 1996
Forsythe, Dall W., *Memos to the Governor: An Introduction to State Budgeting*, Washington, Georgetown University Press, 1997
Howard, S. Kenneth, *Changing State Budgeting*, Lexington, Kentucky, Council of State Governments, 1973
Hyde, Albert C. and Jay M. Shafritz, Eds., *Government Budgeting: Theory, Process, Politics*, Oak Park, Illinois, Moore Publishing Company, Inc., 1978
Wildavsky, Aaron, *The Politics of the Budgetary Process, Second Ed.*, Boston, Little, Brown and Company, 1974

## Periodicals

Key, V. O. Jr., *The Lack of a Budgetary Theory*, The American Political Science Review, December, 1940, pp. 1137-1144
_____, *The politics of Mr. Nixon's economics*, Life, February 13, 1970, p. 28

## CHAPTER 7

## Books

Charney, Cy, *The Manager's Tool Kit: Practical Tips for Tackling 100 On-the-Job Problems*, New York, American Management Association, 1994
Davis, Lanny J., *Truth to Tell: Tell It Early, Tell It All, Tell It Yourself: Notes From My White House Education*, New York, The Free Press, 1999
Deaton, Angus, *The Great Escape: Health, Wealth, and the Origins of Inequality*, Princeton, New Jersey, Princeton University Press, 2013
Fisher, Roger, William Ury, and Bruce Patton, *Getting to YES: Negotiating Agreement Without Giving In, Second Ed.*, New York, Penguin Books, 1991
Neustadt, Richard E. and Ernest R. May, *Thinking in Time: The Uses of History for Decision-Makers*, New York, The Free Press, 1986
Simon, Herbert A., *Administrative Behavior: A Study of Decision-Making Processes in Administrative Organization, Third Ed.*, New York, The Free Press, 1976

Tamm, James W. and Ronald J. Luyet, *Radical Collaboration: Five Essential Skills to Overcome Defensiveness and Build Successful Relationships*, New York, Collins, 2004

## Newspapers

Bryant, Adam, *Corner Office: Cathleen P. Black, New York Times*, Business p. 2, December 19, 2010

\_\_\_\_\_, *Corner Office: Shivan S. Subramaniam, New York Times*, Business p. 2, November 14, 2010

# CHAPTER 8

## Books

\_\_\_\_\_, *Transition and the New Governor: A Planning Guide*, Washington, National Governors' Association Office of Management Services, 1998

# CHAPTER 9

## Books

Bissinger, Buzz, *A Prayer for the City*, New York, Random House, 1997

Keyes, Ralph, *The Quote Verifier: Who Said What, Where, and When*, New York, Macmillan, 2006

Reedy, George E., *The Twilight of the Presidency*, New York, The World Publishing Company, 1970

Smith, Hedrick, *The Power Game: How Washington Works*, New York, Random House, 1988

## Newspapers

Bryant, Adam, *Corner Office: Brent Saunders, New York Times*, p. B2, May 28, 2013

\_\_\_\_\_, *Corner Office: Carla Cooper, New York Times*, p. B2, December 13, 2013

\_\_\_\_\_, *Corner Office: If You Want to Win, Just Say Yes: Bernard L. Schwartz, New York Times*, p. Business 2, June 15, 2014

Seib, Gerald F., *In Crisis, Opportunity for Obama, Wall Street Journal*, p. 1, November 19, 2008

## Online

The Quotations Page, http://www.quotationspage.com/quote/4758.html

# CHAPTER 10

## Books

Ehrenhalt, Alan, Ed., *Politics in America: Members of Congress In Washington And At Home*, Washington, D.C., Congressional Quarterly Press, 1981

\_\_\_\_\_, Ed., *Politics in America: The 100th Congress*, Washington, D.C., CQ Press, 1987

Harris, Joseph P., *Congress and the Legislative Process, Second Ed.*, New York, McGraw-Hill Book Company, 1972

Muir, William K. Jr., *Legislature: California's School for Politics*, Chicago, The University of Chicago Press, 1982

Rosenthal, Alan, *Legislative Life: People, Process, and Performance in the States*, New York, Harper & Row, Publishers, 1981

# CHAPTER 11

## Books

Adams, Scott, *This Is the Part Where You Pretend to Add Value*, Kansas City, Missouri, Andrews McMeel Publishing, 2008

Alterman, Eric, *What Liberal Media? The Truth About* Bias *and the News*, New York, Basic Books, 2003

Fallows, James, *Breaking the News: How the Media Undermine American Democracy*, New York, Pantheon Books, 1996

Grossman, Lawrence K., *The Electronic Republic: Reshaping Democracy in the Information Age*, New York, Viking Penguin, 1995

Jamieson, Kathleen Hall and Paul Waldman, *The Press Effect: Politicians, Journalists, and the Stories That Shape the Political World*, New York, Oxford University Press, 2003

Manjoo, Farhad, *True Enough: Learning to Live in a Post-Fact Society*, Hoboken, New Jersey, John Wiley & Sons, Inc., 2008

Phillips, Brad, *The Media Training Bible: 101 Things You Absolutely, Positively Need to Know Before Your Next Interview*, Washington, D.C., SpeakGood Press, 2013

Rosenfeld, Richard N., *American Aurora: A Democratic-Republican Returns—The Suppressed History of Our Nation's Beginnings and the Heroic Newspaper That Tried To Report It*, New York, St. Martin's Press, 1997

## Newspapers

Carr, David, *Newspaper Barons Resurface, New York Times*, p. B8, April 9, 2012

## Online

The Almanac of Theodore Roosevelt, http://www.theodoreroosevelt.com/trsorbonnes-peech.html

Morales, Lymari, *U.S. Distrust in Media Hits New High*, Gallup Politics, http://www.gallup.com/poll/157589/distrust-media-hits-new-high.aspx, September 21, 2012

# CHAPTER 12

## Books

Adams, Walter and James W. Brock, *The Bigness Complex: Industry, Labor, and Government in the American Economy, Second Ed.*, Stanford, California, Stanford University Press, 2004

Sclar, Elliott D., *You Don't Always Get What You Pay For: The Economics of Privatization*, Ithaca, New York, Cornell University Press, 2000

Vogel, David, *Fluctuating Fortunes: The Political Power of Business in America*, Washington, D.C., Beard Books, 2003

## Monographs

Bureau of Justice Assistance, *Emerging Issues on Prison Privatization*, Washington, D.C., February, 2001

General Accounting Office, *Report to the Subcommittee on Crime, Committee on the Judiciary, House of Representatives: Private and Public Prisons—Studies Comparing Operational Costs and/or Quality of Service*, Washington, D.C., August, 1996

## Newspapers

Associated Press, *Idaho: F.B.I. Enters Investigation Into Prison Operator*, New York Times p. A12, March 8, 2014

Bryant, Adam, *Corner Office: Susan Lyne*, New York Times, Business p. 2, October 4, 2009

Dolnick, Sam, *As Escapees Stream Out, a Penal Business Thrives*, New York Times, p. A1, June 16, 2012

Weiser, Benjamin, *To Curtail Lawsuits, City Decides It's Time to Fight*, New York Times, p. A19, February 26, 2013


# BIOGRAPHIES AND AUTOBIOGRAPHIES OF MANAGERS AND LEADERS

## Books

Brownlow, Louis, *A Passion For Anonymity: The Autobiography of Louis Brownlow—The First Half*, Chicago, University of Chicago Press, 1955

Caro, Robert A., *The Years of Lyndon Johnson: The Path to Power*, New York, Alfred A. Knopf, 1982

——, *The Years of Lyndon Johnson: Means of Ascent*, New York, Alfred A. Knopf, 1990

Chace, James, *Acheson: The Secretary of State Who Created the American World*, New York, Simon & Schuster, 1998

Cray, Ed, *General of the Army: George C. Marshall, Soldier and Statesman*, New York, Simon & Schuster, 1990

Cuomo, Mario, *Diaries of Mario M. Cuomo: The Campaign For Governor*, New York, Random House, 1984

Manchester, William, *American Caesar*, New York, Dell Publishing Co., Inc., 1978

McCullough, David, *Truman*, New York, Simon and Schuster, 1992

O'Neill, Tip and William Novak, *Man of the House*, New York, Random House, 1987

Reich, Robert B., *Locked in the Cabinet*, New York, Alfred A. Knopf, 1997

Riordan, William L., *Plunkitt of Tammany Hall*, New York, E. P. Dutton & Co., Inc., 1905

Smith, Jean Edward, *Lucius D. Clay: An American Life*, New York, Henry Holt and Company, 1990

Udall, Morris K., Bob Neuman, and Randy Udall, *Too Funny To Be President*, Henry Holt and Company, 1988


# AMERICAN GOVERNMENT

## Books

Bardes, Barbara A., Mack C. Shelley II, and Steffen W. Schmidt, *American Government and Politics Today: The Essentials, 2013-2014 Ed.*, Boston, Wadsworth, Cengage Learning, 2014

Bent, Alan E. and Ralph A. Rossum, Eds., *Urban Administration: Management, Politics, and Change*, Port Washington, New York, Kennikat Press, 1976

Ladd, Everett Carll, *The American Polity: The People and Their Government, Second Ed.*, New York, W. W. Norton & Company, 1987

Levy, Frank S., Arnold J. Meltsner, and Aaron Wildavsky, *Urban Outcomes*, Berkeley, California, University of California Press, 1974

Lineberry, Robert L., *Equality and Urban Policy: The Distribution of Municipal Public Services*, Beverly Hills, California, Sage Publications, 1977

Morgan, David R., *Managing Urban America: The Politics and Administration of America's Cities*, North Scituate, Massachusetts, Duxbury Press, 1979

Seidman, Harold, *Politics, Position, & Power: The Dynamics of Federal Organization, 2nd Ed.*, New York, Oxford University Press, 1976

Shea, John C., *American Government: The Great Game of Politics*, New York, St. Martin's Press, 1984

Wilson, James Q., *American Government, Tenth Ed.*, Boston, Wadsworth, Cengage Learning, 2012

# Index